MOTHERHOOD, EMBODIED LOVE AND CULTURE

About Bioethics Series

About Bioethics, Volume One: Philosophical and Theological Approaches
(Connor Court, 2011)

About Bioetics, Volume Two: Caring for People Who are Sick and Dying
(Connor Court, 2012)

About Bioethics, Volume Three: Transplantation, Biobanks and the Human Body
(Connor Court, 2012)

MOTHERHOOD, EMBODIED LOVE AND CULTURE

Nicholas Tonti-Filippini

Published in 2013 by Connor Court Publishing Pty Ltd

Copyright © Nicholas Tonti-Filippini 2013

ALL RIGHTS RESERVED. This book contains material protected under International and Federal Copyright Laws and Treaties. Any unauthorised reprint or use of this material is prohibited. No part of this book may be reproduced or transmitted in any form or by any means, electronic or mechanical, including photocopying, recording, or by any information storage and retrieval system without express written permission from the publisher.

Connor Court Publishing Pty Ltd.
PO Box 224W
Ballarat VIC 3350
sales@connorcourt.com
www.connorcourt.com

ISBN: 9781922168603 (pbk.)

Cover design by Ian James

Printed in Australia

Scriptural quotations, unless otherwise noted, are from the Revised Standard Version of the Bible. Excerpts of Vatican documents are from the English translation found on the Vatican webpage, www.vatican.va

CONTENTS

Preface.. xi
1. Introduction... 1
2. The Human Body... 15
3. Prenatal Diagnosis and Reproductive Discrimination.... 40
   3.1 Prenatal Diagnosis
   3.2 Morality and Prenatal Diagnosis
   3.3 Morality and Pre-implantation Genetic Diagnosis
   3.4 Reproductive Discrimination
   3.5 Human Embryo Experimentation and Cloning
4. Perinatal Palliative Care and Support........................ 61
   4.1 Introduction
   4.2 Perinatal Palliative Care
   4.3 False Reassurance and the Need for Counselling Prior to Testing
   4.4 Patients' Experiences
   4.5 Gaps in Service Delivery
   4.6 The Effects of Offering Perinatal Palliative Care
   4.7 Decision-Making Counselling
   4.8 Conclusion
5. Assisted Reproductive Technology........................... 80
   5.1 Infertility
   5.2 Assisted Reproduction
   5.3 The Moral Status of the Embryo
   5.4 Embryo Loss
   5.5 Reproduction and Equal Respect for Persons
   5.6 Donor Gametes
   5.7 Surrogacy
   5.8 A Child is not a Cure for Infertility
   5.9 Viable Alternatives

6. Embryo Rescue.. 112
7. A Woman-Centred Approach to Abortion............................ 118
8. Early Induction and Late Term Termination of Pregnancy 128
9. Ectopic Pregnancy... 138
10. Professional Conscience and Obstetrics and Gynaecology 146
11. Amending the *Abortion Law Reform Act* 2008.................. 151
   11.1 Summary
   11.2 Freedom of Conscience of Health Practitioners
   11.3 The Abortion Law Reform Act 2008
   11.4 Amending the Act
12. Post Coital Intervention: "Emergency Contraception", "The Morning After Pill", or "Contragestion".................. 162
   12.1 From Fear of Pregnancy to Rape Crisis
   12.2 Case Study
   12.3 A Common Problem
   12.4 Post-Coital Intervention
   12.5 Identifying Fertile and Infertile Phases
   12.6 An Alternative to Abortifacience
   12.7 Managing Pregnancy Scares
   12.8 Rape Crisis
13. When Pregnancy is a Maternal Danger: The Lysaught Opinion and a Deeper Malaise of an Anthropocentric Morality... 180
   13.1 Introduction
   13.2 Direct and Indirect Abortion
   13.3 Rhonheimer and Vital Conflicts
   13.4 Grisez's Analysis
   13.5 Conclusion
   13.6 Like Cases
14. Why Reject Contraception?... 228

15. Prevention of Sexually Transmissible Infection: Was the Church wrong?...240
15.1 The Issue
15.2 Criticism of Church Policy
15.3 Does the data support the claim?
    15.3.1 What Caused the HIV Decline in Uganda?
    15.3.2 What Happened in Uganda?
    15.3.3 Were Condoms the Solution in Uganda?
15.4 HIV Prevention in Australia
15.5 Did STIs in young people fall?
15.6 The Education Issue

16. The Oral Contraceptive Pill and Society: Fifty Years On.... 252
16.1 Social and economic Effects
16.2 Medical and Relationship Effects

17. Gender Reassignment and Catholic Schools...................... 260
17.1 Introduction
17.2 Disorders of Sex Development
17.3 Gender Dysphoria.
17.4 Is Gender Identity Disorder (GID) a Delusion?
17.5 Is Gender Reassignment Corrective or Mutilating?
17.6 A Teacher in a Catholic School
17.7 A Child in the Classroom
17.8 A Draft Letter to Parents

18. Homophobia... 283
18.1 Homophobic Harassment
18.2 Effect on Free Speech and Religion
18.3 Should "Homophobic Harassment" Be an Offence?

19. Same Sex Attraction..294
19.1 Not a Choice
19.2 A Vocation to Love

19.3 Discovering Gender
19.4 Integration of Sexuality
19.5 Witness to God's Love
19.6 Jesus Calls Us
19.7 Giving Ourselves in Love

20. Marriage is More than Romance 299
20.1 Redefining Marriage
20.2 Biological Marriage
20.3 Removing Motherhood and Fatherhood
20.4 Same Sex Unions and Step-children
20.5 Role of the State and Marriage
20.6 Conscientious Objection
20.7 Marriage is about Sexual Intimacy
20.8 Same Sex Unions are not Marriage

21. Masturbation and Pornography 306

22. The Catholic Church and Paedophilia 311
22.1 Introduction
22.2 The Incidence of Paedophilia in Clergy and Religious
22.3 Formation
22.4 Misprision
22.5 The Puzzle about Managing Suspicion of Serious Crime
22.6 Ignorance about Paedophilia
22.7 Church Authorities Not Alone
22.8 A Grave Misjudgement
22.9 Parallels
22.10 The Historical Obligation to Try and Punish a Serious Crime
22.11 The Obligation to Protect Children
22.12 The Future
22.13 Response to the Commission
22.14 Current Thinking

22.15 A Third Tier?

22.16 Issues in Clerical Formation and Professional Development

23. Sex Education and the National Curriculum..................... 342

23.1 The National Curriculum

23.2 Literature Review

    23.2.1 Introduction

    23.2.2 National Strategies and Programmes in Australia and U.S.A.

    23.2.3 The Main Directions of the Research

    23.2.4 Sexually Transmitted Diseases and Sexual Education

    23.2.5 Teenage Pregnancy and Sexual Education

    23.2.6 School Curricula and Sexual Education

    23.2.7 Methodology of Research

    23.2.8 What Should Be Done for Improvement of the Research?

    23.2.9 Types of Programmes for Young People: Do They Work?

23.3 Education in Sexuality: Needs, Objectives, and Methods

    23.3.1 The Goals of Education in Sexuality

    23.3.2 Partners in Sex Education

    23.3.3 Foundations of Education in Sexuality

    23.3.4 Methods of Education in Sexuality

23.4 Ethics and the Evaluation of Effectiveness of Education in Sexuality and Relationships

23.5 Focus on Context: What Does Work in Sex Education

24. Mothers, Grandmothers and Others: Some Reflections... 390

Bibliography.. 425

Index.. 441

Preface

As a man, I am at something of a disadvantage in writing about motherhood. However, given that so much of bioethics is about reproductive technology, the *About Bioethics* series would not have been complete without it. A second source of discomfort was whether to use the word "motherhood" at all. It is almost inevitable that a male using the term will commit politically incorrect indiscretions and cause offence. However, I wanted to focus on the human aspect of applying the technologies, and that is motherhood in the first instance. We have developed a culture of *technicism* – the belief that all problems can be resolved by technology.[1] A similar point is made by what is often called, the "technological imperative" – if it can be done, it will be done. This is no more evident than in the takeover of healthy women's bodies by technology, including the pill, emergency contraception, abortion and reproductive technology and the mantra of choice that inevitably devalues women and their bodies and perceives motherhood as a restriction on freedom.

No area has been fraught with more social tension than the fact that there is an area of life in which men and women are not equal. Nothing can make me a mother. I will always be an outsider. Much as I love my own mother, my wife, my daughters and my sisters and other female relations, they will always be strangers to me, a mystery, wonderfully so, but also so challenging. There are whole aspects of my life in which they are inclined to look at me with a strong sense of their superiority, rather in the same way an adult looks at a child, mildly amused at the child's stumbling efforts towards understanding.

Men and women are so different in their responses to sexuality. We can examine such matters intelligently, but physiologically we are so different and the physical and biological differences are experienced affectively and in the way in which we make sexual and relationship decisions. In sexual

---

1 Rodríguez Gómez Rodríguez, *Theory and History of Ideological Production*, Associated University Press: Cranbury, New Jersey, 2002, p. 123

relationships the relative risks and consequences for men and women are also quite different. In so many ways we remain mysteries to each other. After sharing a bedroom, and so much else, with the one person for nearly three decades, I still find myself bemused and surprised and consequently full of joy and admiration at the sheer wonder and unpredictability of the mystery of Mary's femininity.

As I struggle to grapple with my emotions, to "name, claim, aim and tame" them, as Aristotle would have it in his *Nicomachean Ethics*,[2] I am conscious that what for me and, seemingly for most men, is a struggle, is taken for granted by most mature women. Many people, far more professionally qualified in the appropriate disciplines than I, have analysed the evidence and undertaken studies on the relative emotional maturity of men and women. I do not presume to attempt to write authoritatively on these questions. But I have had a lifetime struggle, trying to be a good man, a good husband and father, in a world in which at least half are women, and so very different. Even now I will occasionally find, by the nature of reactions, that I have again got it wrong and overlooked something of major significance or misrepresented it in something I have said.

Marriage has been the most wonderful adventure, a mystery that unfolds each day, not only in my understanding of Mary, but also the changes that occur in myself with age and with changing demands and circumstances, including illness. There is a sense in which, no matter how good it has become, the changes as they occur always seem to bring about a deepening of our love and understanding. There has been no plateau, just constant change. What went before always seems so weak and inadequate in the face of what has succeeded it. Perhaps the future will not be so, especially if either of us becomes cognitively disabled, but perhaps if that happens, it will bring new challenges that require a different depth of personality.

The strength of marital love is not because it is a contract, but because, for a Christian at least, it is a covenant. We give our love mutually, but we

---

2 Aristotle *Nicomachean Ethics*, translated by W.D. Ross). Accessed 26/12/12 from http://classics.mit.edu/Aristotle/nicomachaen.8.viii.html Also, see the analysis by Sherman, Nancy. (2007) 'Virtue and a Warrior's Anger', in R.L. Walker & P.J. Ivanhoe eds., Oxford UP, 2007, pp. 251-278

give our love as though it were unilateral, without price, measurement or comparison. At least we do when we are trying. I have no shortage of human weaknesses, of pride, resentment and making unreasonable demands. But we share a knowledge that essentially the other will give without counting the personal cost, and that is what makes the relationship strong. A most important aspect of love is ensuring that one neither seeks to dominate nor to possess the other. Love is the opposite of mere use. For each the gift is unilateral, not a bargain or exchange, even though so much of what we do is governed by an underlying sense of balance or fairness. Love precedes justice, but is never unjust.

The most interesting aspect of marriage is our gender difference. That is expressed in everything we do, constantly enriching the relationship with unpredictability and a source of so much joy and humour. Being a man to her being a woman is what I do, every conscious moment of our shared lives, and, I suspect, many of our less conscious moments. It was played out particularly in our shared task of parenthood. I greatly enjoy watching Mary's motherhood and delight in her friendships with each of the children. I depended so much on her advice and direction in seeking to be a father to them, so often being dependent on her quicker and deeper appreciation of their emotional and other needs. It is no secret that given a choice, a child who is hurt usually turns first to his or her mother. Fathers have their uses but often it is a secondary role. Often his role is one of support for her, trying to create the circumstances that best serve her, that foster peace and tranquillity. By meeting her needs, including taking his share of meeting the needs of the children, his fatherhood flourishes amongst them and in love of her. It has been wonderful journey for which I am deeply grateful to Mary but also to Claire, Lucianne, Justin and John. Fathers anchor the family in their love for their wives and their willingness to sacrifice themselves for her so that she can go about her task of motherhood secure in his support for her.

Physiologically, husbands and fathers have an hormonal stability that predisposes to emotional stability in contrast to a woman's hormonal variability and mood changes. That should make us emotionally more dependable. That is not to say that men do not have moods. We are as susceptible to our glucose levels as anyone. But women have an extra dimension of variability and a particular closeness to the gift of life made so evident in the hormonal changes that so regularly produce a fertile window and the option of conception. The differences between motherhood and fatherhood, and the relative vulnerability of our bodies in sexual intimacy, profoundly affects us emotionally and the way we relate.

Recently, when John, our youngest, completed secondary school and left for his gap year travels before starting a medical course, we found ourselves on our own for the first time since Claire arrived. It felt like we had completed a twenty-seven year survival course. When the children were young and then when they were teenagers, life outside of work focussed on our meeting their needs, and that was made more than usually complicated by my being dependant on dialysis for all of John's life and most of the lives of the others. So much has fallen to Mary. The children have all been strong achievers and we have little to complain about, but every child needs attention, sometimes more than others.

One of the most interesting aspects of Mary's motherhood has been the fact that her own mother died when Mary was just seven years old. She had no immediate example to follow for being a mother to older children. Her father, however, seems to have been a wonderful combination of fatherly tolerance and acceptance while communicating clearly his values. He seems to have coped well with the mini-skirt era, of which there is photographic evidence of Mary's participation, albeit more modestly than some, and the other challenging developments of having a child become an adult in the 1970s, while maintaining a diplomatic silence. There were housekeepers and adult female friends, but that is not quite the same as having the presence of a mother. Both Mary's parents did not survive to be grandparents and Mary has had much to explore without their contemporary example and advice.

Without the example of her own mother, Mary has managed the role intelligently. The children always knew that they had her love and support in whatever they did, and her willingness to be enthusiastic and cheerful for them and their ideas, helping them to participate in sport and other extra-curricular activities. Having decided against home-schooling, we took the view that we should actively contribute to their schools. I was chairman of the Board of Directors of the girls' school and Mary was a busy member of the parents' committee of the primary school and the boys' school. We were greatly privileged to be able to work with other parents and the principals and leadership teams and learn from them.

When the children were in primary school, there was an occasion when Mary attended a sex education program run at the school for grade three children and their parents by an outside body called "Family Life". We were concerned because what was offered was claimed to be "value neutral" and it contained material that did not seem age appropriate for eight-year-olds. Not sure what to do, we decided to approach the school leadership and to encourage the school to design its own program and to consult parents about content and method. There was some reticence about talking about values, and about marriage particularly, given the knowledge that in many families the children were not living with both their natural mother and father, with many families having irregular circumstances, including blended families and single parents. Male teachers also expressed reluctance to discuss sexual matters in the classroom.

We explored what materials were available and assembled bits and pieces from a range of available programs including a program that had been developed by the Adelaide archdiocese and another from Philadelphia. With our encouragement, the school formed a small parent consultation group, including Mary as a doctor, and they conducted a consultation, to which all parents were invited, to discuss which of the material we had made available for display might be used and at what level. It was interesting to see confidence grow amongst the teachers and the leadership as they realised that all parents wanted values taught, including about the ideals of marriage, especially from those whose own circumstances, on their own admission, were not necessarily regular. It was as though they wanted the school to provide assistance on those matters they might find difficult. When the male teachers saw that much of this was about gender identity and relationships, and not about sexual intimacy, they became willing to be engaged. The principal, Mr Tony Breen, and the deputy principal, Mrs Alice Green, were wonderful in the time and effort given to finding and developing materials and being open to our suggestions. They led a process which resulted in a complete sexual education program for all levels of primary school, and one which engaged the parents in activities with their children. I regularly put that program before my students inviting them to criticise it and other alternatives, in the light of the evidence – see chapter 23.

Later, our school parent experience was very helpful when Mary and I were engaged as consultants to undertake some research into existing school programs and to assist the Catholic Education Office in Melbourne to develop a document that Archbishop Denis Hart later issued as "Directives for Education in Sexuality". Guided by the Pontifical Council for the Family document, *Truth and Meaning of Human Sexuality: Guidelines for Education within the Family*[3], the document outlines the principles to be applied, including especially respecting the role of a child's parents as primary educators, with whom the teachers are in partnership, and protecting the ages of innocence, while providing education in the knowledge, skills, behaviour and attitudes the children needed at that time and then later. Primary education, when the children are more receptive, is an especially important time to develop skills, behaviours and attitudes that respect their own dignity and the dignity of their peers.

We developed the mantra, "Understand, appreciate, protect", in relation to sexuality, fertility and the human body. Accurate knowledge of self and one's body leads to the right values and the right values leads to the right behaviour. Central to that approach was knowledge about good relating within the family and with friends, and about themselves, but also useful knowledge about the female cycle of fertility, centred not on menstruation, but on understanding ovulation, its observable signs and symptoms, and its wonderful power to generate the possibility of new life in every cycle. By appreciating the complexity of their reproductive systems and by relating the girl's cycle to her affectivity, both young men and women could learn to value and protect their fertility. With that went learning about behaviours to protect their health. We focused also on ensuring that parents had access to good materials, knew the timing and would be invited, through shared projects with the children, to actively contribute. That was especially important for sensitive matters that might be embarrassing in the classroom,

---

3   http://www.vatican.va/roman_curia/pontifical_councils/family/documents/rc_pc_family_doc_08121995_human-sexuality_en.html

but which could more easily be managed by a parent of the same gender in possession of helpful material.

The biology and psychology of gender differences, presented in a positive way, generate a set of universal values of love and respect for others, and focus relationships toward securing commitment in which a family can thrive. That the nature of gender difference is the potential for motherhood and fatherhood, profoundly alters the way we think about relationships between men and women. To make sense of sexuality in our overly sexualised society, our children benefit greatly from ensuring that sex education puts the extraordinary power to generate a child front and centre. Nothing delights a class of school children more than having a young parent bath an infant in front of the class. Nothing makes the values involved in sexuality make more sense. When a young women is attracted by a young man and vice versa, that the other might be a father or mother to future children ought to be a significant part of their thinking and with that thought goes a remarkable set of values and priorities.

I hope that you find this book satisfying for the response it offers to contemporary questions. I wish to acknowledge all the women who have contributed to shaping who I am and to my maturing. I particularly wish to acknowledge Mary, for thirty years of friendship and twenty-eight years of marriage. I owe her my continued existence, for without her I would not have continued the burden of the treatment regime that keeps me alive, and has done so for twenty-one years. Her love and the love of my children sustain me. With God's grace, Mary made me a father and being a father is a most extraordinary privilege. I acknowledge the contribution that my daughters, with their brothers, have made to my emotional intelligence. A father's relationship to a daughter is full of wonder as the child becomes a woman and he has a behind-the-scenes perspective, so to speak, of the complex dynamics of female virtues. It is the role of a parent to nurture a child, but so much of that, in reality, is no more than trying to maintain a safe environment for them to do their own growing up and supporting their endeavours. As parents we develop with our children to meet their needs. I am very grateful to Claire, Lucianne, Justin and John for giving me so much. Parenthood has its burdens, but so many of the tasks we do for our children are in fact delightful. Few things are more pleasurable then reading to a child at night, constructing a make-believe story for an ever appreciative audience, or hearing their nightly prayers, followed by the sheer bliss of standing at the door to look down at a child in untroubled sleep. They are never more beautiful. Those days are long gone for us, to be replaced with the special friendship that one has with one's adult children, experts now in their own disciplines, and shaping the world anew with their own talents and the energy and certainty of youth. They are still beautiful but with their own maturity and life choices that necessarily take them away from their parents.

In earlier volumes I have acknowledged those who have contributed to my professional development especially those at St Vincent's Hospital and contemporarily at the John Paul II Institute for Marriage and Family, and I will not repeat the acknowledgements here.

I am conscious of the autobiographical nature of this preface. In fact I had originally included much more autobiographical material, but thought it too long. However, I have retained that material as chapter 24. I have included that chapter by way of explaining my understanding of motherhood and sexuality. I accept Alasdair MacIntyre's approach to moral thinking that recognises that we are the product of our cultures[4] and in this preface and the reflection that is chapter 24, I offer an account of the main cultural influences that shaped who I am. A reader might well choose not to be bothered with these personal matters, which is why they are included as an afterword as it were, but you might just as well choose to read chapter 24 before proceeding.

---

4 Alasdair MacIntyre, *After Virtue*, University of Notre Dame Press, 2007.

1
Introduction

The title *Motherhood, Embodied Love and Culture* intentionally focusses on motherhood and, by implication, fatherhood, and on the fact that gender and sexual intimacy are about being bodies. The cultural imperatives have separated sexual intimacy from what gender actually means. Apparently it is proper to speak of parenthood but not in a gendered way. The culture has become heavily sexualized but with the emphasis on recreation, not family formation, and it is improper to refer to gender as a biological difference. Instead gender is considered to be a social construct only and therefore elective. The cultural imperatives have also medicalized pregnancy and childbirth so that prenatal testing, including invasive testing, is assumed to be normal and medically assumed to be necessary to make selective abortion available.

The divide between contemporary Western culture and its Christian origin is most evident in attitudes to the human body and sexuality. At the same time, there has been an exciting reform in the Catholic Church, begun at the Second Vatican Council and continued by Popes John Paul II and Benedict XVI. The reform is in the theology of marriage, of the body and of sexuality. At the Institute our subject on the *Theology of the Body* is by far the most popular, with people willing to travel long distances for that subject alone, including students travelling from India and Singapore.

Somehow, the imaginations of many young Christians and others, have been captured by moving away from the old scholastic and natural law approaches to sexuality, to approaches that are clearly Christocentric and Scriptural. It is as though we have recaptured something of the focus of the early Fathers on Jesus and on the *imago dei*. Human beings are meant to imitate the God of love, and no more so than in the complete gift of self in the marital union. Further, God's love is both *agape* and *eros*. God's love is not just disinterested. God desires our love. What we do matters to God.

This is an exciting development that holds out much promise for a genuine celebration of our sexual selves and understanding the theological significance of being gendered. Gender has never been so important.

Wanting to make a positive start and to respond to the challenges to motherhood and sexuality constructively, I decided to follow this introduction by having Chapter 2, explore the topic "The Human Body".

Having begun with sexuality and its embodiment and links to parenthood, it seemed appropriate to follow with one of the main areas of medicalization: prenatal testing. Discussion of the developments is aimed at assisting women to make choices that respect them, their bodies, motherhood and the life a woman may nurture within her.

In contemporary Western society, it has become common practice for women to undergo prenatal screening and testing. As time has gone by, the screening and testing has become more sophisticated at the same time as becoming commonplace. When a woman is referred to an obstetrician for antenatal care, the arrangement to have the screening and testing done may even be made by the receptionist before the patient sees the obstetrician. In other words, the screening and testing are so commonplace as to be considered not to need a session to explain to her the nature of the tests and their implications before they are undergone. It does seem strange in an era in which we emphasise patient autonomy that, in this instance, there is insufficient respect for the woman's autonomy to require an information session and the opportunity to discuss the options beforehand, especially tests that have risks for her or for the child.

As a result, many women find themselves on something of a treadmill progressing from non-invasive screening towards more invasive testing if the screening proves to be positive. Many women are unaware of the difference between screening and testing. They are also unaware that there is a sequence to be followed in the event of a positive result. The evidence also indicates that women are also usually unaware that the medical reason for screening and testing is to make available the option of selective abortion in the event of a positive test result. The evidence indicates that women generally have the tests seeking reassurance that all is well with the child, but doctors offer the tests in order to make selective abortion available.

Chapter 3 explores the issues involved in prenatal diagnosis and the way in which our culture has accepted reproductive discrimination. By reproductive discrimination, I mean intervening to seek to prevent the birth of a child with an abnormality.

A consequence of prenatal testing is that, of those women in Australia who have a diagnosis of a life-limiting condition in the child during pregnancy, approximately 90% decide to have an abortion. There is an alternative in which the woman is encouraged to continue the pregnancy until birth, even if the child is likely to be stillborn or die soon after birth. The phrase used for this is "perinatal palliative care and support". In places where perinatal palliative care and support are offered the proportion of women who choose abortion after receiving a life-limiting diagnosis of a child is significantly reduced. This possibility is discussed at length in Chapter 4.

Sadly, many couples, after months of trying to conceive, find they have a difficulty. Around fifty per cent of those who do not conceive within 12 months will still have a child within five years. However, many are referred to reproductive technology which tends to have replaced medical and surgical treatments to restore natural fertility.

The generation of human life in the laboratory raises many ethical issues, including those related to the destruction of human embryos and those related to the technology displacing the sacredness of the marriage act in the origin of the child. The technology is also not as successful as the publicity would indicate. The official figures gathered by the Victorian Assisted Reproductive Technology Authority indicate that 77% of women who have IVF procedures do not achieve the birth of a child. Also there are marginally higher rates of congenital abnormality, and recent data, following up adults who were IVF-conceived, is indicating that they have a higher incidence of some adult onset diseases, such as those related to insulin resistance.

Chapter 5 explores the above issues facing infertile couples and the choices they face, and options for seeking to maximise their natural fertility. It also includes discussion of the new concept of *peri-conception health*. The evidence now indicates that the health of *both* husband and wife prior to conception has a bearing on the long term health of their child. Animal studies show that, for instance, obesity in either parent prior to, or at the time of, conception can cause epigenetic changes related to obesity in the offspring. It might also cause infertility. Pre-existing illness in either can cause problems for the child. It is sound advice for both men and women to have a medical assessment before seeking to achieve pregnancy.[1]

The pro-life community has been divided over the issue of what might be done with embryos that are held in storage on IVF programs but which are no longer wanted by the women for whom they were developed. There are thousands of embryos that are thus considered to be surplus to requirements. Some have argued that "embryo rescue" or "heterologous embryo transfer" is akin to adoption and have therefore advocated that some women might offer to "prenatally adopt" abandoned embryos. Others have argued that this involves a woman being made pregnant from outside marriage and have raised concerns about the morality of doing so. This issue is discussed in Chapter 6.

---

1 Germaine M.B. Louis, Maureen A. Cooney, Courtney D. Lynch, Alexis Handal, "Periconception window: advising the pregnancy-planning couple", *Fertility and Sterility*, Volume 89, Issue 2, Supplement, pp. 119-121, February 2008.

Chapter 7 approaches the most obvious application of technology to motherhood, the widespread practice of induced abortion. Several years ago, John Fleming and I published *Common Ground? Seeking an Australian Consensus on Abortion and Sex Education* (St Paul Publications: Sydney 2007) in which we comprehensively reviewed Australian attitudes and data on the issue. In Australia, 25% of pregnancies end in termination. One in three women and their partners will experience a termination of pregnancy. So, for many women, their motherhood is profoundly affected by the practice. However, motherhood does not end with termination of pregnancy.[2] A woman who has carried a child will always be a mother. Though our society has dealt with that question by being in a state of denial, even the abortion clinics now recognize what they refer to as "post abortion syndrome".[3] Women report quite different experiences in relation to termination of pregnancy.[4] It is not for me to try to define what that experience might be like. What I attempt to do is to explore how we as men may behave appropriately in relation to women who may be in difficulty in relation to having become pregnant.

The reality is that it is women who become pregnant and who carry the primary responsibility. On the other hand, women become pregnant in a relationship to a man and he has responsibility towards her and to the child who is the result, usually, of their joint decision to make love. The exercise of the man's responsibility, however, can only be exercised through his relationship to her. That reality has led to what John Paul II calls the need for a woman-centred approach. Whatever we might say of the practice of abortion, we, as men, can do nothing useful except in terms of how we serve women.

---

2 The Hon Christine Campbell MP, in a private conversation, October 2012.
3 See for instance the websites: http://mariestopes-px.rtrk.com.au/our-services/women/abortion?utm_source=ReachLocal&utm_medium=PPC&utm_campaign=abortion_vic; or http://www.fcc.com.au/
4 Melinda Tankard Reist has chronicled women's experiences in her two collections *Giving Sorrow Words: Women's Stories of Grief After Abortion*, Duffy & Snellgrove, 2000; and *Defiant Birth: Women Who Resist Medical Eugenics*, Spinifex Press, 2006.

This chapter thus deals with developing the concept of a woman-centred approach to abortion, but focussing mainly on how men might best approach a matter in which our role is always secondary.

There is a distinct difference between termination of pregnancy before, and after, the child becomes viable. After the child has begun to be viable, the pregnancy can be brought to an end without ending the life. Ending the life is a decision to kill the child that is separate from ending the pregnancy. Often there are separate actions, such as, injecting the child's heart with potassium chloride so as to cause a cardiac arrest and death before delivery, or partial birth abortion in which an instrument may be thrust into the child's brain during delivery.

Obviously if there are medical risks to either the mother or the child in the pregnancy continuing, then there may be good reason to end the pregnancy. The terrible conflict that may arise prior to viability, between the medical interests of the mother and the medical interests of the child, no longer exists after viability.

Late-term termination of pregnancy is thus a very different issue from early abortion because there is the option of bringing about a live birth. The obvious motivation involves deliberately bringing about the death of the child.

Chapter 8 deals with the particular issues associated with late term termination of pregnancy.

Sometimes pregnancy occurs outside the uterus. Most often ectopic pregnancies miscarry and the issue resolves naturally. However, an ongoing ectopic pregnancy is a grave risk to the life of the mother. There have been tensions over the different options for the medical or surgical management of ectopic pregnancy. The Catholic Church has tended to deal with this as an application of double effect reasoning. It is a complex matter. Chapter 9 explores the complexities.

The practice of obstetrics and gynaecology has developed in numerous ways based on assumptions that involve significant ethical conflicts over the status of the child before birth, the status of the human embryo in the laboratory, and the variety of ways in which women's bodies may be manipulated. The negativity of the latter would seem to be reflected in the high cost of medical indemnity insurance for obstetrics and gynaecology which is on a par with cosmetic surgery. I suspect that the high risks for both areas relate to negative perceptions about whether the interventions are always necessary. It cannot be that there is greater negligence in these specialties.

I was approached by the Royal Australian and New Zealand College of Obstetrics and Gynaecology and asked to write an essay on how a doctor with religious beliefs practising in the area could deal with not being able to provide reasonable care because of his beliefs. That was obviously a loaded question, assuming that the caution required by religious beliefs would not be reasonable. I would argue, on the other hand, that often there is a medically and morally better option than the interventions that have become accepted as commonplace, such as,

- surgical or chemical termination of pregnancy,
- sterilization,
- post-coital chemical intervention,
- Methotrexate as a way of managing ectopic pregnancies,
- the use of IUDs, condoms, and the contraceptive pill,
- the range of options now available under the heading "reproductive technology" and
- prenatal diagnosis and pre-implantation genetic diagnosis (PGD) linked to selective destruction of an unwanted embryo or foetus.

There seem to be so many interventions that are ethically fraught but that have become an accepted part of gynaecology and obstetrics.

Chapter 10 explores the issue of professional conscience and its standing within the regulation of medical practice, especially obstetrics and gynaecology, in an essay that was published by the College in their magazine.

In many Western jurisdictions, there is tension over equal opportunity law and freedom of conscience and freedom of religion. In Australia, there is now an issue about professional freedom of conscience, because freedom of conscience and freedom of religion are not protected by Australian law and in the State of Victoria, the 2008 *Abortion Law Reform Act* overrides freedom of conscience. This is discussed in Chapter 11.

Chapter 12 is an essay that Mary and I had published in a well-regarded peer reviewed journal. The essay is on post-coital intervention known variously as the "morning after pill", "emergency contraception", or "contragestion". The article has led to some discussion about what a Catholic facility might offer, especially for a woman who fears pregnancy after rape or other circumstances not involving the good of marriage. We also suggest a protocol that would identify when women would have no reason to consider using post-coital intervention. By identifying whether she is unlikely to be at a possibly fertile time, intervention may be avoided. It is also possible to identify whether intervention is more or less likely to cause loss of nascent human life, rather than preventing fertilization.

Chapter 13 is a discussion of the issue of managing threats to the mother's life during pregnancy, and the particularly difficult problem of early pregnancy being itself a risk to the mother's life. This has given rise to major differences of opinion about what are called "vital conflicts" and double effect reasoning.

In Chapter 14, I have addressed the vexed issue of contraception which has caused such division amongst Catholics and in many ways separates the Catholic Church from other denominations, with most others taking a more liberal view. The reform known as the Theology of the Body, discussed in chapter 2, has provided some new insights based on a Scriptural understanding of marriage.

Chapter 15 looks at claims that the Church was wrong to oppose the promotion of condoms to prevent sexually transmissible infections (STIs). The Church is often accused of being responsible for deaths from STIs, such as HIV/AIDS or Hepatitis B or C, particularly in developing countries. Is the Church clinging to a dangerous and outmoded dogma? What can we learn from looking at the different approaches adopted by African countries in relation to condom use and policies in relation to educating people about the causes of the AIDS epidemic and seeking to change behaviour.

The oral contraceptive pill is widely acknowledged as having caused significant social change over the past fifty years since it was rapidly taken up by women in the 1960s. The Pill is credited with allowing women greater freedom to pursue careers by liberating them from unwanted pregnancy and permitting them to plan to have a family or not, at a time that suited their careers, as well as limiting family size. In developed countries, the birth rate is well below replacement level, and many developing countries are trending in that direction, with only the least developed countries having birth rates at significant growth levels. There are, however, questions about the impact of the Pill on women, on their health certainly, but also on their relationships and even on their economic options. Chapter 16 examines some of the claims being made about the social impact of the Pill, particularly for women.

In our discussion of gender, there are two groups who are often overlooked, especially in theological discussion. Theological discussion often assumes that people are either male or they are female. Of the two groups who are overlooked, the first are those people who are born without a clear gender and who, in the past, were often operated on as infants to make them appear more like one gender than the other, even though most remained infertile. These "intersex conditions" may be caused by genetic abnormalities affecting the X or Y chromosome. However, they may also be to do with gene expression during development in a genetically normal male or female, resulting in a failure to develop normal sexual and reproductive organs.

The other group includes those who suffer from what has been called "gender dysphoria". This describes people who are firmly of the belief that they are the gender opposite to their biological gender identity.

Sometimes this is referred to as a man trapped in a woman's body or a woman trapped in a man's body. Both conditions are considered disorders of gender development.

At the time of writing, there was no official Catholic teaching specifically dealing with sexual reassignment, but generally amongst Catholic theologians there has been an acceptance of procedures to establish some approximation of one gender or the other in those with an intersex condition, but a rejection of gender reassignment in the circumstances of gender dysphoria.

In recent times, paediatricians have tended to delay surgery to treat intersex conditions following complaints that they made the wrong choice. They tend to wait until there is greater indication of which gender characteristics are more likely to be dominant. In addition, it has become more common for parents, doctors and the Family Court to decide to intervene to prevent puberty developing in children who suffer from gender dysphoria and for hormonal and surgical reassignment to follow after they turn 16. In both instances, it may mean that a Catholic school could face gender reassignment in a child at the school.

There have also been cases of a teacher in a Catholic school announcing a gender change and the intention to have the hormonal treatment and surgery. This creates some pastoral difficulties for a Catholic school in relation to both the vulnerability of the person involved, including a high risk of suicide and self-harm, and the impact on those in the school community of the teacher's handling and representation of the moral issue of what may involve the destruction of healthy sexual and reproductive organs.

Having been consulted about cases involving the circumstances of a child and the circumstances of a teacher, I published an article based on the advice that I had prepared and have included it here as chapter 17. I have added a draft letter that I school might adapt if it were seeking to explain the fact that a child had enrolled as one gender but now wanted to be treated as the opposite gender.

In recent times also, the complex matter of same sex attraction has been widely discussed. It was not so long ago that most Western countries removed the offence of sodomy from the criminal law. During the first response to the HIV/AIDS epidemic much was done to target education to men who had sex with men as one of the groups most at risk, alongside intravenous drug users. The need to bring the practice more out into the open, for education purposes about the risk of infection, led to much greater acceptance of same sex attraction. Coupled with increasingly liberal ideas about sexuality and, through the advent of modern contraceptives, the separation of sexual intimacy from reproduction, same sex relationships have become much more widely accepted. Further, in recent times there has been advocacy for so-called "marriage equality" and the widely perceived need to change the legal definition of marriage to permit two people of the same gender to be "married" under the law.

The revelation that a son or a daughter is attracted by those of the same sex can be difficult for parents and for other family members. Traditionally, the Christian churches have condemned sexual intimacy between people of the same sex and have found support for that view in the Scriptures. The issue of same sex marriage has also divided our communities.

There has also been much discussion about homophobia – that is, fear or hatred of people who are living a life style involving sexual intimacy with someone of the same sex. No doubt there have been inappropriate responses and people who are attracted by those of the same sex have been treated very badly.

The issues of homophobia, same sex attraction and same sex marriage are the tropics of chapters 18, 19 and 20.

Amongst the range of sexual issues is the issue of masturbation. Often contemporary medical and psychological texts will portray it as a normal activity, but for a Christian it has the status of biblical condemnation and moral censure. It is an uncomfortable topic for parents and educators in

Christian sexuality. Masturbation is usually a solitary activity. It has no victim. It is arguably a normal part of adolescent development. What can be said about it now and where does it sit within the theology of the body reforms?

Related to masturbation may be the use of pornography. What may be said about the latter?

These are the topics for chapter 21.

Recently, the Australian Federal Government announced that it would establish a Royal Commission into sexual abuse of children and the response to complaints by alleged victims by Churches, other non-government agencies and government agencies. At the time of writing, the terms had been announced. At the forefront of the issue has been the Catholic Church with frequent allegations made against some clergy and religious that they have abused children, and also that the Church leaders failed to respond adequately, and may even have assisted to cover up criminal activities or otherwise failed to prevent offenders or suspected offenders from continuing to commit criminal offences against children.

These are difficult matters for the entire Church community. Was it just that the leaders were naïve and that the Church was an easy target for paedophiles who saw an opportunity to achieve convenient respectability as a celibate priest or religious while at the same time taking advantage of children entrusted to their care? Alternatively, was there something wrong with the selection and training of those who chose committed celibacy within the Church, something wrong with celibacy or something wrong with the approach that the Church takes to sexuality that led to men who were poorly formed, or sexually maldeveloped such that they later exploited vulnerable children in this way? It has been argued that because some of the religious communities accepted males as young as 14 and many joined immediately after completing secondary school, they were denied an ordinary adolescence because they lived in all male celibate communities from such an early age while they were still maturing sexually and emotionally.

There are also questions about whether there was cooperation between paedophiles within the Church, so-called "paedophile rings", in which they would protect each other and groom and pass victims on from one to the other.

Most Catholics accept that there will always be people who behave badly in any group and the Church is a human church and no different, even if we have higher expectations for those who are our priests and religious. What is concerning is, first, if paedophiles are disproportionately represented amongst priests and religious, and, second, the extent to which paedophiles may have been protected or their activities covered up, and the perceived failure to ensure that those who committed criminal offences were brought to justice. This is the topic of chapter 22 and includes some speculation about how we might lance the boil, so to speak, and move on from what are hideous circumstances, while ensuring that victims are adequately supported and compensated for harm. The latter raises issues about the extent to which the responsibility for harm rests only with the individual criminals or whether the Church community also bears some responsibility.

Chapter 23 addresses the inclusion of education in sexuality and relationships in the new Australian National Curriculum. The aims and purposes are discussed and how religious people and others might best ensure that their children are well formed in these respects. The chapter looks at the trends and the approaches that have been taken to sex education, what works and what does not, according to the evidence. It also addresses the need for research according to parameters that include not just pregnancy and STI rates, but also the effect of sex education on delaying sexual initiation and on the dangers of promiscuity.

The chapter discusses the importance of developing approaches that meet the actual needs of young people, that recognize the importance of a child's parents and family in his or her formation and sexual and emotional maturing, and that acknowledge the significance of the peer group and its importance in any sex education strategy. The evidence is quite significant in indicating that most of what is called "sex education" for young people, in the classroom or in formal government programs, is ineffective in terms of the parameters of pregnancy rates, abortion rates, incidence of sexually transmissible infections and risk behaviours, such as early sexual initiation, unprotected sex and multiple sexual partners. In fact, it appears that neither abstinence-only nor harm reduction, so-called "safe sex", programs make a significant difference to behaviour and attitudes. The factors that do make a difference tend to be contextual, rather than anything to do with what generally passes for sex education. On the basis of the evidence about what does work, some suggestions are made about how best to implement the National Curriculum in relation to education in sexuality.

As discussed in the preface, the final chapter was originally written as part of the preface. It is autobiographical in its reflections on the influences that have influenced my understanding of these issues. In talking about my mother and father, their relationship and my grandmothers and others who affected my maturing, I have tried to explain why I approach gender, parenthood, sexuality and relationships as I have. The purpose was to explain approaching relationships between men and women as a source of joy and wonder, but to acknowledge how difficult our individual journeys are, especially for those who like me, have never felt that they have mastered what it is to be a man and the complexity of relating to the opposite gender. At the same time I wished to explain how that journey is so vitally linked to faith and our vocation to seek communion with our Creator. That vocation is a quest to give witness to God's love for all creation, but especially those who share our status in being the kind of being who is made in the divine image of God and thus with the inherent capacity to give ourselves in love. To love God and neighbour is not an arbitrary teaching of Christ, but what essentially makes sense of our identity as human beings and of this gendered complementarity that is the way we were made to be.

2
The Human Body

Central to the topics of motherhood and embodied love is the way in which we understand the human body. Our culture tends to see the human body instrumentally, something we do things to and do things with, and that implies a dualism in which we somehow have an identity that is separate from the body. On the other hand, the international human rights instruments clearly see the human person as embodied, with bodily needs, and that the person as a body is inviolable.[1] If we identify ourselves as bodies, then we will regard the human body and relationships between bodies as sacred. We will also see motherhood for the extraordinary phenomenon that it is, in which a life comes into existence within a woman's body. That phenomenon forms a new and unique relationship in which she alone is that person's mother, forever changing her status and thus changing the nature of her existence.

In ordering the chapters, I was unsure where to start but decided to start with this chapter, firstly, because how we see the body underlies the issues that are discussed in this book, and second, because of the reform in relation to marriage and sexuality in the Catholic Church, begun at the Second Vatican Council and continued by Popes John Paul II and Benedict XVI.

Somehow the imaginations of young people, and others, have been

---

1 Nicholas Tonti-Filippini, *Human Dignity: Autonomy, Sacredness and the International Human Rights Instruments*, Philosophy Department, University of Melbourne 2000 http://dtl.unimelb.edu.au/R/1VU5TM5MCV5HF6L8YCKBP63YK8QG5G73HNB1YIU3BSE8MUETCT-00920?func=dbin-jump-full&object_id=66021&local_base=GEN01&pds_handle=GUEST

captured by moving away from the old natural law approaches to sexuality to approaches that are clearly Christocentric and Scriptural. It is as though we have recaptured something of the focus of the early Fathers on Jesus and on the *imago dei*. We are meant to imitate the God of love, and no more so than in the complete gift of self in the marital union. God's love is both *agape* and *eros*. It is both given without expectation of return, but God also wants our love.

Because this new development has changed so much of the way in which I, and many others, reflect on these issues, Mary pointed out that it would have been strange to start anywhere else, even though that meant a very theological beginning to the book, perhaps an otherwise strange thing to do for a philosopher. But as a philosopher, I do think it appropriate for me to analyse what Holy Scripture offers, while respecting the Sacred Texts, but at the same time considering what they say to us in our state of weakness and vulnerability to sin. In this day and age the teaching of Christ is a part at least of Western culture and contains explanations and ideas that vie for acceptance and influence in their own right, even for those who have no faith. I found that on secular committees, there was a place for offering a Christian alternative in seeking to identify the best and the ideal in human relating between health professionals and their patients and research subjects. Love as gift of self, and equal respect for the inviolability of each person are rich concepts which stand as alternatives, especially within the redemptive meaning of Christ's life, suffering and death and His teachings. Leaving to one side contemporary scepticism and cynicism about His divinity or His resurrection, how could we ignore the ideas and the influence of the Sermon on the Mount on Western culture, and even on the moral languages we share?

The marriage relationship is offered repeatedly in Scripture as an analogy for God's love. The intimacy between husband and wife thus assumes a unique dignity, the sacredness of being a witness to God's love: the love between the Father and all creation, the love between Christ and the community of His faithful, and the love between the Persons of the Holy Trinity and between the Holy Trinity and the people of God.

Note that this reform known as the "Theology of the Body" and developed principally through the Wednesday audience catechesis of Pope John Paul II, has been open to misrepresentation. In well-meaning attempts to popularise it, there has developed an approach that might be described as prurient and lacking a foundation in Scripture and without philosophical rigour. It is important to acknowledge and to be grateful for what has been done to popularize Pope John Paul II's catechesis, but it is important also that pastoral teaching and other work in the field, so to speak, retains a sound basis in scholarship and expresses a sense of sacramentality and reverence founded upon the tradition of Scriptural analysis and combined with historical accuracy. We are embodied and made in the image and likeness of God, and the latter gives great dignity to marital intimacy. The *Theology of the Body* should not be an excuse for prurience, but should instead respect the sacredness of marital intimacy and its fundamentally private nature.

This reform is an exciting development that holds out much promise for a genuine celebration of our sexual selves and understanding the theological significance of being gendered. Gender has never been so important, because we are in danger of developing an anthropology that sees it as merely a social construct and thus able to be treated as dispensable, rather than as essential to understanding our individual human identity, and crucial to our relating.

Soon after his pontificate began, Pope John Paul II, as noted, began a catechesis of marriage and celibacy known as the Theology of the Body. The first lecture was delivered on 5 September 1979 and he delivered the 129th audience on the Theology of the Body on 28 November 1984.[2]

What was distinctive about this treatment of sexuality was that it based the teaching on sexuality not in natural law, but in Holy Scripture.

---

2 Pope John Paul II, *Theology of the Body: Marriage and Celibacy in the Divine Plan*, Pauline Books, 1997.

An analysis of the Theology of the Body needs first to address "what is theology?"

Theology means thought and talk about God. Theology is also about ourselves (and everything else) considered in relation to God. That leads us to reflect upon the sources in which the truth of faith is articulated. Often theology is divided into:

- natural theology or theodicy – philosophical theology – applying the light of reason;
- sacred theology – applying the light of faith;
- systematic theology – seeking to determine the relationship between the truths of faith and other propositions that are not revealed.[3]

Theology of the Body is the study of human beings as physical beings in our relationship to God and it includes topics such as:

- theological anthropology;
- creation of humanity;
- incarnation of Jesus;
- eschatology (discussion of life after death) and the body.

Theology of the Body is both contemplative and moral. It is contemplative in that it involves reflecting on who we are in relationship to God. It is moral in that it involves reflecting on how we should act given who we are.

Pope John Paul II began his analysis by reflecting on Jesus' comments on divorce:

> "Haven't you read," he replied, "that at the beginning the Creator 'made them male and female,' and said, 'For this reason a man will leave his father and mother and be united to his wife, and the two will become one flesh'? So they are no longer two, but one.

---

3 Germain Grisez, *The Way of the Lord Jesus Volume One: Christian Moral Principles*, Franciscan Herald Press, 1983, p. 3ff.

Therefore what God has joined together, let man not separate."
[Matthew 19:3ff]

Pope John Paul understood this to be a reference to Genesis.[4] In Genesis 1:27 we read:

> So God created man in his own image,
> in the image of God he created him;
> male and female he created them.

and in Genesis 2:24-25:

> For this reason a man will leave his father and mother and be united to his wife, and they will become one flesh.
> The man and his wife were both naked, and they felt no shame.

In this there is a key metaphysical concept (to do with the nature of being), that human beings exist as a body and that we are gendered.

Important also are the notions of original innocence and the fact that in that state our first ancestors felt no shame and they were equal – both made in the image and likeness of God. They also existed in a state of original unity and innocence – they had no knowledge yet of good and evil.[5]

The significance of the Fall through sin – their own choice – is that there was enmity between them, they began to seek to dominate and own each other and they lost that sense of equal respect for each other.[6]

Jumping forward to the New Testament, we know that by his life, suffering and death, Jesus redeemed us from the effects of sin so that through him we can again seek full communion with God.[7]

The phrase the "nuptial" or "conjugal" meaning of the body is often used in the Theology of the Body.[8]

---

4 Pope John Paul II, Op Cit, General Audience, 5 September 1979.
5 Ibid., General Audience, 26 September 1979.
6 *Genesis* 3:14-19.
7 *John* 10:10.
8 See for instance, Pope John Paul II, Op Cit, General Audience, 9 January 1980.

The human body, with its gender, its masculinity or femininity, seen in the very mystery of creation, is not only a source of fruitfulness and procreation, but is part of the whole natural order. It includes, right from the beginning, the nuptial attribute, that is the capacity of expressing love, that love in which the person becomes a gift and – by means of this gift – fulfils the meaning of his or her being and existence.[9]

In our fallen state, we perceive the original innocence before the effects of sin very dimly. The Theology of the Body seeks to understand what it was that we lost through sin, and must be understood from the perspective of our beginning in original innocence, without shame, without sin, created male and female in the image and likeness of God. Scripturally it was a time when men and women did not seek to dominate or possess each other, but were equal and unaffected by sin.[10]

Essentially man and woman were made to be a perfect gift to each other. In original innocence, woman is given to man by the Creator and received by him as a gift. In giving herself she rediscovers herself at the same time because of the way she is welcomed and received by man *for her own sake*.[11]

We understand that we are made in the image and likeness of God, and God is not one person but three persons in perfect relationship to one another in which each perfectly loves the other, each is a perfect gift to the other and their love is fruitful. They are a communion of persons. Thus in being made in their image and likeness, man and woman are made to be a communion of persons freely giving themselves completely to each other in reciprocal relationship, and in a way that is fruitful.[12]

Created male and female in the image and likeness of God, they form a communion from a state of individual solitude. This is often called the Trinitarian Concept of the "Image of God." In the mystery of creation

---

9 Ibid. General Audience, 7 November 1979.
10 Ibid. General Audience, 26 September 1979.
11 Ibid. General Audience, 2 January 1980.
12 Ibid. General Audience, 19 December 1979.

– on the basis of the original and consistent "solitude" of his being – human beings were endowed with a deep unity between what is, humanly and through the body, male in them and what is, equally humanly and through the body, female in them. Being made in the image and likeness of God, their unity imitates the unity between the Divine Persons of the Holy Trinity.[13]

If man and woman cease to be a disinterested gift for each other, as they were in the mystery of creation, they recognize that "they are naked" (Genesis 3). Then the shame of that nakedness, which they had not felt in the state of original innocence, will spring up in their hearts. Sin has affected their relationship.

Maleness and femaleness of humanity was part of the design of creation: "And God saw everything that he had made, and behold it was very good" (Genesis 1:31).

That spousal relationship was the primordial sacrament, a visible sign of truth and love which has its source in God, the Creator. The unity of man and woman "in one flesh" is the conjugal mystery in which they give of themselves completely and in that way their relationship is a likeness to the perfect love of the communion of persons that is the Holy Trinity. The sacrament of marriage therefore is itself a sign and a witness to God's love: the love between the persons of the Trinity and the love between God and humanity. Christ refers to himself as the bridegroom, choosing the marriage relationship to indicate the gift that he makes to humanity including his willingness to suffer and die for the other, for us.[14]

In this understanding, conjugal knowledge is a definitive discovery of the meaning of the human body in which two persons become an unrepeatable female-male "self", each becoming part of the other's knowledge of self. This does not mean the sexual life together of husband and wife. They are not passive objects defined by their bodies

---

13 Ibid, General Audience, 10 October 1979.
14 Ibid, General Audience, 20 February 1980.

and their sexuality. Rather this means that through their mutual gift of love in marriage, man and woman form a new "self".

When we experience shame as man or as woman it is because we are regarded by ourselves or others as an object.

The significance of the Genesis story of our beginning is that our ancestors in their original innocence before they were affected by sin, were mutually conscious of their spousal nature as gift for each other and hence in their innocence experienced no shame. They were not objects, but a true and perfect gift to each other.

When with the fall they ceased to give in that disinterested way, they came to view each other as objects of desire and that made their sexuality shameful.

The Theology of the Body thus proposes questions about gender, complementarity and reciprocity.

What is gender? It refers to the properties of belonging to the male or female sex. Sex means either of the main divisions (male and female) into which living things are placed on the basis of their reproductive function. Inherently gender is determined by our capacity to be a mother or a father.

Recognising gender is thus the identification of those properties by which a being may be classified male or female. Whether one is the kind of being who has the biological capacity to mother or alternatively to father offspring is usually determined in humans genetically by the two sex chromosomes, females are generally XX and males XY.

There are of course some gender disorders such as in children who at birth possess XO, XXY and XYY combinations. The disorders of the X or the Y chromosome include:

- intersex conditions;
- androgen insensitivity syndrome caused by damaged X chromosome;

- congenital adrenal hyperplasia – a hormonal disorder causing ambiguous genitalia in girls and excessive masculinization in boys;
- gender identity disorders.

Gender identity disorder is a mental disorder involving the desire to be, or the insistence that one is, of the other sex (other than as determined by one's biology). It is a persistent discomfort about one's assigned sex or a sense of inappropriateness in the gender role of that sex and often involves significant distress or impairment in social, occupational, or other important areas of functioning.[15]

Sex reflects reproductive function, thus the significance of gender is in the capacity to become a father or a mother, and the relationship by which one becomes a mother or a father. Gender is therefore essentially about that fruitfulness by which one becomes a parent. The different capacity for fruitfulness in either fatherhood or motherhood essentially delineates male from female

Gender differentiation is biological in the first instance, according to reproductive organs, and we recognize physical and psychological properties of individuals which, through experience, we come to associate as differences between the sexes. We are very good at determining human gender at first glance in fully clothed individuals and at distance!

An important fact of our experience of gender is that it is a fallen experience, marred by sin. Thus we tend to experience inequality and disunity. Gender complementarity is poorly developed against a background of individualism. Individualism spawns the desires to dominate, possess, compete against and use. Therefore a view of complementarity as competing psychological and physical advantages and weaknesses is mistaken.

The primary questions about gender are to do with our anthropology and the *imago dei* and the original unity and equality that we initially

---

15 American Psychiatric Association, *Diagnostic Services Manual IV*. http://www.psychiatryonline.com/referral.aspx?gclid=CNGV7LKczKECFRM3bwodF27ncQ

lost through sin. Redemption through Christ Jesus opened the door to recovery. In that redemption, gender complementarity has a non-exploitative place as loving gift. We recognize man and woman being made for each other and complementarity is our ability to give completely to another, at all levels, physically, cognitively, emotionally and spiritually, and our yearning to express ourselves in that giving.

In the creation of Eve we are told,

> It is not good that the man should be alone. I will make him a helpmate. (Gn 2:18-19)

In the beginning therefore man yearned to give himself.

In the passage, "This at last is bone from my bones. This is to be called woman for this was taken from man" (Gn 2:23), Pope John Paul II notes the recognition of another who is like me, another "I," and the unity of two as the personal character of a human being.[16]

This is a dual unity in which, but for the exception of the intersex disorders, a human being exists only and always as a masculine or a feminine being. Pope John Paul teaches that "helper" is to be understood reciprocally not subordinately. This is a relationship of identity and difference in which there is absolute equality of each as a being created by God for his or her own sake but different physically and psychologically.[17]

The difference of the sexes belongs to human nature as a being made in the image of God, and sexuality is not reducible to animality, nor to spirituality. The existence of an intersex condition is thus a matter of profound significance and difficulty. It is not just a physical matter and it is not resolvable by considering it only cognitive or only spiritual. The differences between the genders is the basis of spousal love and spousal love is of great theological significance.[18]

Spousal love is the principal analogy for every kind of love. The

---

16 Ibid, General Audience, 7 November 1979.
17 Ibid.
18 Ibid.

nature of consecrated celibacy and marriage is "conjugal" and finds its expression in being a gift of self.[19]

In his reflection on the notion of "helper" in Genesis 2:18-25, Pope John Paul II teaches that in the passage, "I will make him *a helper fit for him,*" the biblical context enables us to understand this in the sense that the woman must "help" the man – and in his turn he must help her – first of all by the very fact of their "being human persons." In a certain sense this enables man and woman to discover their humanity ever anew and to confirm its whole meaning. We can easily understand that, on this fundamental level, it is a question of a "help" on the part of both, and at the same time a mutual "help." [20]

In his reflection on gender, Pope John Paul explains that gender is the intrinsic polarity intended for dual unity – identity and difference converge. Solitary man or woman is whole in him or herself, made in the image and likeness of God, but yearns for opportunity to give of self to another. This yearning is bio-instinctual but not merely so. It is free and rational and thus expressive of the *imago dei*. Gender difference yields the opportunity for complete gift of self in imitation of God's love. Complementarity represents that within oneself which may be given beneficially to the other within the unity of mutual love and intersubjectivity.[21]

Yearning to express oneself in gift finds opportunity for complete gift of self in recognising in oneself that which may be given beneficially to the other within the unity of the two, which presents itself in a contingent reality within an intrinsic polarity.[22]

That intrinsic polarity is experienced in differences recognized psychoanalytically and physically. Such differences are an experienced but variable mysterious reality. There is great variation between different couples and how their genders are experienced.

---

19 Pope Benedict XVI, *Deus Caritas Est* (2005), n. 5.
20 Pope John Paul II, *Mulieris Dignitatem* (1989) n. 6-7.
21 Pope John Paul II, *Theology of the Body* op. cit. General Audience, 6 February 1980.
22 Ibid. General Audience, 2 April 1980.

The gendered gift of love is Trinitarian. It reflects the reality that there is unity in one divine nature, but there are different persons within that one nature. Difference and unity thus reside together in the Trinity. Jesus was born of woman conceived by the Holy Spirit. The Holy Spirit is thus a model for the fruitfulness of the conjugal union.

The Trinity is the model for conjugal love and thus for the dual unity of gender as identity and difference, and it is a model for its fruitfulness.

> The fact that man "created as man and woman" is the image of God means not only that each of them individually is like God, as a rational and free being. It also means that man and woman, created as a "unity of the two" in their common humanity, are called to live in a communion of love, and in this way to mirror in the world the communion of love that is in God, through which the Three Persons love each other in the intimate mystery of the one divine life. The Father, Son and Holy Spirit, one God through the unity of the divinity, exist as persons through the inscrutable divine relationship. Only in this way can we understand the truth that God in himself is love (cf. *Jn* 4:16).[23]
>
> The Lord Jesus, when he prayed to the Father "that all may be one ... as we are one" (*Jn* 17:21-22), opened up vistas closed to human reason. For he implied *a certain likeness* between the union of the divine Persons and the union of God's children in truth and charity. This likeness reveals that human beings, who are the only creatures on earth which God willed for their own sake, cannot fully find ourselves except through a sincere gift of self.[24]

This gendered gift of love in the nuptial mystery is Christological. It is the mystery of Christ and the Church with Christ as Bridegroom, Church as bride. Conjugal love is also a gift of self as Christ gave himself completely on the Cross.

In the story of the Fall, to the woman God said: "Your yearning shall be for your husband, yet he will lord it over you" (Gn 3:16).

---

23 See John Paul II, *Mulieris Dignitatem* (the Dignity of Women), n. 7; and in the Second Vatican Council document, *Gaudium et Spes*, n. 24.
24 Ibid.

Possessiveness and dominance are thus consequences of the fall, the original equality destroyed. Therefore ownership and subordination are not part of original creation but a consequence of failure due to human choosing.[25]

That prompts the question: What was the sin of Adam and Eve?

The Second Vatican Council notes, "Although he was made by God in a state of natural justice, from the very dawn of history man abused his liberty, at the urging of the Evil One. Man set himself against God and sought to find fulfilment apart from God."[26]

This was the rejection of God as the source of unity: "Creating man in his image and likeness, God wills for them the fullness of good, or supernatural happiness, which flows from sharing in his own life. *By committing sin man rejects this gift* and at the same time wills to become "as God, knowing good and evil" (GN 3:5), that is to say, deciding what is good and what is evil independently of God, his Creator. "Sin brings about a break in the original unity which man enjoyed in the state of original justice: union with God as source of unity within his own 'I,' in the mutual relationship between man and woman [*communio personarum*] as well as in regard to the external world, in nature."[27]

God is the source of the man-women unity. Loss of that acknowledgement of God as source is a loss of the sense of submission to each other as a gift given by God, as an opportunity to express personality in that mutual gift of self to the other, a loss of conjugality.

Submission to the other in love is then replaced by the desire to possess or to dominate.

The yearning becomes a desire to use rather than to give of oneself. Losing focus on God, we lose the meaning of love. John refers to the threefold concupiscence (Jn 2:16):

---

25 Ibid. General Audience, 26 September 1979.
26 *Gaudium et Spes*, n. 13.
27 Ibid.

- lust of the eyes;
- lust of the flesh;
- pride of life.

Delineating what we were made to be from what we became, equality means that neither is superior, but each is made in the image and likeness of God. Gender complementarity means yearning to give of oneself in a way that relates to the needs of the other and of the dual unity, rather than desiring the other as a mere object of pleasure. Gender creates the opportunity for complete gift of self, expressed in the conjugal union. That conjugal unity has a focus on fruitfulness, not unity for its own sake.[28]

Pope John Paul II goes on to say,

> ... conjugal love, while leading the spouses to the reciprocal "knowledge" which makes them "one flesh," does not end with the couple, because it makes them capable of the greatest possible gift, the gift by which they become co-operators with God for giving life to a new human person. Thus the couple, while giving themselves to one another, give not just themselves but also the reality of children, who are a living reflection of their love, a permanent sign of conjugal unity and a living and inseparable synthesis of their being a father and a mother.[29]

In relation to the Women's Rights Movement, he teaches that domination by women is not a solution to a history of male chauvinism, but instead we need a rediscovery of gendered equality and gendered gift of self.

> The personal resources of femininity are no less than the resources of masculinity: they are merely different. Hence a woman, as well as a man, must understand her "fulfilment" as a person, her dignity and vocation, on the basis of these resources, according to

---

28 John Paul II, *Familiaris Consortio*, n.14.
29 Ibid.

the richness of the femininity which she received on the day of creation and which she inherits as an expression of the image and likeness of God.[30]

Man is not the reference point for "otherness" of woman. The reference point for human personality is the *imago dei*. Man and woman discover that within that equal personhood of the *imago dei* they are different and the differences are an opportunity for the gift of self, recognising in oneself that which may be received by the other as truly beneficial.[31]

In *Corinthians*, 11:2-16, St Paul taught:

- Christ is head of every man.
- Man is head of woman.
- Man is image of God's glory.
- Woman is reflection of man's glory, as woman came from him.
- Man was not created for sake of woman, but woman created for the sake of man.

In relation to this passage, John Paul II teaches in the Theology of the Body (p. 382) that the motif of "head" and of "body" is not of biblical derivation, but is probably Hellenistic. In Ephesians this theme is utilized in the context of marriage (while in First Corinthians the theme of the "body" serves to demonstrate the order that reigns in society). From the biblical point of view the introduction of this motif is an absolute novelty.[32]

In *Ephesians*, 5:22-33, St Paul also taught:

- Defer to one another in obedience to Christ.
- Wives should regard their husbands as they regard the Lord.
- Christ is head of the Church and saves the whole body, so is husband head of wife.

---

30 *Mulieris Dignitate*, n. 10.
31 Ibid.
32 *Theology of the Body*, Op Cit. General Audience, 4 February 1981.

- The Church submits to Christ, wives to their husbands.
- Husbands should love their wives as Christ loved Church and sacrificed himself for her.

In *Mulieris Dignitatem n. 24*, Pope John Paul II teaches that this passage is rooted in customs of time and should be understood in terms of mutual subjection out of reverence for Christ and that the husband is "head" only in order to give himself up for the wife. "Subjection" is not one-sided but mutual.

In *Familiaris Consortio* (n. 25), he taught that authentic conjugal love presupposes and requires that a man have a profound respect for the equal dignity of his wife: "You are not her master," writes St. Ambrose, "but her husband; she was not given to you to be your slave, but your wife ... Reciprocate her attentiveness to you and be grateful to her for her love." With his wife a man should live "a very special form of personal friendship". As for the Christian, he is called upon to develop a new attitude of love, manifesting towards his wife a charity that is both gentle and strong, like that which Christ has for the Church.

Above all, it is important to underline the equal dignity and responsibility of women with men. This equality is realized in a unique manner in that reciprocal self-giving by each, one to the other, and by both to the children, which is proper to marriage and the family. What human reason intuitively perceives and acknowledges is fully revealed by the word of God: the history of salvation, in fact, is a continuous and luminous testimony of the dignity of women.[33]

In the Theology of the Body, Pope John Paul II teaches that love is ever seeking, never satisfied. The love between spouses is a love between equals who respect the other as divine gift, designed by God to be different and complementary so that their relationship is an opportunity to be a communion of persons that is a witness to the communion of persons of the Holy Trinity and their unitive and fruitful love for each other.[34]

This Scriptural understanding has its origins in the teaching of Christ and the early Fathers, in St Augustine, St John Chrysostom and later in St

---

33 *Familiaris Consortio*, n. 22.
34 *Theology of the Body*, op. cit. General Audience of 6 June 1984.

Thomas Aquinas, so it is not novel, but in a way it is novel because it is not based on the natural law tradition that also developed within the Church and found expression in Catholic teaching, especially the teaching prevalent in the majority and minority opinions of the Papal Commission on Birth Control after the Second Vatican Council. My students are usually shocked and dismayed by the absence of a Scriptural understanding of marriage and the apparent physicalism of what is referred to as natural law in the two opinions. It seems strange to discuss marriage without the Sermon on the Mount.

Servais Pinckaers OP saw the problem as a separation between morality, on the one hand, and virtue, on the other. The virtues that Jesus taught, on that view, are a call to seek perfection available to a few but not demanded of all, but morality reflects universal requirements. The contemporary Theology of the Body embraces all that Jesus taught and lived in which we are called to seek perfection in witness to God's love. Marital intimacy is thus not a secondary state for those too weak to be completely holy. By adopting marriage as the analogy for divine love, Scripture shows us the marriage vocation as an aspiration to perfect holiness. Christ redeemed us, giving us the sacraments as a source and a sign of our unity with God, and the sacrament of marriage, especially giving oneself in loving sexual union in the celebration of that sacrament and open to God's grace and to being a witness to the perfection of divine love, is a way to aspire to human perfection.[35]

I was fascinated to find that the old manualists, such as Henry Davis SJ (*Moral and Pastoral Theology*, Heythrop Series II, London: Sheed and Ward, 1930) saw this way of thinking as heretical as late as the 1930s. I was also fascinated that the official English translation I possess from the time of Pope Pius XI's *Casti Connubii*, in 1930, excludes section 24 which expresses this view of perfection in marriage, which is a recurring theme in *Humanae Vitae* n. 8 and in the writing of Pope John Paul II in *Familiaris Consortio* and the Theology of the Body Wednesday catechesis.

---

35 Servais Pinckaers, "The Return of the New Law to Moral Theology", in Berkman, John, and Steven Titus, Craig, *The Pinckaers Reader: Renewing Thomistic Moral Theology*, Catholic University of America Press, 2005, pp. 369-384; Pinckaers, Servais, "Conscience and the Virtue of Prudence" in Berkman *et al*, op. cit., p. 346.

What is now attracting people to reconsider the teaching of the Catholic Church on marriage and sexuality is an aspirational concept of human sexuality and gender in which gender really does matter in the lived experience of the sacrament, and there is a radical call to men and women to celebrate their sexuality in all its mystery and wonder in being a mutual gift of love in witness to the unity, equality and fruitfulness of divine love. Far from taking the fun from sex, the Church calls on us to celebrate it for its extraordinary power and meaning. We have a vocation to both give ourselves in love and be received in love as a complete and unilateral gift of self. Such a decision to give is not to be taken lightly, but it is also to be celebrated not just by the couple, but by all those who love them. It is such a wonderful happening, when two people make a mature and intelligent decision to completely surrender their vulnerability to the other and to rely upon God's grace to sustain them in that love, and accept the possibility that a consequence of God's grace will be that they may become parents together and thereby build their community of love.

Cynically, marriage may be described as the piece of paper representing the consent event. But the happy tears of families at a wedding indicates something much more because they reflect the depth of their mixed feelings and the complexity of both joy at this extraordinarily complete, fully human and totally mutual gift of love, and sadness at knowing how challenging that choice may be, a challenge demonstrated by the unhappiness of frequent marriage failure in our generation. That failure only happens because one or other or both did not sustain their giving. Amongst the joy and the tears, the friends and families also know that what is being given has a price, and that price can involve great suffering. Marriage and parenthood calls for every element of skill and reserve that each spouse possesses, including dealing with failure. The pass mark is survival of the relationship despite failures along the way. The experience of love is at its greatest not when all is going well, but when it is not. The loveliest moments are often immediately following the lowest moments when one or other or both has had to surrender once more his or her pride, his or her needs, and to plumb the depths of a love that may have been sorely tested. Marriages are sustained by making up after differences and hurt. Without the arguments, so much would be missed.

As we stand at a wedding celebration, all these matters give rise to our tears as we wish the couple not just joy when all is going well, but also many shared triumphs of love over self, of giving and receiving love despite the challenges of things not going so well.

The physical, emotional, cognitive and spiritual nature of marital intimacy celebrates the diversity and mystery of gendered difference and equality, and is the opposite of domination and possessiveness. Marriage is therefore wonderfully liberating, the liberation of launching a great adventure of human discovery, a voyage that will plumb unknown depths and is completely at the whim of fate and the winds that may blow. All we have is the commitment to a democratic communion founded on an overriding commitment to equal love and respect and the willingness to give one's life for another.

The public event celebrates an intensely private happening on the wedding night and all that follows from it. The consent event of the exchange of vows is not what is important, just a legal formality. What we celebrate in the public event is not the consent, but what we expect to follow it, a sweet and holy intimacy which transports the lovers closer to God in the grace of choosing to be a living witness to God's love, open to the divine will for them and whatever may follow. Even if a couple have been living together before marriage, as many now do, the fact of committing permanently to each other in the sight of God (and their families and friends) introduces something completely new to their relationship. By committing themselves to the divine plan for their union, their love-making thereafter is transformed to becoming their vocation to not just love each other, but to love God through their love for each other, willingly open to God's design for them, including becoming parents. Before marriage they stand solitary before God as individuals, but in marriage they ask God to bless their union, and together they wish to do God's will, standing before God as a communion of persons.

It is sad that young couples often choose to delay marriage, but still elect to give each other the fruits of marriage by "living together". In Australia, the majority of couples registering their marriage in 2011 cohabited prior to marriage (78.2%). However, the proportion slightly decreased from a peak of 78.5% from 2010 to 2011, so there may be a trend in the other direction after years of increasing proportions of couples cohabiting before marriage.[36] Of course, that they have not chosen to marry, in the formal sense of having a public ceremony, does not mean that they are not committed. They may, in a natural sense, be married, having made a private commitment. There seems to be a common scenario in which they have that understanding, but choose to either delay making a public announcement of their intentions, or not ever to make it a public event. The latter view goes with an idea that their relationship is entirely a private affair. It seems that a catalyst to a public event is having children or intending to have children and the realisation that the public declaration is relevant to children. That would indicate that, in their minds, they have separated sexual intimacy from procreativity, with the latter being an add-on option.

Where there is no indication of commitment, there is reason to feel sad for them because there is likely to be significant inequality in a number of ways. Often one rather than the other is choosing to delay either asking or acceding. One or other wants to commit or to commit sooner than the other, and that creates a power imbalance that the other party might not want to lose. When they do eventually commit, that party may then feel the subsequent loss of power as entrapment into marriage. A second aspect of the inequality is the differential of risk. The woman is risking pregnancy without his commitment to support her or the child. She has much more to lose economically, and in many other ways, including possibly her full-time employment and thus her career, if she does not have the security of his exclusive commitment to her and any child who results. If the relationship does not survive pregnancy and birth of a child, then she is greatly disadvantaged economically. Further, few relationships survive abortion (see chapter 2), if she takes that course. Young couples often overlook risk of pregnancy, having confidence in prophylaxis, but, as has been discussed elsewhere (see Chapters 7, 12 and 15), the pregnancy rates for all the usual methods of contraception are significant (at least 3-6 per hundred women years in actual use).

---

36 Australian Bureau of Statistics, *Marriages and Divorces, Australia*, 2011. Accessed 19/1/13 from: http://www.abs.gov.au/ausstats/abs@.nsf/Products/3310.0~2011~Chapter~Marriages?OpenDocument

The US evidence about the outcome of cohabiting before marriage is sobering:

- More than eight out of ten couples who live together will break up either before the wedding or afterwards in divorce.
- About 45 per cent of those who begin cohabiting, do not marry.
- Couples who do marry after living together are 50% more likely to divorce than those who did not.
- Only 12 percent of couples who have begun their relationship with cohabitation end up with a marriage lasting 10 years or more.[37]

In Australia, direct marriages (not cohabiting before) were significantly more likely to survive than indirect marriages (cohabiting before). For instance, ten years after marriage, the survival rates for the total sample were 83 per cent and 71 per cent respectively (a gap of 12%); and by 20 years, the rates were 68 per cent and 51 per cent respectively (a gap of 17%).[38]

Inequality and the exercise of power in a relationship are very damaging because they are the opposite of love. Love implies equal respect and equal respect for each other requires no domination, no possessiveness. A second aspect of the absence of public commitment is the privatisation and resultant uncertainty of the relationship denying opportunities for others, friends and family, an event or events to mark the occasion and to support the couple. A couple who cohabit without public commitment are very much alone in securing the relationship, denying themselves the support of others because others, family and friends, simply do not know whether there is anything definite to support.

---

[37] Michael McManus, *Marriage Savers: helping your family and friends avoid divorce,* Zondervan Publishing House, 1984, pp. 27-28; cf from http://www.rayfowler.org/2008/04/18/statistics-on-living-together-before-marriage/ accessed 20/1/13.

[38] David de Vaus, Lixia Qu and Ruth Weston, "Does premarital cohabitation affect the chances of marriage lasting?", Australian Institute of Family Studies Eighth Australian Institute of Family Studies Conference, *Steps forward for families: Research, practice and policy,* Melbourne, 12–14 February 2003, http://www.melbourneinstitute.com/downloads/hilda/Bibliography/Conference_Papers/deVaus_etal_Does_premarital_cohabitation_affect_the_chances_of_marriage_lasting.pdf

The difference in gender means being potentially either mother or father, it also means so many differences in how love is given and received. Bill May writes movingly about the wife receiving in a giving kind of way and the husband giving in a receiving kind of way.[39] The marriage act itself is both expressive and symbolic of their love and it depends on their bodies being made for each other. Every couple will find their own unique combination of individual strengths and weaknesses that contribute to the capability and resourcefulness of their union, but divine wisdom saw to it that the combination of maleness and femaleness are so wonderfully a balance for each other. Marriages survive on the mystery and wonder of the other and so often the humour that arises. So much depends on never taking yourself so seriously that you do not laugh at yourselves. The human body and the marriage act are so sacred, but also so amusing. Nakedness is both funny but also so beautiful, and God gave it to us so we could enjoy the other completely. The combination of joy and beauty in marital love is the inspiration of the Song of Songs, great reading for married couples.

The Theology of the Body recognizes that if we love God, then God will be in our minds, in our hearts and on our lips, and in our embraces, as we celebrate being able to give ourselves in this way, not just in sexual intimacy, but every moment of our finite time together. The God of love is in the marriage bed celebrating with the couple their extraordinary gift to each other, perhaps to cooperate with them in the coming to be of a new life, a new beginning of another who is also made in God's image. The extraordinary power for both the unity and the fruitfulness of marital love is overwhelming in its significance, and the realisation that what they do together means so much more than just their love for each other. Marital love, reaches out from the privacy of that marriage bed to be something so much more, for their communion is in the image and likeness of the love for each other of the Father, Son and Holy Spirit, and the image and likeness of the love of Jesus for all creation, and, like that divine love, it is fruitful.

Every married couple needs to never lose their consciousness that their love is not just about them. It does not stop at being mutually self-serving,

---

39 William E. May, Marriage and the Complementarity of Male and Female, *Anthropotes: Rivista sulla persona e la famiglia* 8.1 (1992) 41-60 republished at http://www.christendom-awake.org/pages/may/marrcomp.htm

for it is designed to be the image of a love that willed all creation to come to be. Marital love is a common project that wills itself to be fruitful, not just in conceiving but in all that parenting requires (even what it takes to be a parent to adult children!). Marital love is strongly linked to parenthood and all that the latter will demand of them both, including the shared partnership of being mother and father together, of helping the other to be a better mother or father, and finding in the marital embrace the love that will surround the children in love. Marital love is a wellspring of divine love and unity in the household. Many of my fondest memories are of a child (at any stage) coming into our bedroom in the morning or evening to talk to us both, while we were still in bed. Somehow that emphasised our common project and the strength and importance of our love for each other as a source of love for them, serving the whole household in being in God's image. At a practical level, it also emphasised our complementarity, bringing both sets of resources to bear on their issues, tempering our responses.

The sadness of infertility reflects loss of the common project of parenthood. I suggest to infertile couples that the tragedy of infertility risks drawing them apart in the absence of such an overwhelming common project. They need to find other common projects that require their complementary knowledge, skills and capacities. Chapter 5 addresses the issues involved in infertility.

The difficulty of same sex attraction becomes evident when one reflects on a theology of marriage based on understanding the significance of the human body and the importance of gender. The arguments for same sex unions inevitably reject the significance of gender. This issue is discussed later in Chapters 18, 19 and 20.

The Theology of the Body celebrates maleness and femaleness, not as stereotypes, but in all the many different ways in which we experience gender and gender difference, and the unique combination of complementary gifts that a man and a woman find in their union. The theology recognizes that each marital act is the celebration of the sacrament for which the couple are the ministers. In the love they express, they give witness to the unity and fruitfulness of God's love. The attraction of the theology is the way it celebrates human embodiedness centered on the Incarnation, and informed by the teaching, life, suffering and death of Jesus. The Theology of the Body is Scriptural and Christological and fully human.

The debate over contraception, before and after *Humanae Vitae*, now appears to have been greatly impoverished in its emphasis on what seemed to be a pure reason account of natural law, and sterile debates over authority and infallibility in relation to a tradition that was not being well explained.

The Catechesis on the Theology of the Body restored a focus on the Word of God and on the Blessed Lord, unifying the Tradition to the early Fathers, to St Augustine, St John Chrysostom and to St Thomas Aquinas amongst others. That unification is brought to a greater completion by Pope Benedict's encyclicals on the theological virtues. In Divine love is the source of human love, with marital love being celebrated for its witness to that divine love.

My parents' generation in the Catholic Church often discussed the way in which they were made to feel that their marital state was very much inferior to the celibate state. They referred to the practice of cleansing mothers of newborns with a blessing after the child was born, as though the women had somehow been defiled by sexual intimacy. Many had very large families: my parents had eleven children (ten surviving) and my cousins were mostly in similarly large families. There was something of an attitude that regarded sexual intimacy as existing primarily for procreation and that the unitive dimension was very secondary. That was very sad and a cause for some resentment.

In contrast, the Theology of the Body makes very clear that the love expressed in the intimacy between husband and wife is sacramental in its witness to God's love, both Agape and Eros, and that couples were meant to seek perfection through their sexual intimacy and not in spite of it.

The Theology of the Body opens up a renewal of marital spirituality, even though recognising the solitude of each spouse before God. We do not lose our individuality and are called first to love God. Christ came to redeem each of us individually from the effects of sin. But His teaching wonderfully liberates marital intimacy as an avenue for seeking to be like Him, by giving of ourselves in love to another as a complete gift of self that parallels His gift on the Cross, but also parallels His desire to be loved. There is so much work to be done for each couple to make the marriage bed the altar on which they celebrate the sacrament. For that to be truly and fully the case, they do need to prepare for that witness to God's love and their openness to the divine grace of the sacrament. They need to make the sacramental nature of what they do the subject of their prayers and of their reading, and to connect the sacramentality of their marriage with the other sacraments, especially Penance and the Eucharist, both of which enrich the marriage. Through their love for each other they make each other holy, finding the divine image in each other and bringing each other closer to Christ

Marital intimacy should never be treated lightly because through it we come closer to the Father, to Jesus Himself and to the Holy Spirit. There is much for us to do to make that so. It is a good thing for couples to read and pray in connection with their love making. That does not necessarily mean a direct connection, a kind of barrier to be overcome first. It is just that their prayer life and their ongoing spiritual formation, in their love for each other, need to be linked.

3
Prenatal Diagnosis and Reproductive Discrimination

3.1 Prenatal Diagnosis

Most pregnant women are advised to undergo antenatal blood tests and ultrasound screening to ensure that the baby is developing as expected and to find out information that may be relevant to managing the pregnancy and the birth, such as the location of the placenta and whether there are twins.

Women are also advised that prenatal screening is normal to determine whether the child may have a serious abnormality. There is a distinction to be made between screening and diagnostic testing. A screening test is usually very sensitive but not very specific. In other words, it will have a high false-positive rate. It may, for instance, indicate that a woman has a higher risk of her child having an abnormality, such as the risk of one in 150. In the event that the screening test is positive, the woman would be advised to have a diagnostic test which is more accurate. However, some diagnostic tests are more intrusive and risk harm to her or the child.

The tests most often used include a maternal blood test and the Nuchal Translucency ultrasound test for Downs Syndrome, which are screening tests, and Amniocentesis and Chorionic Villus Sampling, which are diagnostic tests. The Nuchal Translucency Test uses ultrasound and measures the thickness of an area in the neck, which is usually thicker in children with Down's Syndrome, and this is then used as an indicator to undertake amniocentesis to confirm the diagnosis.

Amniocentesis involves using a long needle, guided by ultrasound, to take a sample of the amniotic fluid and genetically testing the foetal cells within it. Chorionic Villus Sampling involves using a device to take some tissue from the chorion, part of the placenta, and genetically testing it. These two tests have significant miscarriage rates and may also damage the child. The results are not usually directly relevant to managing birth, but are done in order to provide the option of abortion if the child carries a serious abnormality. However, it is claimed that knowing that the child has an abnormality may lead to closer examination for other related conditions, such as heart abnormalities detectable by ultrasound, in a child with Downs Syndrome, and the information may assist the mother and her partner to prepare for the birth of the child with a disability. The issue is whether those benefits outweigh the risk of loss of life. Amniocentesis has a miscarriage rate of around 1% and chorionic villus sampling has a higher loss rate. A question parents might consider is what benefits would lead them to take such a risk with a child who had already been born.

Women on IVF programs are also offered Preimplantation Genetic Diagnosis (PGD), using embryo biopsy, so that abnormal embryos can be excluded and not transferred to the woman's uterus.

3.2 Morality and Prenatal Diagnosis

The Congregation for the Doctrine of the Faith states that prenatal diagnosis presents no moral objections if carried out in order to identify medical treatment that may be needed by the child in the womb. However it is problematic if it is done to provide opportunities for proposing and procuring an abortion. This is eugenic abortion, justified in public opinion on the basis of a mentality – (mistakenly held to be consistent with the demands of "therapeutic interventions") – that accepts life only under certain conditions and rejects it when it is affected by limitation, handicap or illness.

When they do not involve disproportionate risks for the child and the mother, and are meant to make possible early therapy or even to favour a serene and informed acceptance of the child not yet born, these techniques are morally licit. But since the possibilities of prenatal therapy are today still limited, it not infrequently happens that these techniques are used with a eugenic intention which accepts selective abortion in order to prevent the birth of children affected by various types of anomalies. Such an attitude is rejected by the Church as "shameful and utterly reprehensible", since it presumes to measure the value of a human life only within the parameters of "normality" and physical well-being, thus opening the way to legitimizing infanticide and euthanasia as well.[40]

It is important that women make clear to their doctors if from the outset that they would not contemplate abortion and would not have any tests that are done only for the purpose of making abortion of an abnormal child an option, or which would pose a significant risk of miscarriage. If this is not made clear, doctors in our culture are likely to proceed on the assumption that the option of aborting a child must be provided by doing the screening and testing. This is seen as routine rather than as an option to be explored.

3.3 Morality and Preimplantation Diagnosis

The Congregation for the Doctrine of the Faith writes that preimplantation diagnosis – connected as it is with in vitro fertilization, which is itself always intrinsically illicit – is directed toward the *qualitative selection and consequent destruction of embryos*, which constitutes an act of abortion. Preimplantation diagnosis is therefore the expression of a *eugenic mentality* that "accepts selective abortion in order to prevent the birth of children affected by various types of anomalies". Like prenatal diagnosis, this is also problematic since it presumes to measure the value of a human life only within the parameters of 'normality' and physical well-being.[41]

By treating the human embryo as mere "laboratory material", the dignity of embryo is also subjected to alteration and discrimination by the practice of prenatal diagnosis and selective abortion or the practice

---

40 John Paul II, Encyclical Letter *Evangelium vitae*, 63: *AAS* 89 (1995), 502.
41 Congregation for the Doctrine of the Faith, *Dignitatis Personae*, 2008 n. 22.

of PGD and embryo selection. Dignity belongs equally to every single human being, irrespective of the parents' desires, or the person's social condition, educational formation or level of physical development. If at other times in history, while the concept and requirements of human dignity were accepted in general, discrimination was practised on the basis of race, religion or social condition, today there is a no less serious and unjust form of discrimination which leads to the non-recognition of the ethical and legal status of human beings suffering from serious diseases or disabilities. Sick and disabled people are not some separate category of humanity; rather, sickness and disability are part of the human condition and affect most individuals at some stage. Such discrimination is immoral and a law that did permit such discrimination must therefore be considered unacceptable. There is a duty to eliminate cultural, economic and social barriers that undermine the full recognition and protection of people who have a disability or illness.[42]

3.4 Reproductive Discrimination

The expectation that gene therapies would rapidly develop has not been realised. No gene therapies have yet become established therapy; however, as a spin-off of the techniques developed from the Human Genome Project, there is a rapidly increasing capacity to identify genetic difference or abnormality and to correlate this with disease states or propensity for disease. Melbourne IVF has been advertising full chromosomal analysis following PGD. Anecdotally, it has been reported that 2012 may have been the first year in which the majority of IVF patients in Victoria were not suffering from infertility, but were instead using the technology either for genetic selection purposes or for the purpose of egg donation including for same sex couples, including using surrogacy arrangements.

Much has been written about the possibility of the use of genetic information in discriminatory ways in relation to employment, financial institutions, personal insurance, superannuation and pension

---

42 Ibid.

entitlements. But as discussed above, an area of discrimination that has already become well-established is the area called "reproductive discrimination," a term that may itself provoke debate.

3.4.1 Reproductive Rights?[43]

In 2004, the National Health and Medical Research Council promulgated "Ethical guidelines on the use of assisted reproductive technology in clinical practice and research." Compliance by Australian IVF teams with the guidelines is secured by the terms of the funding agreements with the Commonwealth and by adoption of the guidelines by the providers and their association.

The guidelines require that pre-implantation genetic diagnosis of embryos (PGD) must not be used for:

- prevention of conditions that do not seriously harm the person to be born;
- selection of the sex of an embryo except to reduce the risk of transmission of a serious genetic condition; or
- selection in favour of a genetic defect or disability in the person to be born.

This restriction may challenge those who uphold the notions of *reproductive rights* and *reproductive freedom*, especially those who are of the view that it is their right to choose the sex or other genetic features of their child. As a member of the Australian Human Ethics Committee at the time, I found myself targeted by private correspondence from people wanting to use IVF for sex selection purposes and so-called "family balancing".

---

43 The following sections on "Reproductive Discrimination" are reproduced with permission with section and footnote numbering changes only from an article published as Nicholas Tonti-Filippini, "Reproductive Discrimination", *University of New South Wales Law Journal*, The, Vol. 29, No. 2, 2006: 254-260.

The guidelines also expressed reservations that the practice of selecting against some forms of abnormality may threaten the status and equality of opportunity of people who have that form of abnormality, and that the procedures involve the disposal of some healthy embryos.

The overall rationale adopted for restricting choice in the use of reproductive technology was, "Clinical decisions must respect, primarily, the interests and welfare of the persons who may be born, as well as the long-term health and psychosocial welfare of all participants, including gamete donors."[44]

The jurisprudential dialogue about reproductive rights occurs against the background of the legal tradition that the interests of the child are paramount. This principle found expression in the UN *Convention on the Rights of the Child*, which recognizes, amongst other matters, the rights of the child to an identity, nationality, family relations, and, to personal relations and direct contacts with both parents. In this respect too, family law has been based on the notion that the interests of the child are paramount. Family law restricts parental choices and resolves conflicts in favour of the welfare of children.

The philosophical point to make is that the child, as a member of the human family and thus a bearer of inalienable rights (in the terms of the international human rights instruments) cannot be the object of another's rights. Reproductive rights, therefore, do not and cannot, in principle, include a right to a child. Given that reproduction is about producing children, then what exactly is the scope of so-called "reproductive rights"?

There is international recognition of the right to form a family, but it is limited, in the *International Covenant on Civil and Political Rights*, to the right of men and women of marriageable age to marry and form a family. There have been court judgements about access to reproductive technology, but these have tended to focus on the matter of access

---

[44] National Health and Medical Research Council promulgated *Ethical Guidelines on the use of Assisted Reproductive Technology in Clinical Practice and Research*, Australian Government, 2004.

to a medical service, rather than the broader issue of whether what is involved is a right to a child.

In the NHMRC document, acknowledgement is made of an ongoing debate on these topics and to that end, there is an appendix that lists issues that need to be debated. One such area is the matter of using genetic technologies in conjunction with reproductive technology.

The document offers reasons for opposing or limiting the use of genetic technologies associated with ART:

- Use of genetic technology implies that admission to life is no longer unconditional.
- Use of genetic technology may foster reproductive discrimination.
- Use of genetic technology establishes the principle that parents may choose the qualities their children have.
- The handling, testing and manipulation of embryos in genetic technology procedures may expose them to significant risk of harm. (The weight of this consideration may depend on the seriousness of the outcome that the technology is being used to avert.)
- The likelihood that the social effects of general acceptance of ART (with genetic technology) as an alternative to natural reproduction will include a diminished tolerance for difference.
- Ethical guidelines on the use of assisted reproductive technology in clinical practice and research
- Though avoidance of serious disease may be a reasonable use of genetic technology, shaping babies to parents' ideas of perfection (were this to prove possible) is not.
- Otherwise normal (so-called 'carrier') embryos that would be expected to have a normal life will be discarded.[45]

---

45 Ibid.

3.4.2 What is Reproductive Discrimination?

Two decades ago, Jonathon Glover[46] asked the question, "What Sort of People Should There Be?" He referred to the "genetic supermarket" and envisaged that the development of gene therapies would result in parents being able to choose the genetics of their children.

Since then the Human Genome Project (HGP) reached the end of the first stage when the human genome had been mapped. The second stage, identifying the functions of each of the individual genes, has not yet been achieved.

The expectation that gene therapies would rapidly develop has not been the reality. It is still the case that, at the time of writing, no gene therapies have become established therapy. What has developed as a spin-off of the techniques developed for used in the HGP is a rapidly increasing capacity to identify genetic difference or abnormality and to correlate this with disease states or propensity for disease.

Much has been written about the possibility of the use of this information in discriminatory ways in relation to employment, financial institutions, personal insurance, superannuation and pension entitlements. But there is an area of discrimination that has already become well-established, that is the area which the NHMRC calls "reproductive discrimination".

Reproductive discrimination happens when a person or a couple experience pressure not to reproduce a child who has their familial genetic traits, or where a particular type of person is not reproduced because it is judged that his or her genetic traits ought not be reproduced.

Reproductive discrimination may happen through pressure or influence for the purpose of preventing conception or birth of a child with a particular genetic trait:

- Pre-nuptially – by screening individuals who have decided to have a child
- Pre-fertilisation – by screening or altering gametes, or somatic cell nuclear transfer

---

46 Jonathon Glover, *What Sort of People Should There Be?"*, Penguin, Harmondsworth, 1984.

- Pre-transfer – by embryo biopsy and selection.
- Pre-birth – by pre-natal diagnosis and selective abortion.
- Peri-natal – by infanticide.

The reasons for selection may be to

- Select against disability.
- Select for disability (e.g., deaf parents wanting a deaf child).
- Select for or against non-disease traits – gender, sexual orientation, enhanced capacities.

Some would argue that reproductive discrimination is not discrimination at all, but simply a matter of respecting the individual choice of the woman and her partner. However, to say that an act of discrimination is an act of individual choice, does not make that choice any less discriminatory. Discrimination is almost always a matter of individual choice. What matters is when that discrimination forms something of a pattern so that a group or category of individuals suffers as a result of those choices.

3.4.3 Discriminating Against Those Who Have Genetic Differences

The reasons currently being offered by Western medical authorities for reproductive discrimination concern abnormalities or genetic difference. This matter has been the subject of much discussion internationally for it re-opens the debates about eugenics and the debate has become particularly intense in the discussion of the implications of the world-wide human genome project.

The United Nations Educational, Scientific and Cultural Organisation (UNESCO) prepared a draft *Declaration on the Human Genome and Human Rights* (from hereon referred to as "the *Declaration*"). The draft was prepared at the request of the Director-General of the UN for a committee of governments to discuss in 1997 for presentation for adoption by member States in 1998. It is worth noting that the draft which was launched by the French President, Francois Mitterand, in November 1996, explicitly rejected eugenic practices, but the final draft that emerged after the consultation with national governments had lost all reference to eugenics. At the time there was a concerted, and eventually a successful effort, by those who were both involved with the Human Genome Project and party to UNESCO's International Bioethics Committee discussion, to exclude the reference to eugenics. Preventing the coming to be of people who were genetically different in the sense that they might be less able in some way was held to be acceptable and the practice was not to be given such a pejorative label. Of course, the reality is that the motivation is eugenic, even if the means used is medical suasion of the parents, or would-be parents, rather than downright force, even though the former may be of such authority and supported by social pressure that the effect and the sense of loss of choice may be much the same.

In November 1996, the Council of Europe issued the *Convention for the Protection of Human Rights and Dignity of the Human being with Regard to the Application of Biology and Medicine: Convention on Human Rights and Biomedicine.*

The Convention embraced the same purpose of the UN *Declaration*, to ensure a development of human genetics that fully respects human dignity and human rights, and benefits the whole of humanity, to set out principles which, if universally respected, will make it possible to prevent abuse, and to affirm the need for democratic debate, the dissemination of knowledge and the promotion of the teaching of bioethics.

The actual wording of the preamble to the draft UN *Declaration* that was launched in 1996 stated,

> the applications of genetic research must, however, be regulated in order to guard against any eugenic practice that runs counter to human dignity and human rights.

The removal of these words was disturbing. There are those who see these matters as individual decisions and matters of privacy, and those who argue, to the contrary, that many private discriminatory decisions ultimately constitute widespread discrimination. This is precisely the point of anti-discrimination legislation: one person's individual personal preference, when part of a broader trend involving many people, creates the injustice of discrimination against a whole class or category of other people. In this case it is discrimination against the somehow genetically inferior or in favour of the somehow genetically superior, whether that discrimination is on the basis of disability, disease, race, intellectual capacity, appearance, or gender.

There are many quandaries in this debate. Confronted with Sally, a person with a genetic abnormality, I may say of Sally that it is a good thing that she exists. But many would seem to accept that proposition but also a second, seemingly contradictory proposition, that it is not a good thing that there be people in future generations with Sally's abnormality. This latter proposition would seem to underlie the widespread practice of genetic counseling and genetic screening, and of pre-natal diagnosis and selective abortion, and PGD and embryo selection, as well as more recent developments such as overcoming mitochondrial disease by germ cell genetic manipulation involving embryonic nuclear transfer to an enucleated egg or embryo.

The proposition is challenged. An international organization representing disabled people *Disabled People's International* published a statement entitled "the Right to Live and be Different" in which they asserted that a society without disabled people would be a lesser society and they demanded an end to the bio-medical elimination of diversity and an end to gene selection.[47] This raises broader issues than abortion because the genetic constitution of future generations could be controlled without abortion by simply screening would-be parents and persuading or coercing carriers of genetic abnormality to not have children. As mentioned, genetic selection can also occur at the level of screening embryos in IVF programs, is promoted by IVF programs and is held to be a reason even for fertile couples to use IVF.

Article four of the draft *Declaration* which was launched in 1996 stated:

> The protection of the individual with respect to the implications of research in biology and genetics is designed to safeguard the integrity of the human species, as a value in its own right, as well as the respect for the dignity, freedom and the rights of each of its members.

The concept of *safeguarding the integrity of the human species* raised

---

47 cf. Christopher Newell, "The Right to Live and be Different: An exploration of the DPI Europe Declaration on Bioethics and Human Rights", in *Interaction*, v. 13, N. 3, 2000.

concerns with many of those at the Paris meeting, because, apart from being ambiguous, it implies a eugenic aim. This clause was later removed, but the sentiment that wanted it removed was not given expression in the final document.

Safeguarding the integrity of the human species is considered a "value in its own right" in the draft statement. The final part of the sentence seems to me to put the value of the integrity of the human species against respect for the dignity, freedom and the rights of each of its members. This separation of some sort of reductionist notion of species integrity separable from members of the human family, and as something to be valued distinctly from the dignity of human individuals, appears to conflict with human rights objectives founded upon the inherent dignity of every member of the human family.

Perhaps the Council of Europe's *Convention on Human Rights and Biomedicine* is less ambiguous:

> Article 13
>
> An intervention seeking to modify the human genome may only be undertaken for preventive, diagnostic or therapeutic purposes and only if its aim is not to introduce any modification in the genome of any descendants.

But there is an avoidance of a major issue in both documents. The trend toward elimination of genetic diseases through

- controlled reproduction using artificial reproduction techniques in conjunction with embryo biopsy for selection purposes or the use of donor gametes,
- the practice of ante-natal diagnosis in conjunction with selective abortion,
- the identification of carrier status in conjunction with policies influencing decisions to marry and form a family,
- sterilisation (voluntary or involuntary) of carriers, and
- infanticide of those with undesired genetic features either by

fatal intervention or by neglect of reasonable care including the failure to provide adequate nutrition and hydration[48], will ultimately affect the human gene pool with fewer people with genetic abnormalities reproducing and hence some human genes heading for extinction. Further, this change to the human gene pool need not be restricted to serious genetic diseases. More and more it is genetic susceptibility to disease rather than disease itself that is being identified. There is also a growing scope for selection for or against genetically determined characteristics other than disease states. Height, intelligence, appearance and behavioural traits are just some of the aspects which have a genetic component and which may be the subject of parental or social preference, once the genetic determinants become identifiable.

These issues raise profound questions about

- what sort of people there should be,[49]
- what constitutes disease, what is normality,
- whether the genetic disease variations in human individuals constitute part of the integrity of the human genome that should be protected,
- whether the latter question makes sense when asked in this reductionist way as though the genes were separate from the people who are the bearers or instantiation of those genes,
- whether the individual member of the human family, including his or her particular genetic structure, should be considered an artefact or an icon,[50]
- whether respect for the inherent worth and dignity and

---

48 It should be noted that infanticide and abortion for reasons of male selection are common practice in China and India, abortion for sex selection is not unknown in Australia, and the withdrawal of ordinary care such as feeding is a common practice in Australia and other Western countries for infants born with serious abnormalities.
49 Jonathon Glover, *What Sort of People Should There be?*, Penguin, Harmondsworth, 1984.
50 Rev Robert Brungs SJ, "The Human Body: Artefact or Icon?", *Proceedings of the 1983 Annual Conference of St Vincent's Bioethics Centre,* Edited by Joseph N Santamaria and Nicholas Tonti-Filippini.

inalienable rights of an individual member of the human family warrants protection before birth as well as after birth,[51]

- the right of men and women to marry and form a family?[52]

Article 14 of the *Declaration* gives some recognition to this problem:

> States must guarantee the effectiveness of the duty of solidarity towards individuals, families and population groups that are particularly vulnerable to disease or disability linked to anomalies of a genetic character.

A relevant distinction is between treating a person who has a genetic disease, and seeking to eliminate the disease by eliminating the diseased, by ensuring that persons and others like him or her do not reproduce, or their affected offspring are eliminated by embryo selection, abortion or infanticide. It is worth noting that such an approach has now become commonplace in ante-natal care and in reproductive technology.

That this may happen with the consent of the parents, or would-be parents, does not alter the fact that the concentration on early diagnosis is for the purpose of elimination of the diseased rather than the treatment of the disease. I am prompted to ask: What will be the impact of elimination strategies as the potential pool of those who have an identifiable genetic disadvantage becomes much greater as the capacity to achieve genetic profiling develops? This is rapidly becoming the reality with the offer, mentioned earlier, of full chromosomal testing of all twenty-three pairs, and the new development of maternal serum testing during pregnancy to isolate foetal cells or chromosomes in her blood and test them to diagnose genetic abnormalities. This is becoming an alternative to the current diagnostic tests that are intrusive and risk miscarriage. It may soon be possible to offer a complete genetic profile of the unborn child, including predictions for propensity for disease in adult life, as well as diagnosis of actual disease. The possession of such information is not only an issue for abortion and embryo selection: it raises questions about the impact on parenting. For instance, what would be the effect on parents, and their parenting, if they

---

51 United Nations, *Convention on the Rights of the Child*, Preamble.
52 United Nations, *International Covenant on Civil and Political Rights*, Article 23.

were informed that their child had a greater likelihood of a disease causing behavioural problems, or a greater likelihood of being same-sex attracted?

3.5 Embryo Experimentation and Cloning

The status of human embryos arose as a separate issue when experiments began to try to achieve fertilization in the laboratory, ultimately resulting in the birth of Louise Brown in 1978. What may or may not be done to those embryos often involves issues of women's rights, particularly since women may be exploited by the technology as the sources of ova, and as gestators for the embryos conceived in the laboratory; but unlike the abortion of human foetuses, human embryo experimentation need not involve use of the woman's body. It may even be possible now to achieve a human embryo without involving a woman as a source of ova. There are reports of attempts to achieve cloned human embryos using animal ova, in which the animal nucleus is replaced by a nucleus from an ordinary somatic cell from a human being, known as "trans-species somatic cell nuclear transfer". Also it may be possible to form sperm or ova using the technology involved in inducing pluripotency, thus avoiding having to harvest eggs.

In his treatment of human embryo experimentation, Peter Singer (with Helga Kuhse), an advocate of human embryo experimentation, admits the validity of the claim that a human embryo is a human being, but challenges the claim that every human being has a right to life. Not everyone accepts that a human embryo is a human being, but that may be simply a matter of semantics. Kuhse and Singer's point is straightforward:

> the embryo is clearly a being, of some sort, and it can't possibly be of any other species than *Homo sapiens*. Thus it seems to follow that it must be a human being.[53]

A human embryo may be human in the trivial sense that even a human hand is human. Saying that it is a human *being*, however, is to say that it is much more than a mere part of a human being, or even a discarded or separated part of a human being, as in the case of sperm. "Being" denotes

---

53 Helga Kuhse and Peter Singer, "Individuals, Humans and Persons", in Peter Singer *et al, Embryo Experimentation,* Cambridge University Press, 1990, pp. 65-75.

an existence, even a life of its own, which is not true of a human hand, for instance, or of sperm.

There is some debate, to which Kuhse and Singer refer, about when a human embryo actually begins and when it can be considered an individual being, given the capacity of the early embryo to divide to form identical twins. The twinning argument only has relevance to the first week or so. After that it does not occur as the cells become differentiated, losing their totipotentiality. I could concede that first stage without affecting the basic point of interest, which is to defend the status of immature members of the human family including "the child before birth," and to make the claim that infants are considered worthy subjects of protection and human dignity, with equal and inalienable rights.[54]

My view is that a new member of the species comes into existence when a new cell, the human zygote, is formed for the first time with the completed capacity of being able to develop to human adulthood, given nourishment and a favourable environment. That is a biological reality. We may differ about the moral or social significance of that biological reality.

We now have to accept that while, in our experience, human zygotes have only come into existence through the fusion of an ovum and sperm, it may eventually be possible that such a cell could be artificially constructed through altering or substituting the genetic constitution of an ovum, or, even more remotely possible, by bringing about the de-differentiation and activation of a somatic cell so that it acquires the totipotentiality of a zygote. The event known as "Dolly the sheep," which Professor Ian Wilmut claimed to have achieved in his now famous cloning experiment,[55] opened the possibility of cloning in humans.

I see no more difficulty for identity and individuality in the twinning issue – asexual reproduction – than in ordinary sexual parenthood. In the one case a new being comes into existence from another with the first continuing throughout the process. In the second case a new individual comes into existence from two others. I suspect that the twinning debate

---

54 See for instance, the preamble to the UN *Convention on the Rights of the Child.*
55 Ian Wilmut, A.E. Schnicke, J. McWhir, A.J. Kind and K.H.S.L. Campbell, "Viable offspring derived from fetal and adult mammalian cells", *Nature,*1997, 385, pp. 810-3.

over identity and individuality lost its relevance when it became a possibility that an adult human being might also be cloned – also asexual reproduction. Conceptually, it is no more a challenge to the identity of an embryo that a cell, or cells, might become isolated and form another individual, than it is for a cell to be isolated from an adult and become activated to act as an embryonic cell commencing development toward adulthood. In that sense we are all potentially more than one individual, in that we can be twinned by cloning, but that does not alter the fact that we are now individuals.

Kuhse and Singer also raise the question of chimera formation. This is when two embryos are combined to form one individual, which in some species has been shown to develop to adulthood containing two different genomes. In some cases, the combination was trans-species so that an animal had some cells belonging to one species and some belonging to the other. This is quite distinct from cross fertilization between species, in which a single genome is formed and may be found in every cell in the body of the animal. With the formation of a chimera, a new individual is formed which is distinct from the two individuals that ceased to live as distinct entities when they united. The individuals that they were cease to be. If it were possible to unite two people to form one person, it is difficult to imagine how this could happen in a way that preserves their individual identities. If this were to be true merging, their brains would have to unite to form one brain and one mind. In those circumstances the person would presumably have memories of "when I was two people" but that poses so many problems for identity that it is difficult to imagine that one could survive the addition of the other. Rather it would seem more like the loss of two people and the formation of a third very strange person. There is saying that we are what we eat. But of course this is false. I am not a lettuce or the beans or the lamb I may have had for lunch. They lose their identity when they are assimilated through my digestion, if not during the processing before being eaten. Who I am, as an identity, is a bundle of continuities in space and time in one integrated entity. Whether that identity persists through the changes that may occur, depends on those continuities in the one entity. It would seem that chimera formation breaks those continuities in relation to the loss of the separate entities and that would be the case in either adults, if that were possible, or in embryos. What is formed would be a different being altogether. But for my purposes here, this discussion, like the twinning discussion, need not be pursued; chimera formation is no longer possible after the first few days and there remains the issue of the status of the immature being, from that time, right through to some time in his or her development when he or she exhibits the higher order characteristics we particularly value in human beings.

But membership of the species may not be what is meant by "human being"; the adjective "human" has meanings other than merely belonging to the species *homo sapiens*, such as having the characteristics of humankind,[56] especially the better characteristics or those that seem particularly unique to human beings, such as those which involve higher intelligence. In this debate some have taken that line, rather than accept as Kuhse and Singer do that a human embryo is a human being. The embryo, they may say, lacks those characteristics that are so significant in adult human beings: it may be a member of the genus as a biological entity, but it is not yet human in that sense of having valuable human characteristics. Therefore, they might claim, the human embryo is not a human being.

But while Kuhse and Singer accept that the embryo is a human being, they attack the proposition that every human being has a right to life. In fact they do not recognize a right to life of any human being: even an intelligent, self-conscious human being only has his or her right recognized as a rough rule of thumb which, at a level of critical moral thinking, may be overridden when a calculation of preferences would indicate greater satisfaction of preferences through killing the person.[57]

The argument is familiar. In order to explain our particular objection to killing human beings over and above other species, we are moved to resort to an appeal to some particular characteristics of human beings not possessed by animals, typically those characteristics requiring higher levels of intelligence. In making that move, we exclude immature human beings because they lack that status. Any appeal that we make for special consideration of human beings on the basis merely of their membership

---

56 *The Concise Oxford Dictionary*, 9th Edition, 1995.
57 By "critical moral thinking" I am here referring to the type of thinking which R.M. Hare describes in his *Moral Thinking: Its Level, Method and Point*, Clarendon Press, Oxford, 1981.

of our species, will be subject to a charge akin to racism, that species membership, like membership of a particular race, is itself morally irrelevant.

There is a difficulty for Kuhse and Singer in relation to mature human beings who temporarily lose those higher characteristics for which they are valued, which happens regularly with sleep and with any other occasions of lost or diminished consciousness. In *Practical Ethics*, Singer resorted to referring to a sleeping adult human being as a being *of a kind* who has valued characteristics. If this move is permitted, then it seems that the door is open to those who are of the kind of being who, normally, when adults, would have those valued characteristics – that is, immature human beings.

The third string of their argument is to raise the matter of potential persons. Rightly, they dismiss potential human beings as of no significance. A sperm and an ovum, together before fertilization, constitute a potential human being, but nobody, it seems, claims that the gametes should be given equal and inalienable rights.

However, I have never heard or read an argument from someone proposing that an immature human being – zygote, embryo, foetus or newborn – should have rights *because they are potential human beings or potential persons*. The latter claims that Kuhse and Singer tackle at this point, would seem to be something of a straw man of their own construction. I have heard an argument expressed along the lines that an immature human being is valuable because as a human being he or she has the potential for exhibiting valuable human characteristics; that is, a human being with potential rather than a potential human being. An immature human being differs from sperm and ova because he or she has come to be as a being with the completed capacity for continued development as a human being, which capacity is *only* potential in the sperm and the ovum. One cannot rightly say of a sperm or of an ovum that it is the kind of being that will, unless there are mishaps, have higher order characteristics. That being only exists once the sperm and ovum unite to form the new cell with the completed genome and human constitution which determines that capacity. As sperm or ovum, they are incapable of further development.

Kuhse and Singer claim that damage to an embryo, if it never becomes a sentient being, does not harm it, because its total lack of awareness means that it never has had any interests at all.

The truth or otherwise of this proposition depends very much on what is meant by "harm" and what is meant by "interests". There is a simple way in which it is false. If I poison a rosebush so that its leaves blacken and shrivel and it dies, I have harmed it. Whether that harm has any intrinsic moral significance is a different matter.

Similarly, what is meant by interests is not simple. It is commonly claimed that interests are related to desires, but the nature of the relationship is not clear. A person can desire what is not in their interests, not only mistakenly through lack of information, but also deliberately. I can choose to act in someone else's interests rather than my own, and for altruistic reasons may prefer, desire or choose to further another's interests in a way that is contrary to my own interests. I can knowingly desire something that is harmful to me. Once it is admitted that there is some sense of what is good or advantageous for me in terms of meeting vital needs for my development, flourishing or fulfilment, then some other standard than desires may be applied. It may even make sense to speak of what is in the interests of even a non-sentient being, such as a tree. Something is in the interests of a tree if it is necessary for or results in the flourishing of the tree. Whether that notion of interests has moral significance would seem to depend on whether trees have moral standing.

However, it is not necessary to argue for non-sentient interests to justify considering immature human beings to have interests. That an immature human being exists as a being of a kind which, in maturity, normally has significantly valuable characteristics, such as rational autonomy, and all that autonomy or free will makes possible, justifies referring to what is or is not in the person's interests, and makes it possible that he or she may be harmed. The question is whether those interests or that harm is morally significant. I would argue that damaging an immature human being so that he or she loses the capacity for rational autonomy is to do grave harm to him or her, harm of a morally significant kind akin to damaging an adult human being so that he or she loses rational autonomy.

Such a claim will depend on the theory of dignity, equality, rights or morality applied. But those theories that contain a notion of dignity inclusive of inviolability or sacredness, I will argue, ought yield just such a moral conclusion.

Singer's account in this respect has some gaps, and it is not clear that even his preference utilitarianism would exclude consideration of an immature human being who is of a kind that will, unless mishap occurs, have self-conscious preferences, any more than those who are sleeping would be excluded. As I have discussed, a major gap in Singer's account is that his account of the wrongness of killing does not yield the protection of the individual that is claimed, for instance, in the international human rights instruments based on a notion of inherent dignity, inclusive of inviolability or sacredness, and which yields inalienable rights. For Singer such notions can only be rules of thumb, contingent upon the results of critical analysis in any given circumstance.

Nevertheless, the issue of induced abortion has highly charged the issue of respect for the life of a human being before birth, and what I have argued may have been dismissed simply because it is seen to challenge an entrenched acceptance of the practice of induced abortion. The major difference between the issue of induced abortion and embryo experimentation, however, is that abortion involves a woman who is pregnant and this, whatever happens to the child, involves her.

The issue of embryo experimentation, though it is likely to involve a woman as a source of eggs and possibly a man to provide sperm, or someone else if cloning is used, is less complicated than abortion in that the embryo comes to be in the laboratory. There is no conflict with the woman's right with respect to her body. The issue can be considered therefore entirely in terms of whether the embryo can be treated as mere biological material or whether it is a nascent human life. The separate issue of the moral status of the embryo in reproductive technology is discussed in chapter 5.3 and the complex issue of induced abortion is discussed in Chapter 7.

4
Perinatal Palliative Care and Support[58]

4.1 Introduction

The concept of perinatal palliative care for women who experience a diagnosis, during pregnancy, of a life limiting abnormality for the child before birth, is well developed in the literature but seemingly not so in practice in Australia. *Perinatal palliative care* is a system of interdisciplinary "care to prevent and relieve infant suffering and improve the conditions of the infant's living and dying. It is a team approach to relieving physical, psychological, social, emotional, and spiritual suffering of the dying infant and the family"[59] when a diagnosis of a life limiting condition is made in the child during pregnancy.

There is a significant dislocation between medical perceptions that prenatal testing[60] is for the purpose of providing the option of termination and the perspective of those women who opt for the tests in the false belief that the test results provide reassurance. It seems that women who do

---

58 This chapter was jointly authored with Dr Mary Walsh MBBS FRACGP who is a general practitioner who undertakes shared obstetric care with the Mercy Hospital for Women in Heidelberg, Victoria. This chapter was published in the journal *Ethics Education* vol 18, Issues 1 and 2, December 2012, and is reproduced unchanged with permission.
59 Anita Catlin and Brian Carter, "Creation of a Neonatal End-of-Life Palliative care Protocol," in *Journal of Perinatology*, 2002, 22: 184-195.
60 Note that the term "prenatal testing" tends in practice to be differentiated from "antenatal testing". Antenatal testing is used for tests related to the health of the mother or the child that are primarily focussed on improving the care provided during pregnancy and child birth. Prenatal testing tends to be used for identifying life limiting conditions in the child which may have a bearing on decisions to terminate pregnancy. There is sometimes some overlap between the uses.

receive a positive screening result may be shocked and unprepared for its significance and the sequel of being offered invasive diagnostic tests.[61]

As a matter of some urgency, women need to be offered supportive decision-making counselling before they embark on a course of prenatal testing that may lead to invasive tests, risk of miscarriage and the predicament of being offered termination of pregnancy.

There is a need for GPs, nurses, clergy and others who provide information and counselling to women to be better informed and to provide early advice to women about what they are likely to expect, including the major medical objective (making termination available), the accuracy of the tests and the risks involved. Though routine antenatal tests are important for managing pregnancy and delivery, women should be informed that the prenatal screening and diagnostic tests for life limiting conditions are not mandatory and not usually needed as part of good routine care.

Obstetricians and maternity services also need to ensure that, prior to any prenatal screening or diagnostic testing, there is an opportunity to discuss the issues with a counsellor to enable informed decisions about the sequence of events that may be triggered by the tests.

The available evidence suggests that offering perinatal palliative care reduces the proportion of women who opt for termination. At all stages of the process, the option of perinatal palliative care should be made known so that women are aware of this choice from the outset, and are not left with the impression that the only medically supported option, in the event of abnormality, is termination of pregnancy or induction and foeticide.

---

61 An invasive test, such as amniocentesis, involves using needle aspiration under ultrasound diagnosis to remove some amniotic fluid from around the foetus and testing foetal cells it contains. Done at about 16 weeks when it is usually recommended, it risks causing a miscarriage (approx. 1%) or otherwise permanently damaging the child. Chorionic Vilus Sampling (CVS) involves using needle aspiration to take a sample of the chorion, which is part of the placenta, and has a much higher risk of miscarriage (approx 2-3%) and harm. It is usually recommended to be done during the first trimester so that, if abortion is chosen, it is less physically and emotionally traumatic for the women. Both procedures are safer if done later. The risk of miscarriage does vary depending on the skill and experience of the operator.

Perinatal palliative care is an alternative to the current circumstances in which women who terminate a pregnancy on medical grounds often report powerlessness.

The outcome of perinatal palliative care is much less certain than the alternative of termination of pregnancy, where the aim is to end the life of the child. However, for those women (and their partners) who have recognized the identity of their foetus as a child, and perhaps bonded, but also for those women who have not, offering perinatal palliative care creates hope and the opportunity to do the best to care for their child, however limited his or her existence may be, and knowledge that there are health professionals who will assist them to do so. The availability of perinatal palliative care demonstrates that their child is respected and valued by others. Perinatal palliative care is thus a vital service.

4.2 Perinatal Palliative Care

In Australia, a perinatal death is one that occurs between 20 weeks gestation and a month after birth.[62] In 2008, there was one perinatal death for every 100 births. 73 % were dead at birth and 27% after being born alive. 292 women experienced perinatal loss.[63] It is not a huge number nationally but still significant.

In recent years, an extensive literature has developed about the concept of "perinatal palliative care". Perinatal palliative care staff assist families who have a diagnosis of a life limiting condition for their foetus or unborn child to plan for, and cope with, the remainder of their pregnancy and the time around delivery. The goal is to support families as they face the unimaginable and to help them down a path of healing.[64]

This is done in a multidisciplinary way by:

---

62 http://meteor.aihw.gov.au/content/index.phtml/itemId/327314
63 National Perinatal Statistics Unit, "Australia's mothers and babies 2008" http://www.preru.unsw.edu.au/PRERUWeb.nsf/page/ps24
64 David Munson, Martha Hudson, Stefanie Kasperski, "Perinatal Palliative Care Initiative", Philadelphia Children's Hospital, Accessed 20/12/2010 from http://www.chop.edu/service/fetal-diagnosis-and-treatment/about-our-services/perinatal-palliative-care.html

- Helping prospective parents create a birth plan that is consistent with their hopes, goals and values.
- Exploring the possible pathways that lay ahead.
- Bolstering the family's coping strategies.
- Exploring medical decisions.
- Considering memory making options.
- Providing a safe environment for families to talk about what they are experiencing.[65]

The term "life limiting condition" has been adopted by the Murdoch Children's Research Institute,[66] instead of "lethal abnormality" still used in some publications. Prognosis is often uncertain in circumstances in which the diagnosis may refer to a range of conditions of variable severity and when there may also be intercurrent illnesses. Death may be expected at or before birth, but the child may survive against that expectation.

Unfortunately, there is a misconception in our community that palliative care is basically the management of death. The National Health and Medical Research Council describes palliative and supportive care as including a multi-disciplinary range of professional services that are focussed on supporting a person and his or her family physically, socially, emotionally and spiritually; and on relieving painful or uncomfortable symptoms, while maintaining function including, when possible, lucidity. Palliative care may be engaged when there is no hope of curing the underlying condition, but it may also be an adjunct to curative intervention. The NHMRC insists the palliative care should happen through out a person's illness not just in the terminal phase.[67] This is true also of severe perinatal conditions: multidisciplinary support is needed throughout the process: in preparation for testing and from diagnosis until birth, and then from birth and throughout the life of the child until death.

---

65 Ibid.
66 Alice Horwood and Sibel Saya in discussion at a meeting on Perinatal Palliative Care, John Paul II Institute for Marriage and Family, East Melbourne, 7 December 2010.
67 NHMRC *Ethical Guidelines for the Care of Persons in Post Coma Unresponsiveness (Vegetative State) or a Minimally Responsive State* http://www.nhmrc.gov.au/_files_nhmrc/file/publications/synopses/e81.pdf+NHMRC+unresponsive+state

The above list reflects important aspects of perinatal palliative care in which the parents are given the option of continuing with the pregnancy, and care is provided as appropriate for the foetus or unborn child to minimise any distress caused by the condition, while assisting the family to cope with the diagnosis and prognosis, and then providing the care necessary when the child is born. Offering perinatal palliative care is also an alternative to the powerlessness that women who terminate a pregnancy on medical grounds often report.[68]

4.3 False Reassurance and the Need for Counselling Prior to Testing

Prenatal testing identifies abnormalities in approximately 5% of pregnancies that are tested and, despite testing, a further 2-3% of abnormalities are not identified until after birth. Approximately 15,000 Australian women receive a diagnosis of congenital abnormality during pregnancy each year. Anecdotally approximately 90% of women who receive a diagnosis of a life-limiting condition in their foetus/unborn child will choose to have the pregnancy terminated.[69]

In one UK study, most of the terminations occurred within 72 hours of the woman receiving the news of the abnormality.[70]

Despite this connection between prenatal testing results and termination of pregnancy, for many expectant couples, the link between prenatal testing and abortion, at least initially, does not exist.[71] Even when birth defects and abortions are explicitly discussed, the pregnant woman and her partner often simply do not link this outcome to prenatal diagnosis.[72] There often

---

68 J.-J. Detraux, F.R. Gillot-de Vries, S. Vanden Eynde, A. Courtois, A. Desm, "Psychological Impact of the Announcement of a Fetal Abnormality on Pregnant Women and on Professionals", *Annals of the New York Academy of Sciences*, 5 February 2006.
69 http://www.hopkinsmedicine.org/bin/q/l/patient-Info-Sheet.pdf
70 P. Donnai, N. Charles, R. Harris, "Attitudes of patients after 'genetic' termination of pregnancy", *British Medical Journal*, 1981; 282:621-622, p. 622.
71 Elizabeth Ring-Cassidy and Ian Gentles, "The Impact of Abortion After Prenatal Testing", Accessed 20 December 2010 from http://www.afterabortion.org/prenataltesting.html#6#6
72 O.W. Jones, N.E. Penn, S. Shuchter, C.A. Stafford, T. Richards, C. Kernahan, J. Gutierrez, P. Cherkin, "Parental response to mid-trimester therapeutic abortion following amniocentesis", *Prenatal Diagnosis*, 1984, 4:249-256, p. 250.

appears to be dissonance between the practitioner's understanding of the purpose of prenatal diagnosis and the pregnant woman's perception of the procedure. While the practitioner may view the diagnostic tests as a way of preventing the birth of a "defective" child, pregnant women seek them out for reassurance that their babies are well and healthy.[73]

Antenatal testing is important in the management of pregnancy, identifying matters that are relevant for the management of delivery and, in some circumstances, allowing for in utero procedures to treat problems that might not be so well managed if left until birth, and in some cases preventing stillbirth. The major ethical issue concerns prenatal tests for conditions for which there is no treatment and for which the current major medical justification is termination of pregnancy. Though the possibility of termination is the medical justification for the test, it appears that women who have the tests do so to seek reassurance, rather than with termination in mind. There is therefore a gap between the medical justification and the understanding of the women. This is most obvious in the timing of the tests. Tests done during the first trimester, especially invasive tests which have greater risks when done early, are done at that time for the medical reason that termination is easier the earlier that it occurs. There is no other medical reason for doing the tests so early.

The chances of a serious abnormality at birth are relatively low, approximately 3%, but they may be higher where there are risk factors or a family history of genetic disease. Often the desire for reassurance is based on false beliefs; a negative result of a test does not mean that the baby will be born healthy, and may only indicate a marginal difference in the probability that the child has a serious abnormality. Not only are there false negatives, the tests are only for a limited range of conditions and there remains a 2-3% chance of abnormality, despite negative tests. Thus an average 3% risk that prompted the tests, may still remain only slightly changed by a negative test result. Further, the invasive tests themselves have risks of morbidity and of miscarriage.

---

73 J.M. Green, "Obstetricians' views on prenatal diagnosis and termination of pregnancy: 1980 compared with 1993", *British Journal of Obstetrics and Gynaecology*, 1995 March; 102 (3): 228-232, p. 231; and R. Mander, *Loss and Bereavement in Childbearing*, Oxford: Blackwell Scientific Publications, 1994, p. 44.

Thus if fully informed, the testing is not likely to be reassuring and may even add to anxiety. The aim of eliminating some diseases by termination may justify a 1% risk of miscarriage, in some medical minds, but for a woman, miscarriage is usually devastating and even more so if she is aware that she may have caused it simply because she wanted reassurance.[74] The assessment of risk depends very much on the acceptance and expectation of termination, and the difference between the medical justification and the women's desire for reassurance is relevant and reflects a lack of knowledge on the part of the women in seeking the tests for the purposes of reassurance rather than for the possibility of termination.

Therefore women who opt for the tests for reassurance and without expectation of termination, in the event of abnormality, are choosing the tests without adequate information and therefore without informed consent. The difference between their expectations and understanding and the medical perception is thus of grave concern.

In the experience of providing shared care for women during pregnancy, on many occasions the receptionist has booked the prenatal tests ahead of the appointment with the obstetrician. It seems that the tests are regarded as so normal and routine that they do not even warrant a discussion with the obstetrician of the risks and the possible outcomes. In those circumstances there is thus no opportunity for a discussion with the obstetrician about the purposes of the tests, what may be expected from them, and what the sequel may be in the event of an indication of abnormality.

---

[74] The Royal Australian and New Zealand College of Obstetricians and Gynaecologists advises mothers that there is a – 3% risk of miscarriage following CVS (i.e. between and 3 babies in 100 will miscarry). The test may also involve complications such as infection, limb deformities and trauma to the child. (Royal Australia and New Zealand College of Obstetricians and Gynaecologists *Amniocentesis and Chorionic Villus Sampling (CVS)* January 2007, www.mitec.com.au). Amniocentesis carries a risk of miscarriage, depending on the skill of the operator, of up to 1% (i.e. up to baby in 100 will miscarry), as well as other risks to the child due to amniotic fluid leakage, e.g., abnormalities in posture, infection and respiratory distress. (A. Tabor, J. Philip, M. Madsen, J. Bang, E.B. Obel, B. Norgaard-Pedersen, "Randomised controlled trial of genetic amniocentesis in 4606 low-risk women", *The Lancet* (1986) 352: 1287-93).

Women attending the Mercy Hospital for Women (Heidelberg) for tests are given pamphlets[75] that indicate:

- the combination of maternal serum screening and the ultrasound tests are optional;
- a low probability does not indicate that the child does not have Downs Syndrome;
- the tests do not tell them whether the child will have Downs Syndrome or not;
- they will be offered diagnostic tests; and
- the diagnostic tests have a small risk of miscarriage.

The women are given a list of questions that asks whether they would consider termination. Given that the literature indicates that the women have the tests for reassurance rather than for the option of abortion, it would seem that the information about continued risks of abnormality, the false positive and false negative rates and the risks of the invasive tests may not be well understood. There is little evidence that having this information about the tests alters the proportion who decide to have the tests or to have an abortion in the event of a positive diagnosis. The issue seems to be not so much a matter of possessing the information but about interpreting its significance.

The information is presented as though the tests are simply normal practice. If a women has the view that she would not contemplate abortion and would not unduly risk her child, there is little if anything to flag for her that a 1-2% chance of losing her child as a result of the test needs some substantial benefit to the child or to her to justify such a risk. One might ask: what likely benefits would be needed for a parent to take a 1-2% risk of one-year-old child dying? Such a risk would be daunting for most parents, but with no flagging about the gravity of the risk and the sense that such testing is normal for the management of pregnancy,

---

75 Note that the information given at the Mercy is very similar to that given elsewhere. The point here is not to claim that what the Mercy does is somehow superior.

it appears that many women do not interpret the information in a way that would reflect their values. They tend to be guided by the medical advice that is based on a quite different premise about making abortion available in the event of a positive result. This is why decision-making counselling that helps the woman and her family put the risks of tests and their purposes into context and to make her own decision based on her own values, not the medical assumptions, is so important.

4.4 Patients' Experiences

A colleague who is a senior academic reported that he and his wife had no opportunity to ask questions about the risks of chorionic villus sampling until she was actually on the table about to have the procedure done. On being told that the risk of miscarriage was of the order of 1% she declined to have the test. They were deeply upset that it had been assumed that they would consider that risk to be insignificant and no-one had raised with them that the purpose of the test was to select for termination of pregnancy.

Not only are the tests regarded as normal and routine, but anecdotally many women report being treated badly if on receiving a diagnosis of abnormality they do not terminate. Women who choose not to follow the majority, report experiencing unsupportive attitudes from health professionals. They claim that they were made to feel at fault and that they did not receive the normal antenatal support that women with normal pregnancies are given and instead attitudes were expressed that implied that the child was not worth it.

Pauline Thielle, a nurse, has recently published her experiences[76] in the *Journal of Medical Ethics*. In that account she reports that, following diagnosis of trisomy 18, information about her pregnancy needed for the care of the pregnancy was not recorded and the usual obstetric focus on protecting the well being of her child/foetus did not occur. She received the diagnosis by telephone while driving. She had to battle to be allowed to give birth to Liam in her local maternity hospital, and her experiences between diagnosis and eventual stillbirth were difficult and without counselling support, until late

---

76 Pauline Thiele, "He was my son, not a dying baby", *J Med Ethics*, 2010 36: 646-647.

in the pregnancy when she was eventually referred to a paediatrician who was sympathetic to her plight and willing to advocate on her behalf and on behalf of Liam, who was eventually stillborn.

Another patient has provided a similar account of her experiences from the time that ultrasonography identified a greater probability of trisomy 18, through to having the chorionic villus sampling to confirm the diagnosis and then managing the pregnancy until birth. Her baby, Peter, died soon after birth by Caesarean section.

Peter's mother had a traumatic time beginning with the routine ultrasound in which the likelihood of the condition was identified. The shock was great as she had not been prepared for an adverse result and she had her daughter with her who was only four years old. The ultrasonographer handled the situation with little sensitivity.

From the outset, she felt that the care provided was different from the care that she would have been given if Peter had not been diagnosed with severe disability: there were many responses from health professionals that reflected negatively on her child and on her decision to continue with the pregnancy. The experiences were so traumatic that she changed hospitals seeking acceptance and supportive care for her baby, herself and her family. Even at the second hospital, there were many battles with health care providers to gain acknowledgement and respect for her decision. Their attitude seemed to be that she had "brought this on herself" by choosing to continue with the pregnancy. Her distress was further compounded by the involvement of a doctor, who is a well-known proponent of late term abortion, in her care.

Approaching the time of delivery, she and her husband wanted their child to have the best chance of being born alive and so they requested a Caesarean section to minimise the trauma for Peter. (She had had one previous Caesarean). Her obstetrician initially was reluctant, another source of great distress. Another obstetrician was consulted, who fully supported her decision and raised his concerns with the treating obstetrician. The section was performed, and afterwards she was able to speak very highly of the care received at the time of the birth, with vital support from pastoral care, nursing staff, counsellors, a paediatrician, and her family.

It was a remarkable series of events, with many lessons learned about what is needed to provide adequate support in what have come to be the unusual circumstances of a woman electing not to terminate following a diagnosis of a life limiting condition. One lesson learned is that the length of one's life does not dictate the impact that it will have – Peter and Liam have touched the hearts of so many already, and have been catalysts for change in the provision of perinatal care.

Another patient had an infant who was diagnosed after birth with Spinal Muscular Atrophy. The baby lived for nine months, gradually suffering greater effects of paralysis, until death from respiratory failure. It was a difficult time for both parents, there was not a great deal of support available to manage the illness and dying of the child, and the illness and death clearly influenced their approach to subsequent pregnancies for which they sought prenatal diagnosis and chose abortion for a later pregnancy. They were advised that the child of the later pregnancy might not be affected by the disease to the same extent and might not have the same prognosis, but they elected termination rather than have a child suffer as the first child had done. One wonders what the outcome would have been had the immediate offer of a perinatal palliative team approach been available.

A patient diagnosed by amniocentesis as having a child with Down Syndrome found herself in a situation in which there was immediate rejection of her baby by her husband and conflict over his desire for termination. She experienced such negative attitudes also from health professionals in Australia, as well as from her husband, about continuing the pregnancy that she returned to her country of origin and extended family for the birth. She subsequently returned to Australia after the birth where the relationship with her husband was eventually helped with care and support from friends and her mother-in-law. She had the tests in the first instance simply because they were routine and she and her husband were totally unprepared for what happened.

4.5 Gaps in Service Delivery

There would appear to be significant gaps and inconsistencies in the services available to meet the needs of women and their families who experience diagnosis of a life-limiting condition for their foetus/unborn child.

Sometimes the circumstances are well managed, but on other occasions they seem to fall between the cracks.

The needs for counselling, advice and support can be separated into several distinct stages:

- Prior to and at the time of non-invasive testing, when women need to be prepared for what might eventuate and to be informed that pre-natal screening and testing is a pathway that may result in an adverse diagnosis and a proposal for induced abortion which most women accept in those circumstances, they need to be informed that continuing the pregnancy and palliative care is an available option for which they will be supported.

- Prior to and at the time of invasive testing, women need to know the risks of invasive tests which may harm the child in various ways, including causing miscarriage - even of a healthy child. As there are many conditions for which no prenatal tests exist, women should be informed that a negative result does not exclude abnormality; whereas in the case of a positive result, they should be told that continuing the pregnancy is an alternative for which there will be resources and support. Such support would include perinatal palliative care, and should be described. Finally, they will also benefit from meeting parents of children who have similar conditions.

- Between testing and the induced abortion or birth, there is a need to recognize that the woman may be bonding to her child and may express great love for her child, while grieving over the likely early death. She and her family are likely to need the same care and support needed from multidisciplinary palliative care teams as may be provided when any member of the family is dying. It is especially important that her relationship to the child is recognized, and not *belittled*, and that the child and his or her needs for care are not treated as insignificant because of the life limiting condition. Some women prefer to minimize the trauma for the child, including opting for Caesarean section, despite the grim outlook. It is important that they are not made to feel that that option is useless because of the prognosis.

- There are different sets of needs between the circumstances of a women who loses a child as a result of a miscarriage caused by an invasive test, women who lose a child after opting for induced abortion, and women who continue with the pregnancy and may suffer stillbirth or neonatal death. The needs for support may be on-going in each case.
- At the time of birth, thought needs to have gone into the possibilities beforehand, including stillbirth and how an early death of the child may be managed and plans made perhaps for a funeral and rites to mark death and the grieving.
- Afterwards if the child survives he or she may live for a time, even a long time, with disability, and thought needs to go into the possibility that the child may go home with the parents.

There also appear to be differences between the public and private sectors. In the public sector women are more likely to be referred to genetic counsellors[77] or other health professionals who can provide a contact, advice, counselling and support for the duration of the pregnancy. In the private sector there appear to be gaps, and women may not receive counselling to assist them with making decisions. At a recent meeting on this topic,

---

[77] A genetic counsellor is a person who has received a graduate training in the discipline "... which aims to help individuals, couples and families understand and adapt to the medical, psychological, familial and reproductive implications of the **genetic** contribution to specific health conditions. This process integrates the following:
- Interpretation of family and medical histories to assess the chance of disease occurrence or recurrence.
- Education about the natural history of the condition, inheritance pattern, testing, management, prevention, support resources and research.
- Counselling to promote informed choices in view of risk assessment, family goals, ethical and religious values.
- Support to encourage the best possible adjustment to the disorder in an affected family member and/or to the risk of recurrence of that disorder."

Source: R. Resta, B.B. Biesecker, R.L. Bennett, S. Blum, S.R. Hahn, M.N. Strecker, J.L. Williams, "A new definition of genetic counselling: NSGC task force report", *J Gen Couns.* 2006 Apr; 15(2): 77-83.

a chaplain at a major private hospital reported women proceeding from diagnosis to termination without being offered counselling and support, and without being presented with options to be supported if they choose not to terminate.

In both sectors, women may experience non-invasive testing without much advice about the possibility of a diagnosis of a major abnormality and the decisions that may need to be made subsequently. There appears to be little preparation for the shock that women may experience, the likelihood of being offered invasive testing, and the reality that most women who receive a diagnosis of a major abnormality choose to end the pregnancy.

There would appear to be insufficient funding of genetic counsellors and, consequently, lack of opportunities, for women experiencing tests which may reveal a major abnormality, to have access to counselling at each stage. The issue is not a matter of training. There are many more qualified genetic counsellors than there are places available. Qualified genetic counsellors are being employed in other roles for lack of funded positions for genetic counsellors.

There is also a lack of Australian research into the needs of women in these circumstances. The studies presented were very small scale and the samples not representative of either the health professionals involved nor of women experiencing a diagnosis of a life limiting condition in their foetus/unborn child. The Murdoch Institute is pursuing some grants for research into this area.

How the needs for support through the process of screening, diagnostic testing, considering options and managing pregnancy are met, may significantly affect the choices made and the outcomes.

4.6 The Effects of Offering Perinatal Palliative Care

In a recent UK study,[78] women and their partners were offered perinatal palliative care, following a diagnosis of lethal foetal abnormality, as

---

78 A.C.G. Breeze, C.C. Lees, A Kumar, H.H. Missfelder-Lobos, E.M. Murdoch, "Palliative care for prenatally diagnosed lethal fetal abnormality", *Arch Dis Child Fetal Neonatal Ed*, 2007; 92:F56-F58.

an alternative to termination of pregnancy. The article shows that perinatal palliative care is a significant alternative, because 40% opted for perinatal palliative care compared to the usual 90% who opt for abortion. The study included 20 pregnancies and of the eight parents who chose to continue the pregnancy and pursue perinatal palliative care, six of these eight babies were liveborn and lived for between an hour and three weeks.

The numbers are too small and the sampling not reliable enough to make it possible to draw general conclusions. But it does seem significant that 40%, when offered an option of perinatal palliative care, chose not to terminate compared to the 10% who would normally be expected not to do so. There is a need for more research into whether offering perinatal palliative care would affect women's choices and what the comparative outcomes would be for those women and their families who chose to continue to birth and those who chose to terminate.

This study would seem to indicate how important it is for women to be well informed and given genuine options to continue with their pregnancies. Prenatal palliative care would seem to be insufficiently developed in Australia and much needs to be done to make genetic counselling routinely available prior to women entering into the screening and diagnosis pathway so that they have the time and space to make well informed decisions in accordance with their own beliefs.

4.7 Decision-Making Counselling

Counselling before undertaking prenatal tests and at each stage of the way is obviously important, but it seems that for many women, especially those in the private sphere, it is either not available or at least not offered[79]. Decision-making counselling is important for the opportunity

---

79 This conclusion was reached at a seminar for health professionals held by the John Paul II Institute for Marriage and Family, 7 December 2010, at the Thomas Carr Centre in East Melbourne.

that it gives for women and their partners to take the time to explore in an informed way the issues and their own values before making such vital decisions.

The issue of decision-making counselling is so important that in September 2006, the Australian Catholic Bishops Conference issued interim ethical guidelines for pregnancy counselling that insist upon it.

The Bishops advised that pregnancy-counselling services ought not refer for abortion and that non-directive counselling during pregnancy has an important role.[80] They described pregnancy support as having two components:

a) Counselling to assist with decision-making; and
b) On-going advice, material, emotional and spiritual support during pregnancy.

In their document providing interim ethical guidelines for pregnancy support services,[81] the Bishops said that the aims of decision-making counselling are distinct from pre-procedure counselling. Pre-procedure counselling is for a person who has decided on a course of action and is being guided in what to expect during and after the procedure. They

---

80 Australian Catholic Bishops Conference, "Bishops' Commission for Doctrine and Morals Preliminary Advice on Pregnancy Support and Counselling", 10/9/2006. Published on the Australian Catholic Bishops Conference website http://www.catholic.org.au/index.php?option=com_docman&Itemid=315
81 Denis Fitzgerald, "The features of counselling in a Catholic agency", *Kairos*, Vol 2, No 3, 2007.

supported *decision-making counselling*[82] on the basis that it is client-centred and non-directive and aims to assist a person to make a decision by:

a) Providing emotional support, time and space so that the client can make a decision that is reflective rather than panicked.

b) Assisting a client to talk through the problem(s) facing her by examining options and their implications for the client's own values.

c) Assisting the client to clarify her own sense of self in relation to a new problem and to make reasonable decisions for herself about what she wants now and in the long term.

d) Assisting the client to make reasonable decisions in relation to others.

e) Informing and exploring with the client the availability of emotional and other support.

f) Indicating to the client the need to seek medical or other professional services in relation to her pregnancy and encouraging her to seek that assistance from her own doctor or from another doctor or professional.[83]

The Bishops maintained that decision-making counselling ought not

---

82 Note that "decision-making counselling" as defined here is not a referral service. The counsellors explore what is involved and what values the clients express. To refer would be to be directive. The idea is to assist the client to recognize what decision would be most consistent with her long term critical values. The reason for adopting this approach, as distinct from counsellors being directive about expressing their own values, is the belief that the women are already under pressure and further pressure is only like to lead them to an expedient approach just to be rid of the pressure and not necessarily a decision they can live with in the long term. The trust is that if adequately supported and not pressured through this time, a life affirming choice is more likely. Professional Catholic counsellors, like other professional counsellors, are trained to be non-directive in this way. It does mean having to quietly not intervene in choices with which the counsellor might conscientiously disagree, trusting that just by continuing to listen and be supportive a better outcome may yet be achieved.

83 Australian Catholic Bishops Conference "Bishops' Commission for Doctrine and Morals Preliminary Advice on Pregnancy Support and Counselling", 10/9/2006 http://www.catholic.org.au/index.php?option=com_docman&Itemid=315

to attempt to direct the patient in relation to her pregnancy or toward any particular decision. The client is most likely to make a good choice if the counsellor serves to reduce the sense of panic and urgency and instead assists the client to regain control of her own circumstances. The aim is to give her greater confidence in being able to cope with pregnancy and to assist her to make a reasonable decision for herself. This provides the best chance of a life-affirming choice.[84]

4.8 Conclusion

The concept of perinatal palliative care for women who experience a diagnosis of a pregnancy with a life limiting abnormality is well developed in the literature but seemingly not so in practice in Australia.

There is a significant dislocation between medical perceptions that testing is for the purpose of providing the option of termination and the perspective of those women who opt for the tests in the false belief that the test results provide reassurance. It seems that women who do receive a positive screening result may be shocked and unprepared for its significance and the sequel of being offered invasive diagnostic tests and termination of pregnancy in the event of a positive result.

As a matter of some urgency women need to be offered supportive decision-making counselling before they embark on a course of prenatal testing that may lead to invasive tests, risk of miscarriage and the predicament of being offered termination of pregnancy.

There is a need for GPs, nurses, clergy and others who provide information and counselling to women to be better informed and to provide early advice to women about what they are likely to expect, including the major medical objective (making termination available), the accuracy of the tests and the risks involved. Though routine antenatal tests are important for managing pregnancy and delivery, women should be informed that the prenatal screening and invasive diagnostic tests are not mandatory and may not be needed as part of good care.

---

84 Ibid.

Obstetricians and maternity services also need to ensure that, prior to any prenatal screening or diagnostic testing, there is an opportunity to discuss the issues with a counsellor to enable informed decisions about the sequence of events that may be triggered by the tests.

The available evidence suggests that offering perinatal palliative care reduces the proportion of women who opt for termination. At all stages of the process, the option of perinatal palliative care should be made known so that women are aware of this choice from the outset, and are not left with the impression that the only medically supported option, in the event of abnormality, is termination of pregnancy or induction and foeticide.[85] Perinatal palliative care is an alternative to the current circumstances in which women who terminate a pregnancy on medical grounds often report powerlessness.

The outcome of perinatal palliative care is much less certain than the alternative of termination of pregnancy, where the aim is to end the life of the child. However, for those women (and their partners) who have recognized the identity of their foetus as a child, and perhaps bonded, but also for those women who have not, offering perinatal palliative care creates hope and the opportunity to do the best to care for their child, however limited his or her existence may be, and knowledge that there are health professionals who will assist them to do so. The availability of perinatal palliative care demonstrates that their child is respected and valued by others. Perinatal palliative care is thus a vital service and should be as available in Australia and in our maternity hospitals as it is the United States of America where over forty such services exist.

---

85 In most jurisdictions induction of labour and foeticide may be lawful if the procedures that kills the child happens before the child is completely born. Once the child is outside the body of the mother the law recognizes that killing may be a criminal offence. Usually in the abortion of viable foetuses (those able to be born alive), the procedure includes a step to ensure that the child is not born alive. This is sometimes referred to as "partial birth abortion" in which an instrument may be introduced into the brain of the child as the head appears outside the body of the woman but before birth is complete, with the intention to kill – foeticide. There is also controversy over claims about children being neglected to death after being born alive following a late abortion.

5
Assisted Reproductive Technology

5.1 Infertility

Infertility is a great tragedy. Most young couples, when they marry, expect to have children. These days, it is often the decision to attempt to have children that actually precipitates the decision to marry in order to give the children, and each other, the security of that commitment when the unity is likely to find expression in the relationship being fruitful in that very permanent way.

Not being able to have a child is thus very hurtful, bringing with it not only the frustration of being childless and being denied the joys of parenthood, but also feelings of inadequacy in not being able to achieve something that most people find relatively easy to achieve and spend a good part of their lives trying to avoid. The hurt is not restricted to the couple, as often their families, the would-be grandparents especially, are also affected.

Infertility seems even more tragic if choices have been made earlier to have an abortion or if the infertility results from avoidable causes, such as a decision to be sterilized, or as a result of sexually transmitted infection. For many couples it is simply a matter of leaving it too late, as infertility declines with age for both men and women, but more so for women.

5.2 Assisted Reproduction

Many couples in Western society, if they have been unsuccessful in conceiving for more than twelve months, are likely to be referred to in vitro fertilization (IVF).

Infertility generally means being unable to achieve pregnancy after trying for more than 12 months and somewhere between 12% to 28% of couples will suffer the problem, though the range in Western countries is usually given as between 12 and 15%, up to one in six couples. Approximately 11% of women will not have children but that includes many who choose to be childless. Involuntary childlessness, that is women who are childless at age 45 after having attempted to conceive, is between 3% and 8%.[86]

Reported clinical experience indicates that of those couples who have tried unsuccessfully for more than 12 months, approximately 70% will eventually have a child, with 27% having a child within the next year and 50% within five years.[87]

Nevertheless, many are referred to reproductive technology, especially as age is a factor and the opportunities may be dwindling. Of the 60,687 IVF cycles in 2010, 21.7% were done for male infertility factors as the only cause of infertility; 38.6% reported only female infertility factors; 13.8% reported combined male-female factors; 25.2% reported unexplained infertility; and 0.7% were not stated.[88]

As mentioned, fertility in both men and women declines with age, but markedly in women over the age of 35, and that is mirrored in the IVF success rates. The success rates for IVF/ICSI are also not as great as the media reporting would indicate. The most reliable source of data is that provided by the Victorian Assisted Reproductive Technology Authority to which the IVF teams have a statutory obligation to report.

---

86 W. Himmel, (1997). "Voluntary Childlessness and being Childfree". *British Journal of General Practice*. 11. http://www.ncbi.nlm.nih.gov/pmc/articles/PMC1312893/pdf/9101672.pdf.
87 Conversations with Prof James B. Brown, Royal Women's Hospital, Melbourne, August 2001, and Dr John McBain, Melbourne, IVF, July 2002.
88 Alan Macaldowie, Yueping A. Wang, Georgina M. Chambers, Elizabeth A. Sullivan National Perinatal Statistic Unit, *Assisted reproductive technology in Australia and New Zealand 2010*, Australian Institute of Health and Welfare, 2012 http://www.aihw.gov.au/WorkArea/DownloadAsset.aspx?id=10737423255

The last completed cycles recorded were for the 2009-10 year, in Victoria, allowing time for the stored embryos to be transferred by 2012:
- 7330 women treated with IVF (inc. ICSI)
- 50,249 embryos formed (eggs fert.)
- 2208 Clinical pregnancies were recorded (elev. HCG)
- 1700 confinements (gave birth)
- 1855 babies born
- 23% of women treated gave birth
- 3.5% of embryos survived to birth.[89]

It is worth noting that a retrospective study undertaken by the Billings organization in Melbourne noted that, of couples who had been trying unsuccessfully for more than 12 months, over 54% conceived within an average of less than five months after learning fertility awareness. It is a strong indication that being able to identify peak fertility using the mucus symptom increases the chances of an earlier pregnancy. It is difficult to draw general conclusions, because there was no control group and no attempt to control sampling. These were women who came to Billings clinics to seek assistance to achieve pregnancy – not a random sample and obviously self-selecting. One would expect that women for whom a definite cause of absolute infertility had been identified would be unlikely to approach a Billings clinic.

When couples are referred to me for advice about reproductive technology, often after they have been sent by their doctors to an IVF clinic, I take them to the website of the clinic to which they have been referred and also to the VARTA website (referred to above) and also the National Perinatal Statistics Unit website. It is important for them to identify the range of decisions they may need to make, and there are many options, and also obtain reliable information. The clinics can be reticent about providing live birth rate data per woman, which is what the couples want to know, preferring instead to talk of clinical pregnancy

---

89 www.varta.org.au/annualreports

rates (raised HCG levels) many of which do not continue to term. They also tend to give data based on women being prepared to have multiple attempts. In fact, because of the cost and the difficulties involved, many women choose not to continue. Thus a success rate of 50-60% may be quoted, when in fact the overall rate, as the above government data indicates, is that only 23% of women who have at least one egg pick up cycle will have a confinement (a birth). The success rate will be related to the age of the woman (and her partner), with younger women having a better chance.

I also encourage couples to explore the possibility of increasing their chances of conceiving naturally. My wife, Dr Mary Walsh, has taken a special interest in this area, and conducts a Fertility Assessment Clinic at the Manningham Medical Centre, with the assistance of fertility tutors or educators who instruct the women in observing and charting their symptoms. Couples are given general health assessments and assistance with factors that would affect the health of the child or their chances of conceiving, including specialist referral if that is indicated. The emphasis is on maximizing the chances of a natural conception and a healthy child. It is often surprising that couples know very little about their natural fertility and even less about treatments that restore it or reduce factors that might cause infertility. At a meeting we attended recently, a senior IVF specialist complained that young gynaecologists tend to refer directly to IVF rather than exploring ways of achieving natural conception.

If a couple can conceive naturally it is would seem better that they do so.

Current Australian data for all pregnancies shows that approximately:

- one pregnancy in six will miscarry
- one baby in 14 will be premature
- one baby in 25 will have a birth defect
- one baby in 100 will die around the time of birth

- one baby in 400 will have cerebral palsy and be disabled[90]

In contrast, between five and six per cent of IVF-conceived babies have a birth defect compared with approximately four per cent of spontaneously conceived babies.[91] That includes higher rates of neural tube defect such an anencephaly and spina bifida. A rare condition called Beckwith-Wiedemann Syndrome (BWS) has been shown to occur in about one in 4,000 IVF babies compared with one in 14,000 to 35,000 spontaneously conceived babies.

The perinatal (after 20 weeks gestation and before 28 days after birth) mortality rate for IVF and Embryo Transfer in Australia in 2010 was 13.5 deaths per 1,000 births, which was lower than the rate of 15.3 deaths per 1,000 ART births in 2009 and higher than the rate of 9.8 per 1,000 births to all women who gave birth in Australia in 2009.[92] That is to say perinatal mortality is 1.3 times the normal. It has fallen slightly as the practice has moved away from multiple embryo transfer and there are fewer multiple pregnancies. The trend is towards transferring only one embryo at a time as the results for the children born are better.

There is increasing concern about the long term effects of IVF on adults who were conceived that way. There is evidence of higher rates of insulin resistance and cardiometabolic disorders.[93]

The data therefore suggests that if couples can conceive naturally it would be safer for the child to do so rather than resort to IVF.

---

90 Victorian Assisted Reproductive Technology Authority, *Possible Health Effects of IVF* http://www.varta.org.au/www/257/1003057/displayarticle/1004681.html
91 Ibid.
92 A. Macaldowie, Y.A. Wang, G.M. Chambers & E.A. Sullivan, 2012. Assisted reproductive technology in Australia and New Zealand 2010. Assisted reproduction technology series no. 16. Cat. no. PER 55. Canberra: AIHW.
93 M. Ceelen, M.M. van Weissenbruch, J.P. Vermeiden, F.E. van Leeuwen, H.A. Delemarre-van de Waal, "Cardiometabolic differences in children born after in vitro fertilization: follow-up study." *J. Clin Endocrinol Metab* 2008 May; 93(5):1682-8.; Acton, Q. Ashton, *Advances in Hyperinsulism Research and Treatment/ 2011 Edition*, Scholarly Editions, Atlanta, Georgia 2012 p. 8.

Increasingly couples are seeking IVF in association with pre-implantation genetic diagnosis in which a cell is removed from the early embryo for testing at about the eight cell stage. The couple then may use the information to discard embryos that have a chromosomal abnormality such as Downs Syndrome. Melbourne IVF have recently been advertising full chromosomal testing of embryos.

PGD has not been a very common procedure and in the past resulted in very few births. In the 2009/2010 year in Victoria, the two centres that practise it treated just 101 women using PGD for the purposes of preventing the birth of a child with a genetic abnormality, resulting in just four births.[94] 164 PGD procedures were undertaken, resulting in 21 clinical pregnancies and 4 confinements. In that process during 164 PGD procedures there were:

- 2227 oocytes collected
- 1821 oocytes inseminated
- 1321 oocytes fertilised
- 108 cycles where genetically suitable embryos were transferred
- 122 embryos transferred
- 80 embryos frozen for future use.[95]

The numbers are too small to provide a basis for accurate predictions, but on these figures a women undergoing IVF and PGD should be prepared for disappointment given that 97.5% of procedures did not result in a birth, and when a pregnancy was achieved, 81% miscarried. Overall about 3% of embryos used in PGD survived to be born. At a Victorian Civil and Administrative Appeals Tribunal at which, as an expert witness, I had presented these figures, I was told that an IVF practitioner had claimed higher pregnancy rates. These are, however, the official

---

[94] Note a further 96 women were treated using PGD for recurrent IVF failure and miscarriage and 3 of those women gave birth.
[95] Victorian Assisted Reproductive Technology Authority *Annual Report 2010* p. 34 http://www.varta.org.au/annual-reports/w1/i1003573/ Accessed 21/2/2011.

data required to be submitted to the Victorian Assisted Reproductive Technology Authority by the IVF teams by Victorian law. It may be that later figures will show an improvement for pregnancy following PGD.

The Catholic Church has expressed strong reservations about using reproductive technology. Basically the Church approves measures that are aimed at assisting a couple to conceive a child through their marital intimacy, but rejects those procedures that replace the marriage act in the origin of the child.

Very simply, there are three principles that the Church suggests are relevant to assisted reproduction:

a) the right to life and to physical integrity of every human being from conception to natural death;

b) the specifically human values of sexuality, which require "that the procreation of a human person be brought about as the fruit of the conjugal act specific to the love between spouses;" and

c) the unity of marriage, which means reciprocal respect for the right within marriage to become a father or mother only together with the other spouse.[96]

5.3 The Moral Status of the Embryo

The debate about the beginning of life is helped by Plato's Theory of Forms[97] and his distinction between *Matter* – stuff, and *Form* – organization, shape or pattern. Aristotle held that there could be no matter without form. Living beings then are informed matter or enmattered form.[98]

---

96 Congregation for the Doctrine of the Faith, *Dignitas Personae*, Vatican City 8 September 2008, n. 12. Accessed from http://www.vatican.va/roman_curia/congregations/cfaith/documents/rc_con_cfaith_doc_20081208_dignitas-personae_en.html See also Fleming, John, *Dignitas Personae Explained*, Connor Court, Ballan, 2009.

97 Marc Cohen, *Philosophy 320: History of Ancient Philosophy*, University of Washington Philosophy Department, 2006, http://faculty.washington.edu/smcohen/320/thforms.htm.

98 Lloyd P. Gerson, *Aristotle and Other Platonists*, Cornell University Press, 2005.

Often we speak of the soul and the body as though they were separate, but the reality of our lived experience is that, as Aristotle explained it, there is no matter without form and we are a unity of the body and soul. Aristotle expressed the unity of matter and form in the following way:

> ... the proximate matter and the form are one and the same thing, the one potentially, and the other actually ... for each thing is a unity, and the potential and the actual are somehow one.[99]

The philosopher René Descartes[100] discussed the mind and body as though they were separate, a view described as *dualism*, but the only experience we have is an embodied experience. On a dualistic account, the mind is an entirely immaterial thing without any extension in it whatsoever; and, conversely, the body is an entirely material thing without any thinking in it at all. This also means that each substance can have only its kind of modes. For instance, the mind can only have modes of understanding, will and, in some sense, sensation, while the body can only have modes of size, shape, motion, and quantity. But bodies cannot have modes of understanding or willing, since these are not ways of being extended; and minds cannot have modes of shape or motion, since these are not ways of thinking.[101]

A major problem for dualism is that there is obviously a causal relationship between the mind and the body. It as a body that I think and act.

The empiricists assert *materialism*[102] and the idea that there is only the material existence. That is to say they deny the existence of the human being as a spiritual being.

---

99 E, Berti, "Multiplicity and Unity of Being in Aristotle", *Proceedings of the Aristotelian Society*, Volume 101, 2001, pp.185-207.
100 René Descartes, *The Philosophical Writings of Descartes*, trans. John Cottingham, Robert Stoothoff, Dugald Murdoch and Anthony Kenny, Cambridge: Cambridge University Press, 3 vols. 1984-1991.
101 Internet Encyclopedia of Philosophy http://www.iep.utm.edu/descarte/#SH7b
102 A.J. Ayer, *Logical Positivism*, Dover Publications, 1952.

Some traditions, such as Hindhu traditions, see the *spiritual reality* as the only true reality, and freedom only attainable by freeing ourselves of the impediment of the body. The Absolute is a state of mindfulness unfettered by the body.[103]

The Catholic tradition, however, sees human existence as an embodied existence in which our immortal souls provide form to the matter in which each one of us is instantiated, and we accept Christ's ascension body and soul, Mary's assumption into Heaven, body and soul, and our own resurrection as a glorified body. The doctrine that we are a unity of body and soul in which the soul forms or informs the matter of the body was first proclaimed by the Council of Vienne[104] in the Middle Ages and has been affirmed many times since.

The first issue to resolve in any discussion of when life begins is the question about what life is. Life is a condition distinguished by capacity for growth, functional activity and change.[105] In that respect we make a distinction between organic and inorganic matter, between that which is animate and that which is inanimate.

In considering different life forms, we can distinguish between vegetative life, animal life and human life. In contemplating the beginning of a human life, the issue is one of individuation, of considering not just life, but a life. As human beings we are part of humanity and humanity goes on as a life form with each of us playing a short role in that on-going existence. The questions that most concern us about this individual existence are:

- What is an individual?
- What can be meant by the beginning or end of an individual?

---

103 The Teachings of Sri Ramana Maharshi, The nature of Individual self and of liberation http://www.hinduism.co.za/mind1.htm
104 Council of Vienne 1312. Accessed from: www.papalencyclicals.net/Councils/ecum15.htm
105 *The Concise Oxford Dictionary*, English Edition, 1991.

- What relationship can an individual have to other individuals concerning his or her beginning or end?
- What is a human person?[106]

The notion of being an organism is central to being a human individual. Biologically an organism may be roughly defined as a living agent that belongs to a reproductive lineage, some of whose members have the potential to possess an intergenerational life cycle, and which have minimal functional autonomy.[107]

An individual life can be understood to have begun when the process of reproduction results in a new organism that exists then as a distinct living agent, belonging to an intergenerational life cycle and having functional autonomy. In mammals, that organism usually begins as a result of fertilization and the formation of a new cell that has the capacity for embryogenesis and thus is the first stage of this new system that is an individual life. The individual ends when that system permanently ceases to operate as a living organism. It ceases to be alive when it ceases to have capacity for growth, functional activity and change. It ceases to be an organism when it loses the organization and integration of organs that makes it a single living agent.

The issue of the end of life is discussed extensively in volume three. The issue that concerns us here is the beginning of life. In mammals the first cell formed by fertilization of an egg by sperm can be considered the beginning of the organism because that cell is different from other cells in two important respects. It is formed with a new genome that contains parts of the genome of both parents; and it has the capacity for embryogenesis. It contains the organization, the information that directs

---

106 T.V. Daly SJ, "The Status of Embryonic Human Life: A Crucial Issue in Genetic Counselling," in Nicholas Tonti-Filippini, *Health Care Priorities in Australia*, St. Vincent's Bioethics Centre, 1985.
107 Evelyn Fox Keller, "Beyond the Gene but Beneath the Skin," in Susan Oyama, Paul E. Griffiths, and Russell D. Gray (editors), *Cycles of Contingency: Developmental Systems and Evolution*, Cambridge, MA: MIT Press, 2001, pp. 299-312.

its development from thereon. All it needs is a favourable environment. No further information is added. It is the beginning of a new system that is a unique organism that will have its own life history, with individual cells living for a time and dying, but forming a single living entity.

What makes that organism a human life is an interesting question. The Church has been content to refer to the fruit of human generation as a human being. Biologically we can identify that organism, with its inherent capacity for organogenesis and embryogenesis, to be human because it has a human genome.

So, biologically, a new human individual is formed when the first cell is formed with a human genome and capable of embryogenesis. Earlier I referred to fertilization, but of course that is not the only way in which a new life can come to be, now that cloning is a possibility. It is possible to form a new life by fusing an enucleated egg with an ordinary cell and, in the future, there may be other ways of producing a cell that is capable of embryogenesis and contains a human genome. It is not beyond the possibilities of recombinant DNA technology that one day a laboratory may succeed in generating a human embryo from first principles. In my view the source of that person would not alter his or her status as a human being.

In the *Research involving Human Embryos Act 2002*, the Australian Parliament defined a human embryo as:

> A discrete entity that has arisen from either:
>
> (a) the first mitotic division when fertilisation of a human oocyte by a human sperm is complete; or
>
> (b) any other process that initiates organized development of a biological entity with a human nuclear genome or altered human nuclear genome that has the potential to develop up to, or beyond, the stage at which the primitive streak appears; and has not yet reached 8 weeks of development since the first mitotic division

The reason for choosing the mitotic division is that the first cell division is the first evidence available that fertilization has succeeded. However the release of the contents of the head of the sperm into the egg and thus the fusion of the sperm and the egg will have occurred around sixteen hours before that division. Australia's National Health and Medical Research Council (NHMRC) recognized this gap and so its *Ethical Guidelines on the use of Assisted Reproductive Technology in Clinical Practice and Research* (2007) stated that the term "human embryo" should also apply to:

- the single entity formed by the combination of two gametes; and
- a single cell or group of cells that is capable of reaching the stage of forming a blastocyst in vitro, because it is considered to have the potential to develop up to, or beyond, the stage at which the primitive streak appears.

It is significant that the legal definition focuses on the "human nuclear genome or altered human nuclear genome." The importance of having a human genome is that the human genome gives the embryo the inherent capacity for intellect and reason.

Modern biology has thus established a clear beginning for the human embryo. Contemporary knowledge has made that possible. That was not true for Aristotle or even St Thomas Aquinas.

Aristotle's account of the beginning of human life is very different:

> The action of the semen of the male in "setting" the female's secretion in the uterus is similar to that of rennet upon milk. Rennet is milk which contains vital heat, as semen does, and this integrates the homogeneous substance and makes it "set." As the nature of milk and the menstrual fluid is one and the same, the action of the semen upon the substance of the menstrual fluid is the same as that of rennet upon milk.[108]

There was a belief in spontaneous generation, for which maggots developing in rotten tissue were evidence. There was a belief that the

---

108 Aristotle, *Generation of Animals*, 11.4 739b 21-27.

menstrual blood which ceased to flow, provide the rotting material for that to happen.

Until well after the Middle-Ages, the thinking appears to have followed Aristotle in believing that the woman's biology was a passive contributor to the process, with the man's contribution being the active component.

The first time that an egg is mentioned in human reproduction appears to have been by William Harvey in his work *On the Generation of Animals* in 1651. Harvey speculated about their being a union of sperm and egg. He had unsuccessfully attempted to find eggs of the deer in the uterus; others, after Harvey's time, mistook ovarian follicles for mammalian eggs.

Karl Ernst von Baer was born on 29 February 1792, in Piep, near Jerwen, Estonia. He first found the true egg in his friend, Burdach's, housedog, a bitch sacrificed for the investigations. In 1827 he published his discovery in *On the Mammalian Egg and the Origin of Man*, in which he said:

> Every animal which springs from the coition of male and female is developed from an ovum, and none from a simple formative liquid.

Pope Anastasius II, in a Letter to the Bishops of France, 23 August 498, referred to blood (from the woman) and semen (from the man) as "faesces" or "dregs" and, with a touch of male superiority, took it for granted that the semen must have an active role to play in generating new life.

Thus St Thomas Aquinas was relying on very weak science when he taught about the beginning of life:

> First, as to the mode of reunion, for some held the separated soul to be naturally reunited to a body by the way of generation. Secondly, as to the body to which it was reunited, for they held that this second union was not with the self-same body that was laid aside in death, but with another.[109]

---

109 St Thomas Aquinas, *Summa Theologiae* III, Q. 79, Art. 1.

On ensoulment, Aquinas believed that there was a succession of souls, the next being more perfect than the one before and including all that was the one before – thus a progression of souls from animal to sensitive to rational.

> We must therefore say that since the generation of one thing is the corruption of another, it follows of necessity that both in men and in other animals, when a more perfect form supervenes the previous form is corrupted: yet so that the supervening form contains the perfection of the previous form, and something in addition. It is in this way that through many generations and corruptions we arrive at the ultimate substantial form, both in man and other animals. This indeed is apparent to the senses in animals generated from putrefaction. We conclude therefore that the intellectual soul is created by God at the end of human generation, and this soul is at the same time sensitive and nutritive, the pre-existing forms being corrupted.[110]

Aquinas challenged the previously-held Aristotelian view that the rational soul entered the foetus "forty days after conception for a male and eighty to ninety days for a female." He held that the "rational soul" enters the foetus of either sex upon quickening, the time when the foetus first moves within a woman's body,[111] which usually happens before sixteen weeks. Aquinas thus believed in the formation the body before ensoulment:

> We do not believe in the fiction of Origen that human souls were created at the beginning with other intellectual natures, nor that they are Procreated together with their bodies by coition, as the Luciferians with Cyril, and certain Latin writers have Presumed to maintain. But we affirm that the body alone is begotten by sexual Procreation, and that after the formation of the body the soul is created and infused.[112]

---

110 St Thomas Aquinas, *Summa Theologiae* I, Q118 Article 2.
111 St Thomas Aquinas, *Summa Theologiae* I, Q 18, Art 2.
112 St Thomas Aquinas, *Disputed Questions on the Power of God*, "De Potentiâ, De Eccles. Dogm". (xiv) http://dhspriory.org/thomas/QDdePotentia.htm#3:10

The matter of how life begins had a place in Scripture. In the Genesis account:

> Then God said, "Let us make man in our image, after our likeness. And let them have dominion over the fish of the sea and over the birds of the heavens and over the livestock and over all the earth and over every creeping thing that creeps on the earth." So God created man in his image, in the image of God he created him; male and female he says, created them. [Genesis 1:26-27]

And Isaiah:

- Isaiah 49:15-16 Can a mother forget the baby at her breast and have no compassion on the child she has borne?
  Though she may forget, I will not forget you!
  See, I have engraved you on the palms of my hands; your walls are ever before me."
- Isaiah 44:2 This is what the Lord says – he who made you, who formed you in the womb, and who will help you ...
- Isaiah 44:24 This is what the Lord says – your Redeemer, who formed you in the womb: "I am the Lord, who has made all things, who alone stretched out the heavens, who spread out the earth by myself..."
- Isaiah 46:3-4 Listen to me, O house of Jacob, all you who remain of the house of Israel, you whom I have upheld since you were conceived, and have carried since your birth. Even to your old age and gray hairs, I am He, I am He who will sustain you. I have made you and I will carry you; I will sustain you and I will rescue you.
- Isaiah 49:5 And now the Lord says – he who formed me in the womb to be his servant to bring Jacob back to him and gather Israel to himself, for I am honored in the eyes of the Lord and my God has been my strength

And Job:

> Did not he who made me in the womb make them? Did not the

same one form us both within our mothers? [Job 31:15]
Your own hands shaped me and modelled me;
And would you now have second thoughts and destroy me?
You modelled me, remember, as clay is modelled, and would you reduce me now to dust?
Did you not pour me out like milk,
and curdle me then like cheese;
clothe me with skin and flesh,
and weave me of bone and sinew?
And then you endowed me with life, watched each breath of mine with tender care. [Job 10: 8-12]

And then the Psalms:

- Psalm 51:5 Surely I was sinful at birth, sinful from the time my mother conceived me.
- Psalm 119:73 Your hands made me and formed me; give me understanding to learn your commands.
- Psalm 139:13-16 For you created my inmost being; you knit me together in my mother's womb. I praise you because I am fearfully and wonderfully made; your works are wonderful, I know that full well. My frame was not hidden from you when I was made in the secret place. When I was woven together in the depths of the earth, your eyes saw my unformed body.

And Jeremiah:

Before I formed you in the womb I knew you, before you were born I set you apart; I appointed you as a prophet to the nations. [Jeremiah 1:5]

And Wisdom

Like all the others, I too am a mortal man, descendant of the first being fashioned from the earth, I was modelled in flesh within my mother's womb, for ten months taking shape in her blood by means of virile seed and pleasure, sleep's companion. I too, when I

> was born, drew in the common air, I fell on the same ground that bears us all, a wail my first sound, as for all the rest. I was nurtured in swaddling clothes, with every care. No king has known any other beginning of existence; for all there is one way only into life, as out of it. [Wisdom 7:1-6]

It is thought that the Alexandrian Jews in the second century BC, to whom the *Book of Wisdom* is attributed, may have been influenced by Aristotelian embryology.

Exodus 21:22-23 and Philo's 1st century version of Exodus refer to the beginning of life also.

In the New Testament the six-month unborn child, John the Baptist, salutes Jesus, probably within a week of Jesus' conception. Then in Luke 1:39-44 just after the angel has just made the announcement to Mary that she will conceive the Son of the Most High, the evangelist reports:

> At that time Mary got ready and hurried to a town in the hill country of Judea, where she entered Zechariah's home and greeted Elizabeth. When Elizabeth heard Mary's greeting, the baby leaped in her womb, and Elizabeth was filled with the Holy Spirit. In a loud voice she exclaimed: "Blessed are you among women, and blessed is the child you will bear! But why am I so favored, that the mother of my Lord should come to me? As soon as the sound of your greeting reached my ears, the baby in my womb leaped for joy.

In the fourteenth century the Council of Vienne (1311-12), presumably following the teaching of St Thomas, decreed:

> [1]. Adhering firmly to the foundation of the catholic faith, other than which, as the Apostle testifies, no one can lay, we openly profess with holy mother church that the only begotten Son of God, subsisting eternally together with the Father in everything in which God the Father exists, assumed in time in the womb of a virgin the parts of our nature united together, from which he himself true God became true man: namely the human, passible body and the intellectual or rational soul truly of itself and essentially informing the body.

In more recent times the Church has taught that life must be respected from conception. The Second Vatican Council taught in *Gaudium et Spes* n. 5, 7, December 1965:

> God, the Lord of life, has entrusted to men the noble mission of safeguarding life, and men must carry it out in a manner worthy of themselves. Life must be protected with the utmost care from the moment of conception: abortion and infanticide are abominable crimes.

The Congregation for the Doctrine of the Faith in its *Declaration on Procured Abortion*, 18 November 1974, declared:

> It is true that in the Middle Ages, when the opinion was generally held that the spiritual soul was not present until after the first few weeks, a distinction was made in the evaluation of the sin and the gravity of the penal sanctions. In resolving cases, approved authors were more lenient with regard to that early stage than with regard to later stages. But it was never denied at that time that procured abortion, even during the first few days, was objectively a grave sin. This condemnation was in fact unanimous.

The embryo had a status in Canon Law with the first papal canon, *Effraenatam*, which was issued by Sixtus V in 1588 and universally imposed a penal penalty of excommunication for abortion. It applied to all abortions and was reserved to the Holy See.[113]

In 1591, the law was modified by Gregory XIV so that the penalty would not apply when a foetus was not "animated" or "ensouled" under the Aristo-Aquinan theory of when human life begins (not before 40 days), and it gave the local bishops control of these cases.[114] This was motivated, at least in part, by the sheer volume of litigation the law had produced ("reserved to the Holy See" meant that *each* case had to be taken to Rome for the excommunication to be lifted).

---

113 http://embryo.asu.edu/view/embryo:1277 70 Accessed 13/3/13.
114 *The 1917 or PIO-Benedictine Code of Canon Law in English*, Ignatius Press: San Francisco, CA, 2001.

In 1869, Pius IX rescinded the animation exception and the change appeared in the 1917 revision of the Code.[115] The canons of the 1917 and 1983 Codes apply to all direct abortions. Abortions incident to otherwise lawful medical care that is required to save the life of the mother (e.g., chemotherapy, hysterectomy of a cancerous uterus) are given an interpretive exception from the rule under the principle of "double effect."

In modern times the debate over the beginning of human life has continued with Helga Kuhse and Peter Singer in their chapter "Individual Humans and Persons: The Issue of Moral Status,"[116] asserting that the embryo is only life like an egg or sperm.

This was despite the biology indicating that life is the capacity that an organized individual has for building up its own structure and powers, and for maintaining and developing these by calling upon external resources that were not part of its own organization, despite the variety of inputs, activities and challenges; and that a human embryo is an organism that has the completed capacity to develop to human adulthood if provided with nourishment and a favourable environment. An ovum or sperm taken on its own will soon die, and has no capacity to develop. It is only when they fuse that there is the capacity to develop.[117]

Others have recognized the continuum of life but the individuality of each member of the human family:

> Life is a continuum passed on from generation. However it can only be handed from individual to individual. Each is a discrete individual. A new life begins when a new cell forms that has the completed capacity to develop toward human adulthood.[118]

---

115 *The 1917 or PIO-Benedictine Code of Canon Law in English*, Ignatius Press: San Francisco CA, 2001.
116 In Peter Singer *et al*, *Embryo Experimentation*, Cambridge University Press, 1990.
117 T.V. Daly SJ, 1986, op. cit.
118 J.J. Diamond, *Abortion, animation and biological hominisation Theologiael Studies*, Volume 36, 1975, pp. 305-324.

The Victorian Infertility (Medical Treatment) Act in 1995 defined an embryo as beginning at syngamy:

> When the two membranes [i.e., of sperm and ovum] open to one another and the contents of the sperm are released into the ovum, the sperm loses its separate identity and the ovum gains a capacity it did not have while simply an ovum, that of developing as a human individual ... The two cells (sperm and ovum) have become a single cell containing many interacting components which by their interaction have the capacity for organizing all the subsequent stages of human development.

Despite the biology, those with an interest, such as IVF pioneers Alan Trounson and Carl Wood, referred to the embryo as just a blob of cells:

> All human beings are, in a sense a blob of cells. The significance of an individual is the organisation and integration of those cells to form just one being and the nature of that being. In the case of a human embryo it is the inherent radical capacity for rationality that is the inheritance of every human being.[119]

In the 1980s and two decades before the Dolly the Sheep cloning process happened in mammals for the first time, some such as Rev Dr Norman Ford SDB raised the issue of twinning as a challenge to the individuality of the embryo. The argument was that because the embryo had been known to form mono-zygotic twins (identical twins), therefore it could not be considered to be an individual or have an indivisible soul until after twinning was no longer possible.[120]

The likely explanation is simply that a second embryo forms asexually from the first embryo, which is no more a problem for individuality than ordinary parenting in which two individuals form a third.

Others dismissed the argument because if it were so that the possibility of twinning excluded individuality, there could never be an

---

119 Alan Trounson and Carl Wood, *Medical Journal of Australia*, Volume 146, 1987, pp. 338-40.
120 Norman M. Ford, *When did I begin?*, Cambridge University Press, 1988.

individual amoeba, or an individual rose bush, since each of these can give rise to a new individual of the same sort. And a mouse would have to be declared non-individual retrospectively if an experiment to take a clone from it should prove successful.[121]

More to the point, since 1997 cloning mammals has been possible. On that basis every human being remains twinnable throughout their lives. That is to say, it is now possible that all adult human beings may be reproduced asexually. On that basis, no human being could be an individual if the Norman Ford argument about twinning were valid.

Interestingly, Aristotle had addressed the matter of asexual reproduction:

> It is a fact of observation that plants and certain insects go on living when divided into segments; this means that each of the segments has a soul in it identical in species, though not numerically identical in the different segments, for both of the segments for a time possess the power of sensation and local movement. That this does not last is not surprising, for they no longer possess the organs necessary for self-maintenance. But, all the same, in each of the bodily parts there are present all the parts of soul, and the souls so present are homogeneous with one another and with the whole; this means that the several parts of the soul are indisseverable from one another, although the whole soul is divisible. It seems also that the principle found in plants is also a kind of soul; for this is the only principle which is common to both animals and plants; and this exists in isolation from the principle of sensation, though there nothing which has the latter without the former.[122]

Another aspect of human reproduction observed in the laboratory is the formation of mosaic embryos in which two embryos fuse and the result develops normally but with two different genomes in different

---

121 Tom Daly, 1987b; Cf St Vincent's Bioethics Centre in Australian Senate Select Committee Evidence, 1986.
122 Aristotle, *On the Soul*, 350 B.C.E. Translated by J.A. Smith. http://classics.mit.edu/Aristotle/soul.1.i.html

parts of the body. It has been argued that as long as this fusion or mosaicism is possible, the embryo cannot be an individual.[123]

The likely explanation is that one individual is absorbed into the other thus losing its own individuality, identity and life.

There have also been those who argue that the embryo does not survive but becomes part of placenta, which is discarded at birth, and hence the embryo cannot be regarded as the beginning of human life. The placenta is an organ of the embryo that is vital for the embryo until birth. The loss of original cells with the placenta at birth is not significant for the individuality of the embryo or the continuity of identity from the zygote to the infant. As human beings we are constantly losing cells. The individual continues despite that process of rejuvenation of tissue.

Arguing on the basis of Aristotle and Aquinas and the early Church's views founded on a mistaken biology, the theologian, Gordan Dunstan, used the views of the early Church to argue that becoming a human being is a gradual process, not an event.[124]

We know from contemporary biology that human development is a process that begins at fertilisation and continues until death. The stages of development of the early embryo no more alter the person's individuality than the stages of development from infant to child to adolescent to adult.

Finally, there are those who concede that human life begins at fertilization, but that personhood does not happen until much later. Peter Singer maintains that the embryo is human being but not a person, because not conscious, knowing, loving, etc.[125]

The issue is whether human dignity is inherent just through being a member of the human family, or whether it is acquired. What or who is

---

123 G. Pastrana, "Personhood and the beginning of life", *Thomist*, Volume 4, 1977, pp 247-94.
124 Gordan Dunstan, "The moral status of the human embryo: a tradition recalled", *Journal of Medical Ethics*, Volume 1, 1984, p. 38ff.
125 Peter Singer, *Rethinking Life and Death*, Text Publishing, 1994.

the embryo when it comes to be? Is it the beginning of another member of the human family with all its inheritance of human capacity complete and intact?

Singer's challenge is that, in asserting human dignity, we are being speciesist, a kind of racism in selecting our own kind in that way. He argues that a human embryo and even a human infant lacks the self-consciousness and hence the desires for the future that would give her a moral status. By contrast he argues that mature animals have a greater moral status.

For the Catholic Church, human beings are a kind of being made in the image and likeness of God with the inherent capacity for rationality and free will. Biological science affirms that the human embryo belongs to the human family because the human genome provides each embryo with the inherent capacity for rationality and free will, and hence the capacity to love, doubt, wonder and affirm. The Church recognizes that as a human being we are each called to communion with God and we each are social beings made for that communion.

There are thus two conflicting views about personhood: that it is inherent, or acquired. From my perspective and that of the Catholic Church, human dignity is inherent and not endowed. It is to do with who we are. From the first moment that the new cell comes to be with a unique human genome and the capacity for embryogenesis and hence differentiation and organogenesis, there is a new individual made in the image and likeness of God, a new individual with the inherent capacity for rationality. The organisation necessary for the development of the individual to the point that it actually expresses rationality is present from the time that the first cell is formed. The beginning of that individual rational being thus begins with the formation of the first cell. If we respect human life because each human life is a rational animal, as Aquinas expressed it, then that individual exists from that time that the sperm and ovum unite to form that first cell, or from the time that that first cell with that radical capacity for rationality comes to be by other means, such as cloning.

5.4 Embryo Loss

In vitro fertilization is of concern first because of the enormous and deliberate wastage of human embryos. As discussed earlier, few places require data to be kept on embryos produced by in vitro fertilization, but in the Australian State of Victoria IVF centres are required to be licensed and to submit their data to a Government authority. As mentioned earlier, according to the most recent data available, 3.5% of embryos produced survived to birth.[126]

It is routine to discard embryos when they are first formed if their development after fertilization is not at a normal rate, and to make a further judgement after freeze-thawing. Often pre-implantation genetic diagnosis is also used in order to undertake chromosomal analysis to identify and discard embryos that are considered abnormal. Finally, the embryo transfer process is not very safe for embryos and many do not survive after transfer. There is therefore concern about violation of the right to life of embryos produced through IVF. It is not so much that the overall loss rate is so high, that can happen following natural conception: my grandmother was the sole survivor of seventeen pregnancies and sixteen miscarriages. No-one suggests that trying for natural conception in circumstances, such as occurred for my great grandmother, are wrong. The problem in IVF is the extent to which the loss rate is a result of deliberately discarding embryos as a quality control measure, or as a result of unnecessary steps such as freezing and storing, because of the use of fertility drugs and the over production of embryos to increase pregnancy rates or because of preimplantation genetic diagnosis or prenatal testing.

When couples come to see me about being on an IVF program, I suggest to them exploring with the team to use the natural cycle rather than ovarian over-stimulation and avoid embryo selection by transferring all the embryos produced, which are likely to be only one or two in a cycle, and so none are frozen and stored.

---

126 www.varta.org.au/annualreports

5.5 Equal Respect for Persons

A second issue involved in IVF is the way in which the child comes to be. Normally in natural conception, a child comes to be as a result of the celebration of love between his or her parents and the child is therefore an embodiment of and an equal third party to their love. That he or she results from their love preserves his or her equal status as a person and therefore worthy of equal love and respect.

In the usual practice of IVF, the parents contribute eggs and sperm to a process in which they are then very interested bystanders. The child actually comes to be not as a result of an act of love, but as the product of a process managed in the laboratory. The relationship formed between the technologist and the child is not a relationship between equals, but a relationship of producer to product in which the producer exercises quality control – hence the selection of embryos during the process, with some being discarded after failing the quality control measures. The child looks back to an origin not in the celebration of love between the parents, but as a product of a process subject to domination by those in the laboratory. This is what the Church means when it refers to IVF violating the specifically human values of sexuality which require "that the procreation of a human person be brought about as the fruit of the conjugal act specific to the love between spouses."[127] The problem with the context of IVF is that it is not an act of love, but a production of a product. The embryo is essentially treated as an object, a product.

5.6 Donor Gametes

The third issue particularly applies to the use of donor sperm or donor eggs. When a couple enters into marriage, they give themselves completely to each other in sexual intimacy, including the ability to become a mother or a father. The gift is fully human, total, exclusive and

---

126 *Dignitas Personae*, n. 12.

faithful for life.¹²⁸ All others are thereby excluded. Using donor sperm or donor eggs involves bringing someone else into the marriage. That other person also becomes a parent to the child as a genetic parent. Parenthood then becomes separable into

- genetic,
- gestational,
- social or nurturing, and even
- a technological parent during the phase in which the embryo is first originated by, and then cared for by the laboratory personnel, and may never in fact ever be transferred to a woman.

For the child, that involves a fragmentation of parenthood, raising questions about who really are the child's natural parents, whatever the law may say in terms of recognizing the birth mother or the genetic mother, depending on the jurisdiction and whatever has been contracted between the parties. The Church considers that using donor sperm or donor eggs violates the unity of marriage. The unity of marriage means reciprocal respect for the right within marriage to become a father or mother only together with the other spouse. That excludes involving another person as a genetic parent of the child.¹²⁹

In practice this fragmentation of the parental roles into genetic, gestational and social or nurturing parents has implications for the child. Psychologists often refer to the phenomenon of *genealogical bewilderment* as children, perhaps later in life, seek to discover their origins and to identify their own identity in circumstances in which the genetic parents may be completely unknown to them or become known to them at a later stage. The relationship between a child and his or her parents is complex.

---

128 Pope Paul VI, *Humanae Vitae* (1968), n. 9.
129 Congregation for the Doctrine of the Faith, *Donum Vitae* Vatican 1987, See especially "Section II Interventions Upon Human Procreation." http://www.vatican.va/roman_curia/congregations/cfaith/documents/rc_con_cfaith_doc_19870222_respect-for-human-life_en.html

So much of our sense of identity is based upon that relationship. When it is fragmented, that can be hurtful and confusing.[130]

5.7 Surrogacy

A surrogate mother is someone who decides to become pregnant in order that the child be given to others after birth.

The surrogate may be genetically a stranger to the embryo because the latter has been obtained through the union of the gametes of "donors;" or she may use her own egg fertilized through insemination with the sperm of a man other than her husband or of her husband. Either way, she carries the pregnancy with a pledge to surrender the baby once it is born to the party or parties who commissioned or made the agreement for the pregnancy, who may or may not be the donors.

The Church teaches that surrogate motherhood represents a failure to meet the obligations of maternal love, marital fidelity and responsible motherhood.[131] That is to say, carrying a pregnancy involves a unique relationship to the child in which the woman becomes the child's mother. As the mother of the child she has obligations to nurture the child.

Second, if the woman is married she has entered into a convenantal agreement in which her capacity to become a mother is given exclusively to her husband, as he gives himself exclusively to her, including his capacity to be a father.

The Church also teaches that surrogacy contracts offend the dignity and the right of the child to be conceived, carried in the womb, brought into the world and brought up by his own parents.[132] This right is also recognized by the United Nations in the Convention on the Rights of the Child, which upholds the child's right:

---

[130] Joanna Rose, *A critical analysis of sperm donation practices: the personal and social effects of disrupting the unity of biological and social relatedness for the offspring.* PhD thesis (2009) Queensland University of Technology. Accessed 9/1/2013 from http://eprints.qut.edu.au/32012/

[131] Congregation for the Doctrine of the Faith, *Donum Vitae*, 1987 A.3.

[132] Ibid.

- to preserve his or her identity, including nationality, name and family relations as recognized by law without unlawful interference (art. 8);
- not to be separated from his or her parents against their will, except when competent authorities subject to judicial review determine, in accordance with applicable law and procedures, that such separation is necessary for the best interests of the child (art. 9);
- not to be separated from one or both parents to maintain personal relations and direct contact with both parents on a regular basis, except if it is contrary to the child's best interests (art. 9);
- to rely on the common responsibilities of both parent for the upbringing and development of the child, and their primary responsibility for the upbringing and development of the child on the basis of the best interests of the child (art. 18);
- that in adoption decisions the authorities shall ensure that the best interests of the child shall be the paramount consideration (art. 21).

The Church also teaches that surrogacy sets up, to the detriment of families, a division between the physical, psychological and moral elements that constitute those families.[133] The woman's capacity to bear a child is implicitly separated from her role as mother to that child and any other children she may have. She must deny any affection she has for the child she carries. One wonders how her other children may regard the fact that she gives a child away and what that means for the security of their relationship to her.

In that respect, the treatment of the surrogate is problematic because it does not recognize the motherhood that exists in becoming pregnant and nurturing the child until birth. The surrogate is implicitly treated as an object, and her body is used as a mere incubator rather than as the child's mother. As the child's mother, she is linked to the child physically, emotionally, cognitively and spiritually and that reality ought

---

133 Congregation for the Doctrine of the Faith, op. cit., A.3.

not be denied. To enter into a contract to the contrary, by which her connectedness is to be rejected, is immoral because it is essentially false.

5.8 A Child is not a Cure for Infertility

One of the things to bear in mind in all this is that, as discussed earlier, most couples (77 per cent) who go on IVF programs do not succeed in giving birth to a child.[134] For most, the procedure fails them. Second, the pain of infertility is not just a matter of being childless. Even if IVF manages to produce a child for them, the couple still remains infertile and that pain will stay with them. Counselling is an important step to assist a couple to come to terms with the tragedy of infertility, whether or not they subsequently seek to have a child via the technology. Whether or not IVF produces a child for them, they will still need to cope with their infertility.

The evidence also suggests that, *if donor gametes are used*, the child may become a symbol of that infertility, particularly if the relationship between the child and the social parent is strained as often happens when a child becomes a teenager. It is important not to infantilize children when discussing the consequences of obtaining a child via assisted reproduction. A baby or even a primary school age child may do just as well on average as other children. The real issues raised by the manner of conception are much more likely to occur later when the child better understands what happened, and in the case of a donor or donors, that there has been a fragmentation of parenthood and there are others who have a parenting relationship to the child. If the matter has been hidden that may cause resentment. If the young person has identity concerns they may be exacerbated and there may be a need to find the hidden donor and other family members.

Further, one of the problems with surrogacy contracts is that they are in effect a decision to adopt a child, and adoption by the commissioning

---

[134] Victorian Infertility Treatment Authority, *Annual Reports*. Accessed October 2012 from http://www.varta.org.au

parents might not be in the best interests of the child and the arrangement may deny the child contact with the mother by birth, and with the man who is the child's father through his relationship to her. Essentially, surrogacy contracts may involve treating both the birth mother and the child as objects, to be used for the benefit of the commissioning couple.

5.9 Viable Alternatives

It is important that couples seek to explore whether they can conceive naturally. One of the failures of contemporary medical approaches to infertility is that doctors can be too ready to go to the IVF technology without addressing how best to engage a couple's natural fertility. The evidence indicates that being instructed in how to recognize when peak fertility occurs in the woman's cycle may increase the probability of natural pregnancy, though no random controlled trials appear to have been done to assess how much greater the probability is. Further, treatment of illness or disease and other factors that may reduce fertility, may also assist her to achieve conception naturally.

In a retrospective study by the Ovulation Method Research and Reference Centre of Australia, of 182 women trying unsuccessfully to achieve pregnancy for more than 12 months, at least 54 per cent achieved pregnancy after Billings instruction within an average of 4.7 months. Twenty of the couples had previously been unsuccessful with IVF, and eight of those couples achieved pregnancy after Billings instruction. That is a success rate of around 40 per cent compared to the IVF success rate of around 26 per cent.[135] The comparison may not be valid, however, because the sampling may be different, in that it is unlikely that couples who were shown to be absolutely infertile would seek Billings instruction.

I should mention a conflict of interests in that Mary conducts a *Fertility Assessment Clinic* supported by the Manningham General Practice in which she practises. As well as seeking to make the most of natural fertility and

---

135 Data supplied by Billings Family Life Centre Melbourne in private correspondence May 2010.

treating conditions that may affect fertility and the health of any child who does result, her clinic also addresses the wider implications that a couple may experience if they have difficulty conceiving. Infertility can be a source not just of disappointment, but also anxiety and depression and can create relationship tensions. The clinic brings together a variety of experts to assist couples, including referral to a psychologist if they would like the opportunity to explore how best to cope. This is a different approach from what is offered to couples on IVF programs where couples who do not conceive may feel that they are failures and where it is often the case that women will appear with a different partner during the course of their treatment for infertility. Infertility is a source of grief and it is often helpful to have the opportunity to have the pain of the situation recognized and understood.

One of my graduate students, Dr Lucia Migliore, has developed a retreat program for couples experiencing infertility difficulties. It is a promising development.

One of the issues in medically diagnosing infertility is the exploration of male infertility. It is common practice in the IVF clinics to obtain semen from the man, either for diagnostic purposes or for fertilizing eggs, by sending him with a specimen jar to a cubicle where he is expected to produce a masturbatory specimen. IVF patients have reported being supplied with mild pornography for the purpose and expressed their discomfort and embarrassment.

There are, however, alternatives. One possibility is to obtain the semen sample from the cervix the morning after the couple have been intimate. The procedure is known as a Hunnar's Test. It is also informative not only in relation to sperm count and motility, but also in relation to the health of the sperm within the woman's cervical mucus which is vital for sustaining the sperm on its journey to the fallopian tube to find and fertilize the egg. The disadvantage is that procedure involved is similar to what is required for a Pap-smear and is invasive and involves some pain and discomfort.

A second possibility involves using what is called a "Male-Factor Pak". The latter involves using a collecting device like a condom to trap some of the ejaculate during marital intimacy. The ejaculate is then removed from this device and placed in a specimen jar for analysis by a pathologist.

Both ways are effective and can be offered to couples as consistent with respect for the sacredness of the marriage act and open to life.

The Australian Catholic Bishops approved the Catholic Health Australia *Code of Ethical Standards for Catholic Health and Aged Care Services in Australia* which on this issue states:

> 2.10 Investigations and remedies for infertility must respect the integrity of marriage and the sacredness of sexual expression in marriage. Semen should only be collected in ways respectful of human dignity and marriage (i.e., surgically or in the context of the marital act).

The latter would indicate that either of the two methods outlined would be appropriate.

Decisions of that nature are obviously a matter for the couple. It is, of course, open to a couple not to have the cause of their infertility diagnosed and to simply leave the matter in God's hands. The reality is that, apart from treating conditions that may have an effect on sperm production, and taking steps to change lifestyle factors that affect health and fertility, there is often not much else that can be done for male infertility. However, that may in part be due to the fact that medicine has tended to concentrate on female causes of infertility. More might be achieved if there were more of a concentration on pursuing natural fertility, rather than bypassing it through reproductive technology.

6

Embryo Rescue[136]

Few places require data to be kept on embryos produced by in vitro fertilization, but in the Australian State of Victoria, IVF centres are required to be licensed and to submit their data to a government authority. From 6220 women treated in 2007/8, 1651(26 per cent) have since given birth. From the 49,389 IVF embryos formed in this process, 3.6 per cent survived to be born.[137] The production and wastage rate of embryos is thus enormous.

The reason for such a large number of embryos is that harvesting the eggs involves the women undergoing a surgical procedure. To minimize the number of surgical procedures, the woman's ovaries are over-stimulated. They normally produce only one or two eggs in a cycle, but in IVF, the average is around 8-12 eggs in a cycle and as many as 50 may be harvested. Eggs are very fragile and attempts to store them have not been very successful. Embryos are much more robust, so the practice is to fertilize all the available eggs. That then creates a reserve of embryos so that several attempts to achieve pregnancy can be made from the one surgical procedure to harvest eggs. The embryo transfer procedure has a low success rate, which is also a reason for creating a reserve supply.

Often, couples on IVF programs still have embryos in storage when they complete their families or decide for other reasons not to continue. As a result there are literally millions of human embryos world-wide which are left in storage, used for research or otherwise discarded.

---

136 I have discussed this matter at length in Tonti-Filippini, Nicholas, "The embryo rescue debate: impregnating women, ectogenesis, and restoration from suspended animation". *The National Catholic Bioethics Quarterly*, Volume 3, Number / Spring 2003, pp. 11-137.

137 Victorian Infertility Treatment Authority *2009 Annual Report* accessed from http://www.varta.org.au/www/257/1003057/displayarticle/1003573.html

The Congregation for the Doctrine of the Faith[138] has rejected using these embryos for research or for the treatment of disease because that would involve treating the embryos as mere "biological material" and result in their destruction. The Congregation also asserts that proposals to thaw such embryos without reactivating them and then using them for research, as if they were normal cadavers, would also be unacceptable.

One suggestion offered has been that a female family member could "adopt" an embryo and have him or her transferred to her uterus. Another often-suggested proposal is that couples with embryos left in storage might donate them to infertile couples who are unable to produce their own embryos.

The Congregation also considered this proposal and held that it too is ethically unacceptable, because it breaches the unity of marriage, which means reciprocal respect for the right within marriage to become a father or mother only together with the other spouse.[139] The Congregation also refers to the practice leading to other problems of a medical, psychological and legal nature.[140]

In relation to so-called "prenatal adoption", the Congregation found that this proposal, praiseworthy with regard to the intention of respecting and defending human life, presents problems not dissimilar to those mentioned above; that is, "pre-natal adoption" breaches the unity of marriage, which means reciprocal respect for the right within marriage to become a father or mother only together with the other spouse.[141]

The Congregation went on to say it needs to be recognized that the thousands of abandoned embryos represent a situation of injustice that cannot be resolved. Pope John Paul II made an "appeal to the conscience of the world's scientific authorities and in particular to doctors, that the production of human embryos be halted, taking into account that there seems to be no morally licit solution regarding the human destiny of the thousands and thousands of 'frozen' embryos which are and remain the

---

138 Congregation for the Doctrine of the Faith, *Dignitas Personae Instruction on Certain Bioethical Questions,* 2008, n.19.
139 Ibid n. 19, 12.
140 Ibid, n. 19.
141 Ibid n. 19, 12.

subjects of essential rights and should therefore be protected by law as human persons."[142]

Prior to the Congregation's publication, there was a vigorous debate on the issue of prenatal adoption. Some, such as Germain Grisez[143], argued that though it was wrong to have produced embryos by IVF, especially in such numbers, and wrong to have subjected them to the freeze-drying process that keeps them in a state of suspended animation in the laboratory, the end or intended outcome of "prenatal adoption" is good, because it rescues the embryos from that state. Grisez also said that the chosen means, thawing, rehydrating and transferring an embryo from freezer to womb, is good. Therefore, he argued, prenatal adoption is morally acceptable.

Grisez argued that procreation is not involved because the child already exists and transfer to womb is akin to a woman volunteering to nurse a foundling at her breast, and that the embryo is in a similar situation to a foundling awaiting adoption. He asserts that prenatal adoption is a service to a baby and not contrary to teaching on surrogacy, which required that a child must be conceived, born and nurtured by his or her natural parents.

Others, such as Mary Geach,[144] have argued that embryo transfer is an unchaste act and violates that couple's reproductive integrity. She argues that what is meant to be a result of a marital act – pregnancy – is now the result of a merely technical procedure, while the sanctity of marriage means that the woman laying herself open to an impregnating intromission is a vital part of the self-giving involved in her part of the marriage act. Geach thus offers an explanation for the teaching of the Congregation, that prenatal adoption violates the unity of marriage.

---

142 John Paul II, Address to the participants in the Symposium on *"Evangelium vitae* and Law" and the Eleventh International Colloquium on Roman and Canon Law (24 May 1996), 6: *AAS* 88 (1996), 943-944.
143 Germain Grisez, *The Way of the Lord Jesus Volume 3, Difficult Moral Questions*, Franciscan Press: Illinois, 1997, pp 239-244.
144 Mary Geach, "Are there any circumstances in which it would be morally admirable for a woman to seek to have an orphan embryo implanted in her womb?" in *Issues for a Catholic Bioethic: Proceedings of the International Conference to celebrate the Twentieth Anniversary of the foundation of the Linacre Centre*, L. Gormally (ed.), The Linacre Centre, London, 1999, pp. 341-346.

The central issue involved is the sacredness of the woman's body and the nature of marriage in which she unites herself bodily to her husband. In that complete gift of love they commit themselves exclusively to one another in that bodily union. Children come about as the fruit of that union, as an embodiment and a symbol of their loving union. In coming to be within the woman's body as a result of their love, the child forms a unique union with his or her mother. For the woman, becoming pregnant is becoming a mother. Pregnancy is, in itself, a union between mother and child. The child is essentially *of her*, not only located within her, but bound essentially, vitally to her. She is literally home to the child, but not home in the sense of merely housing, but home in the sense of a dynamic dependency and interrelationship in which they share an intimate biological and spiritual connectedness. The child's father becomes a father through the child coming to be through the celebration of their loving commitment. The child's mother and father have unique relationships to the child founded upon their own loving union as the origin of the child.

In so-called "pre-natal adoption," the woman's husband has no involvement in her becoming pregnant. She becomes with child, but not within the marriage. The moral issue therefore is that she becomes a mother outside of her marriage and thus in that way breaches the commitment of the exclusive gift of herself to her husband. Her capacity to become with child is part of the gift that she gave exclusively to him.

The central issue is that her capacity to become with child is not something that she is free to give outside of the marriage.

One of the conceptual difficulties we have with all this is the way in which the technology separates the different aspects of parenthood: genetic, gestational and nurturing, social or adoptive parenthood.

Normally a couple become a mother and a father in a way that links all these roles as part of the sacred unity. We used to refer to a woman conceiving a child. Now a child can come to be as an embryo in the laboratory with no-one actually conceiving and we have to distinguish between fertilization and the later step in which a woman may become pregnant. The single event of conception has been in a sense split into two events: fertilization and becoming pregnant. This separates and attenuates the parental roles and leaves the child without the direct connectedness that he or she would normally have to both parents through coming to be within their union and as a result of their love.

"Pre-natal adoption" is a misnomer. For a woman, to become pregnant is not merely adoption, rather it involves a fundamental change to who she is. Adoption is a social solution to a problem in which others substitute for a child's parents, and, for the sake of the child's security, the law gives them the same social status as the natural parents. Of course the legal reality of adoption cannot change the natural reality that an adopted child still has a mother who conceived and gave birth and a father who was at some stage united with her in the marital act.

In becoming pregnant outside of marriage, a woman forms a relationship to her child that is very different from that which an adoptive mother can have to her child. In becoming pregnant she becomes the mother of the child and forms a unique unity with the child. She will remain forever the child's mother even though her own eggs are not involved.

From the perspective of the marriage, "prenatal adoption" and adoption are very different because the latter does not involve either the adoptive mother or the adoptive father having that bond with the child. There is no exclusive and unique bond formed as there is in natural motherhood. There is no sense in which adoption violates the bond of marriage. The relationship that they have with the child comes after gestation and after the period when the child needs such a close and intimate bond with his or her mother.

Some other related issues concern using either an animal or an artificial uterus to gestate embryos left in this predicament of being unwanted, or not needed, by the woman for whom the embryo was produced.

Early in the work on IVF in the Australian state of Victoria, one of the teams led by Professor Carl Wood reported in a publication *Test Tube Conception*[145] that they had been able to generate human embryos for some time; but they could not replicate the success they had had in animals in relation to embryo transfer. Wood reported transferring human embryos to the uterus of a ewe. He said that thankfully they did not survive as it would have been difficult to explain to the community.

---

145 Carl Wood and Ann Westmore, *Test Tube Conception* Hill of Content, Melbourne, 1983.

The possibility of using the uterus of an animal to gestate human embryos was thus not beyond contemplation, though it appears never to have been successful. Choosing to have an animal conceive a human being would raise significant ethical questions, even apart from the obvious health risks.

A related possibility would be to create an artificial uterus. After all, embryos survive for a few days in culture in the laboratory at the start of life prior to embryo transfer, and then they can survive from around the 20th week, routinely surviving outside the uterus beyond 24 weeks in an humidicrib. That does mean for a large part of pregnancy, the gestating role of the mother can be managed artificially, even though in the current state of the technology every child will in fact have a woman who is the child's gestational mother. However, the question does arise whether that role could be replaced by an artificial uterus.

If an artificial womb became possible, would that be morally acceptable? The issue obviously avoids moral issues in relation to women being impregnated inappropriately. However, apart from the woman who supplied the ovum, the child would have no mother at the time of birth. There would be no birth mother. The absence of a relationship to a mother would seem to be the most troubling aspect of this possibility. In the first instance, the status of a child as a citizen, and even as a human being, stems from being born of woman. We simply accept that a child born of woman is a member of the human family. A child born of an artificial uterus would not have that status automatically. His or her membership of the human species would have to be proven. Second, questions about subsequent parenthood would not be determined by the birth mother, as is now the case. It is not clear to whom the responsibility for parenthood would fall. Decisions would need to be made about so-called "social parenthood", but by whom? Without a birth mother, there is no-one with natural parental authority. In the law in most jurisdictions, we do not recognize the parental status of genetic contributors to parenthood as being of automatic significance. Their responsibilities are considered contingent on other factors such as their relationship to the birth mother, or consent to being held to be a parent. Artificial gestation would be very troubling and challenge our existing laws for the status of children. More importantly, for the child there would be absence of that natural relationship. It should also be noted that artificial gestation could only occur as a result of in vitro fertilization.

7
A Woman-Centred Approach to Abortion

Whether abortion takes place is a decision that a woman makes, whatever opinion the law or the culture may follow on the sanctity of the life within her body. Pope John Paul II recognized this in 1995 when he addressed an urgent appeal to women, saying:

> You are called to bear witness to the meaning of genuine love, of that gift of self and of that acceptance of others which are present in a special way in the relationship of husband and wife, but which ought also to be at the heart of every other interpersonal relationship. The experience of motherhood makes you acutely aware of the other person and, at the same time, confers on you a particular task: Motherhood involves a special communion with the mystery of life, as it develops in the woman's womb ... This unique contact with the new human being developing within her gives rise to an attitude towards human beings not only towards her own child, but every human being, which profoundly marks the woman's personality.[146]

He described the way in which a mother welcomes and carries in herself another human being, enabling the child to grow inside her, respecting his or her otherness. Women first learn and then teach others that human relations are authentic if they are open to accepting the other person: a person who is recognized and loved because of the dignity that comes from being a person and not from other considerations, such as usefulness, strength, intelligence, beauty or health.

---

146 John Paul II, Apostolic Letter *Mulieris Dignitatem* (15 August 1988), 18: *AAS* 80 (1988), 1696.

Doctors who deal with women considering abortion note that, even in the circumstances in which she has opted for abortion, a woman will often speak protectively of the child, not wanting to take medicines that would harm the child, conscious of the responsibility of carrying another within her.

The choice of abortion is thus an enormous contradiction that no woman is likely to take lightly. It is a tragedy that many women feel forced to accept, in circumstances that may seem to render them powerless. In a culture that promotes abortion, deciding not to abort can require great courage, especially if her male partner does not support the pregnancy or if he threatens the relationship should she not abort.

A man who only offers the mantra of choice, saying, "It's your choice", in fact offers her no support in his indifference. A young woman may find herself not only abandoned by her partner, she may also be under pressure from her own mother who has other ambitions for her daughter's life and career at that early stage. However, it is men who are often responsible for contributing to the choice to abort.

Too little has been said about the role that we, as men, play in this context and about our responsibility for the consequences of our actions. At the same time, it can be very confusing for a young man to know how he should behave. The culture has adopted the idea of sex without consequence, of sex as harmless, as long as adequate precautions are taken. The facts, however, indicate that despite taking precautions, some women will become pregnant and sex with more than one person risks infection. A sexual relationship is also of enormous significance emotionally, and the break-up of such a powerful bond at a stage of emotional immaturity, can have significant consequences, including suicide. The evidence is discussed in Chapters 15 and 23.

The reality is that young people have been misled. The promotion of prophylaxis often assumes that young people will be sexually active and offers them little choice not to be, and little is made of the consequences of promiscuity. In our culture, young men could be forgiven for thinking that the partner's consent and using a condom is all that responsibility requires for sexual recreation. Over the norm of twenty-five years or more of being potentially fertile and intermittently sexually active, the chances of a woman having an unplanned pregnancy is quite high. As discussed later, the data indicates that even when condoms or oral contraceptives are used, the actual pregnancy rate is somewhere between 3-6 per hundred women years, and, despite widespread sex education in our culture, around 50% of pregnancies are unplanned.

Young people, young men especially, are poor risk takers, and even if they are aware of the data about the likelihood of pregnancy, or the even greater risk of STI transmission, if they or their partner have taken precautions, the outcome of a pregnancy or disease is likely to be a surprise. Mary related a story of a 20-year-old male patient being surprised and angry when she informed him that he had contracted genital herpes, despite always using condoms, as he had been taught to do. He had received and acted upon the "safe sex" message of his sex education classes.

So every day there are young men who are surprised to find that their partner is pregnant and they are likely not to have been told how to conduct themselves responsibly in that eventuality. The emphasis has been placed on abortion being a woman's choice, but how should he behave? He is already a father, but whether he will ever experience fatherhood rests with his partner. In the first instance, it is a question of whether she even informs him. Second, much depends on the character of their relationship and the opportunity that he has within the relationship to provide emotional support for her. An obvious factor is her expectation for him and for his reactions to the information. Continuing pregnancy and the possibility of the birth of their child are likely to be a literally stunning life complication.

The young man may simply try to take his cues from what he perceives are her attitudes and react accordingly, positively, negatively or reflecting her uncertainty. There may be something of a guessing game going on between them with each seeking to anticipate the reactions of the other. He may be overwhelmed by a previously unconsidered possibility of being a father to their child. In the current culture, it is quite likely that there has been no thought given to ongoing commitment to each other, let alone to a child. Given the frequency with which sexually active young people are likely to be moving from one relationship to another and the fact that many have several partners in a year, the young man may well have questions about whether he is the father. He may feel trapped or resentful. If he loves her, that may still leave him uncertain about how to behave, as he tries to read her wishes and intentions, assuming that he can put to one side the enormous consequences for himself. One would hope that, if he loves her, he has the wisdom to express that love for her and his support for her in this new circumstance. The evidence indicates that very few relationships survive beyond the trauma of an abortion. Unplanned pregnancy for a young couple is clearly a very testing time for their relationship.

This is a circumstance that is not at all rare, but there seems to be little offered by way of sex education to young men to prepare them for how they might respond. I have not seen a sex education program that, for instance, role-played this common scenario. It might help young men to consider the decision to have a sexual relationship more carefully, in the first instance, if they were better prepared for this possibility. Given their unpreparedness, we ought not be too harsh on them if they do not behave well, because it is not at all clear how they should behave, especially as the relationship and the couple's feelings for each other are likely to be in a state of uncertainty, especially if they are immature.

The pressures on both the young man and his partner are likely to be enormous. Different problems would arise if either discovered an STI.

In trying to work toward a culture of life, we need to be aware of these pressures on women and their partners, and our first response should be to try to reduce the pressures. We need to create places where a woman, especially, can go to discuss her circumstances with someone who genuinely supports her and offers her the time and the support to consider her options and explore her own idea of herself and her own values. In that way, freed from external pressures, she will be most likely to make a decision that is life-affirming for herself and her child.

It is a mistake to subject a woman who is in distress to further pressure. What she needs is the offer of pregnancy support which has two components:

a) counselling to assist with decision-making; and

b) on-going advice, material, emotional and spiritual support during pregnancy or otherwise.

The aims of decision-making counselling are distinct from pre-procedure counselling. Pre-procedure counselling is for a person who has decided on a course of action and is being guided in what to expect during and after the procedure to ensure that their consent is adequately informed.

Decision-making counselling, in these circumstances, is client-centred and non-directive and aims to assist a person to make a decision by:

a) providing emotional support, time and space so that the woman can make a decision that is reflective rather than panicked;

b) assisting a woman to talk through the problem(s) facing her by examining options and their implications for her own values;

c) assisting her to clarify her own sense of self in relation to a new problem and to make reasonable decisions for herself about what she wants now and in the long term;

d) assisting her to make reasonable decisions in relation to others;

e) informing and exploring with the woman the availability of emotional and other support;

f) indicating to her the need to seek medical or other professional services in relation to her pregnancy and encouraging her to seek that assistance from her own doctor or from another doctor or professional.

Decision-making counselling ought not to attempt to direct the woman in relation to her pregnancy or toward any particular decision. She is most likely to make a good choice if the counsellor serves to reduce the sense of panic and urgency and instead assists her to regain control of her own circumstances. The aim is to give her greater confidence in being able to cope and to assist her to make a reasonable decision for herself. This provides the best chance of a life-affirming choice.[147]

Counselling is an engagement of client and counsellor, of two people. Professional counselling is client-centered, but it is an engagement, of the counsellor as a person who cannot be required to act contrary to his or her own

---

[147] Australian Catholic Bishops Conference, Bishops' Commission for Doctrine and Morals, *Preliminary Advice on Pregnancy Support and Counselling Services* September 2008 http://s2.cam.org.au/~acbcport/index.php?option=com_docman&task=doc_download&gid=246&Itemid=315

conscience. It may be that in that engagement the client asks the counsellor's view, and it may be reasonable in those circumstances for the counsellor to reveal her own view, while stressing that professionally her role is to assist the woman to make her own reasonable decision after informed discussion.

Pregnancy counselling does not direct the woman to obtain a particular service, but does discuss the available options. It is appropriate in circumstances in which abortion is available that the counsellor discusses this option and provides information about what may be involved in abortion, including demonstrated risks and ill-effects. However, referral for a medical procedure is done after medical assessment and is not the task of a pregnancy support agency. It would also compromise the role of a decision-making counsellor if part of the role were to be a referral agency for medical procedures. That would create an interest for the client in a particular outcome – obtaining the referral.

In Germany, counselling was made a prerequisite for termination of pregnancy and the need for obtaining what was in effect a referral by the counsellor badly compromised pregnancy counselling agencies. In Germany in the first trimester:

> If the woman decides to have an abortion (*abtreiben lassen* or *eine abtreibung vornehmen lassen*) she will receive a counselling certificate (*ein Beratungsschein*), which includes her name and the date. The certificate will not contain any details of the discussion between the counsellor and the woman. This certificate is necessary in order to have a legal abortion.[148]

The German experience should inform any attempt to legislate to make pregnancy counselling compulsory. It would be better to make it compulsory for there to a requirement for health professionals, advising or assisting a women who is pregnant, to make independent counselling available, than to require a woman to undergo counselling. The woman may then make her own decision. Compulsory counselling is not really counselling.

---

148 http://berlin.angloinfo.com/information/healthcare/pregnancy-birth/termination abortion/

The problem in Australia is that the abortion providers do not usually offer independent counselling, and the process by which a woman finds herself in the operating room (or being administered chemical abortion) is incredibly streamlined with no medical referral required, as would be the case, for surgical procedures that similarly involved a general anaesthetic and risk of harm to the patient. Yet this procedure is also so complicated by the existence of two patients.

Providing information about pregnancy, about available support and about the stage of development of the foetus would be important elements of providing an informed basis for making a decision.

Like the young men discussed earlier, many women have accepted the advice of the family planning experts and use contraception in the expectation that they will not become pregnant. Many seem to focus on the perfect use figures, so often quoted, and appear not to acknowledge or are not aware that even the contraceptive pill, which has a perfect use pregnancy rate much less than one per hundred women years, in actual use has a pregnancy rate of between 3 and 6 per hundred women years. In talking to senior high school students I have found that few are aware of the actual use pregnancy rates and the significance for them and the high likelihood of an unplanned pregnancy over the duration of the twenty-five years or more of possible fertility, and the risk, therefore, that they will have an abortion. I leave the maths students to provide us with the linear correlation figures over 25 years.

Pope John Paul II decided to speak directly to women who had had abortions, acknowledging the many factors that may have influenced their decisions, and the fact that in many cases it was a painful and even shattering decision. He went on to say:

> The wound in your heart may not yet have healed. Certainly what happened was and remains terribly wrong. But do not give in to discouragement and do not lose hope. Try rather to understand what happened and face it honestly. If you have not already done so, give yourselves over with humility and trust to repentance. The Father of mercies is ready to give you his forgiveness and his peace in the Sacrament of Reconciliation. You will come to understand that nothing is definitively lost and you will also be able to ask forgiveness from your child, who is now living in the Lord. With

the friendly and expert help and advice of other people, and as a result of your own painful experience, you can be among the most eloquent defenders of everyone's right to life. Through your commitment to life, whether by accepting the birth of other children or by welcoming and caring for those most in need of someone to be close to them, you will become promoters of a new way of looking at human life.[149]

That so many (one in three adults)[150] have been involved, through abortion, in taking a nascent human life, must have a significant effect on our culture, upon the psyche of each one of us. That in some maternity hospitals the number of abortions rivals the number of births, must have deeply affected those involved in obstetrics and gynaecology.

That so many women have been victims of abortion, albeit by their own choice, must also have a profound effect on them and on those around them. We need not only to address the factors that lead to abortion, we need also to address its impact on our community.

Recently I heard a Ukrainian priest give an account of the terrible harm done to the Ukrainian population by Soviet rule and by having two war fronts pass through. The atrocities against women including rape for eugenic reasons, the extraordinary loss of life by deliberate ethnic cleansing, and the effects of hostile governments and corruption and mismanagement are difficult to comprehend. Now that they are free of that yoke, however, not all is well. They still have to deal with the aftermath of such shocking brutality and the suppression of freedom for almost a century.

We are nowhere near comparable, but there is something of a similarity with our own hidden holocaust impacting beneath the surface and in secret on so many lives.

Abortion involves the loss of a nascent human life, but it is not as straightforward morally as other forms of killing. This is most obvious in the circumstances of chemical abortion in which there is no direct assault on the child. RU-486, for instance, involves taking a pill to alter the progesterone

---

149 Pope John Paul II *Evangelium Vitae* 1995, n. 99.
150 John I. Fleming and Nicholas Tonti-Filippini, *Common Ground? Seeking an Australian Consensus on Abortion and Sex Education* (St Paul Publications 2007).

receptors and thus causing the endometrium to no longer be able to sustain the pregnancy. In effect, a woman chooses that her body no longer support the child. RU-486 is often used in conjunction with prostaglandin that causes the uterus to contract and expel the child. The child dies when that support is removed and when he or she is forced out of the woman's body. The morality of abortion in such circumstances seems less about direct killing and more about violence to the relationship formed between mother and child and the meaning of her withdrawal of that vital support, as well as the fact that her decision results in the loss of life. The violence is not directly to the child, but to the relationship between the mother and the child. This is much more than just withdrawing life support. It is a rejection of her role of mother to this child who already exists within her body. It is unlikely to be solely because she wants the independence of her own body unencumbered by the body of the child. The issue is not just about enduring the few weeks needed for the child to be mature enough to survive being born and the burdens of being pregnant for that time and the challenges of giving birth – all of which are very significant. Important as those matters are, the much more significant matter is her rejection of being a mother either to this child or to this child at this time. She does *not want motherhood of this child at this time*, perhaps because:

- the relationship to the partner is not yet ready for it;
- in her thinking he is not the right person to be a father to her child;
- this relationship is not the right relationship for the permanent character of shared parenthood;
- the timing is not right for motherhood given her stage in life and career or other lifestyle developments, in her view or the view of those whose opinion she values, such as her partner, friends or family; or
- she fears loss of support from partner, friends or family if she continues as a mother at this time and disrupts her planning and theirs.

Not wanting to be a mother at that time, means not wanting the child to continue to exist. It is not that she just wants the pregnancy to end and to be free of it and its physical effects; she wants the life to end, and with it, the mother-child relationship to end. Abortion is not just termination of pregnancy, it is also the desire that this child no longer continue to be and her motherhood of that child cease. This is much more than withdrawing life support. For the intervention to be successful the child must be dead.

The Church has always condemned abortion and imposes a grave penalty of automatic excommunication on those who procure abortion, though the penalty can be removed by a priest in confession. In the mind of the Church, there is no doubt about the gravity of causing the death of an unborn child and the need to defend every human life, especially those who are so vulnerable.

The concern is for two people and for the predicament in which a woman may find herself after discovering herself to be a mother and in that unique relationship in which another life is totally dependent upon her.

As men we are never in that position. Our role is always secondary to hers in sustaining the child within her. Within the meaning of a Christian vocation to give witness to the image and likeliness of God, love for her means we are called to revere her for the role she plays, for the sacredness of her body, and the sacredness of both her life and the life within her.

Abortion would be much less frequent, if men were more respectful of a woman's capacity for motherhood and included that possibility in their thinking about her, and subsequently being willing to support her in the event that pregnancy occurs. The separation of sexual intimacy from reproduction has done great harm to women, because the significance of motherhood has all but been excluded from our cultural understanding of sexuality. Young men, especially, are unprepared for the consequences of their actions. Motherhood is to be avoided rather than valued, and because the capacity to be a mother is what defines a woman's gender, the rejection of the capacity for motherhood is also a rejection of a defining aspect of her womanhood and thus a devaluing of who a woman is. With the capacity for motherhood not in the picture, a woman is much more likely to be treated as a sex object. Both women and men are profoundly altered by contemporary attitudes to sexuality that separate sexual intimacy from the capacity to be a parent.

The theological significance of this separation and its impact on identity and vocation is discussed in Chapter 2.

8

Early Induction and Late Term Termination of Pregnancy

Sometimes women who are pregnant are confronted late in pregnancy with the information that the child has a serious abnormality. This may even be described as a condition that is "incompatible with life." They are then likely to be encouraged to have an early induction in order that they can get over the grief earlier and try again to have a healthy child. The phrase "incompatible with life" is a misnomer for as long as the child is still alive, even if that life may not survive long after birth.

The reality of such procedures, however, is that they are a termination of pregnancy and often enough the child could be born alive. Early induction late term would be acceptable when the woman or the child is at risk because of the pregnancy and the early induction would reduce grave risks to life for either the mother or the child. Early induction is then not the same as abortion because the aim is to preserve life. The aim would be to continue the pregnancy for as long as is safe for both. Even if the baby will die at or soon after birth, the mother can know that in getting the child to the normal stage of viability she has done her best for the child. Her grieving can also be helped by that knowledge and also the opportunity to hold her dying child after birth.

The major problem in relation to abortion is a conflict between respect for the rights of the child before birth and the rights of women. That is to say, there is a debate to be had over whether the rights of the woman allow her to override the rights of the child in much the way that Judith Jarvis Thompson argues in her much discussed essay[151] on this topic in which she

---

151 Judith Jarvis Thompson, "A Defense of Abortion", *Philosophy and Public Affairs*, Volume 1, Fall 1997, and reprinted in Peter Singer (Ed) *Applied Ethics*, Oxford University Press: Oxford 1987, pp. 37-56.

uses the analogy of the famous violinist being kept alive by a non-consensual sharing of another person's vital organ. The issue of that conflict between the rights of the child before birth and the rights of his or her mother not to be so encumbered are beyond the scope of this discussion, because in this case the child can be born alive if there is a problem in continuing the pregnancy.

The matter of late term induction of birth, therefore, is significantly different from early abortion. Much more agreement may be achievable than in regard to first trimester abortion.

Once the child is capable of being born alive, then his or her removal from the womb, which would otherwise constitute foeticide (the legal term used in the UK late term), becomes separable from foeticide or child destruction (the term used in Australia). The child is capable of an independent existence. Delivery and foeticide become distinct events, distinct medical choices, even though they may be so contrived as to occur simultaneously. The medical, personal, social and jurisprudential implications of this difference are both numerous and manifest. It is these differences that I have chosen to explore because the issue of late term abortion raises significant issues in relation to recognition of the dignity and rights of those who are not yet rational, but are of the kind of being that has the capacity for rationality.

Where a law deprives a category of human beings of the protection which civil legislation ought to accord them, the State is denying the equality of all before the law. When the State does not place its power at the service of the rights of each citizen, and in particular the more vulnerable, the very foundations of a state based on law are undermined.

"Late term termination pregnancy" refers to termination of pregnancy at a stage when the child would normally be capable of being born alive. The gestational age and maturity at which this is so is relative to advances in medical capability and the availability of the technology. Variously, "late term" refers to that period of pregnancy which commences 20-24 weeks after the last menstrual period.

In practice, "late term termination of pregnancy" also includes foeticide as distinct from the "early induction of labour," which is usually used in the circumstances in which a pathological condition endangers the child or the mother during pregnancy, and delivery is warranted in order to overcome the danger to the mother, the child or both. A major medical difference, when the child is capable of being born alive, is the fact that the pregnancy can be ended without ending the life of the child. Foeticide is a distinct medical choice and may even be a distinct procedure before delivery (e.g., saline infusion into the uterus or potassium chloride injection into the heart of the foetus), during delivery (e.g., dismembering prior to extraction), or after partial breech delivery (penetration and suctioning of the child's brain cavity during delivery).

The legal difference between foeticide and infanticide is not the age or maturity of the child, but whether the death is caused before or after complete birth. Whether there is medical effort directed to preserve the health and life of the child, or whether the procedure is done in such a way as to ensure that life does not continue, is a medical decision (albeit based upon whether the mother has decided that the child should live or die). There are obviously different attitudes within the profession about whether late term termination should properly be considered a medical option. A former US Surgeon General, Dr C. Everett Koop, stated in an article in the *New York Times*[152] that with all that modern medicine has to offer, partial-birth abortions are not needed to save the life of the mother, and the procedure's impact on a woman's cervix can put future pregnancies at risk.

Medical and paramedical attitudes to late term termination of pregnancy are likely to be different, not only because the child may be capable of being born alive, but also because he or she will be larger; bone structures will have formed; and there is much discussion in the literature about foetal pain. Response to painful stimulus is evident and there has been much discussion about whether general anaesthesia in the woman would also anaesthetise the child.[153]

The fact that there may be monitoring of foetal heart-beat and foetal movement, and recognition of signs of foetal distress, will obviously affect

---

152 "Why Defend Partial-Birth Abortion?", *New York Times*, 26 September 1996.
153 See for instance a survey of specialist opinion, "For Debate: Do fetuses feel pain?", *British Medical Journal*, 313: 7060 (28 September 1996) 795-798.

the operating room personnel, particularly if the procedure is being aided by real-time ultrasonography.

In such circumstances, there is more likely to be an operating room awareness of the existence of the child. The notion that this is just the removal of tissue is not likely to be sustainable.

There are significant psycho-social sequellae after second trimester termination of pregnancy.

A significant follow-up study of 84 women in West Scotland who had had second trimester terminations of pregnancy for foetal abnormality[154] concluded that within the context of continuing medical care, professionals have a responsibility to learn about this new kind of grief and to recognize (keeping the couples' reticence in mind) the signs that may signal a need for professional mental health intervention.[155] That there is such grief warrants exploration of whether there are matters that have been overlooked in the philosophical debate. I discussed this matter in Chapter 4.

An Oxford study of 71 women who had had termination of pregnancy for foetal abnormality[156] found that in the month after termination of pregnancy many had high levels of psychiatric morbidity (41 per cent) as determined by a standardised psychiatric interview, which is 4-5 times higher than in non-puerperal (10 per cent) and post-partum women (9 per cent) in the general population. 31 per cent still felt guilty and angry 13 months later. Of the 71 women, about a third saw the baby after the termination, and of those who did not, just under a third had wished that they had. 14% arranged funerals for their babies.

The fact that women following late term termination of pregnancy may wish to see and hold the body of their child, the particular kind of grief, the possibility of a need for a funeral and burial, and the fact (discussed

---

154 Margaret C.A. Whit-van Mourik, J.M. Connor and M.A. Ferguson-Smith, "The Psychosocial Sequellae of a Second Trimester Termination of Pregnancy for Fetal Abnormality over a Two Year Period", in *Psychosocial Aspects of Genetic Counselling*, John Wiley and Sons: New York, 1992, pp. 60-74.
155 Ibid., p. 73.
156 Susan Iles and Denis Gath, "Psychiatric Outcome of Termination of Pregnancy for Foetal Abnormality", *Psychological Medicine*, 1993, 23, 407-413.

later) that the cause of death (post twenty-weeks) may be required to be certified by the doctor, are all indications that the medical circumstances for the women and presumably their spouses are distinct. There is much more required in the continuing medical management than would seem to be the case for first trimester termination of pregnancy.

There is something of a medical consensus amongst those who accept the practice, that the indications for late term terminations of pregnancy are narrower than for first trimester termination.

The Medical Board of the Australian State of Queensland reported that terminations are performed after 20 weeks for the following indications:

- risk to maternal life;
- psychotic/suicidal maternal behaviour;
- life-threatening illness;
- lethal foetal abnormality;
- gross foetal abnormality.[157]

There is doubt over whether late term abortion is ever medically indicated as a treatment for psychotic/suicidal maternal behaviour. The procedure itself is a cause of psychiatric morbidity. Where there are risks to maternal life or life-threatening illness, early delivery could presumably be used rather than late term termination. Foeticide is not a treatment for any condition of the mother. Further, in the various enquiries held into this matter, numerous gynaecologists have testified that medical conditions in the mother can always be managed without necessitating late term termination of pregnancy. Given that risks to maternal life in late term pregnancy can be managed, and using early delivery if necessary, then there is no maternal *medical* indication for foeticide in those circumstances.

Life-threatening illness in the mother may raise the matter of whether she wants the child to survive her, but foeticide in such a case is obviously not a *medical* necessity – the indication, if there is one, is social. Without that necessity, such a procedure would, as is discussed below, be unlawful in many jurisdictions.

---

157 The Medical Board of Queensland, *Terminations of Pregnancies in Excess of 20 weeks of Gestation: Project Information Paper*, July 1997, p. 4.

That leaves the matter of late term terminations of pregnancy for reasons to do with lethal or gross foetal abnormality. This is a new practice that has developed with the advances in ante-natal diagnosis. In the medical literature it is highly controversial. No consensus has emerged over what would be considered a serious enough indication.[158] Finally, the social and cultural implications of foeticide as a means of selecting what sort of people there should be have not yet been fully explored. This was discussed earlier under the heading of "reproductive discrimination".

Late term termination has profound personal significance for all those involved, but particularly the mother, her spouse and any other children she may have. A number of features of late-term termination contribute to this:

- Foeticide or child destruction is a distinct medical choice late term because the child can be delivered alive to an independent existence.
- The foetus is more developed, responds to painful stimulus and has solid bone structures such that different procedures are required.
- There are continuing and very different matters of grieving and psychiatric morbidity involved in the termination of a pregnancy when the child is mature enough to be capable of being born alive and the mother is likely to have begun to relate to him or her such that afterwards she may want to see and hold the body of her dead child.

By the time late term termination of pregnancy is contemplated, the pregnancy is likely to be known and discussed within the family. Other children, if any, are likely to be considering the coming of a new brother or sister. The profound significance of a decision to terminate late term cannot be ignored.

Infanticide, in Western culture, is viewed with horror. When a mother kills a neonate, we regard it as such an horrific event, that we, our legislature and our courts readily classify it as a result of a temporary mental state, not something that is likely to have been freely chosen. Medically, there is no clear line between infanticide and foeticide once the child is capable of being born alive.

---

158 See for instance a debate carried out in the *Lancet*, Volume 342, 2 August 1993; 9 October 1993; and 6 November 1993.

The formation of personal morality is a social activity. We form our moral opinions around our own personal identity and self-perception, but in community and in the reflection of the opinions of others. When precisely a new human life is recognized as having the status of an "other," a person to whom respect is due, is a matter of contention and there is a variety of views in the community about it. However, as we move further and further through the stages of development and maturity of a nascent human being, then more and more people will have recognized that moral status.

For some, the child has that status from the moment that the first cell is formed at fertilization; others will give that recognition when the cluster of cells begins to gastrulate and the primitive streak forms; then later others will attach importance to neural development and the capacity to feel and respond to painful stimuli. Quickening, when the woman can feel foetal movement, is another significant stage; then the capacity to be born alive is reached, then birth itself. At each stage the proportion of a woman's family, friends and acquaintances that recognize that her child is owed respect as a member of the human family will have increased.

That accrual of respect for the worth and dignity of the child a woman carries will have a profound impact on her and her family, and on her doctor, as the pregnancy develops, whatever the individual view formed. The nature of moral thinking and its social context makes that so. Self-perception is not entirely separable from the perception of others. How we view ourselves is often through the medium of our relationship to others.

Late term termination of pregnancy occurs at a stage at which that accrual of respect will be relatively advanced. This alone makes it personally very different from early abortion. Further, the medical reality that, once the child is capable of being born alive, foeticide or child destruction is a separate and distinct decision from whether or not delivery of the child is necessitated, also has profound personal significance.

As we have seen the primary *medical* difference in late term termination of pregnancy is that, because the child may be capable of surviving independently, then early delivery and foeticide are separable medical events. Ending the life of the foetus (foeticide) is a distinct medical choice in such circumstances. The conflict between the rights of the mother to control of her own body and the right to life of the child she carries, which is central to the abortion debate, no longer exists with the same meaning once the pregnancy has reached late term. If necessary, the child can be delivered and survive.

Hence, unlike the general debate over termination of pregnancy, the specific debate over *late term* termination of pregnancy is not about a woman's control of her own body. If necessary she can cease carrying the pregnancy by having the child delivered alive. The debate is over whether she and her doctor may decide whether in such circumstances the life of the child should be terminated during that procedure. This is, as the law has categorized it, a debate about *child destruction* in many jurisdictions (foeticide in the UK legal debate).

Matters to do with overcoming grave dangers to the mother's life and health are distinct from the matter of whether foeticide is also to be part of the management. The question of late term termination of pregnancy seems to turn upon whether foeticide is ever legitimate.

The decision of the Victorian Parliament in 2008 to legalise late term termination of pregnancy is difficult to understand. The long-standing law on child destruction was struck down alongside the abortion law. Now, in Victoria, a woman only needs the acquiescence of two doctors to have a late term termination and no medical necessity is required, just their judgement that it is "appropriate in all the circumstances".[159] The two doctors could both be employed by the clinic undertaking the late termination. Section 5 of the *Victorian Abortion Law Reform Act* 2008 states:

5. Termination of pregnancy by registered medical practitioner after 24 weeks

    (1) A registered medical practitioner may perform an abortion on a woman who is more than 24 weeks pregnant only if the medical practitioner-

        (a) reasonably believes that the abortion is appropriate in all the circumstances; and

---

159 *Abortion Law Reform Act* 2008 http://www.austlii.edu.au/au/legis/vic/consol_act/alra2008209/s5.html

(b) has consulted at least one other registered medical practitioner who also reasonably believes that the abortion is appropriate in all the circumstances.

(2) In considering whether the abortion is appropriate in all the circumstances, a registered medical practitioner must have regard to

(a) all relevant medical circumstances; and

(b) the woman's current and future physical, psychological and social circumstances.[160]

A disturbing factor to have emerged in relation to the practice of abortion in the State of Victoria is the quality and competence of the medical staffing of abortion clinics. I have myself seen advertisements in the general practice medical journals for new medical graduates to work in abortion clinics, where they would be trained by the clinic to do the surgical procedure or to administer anaesthesia, and earn proceduralist rates, normally only paid to specialists. In other words, a young medical graduate could move very rapidly to very lucrative levels of payment, and without the usual years of internship experience required even to practice independently as a general practitioner and without further years of study and experience to qualify as a specialist gynaecologist or anaesthetist.

Further, it has also emerged that doctors who have a troubled employment history, such as involving drug addiction, have been employed by private abortion clinics. One such instance in Victoria has resulted in criminal charges against an anaesthetist who allegedly had a history of drug addiction and had self-administered an anaesthetic drug in such a way as to pass on to many women his own hepatitis infection. From his committal hearing it was reported:

> An anaesthetist has pleaded guilty to charges related to infecting more than 50 women with hepatitis C at a Melbourne abortion clinic. James Latham Peters, 63, pleaded guilty in the Victorian Supreme Court today to 55 counts of negligently causing serious injury. It has been alleged in previous court proceedings that Peters infected patients at the Croydon Day Surgery by using pre-filled syringes of

---

160 Ibid.

anaesthetic drugs on himself before administering the remainder to the women.[161]

He has subsequently been sentenced to 14 years gaol.

These matters raise obvious concerns about the quality, experience and competence of the medical staff that women seeking abortion from a private clinic may encounter. Suggestions that the medical practice of abortion requires more stringent regulation have been strongly resisted, including by the 2008 enquiry held by the Victorian Law Reform Commission and whose findings led to the liberalisation of the law. That is tragic because it would appear that women seeking abortion are not necessarily receiving the same standards of care that they would receive for other gynaecological problems.

In terms of regulation, abortion would seem to be on a par with removing warts or other minor skin lesions, and that does not provide women with the kind of support they may need. For other surgical procedures, there is often an opportunity to meet others who have had the experience, and the process of referral for surgical procedures requires first seeing a general practitioner who then refers the patient to a specialist with whom the GP would normally have a history of referring and communication, so that between them the surgeon and the GP can arrange the patient's care and establish a satisfactory level of communication with her. In fact, a pattern of good communication between the specialist and the GP is often a factor in the decisions to continue referring patients, as well as knowledge of the capacity and specific competence of the specialist. Referring patterns often reflect a history of a shared professional relationship, even having trained together.[162] That women often go straight to a specialist abortion clinic without medical referral and thus the medical judgement of competence and two-way communication is not to their medical advantage or in the interests of informed decision-making and good after care.

---

161 "Anaesthetist admits infecting 50 women with hepatitis C at abortion clinic", from: *AAP* November 09, 201211:27AM; *The Australian,* 10 November 2012, http://www.theaustralian.com.au/news/nation/anaesthetist-admits-infecting-50-women-with-hepatitis-c-at-abortion-clinic/story-e6frg6nf-1226513623898

162 Michael L. Barnett, Nicholas A. Christakis, Nancy L. Keating, A. James O'Malley, Bruce E. Landon, "Reasons for Choice of Referral Physician Among Primary Care and Specialist Physicians", *Journal of General Internal Medicine,* May 2012, Volume 27, Issue 5, pp 506-512.

9
Ectopic Pregnancy

Normally a pregnancy may result when an egg is produced by the ovaries and is collected by the fimbria, finger-like structures, at the end of the fallopian tube. Once in the fallopian tube, it may be fertilized by sperm which have moved there from the vagina after sexual intercourse. After fertilization the new embryo would normally be carried down the tube into the uterus where it would implant and continue development. In the condition known as *ectopic pregnancy*, however, the developing embryo lodges outside the uterus and normally in the fallopian tube. The condition can resolve itself with the embryo becoming dislodged without any intervention, but if it continues, then as the embryo becomes larger it may be life-threatening for the mother, with the possibility of the fallopian tube rupturing and severe blood loss from the blood vessels that have developed to support the embryo.

The early symptoms may include abdominal pain, late or missed period, vaginal bleeding, tissue passage from the vagina, and pregnancy symptoms.[163]

If the condition continues until the embryo is much larger there may be significant loss of blood resulting in dizziness and fainting, shoulder pain (referred pain), weakness, racing heart, and bloated and hard abdomen.[164]

The treatment alternatives provide some difficult choices for women and their doctors. Currently there are three possibilities:

- methotrexate, a biochemical agent (often used to treat cancer) that interferes with cell division and hence, because an embryo is growing, ends the life of the embryo;
- salpingostomy, which involves diathermy to seal the maternal blood vessels that are in danger of bleeding if the pregnancy continues, and then flushing out the embryo, who will have died

---

163 S. Mittal , "Non-surgical management of ectopic pregnancy", *Obs Gyn Com*, 1999, 1:23-28.
164 Ibid.

following the loss of the maternal blood supply, leaving the tube intact; or

- salpingectomy, in which the section of fallopian tube containing the embryo is removed.

Both surgical procedures are usually done laparoscopically so that there is minimal incision and lower risk of complications.

In many cases, the condition is detected quite early, and there is the option of expectant management. Expectant management may be offered to an asymptomatic woman where the mass of the embryo is small and the initial level of the hormone associated with pregnancy (human chorionic gonadotrophin) is low. Rising hormone levels, pain, blood pressure changes or evidence from a scan of abdominal bleeding would indicate switching to active management.[165]

The advice from a range of peer-reviewed publications is that approximately 80 per cent of women with a detected ectopic pregnancy and low initial hormone levels will experience spontaneous resolution.[166]

---

165 Ibid.
166 R.J. Carr, R. Evans, "Ectopic pregnancy", *Prim Care*, 2000, 27:169-183; H. Fernandez, C. Lelaldier, V. Thouvenez *et al*, "The use of a pretherapeutic, predictive score to determine inclusion criteria for the non-surgical management of ectopic pregnancy", *Hum Reprod*, 1991, 6:995-998; J. Elito, Jr., A.P. Reichmann, M.N. Uchiyama, L. Camano, "Predictive score for the systemic treatment of unruptured ectopic pregnancy with a single dose of methotrexate", *Int J Gynecol Obstet*, 1999, 67:75-79; M.D. Pisarska, S.A. Carson, J.E. Buster, "Ectopic pregnancy", *Lancet*, 1998, 351:1115-1120; C.M. Farquhar, "Ectopic pregnancy", *Lancet*, 2005, 366:583-591; S. Mittal, "Non-surgical management of ectopic pregnancy", *Obs Gyn Co*, 1999, 1:23-28; M.A. Cohen, M.V. Sauer, "Expectant management of ectopic pregnancy", *Clin Obstet Gynecol*, 1999, 42:48-54; J.E. Buster, M.D. Pisarska, "Medical management of ectopic pregnancy", *Clin Obstet Gynecol*, 1999, 42:23-30; H. Murray, H. Baakdah, T. Bardell, T. Tulandi, "Diagnosis and treatment of ectopic pregnancy", *CMAJ*, 2005, 173:905-912; M. Pansky, "Methotrexate (MXT) treatment for ectopic pregnancy-systemic vs local injection. Scientific presentation at The First World Congress on Controversies" in *Obstetrics, Gynecology & Infertility* Prague, Czech Republic, 1999. Available at: www.obgyn.net/firstcontroversies/prague1999pansky.doc; K.T. Bamhart, G. Gosman, R. Ashby, M. Sammel, "The medical management of ectopic pregnancy: a meta-analysis comparing "single dose" and "multidose" regimens.", *Obstet Gynecol*, 2003; 101:778-784; G.H. Lipscomb, N.L. Meyer, D.E. Flynn, M. Peterson, E. Ling, "Oral methotrexate for treatment of ectopic pregnancy", *Am J Obstet Gynecol*, 2002, 186:1192-1195.

The moral issue that concerns those who wish to respect the life of both the mother and the child is the issue of direct abortion. Even though the embryo cannot survive in the fallopian tube but will die before it can reach viability, destroying the embryo may be seen as something of a pre-emptive strike.

The concern was clarified by the teaching of Pope John Paul II in "*Evangelium Vitae*," No. 58, which defined abortion as the "deliberate and intentional killing, by whatever means it is carried out, of a human being in the initial phase of his or her existence, extending from conception to birth." Further, he declared that direct abortion, that is, abortion willed as an end or as a means, always constitutes a grave moral disorder, since it is the deliberate killing of an innocent human being.

In the same document, however, Pope John Paul II also refers to the possibility of needing indirectly to take the life of an aggressor, even an innocent aggressor in the sense of someone who, like an embryo, is not capable of reason. Moreover:

> legitimate defence can be not only a right but a grave duty for someone responsible for another's life, the common good of the family or of the State.... Unfortunately it happens that the need to render the aggressor incapable of causing harm sometimes involves taking his life. In this case, the fatal outcome is attributable to the aggressor whose action brought it about, even though he may not be morally responsible because of a lack of the use of reason.[167]

The Pope's clarification is important because it would appear to allow indirect ways of resolving the ectopic pregnancy that do not directly kill the embryo, in accordance with the notion of legitimate defence, even when the risk to life comes from someone who is not morally responsible because of a lack of reason.

The definition and account of legitimate defence would seem to be consistent with the traditional view that where the life of the mother is endangered by an ectopic pregnancy then it would be permissible to

---

[167] *Evangelium Vitae* n. 55 the authority for which Pope John Paul II gives as Saint Thomas Aquinas, *Summa Theologiae*, II-II, q. 64, a. 7; Saint Alphonsus De' Liguori, *Theologia Moralis*, l. III, tr. 4, c. 1, dub.3.

do salpingectomy – the removal of the section of fallopian tube that contains the embryo. The embryo would die as a result but the death would be a foreseen result rather than directly or intentionally willed. The immediate objective is to remove the pathology that threatens her life, in this case the segment of fallopian tube that will rupture, or has ruptured, causing life threatening haemorrhage.

Thus the US Bishops, in their 2001 *Ethical and Religious Directives for Catholic Health Care Services*, state:

> 38. Operations, treatments, and medications that have as their direct purpose the cure of a proportionately serious pathological condition of a pregnant woman are permitted when they cannot be safely postponed until the unborn child is viable, even if they will result in the death of the unborn child.
>
> 39. In case of extrauterine pregnancy, no intervention is morally licit which constitutes a direct abortion.

The Catholic Health of Australia *Code of Ethical Conduct* (2001)[168] approved by the Australian Catholic Bishops states:

> An ectopic pregnancy can pose a grave threat to the lives of both a pregnant woman and the embryonic child she carries. Careful monitoring is required and ectopic pregnancies may safely resolve themselves in time. However, a woman's life should never be endangered by an inappropriate delay in treatment. When treatment is required, the pathological situation should be resolved quickly, though not by resort to any procedure or treatment that is abortifacient (in that the death of the embryo is being intended as an end or as a means to the treatment goal), nor by any treatment that involves a surgical or chemical assault on the developing embryo. (section 2.29)

And at section 2.23 the Code states:

> Catholic facilities should not provide, or refer for, abortions, that is, procedures, treatments or medications whose primary purpose

---

168 http://www.cha.org.au/site.php?id=223

or sole immediate effect is to terminate the life of a foetus or of an embryo before or after implantation. Such procedures, treatments and medications are morally wrong because they involve the direct and deliberate killing of an innocent human life in the earliest stages of development.

The issue turns on whether the loss of life of the embryo in order to save the life of the mother is direct or deliberately intended. There seems to be agreement amongst moral theologians that salpingectomy, when the mother's life is at risk, is permissible because the death of the child within the tube when the latter is removed is not directly intended.

A concern with removing the fallopian tube is that the woman's future fertility may be adversely affected. However, there are usually two fallopian tubes and she may not be rendered infertile if the other tube and the ovary on that side are still functioning. However, removal of a fallopian tube may still compromise future fertility.

In more recent times it has been argued that salpingostomy – the direct removal of the embryo – would do less damage to the woman, and that it too is not a direct killing of the embryo.[169] This has been argued by Christopher Kaczor[170] and Stephen Long,[171] amongst others.

Kaczor argues that, as in salpingectomy, in salpingostomy the agent does not endeavour to achieve death nor is a failure to bring about death reckoned as a failure of the agent's proximate or remote aims. Kaczor's argument seems also to be influenced by the claim that in being a removal that does not in itself harm the embryo, the procedure is consistent with the possibility that sometime in the future it might be possible to transfer the embryo back to the uterus.[172]

---

[169] This is argued by Ray Campbell in private correspondence. I am awaiting release of his work on the moral act that will I hope fully explain his view.

[170] Christopher Kaczor, "Moral Absolutism and Ectopic Pregnancy," *Journal of Medicine and Philosophy* 26, no. (2001): 61-74.

[171] Steven A. Long, *The Teleological Grammar of the Moral Act*, Introductions to Catholic Doctrine (Naples, Florida: Sapientia Press of Ave Maria University, 2007), 95-102, 127-129.

[172] I am grateful to Ray Campbell for supplying me with information about the positions taken by both Kazcor and Long and the later account of positions taken by Benedict Ashley, Jerome O'Rourke and Albert Moraczewski.

Long argues, "If it literally means a change of local position with no direct harm inflicted upon the *conceptus*, then it would seem to be permissible."[173] He insists that he is referring to a case where the *conceptus* is simply moved, not scraped, lacerated, speared, crushed or chemically destroyed.

Arguably removal of an embryo lodged ectopically is different from abortion in that the fallopian tube is not the normal place for the embryo to be, whereas the uterus is the normal or natural place for an embryo to develop within a woman's body. The procedure does not directly will the death of the embryo, as the intention is to remove the embryo from where his or her continuing growth threatens the life of the mother. The death of the embryo is not a necessary consequence of the procedure but a foreseen consequence in circumstances in which continuation would threaten the life of both mother and embryo.

There has been a concern expressed by some[174] that the salpingostomy procedure involves simply crushing the embryo. That may have been so, particularly with the older surgical techniques. However, current laparoscopic, thermo and laser surgical techniques would first isolate and seal off the blood vessels around whatever it is that is to be removed, including in this case, an embryo, in order to prevent haemorrhage. In the case of an ectopic pregnancy, the maternal vessels that develop to supply the embryo would be sealed because it is haemorrhage from those blood vessels that would endanger her life as the pregnancy developed. This is different from the older style procedures that did not use thermal techniques and may have been seen as a direct assault on the embryo. In the contemporary procedure, salpingostomy does not involve a direct assault on the embryo. The target is the maternal blood vessels. The consequent loss of blood supply would, however, result in the death of the embryo, but indirectly.[175]

The sealing of the blood vessels would leave the embryo isolated. There would be no point in going further to damage the embryo. In the description of the process, the isolated and dead embryo is then removed by washing

---

173 Long, op. cit., p. 97.
174 This view was put to me by Edward Furton in email correspondence 6/8/10.
175 Maged Shendy and Rami Atalla, "Modern Management of Cornual Ectopic Pregnancy". Accessed 23/1/13 from http://cdn.intechopen.com/

out the fallopian tube. It may be that, in then removing the embryo, damage is done to it, but that would neither be necessary nor sought as an objective, and it would be after death.

Currently, however, the first-line therapy tends to be methotrexate. Though he seems to have changed his position on this question several times, Bill May, while rejecting the direct destruction of the embryo, has at one time argued that the use of Methotrexate in ectopic pregnancy is also not a direct abortion because he claimed:

> Methotrexate attacks the DNA in the trophoblastic tissue that attaches the unborn child to its site within the mother's body; it thus attacks the trophoblast attaching the child to the fallopian tube or cervix or other part of an ectopic pregnancy (I prescind from unborn children implanted in the mother's abdomen insofar as this is very rare and children so implanted usually can survive until birth).[176]

The information that May relied upon is very selective, as is the information that Albert Moraczewski[177] used to reach a similar conclusion, in agreement with Benedict Ashley and Kevin O'Rourke.[178] According to Moraczewski, methotrexate works by preventing the trophoblastic cells from multiplying and preventing the production of the enzymes necessary for penetration into the tubal wall. The moral object of the doctor is to stop the (destructive) action of the trophoblastic cells. He argues that this selective suppression of growth is not a direct killing of the embryo and is morally acceptable. The death of the trophoblast and the embryo follow as a side-effect of the action of the methotrexate.

The information from the US Food and Drug Administration[179] is quite different. The FDA advises that:

---

176 http://www.zenit.org/rssenglish-29448 Accessed 3 August 2010.
177 Albert S. Moraczewski, "Managing Tubal Pregnancies: Part 2," *Ethics and Medics* 21, no. 8 (1996): 3-4.
178 Benedict Ashley and Kevin O'Rourke, *Health Care Ethics: A Theologiael Analysis*, 4th ed. (Georgetown: Georgetown University Press, 1997), 253-54.
179 http://www.drugs.com/pro/methotrexate.html. Accessed 3 August 2010.

Methotrexate interferes with DNA synthesis, repair, and cellular replication. Actively proliferating tissues such as malignant cells, bone marrow, fetal cells, buccal and intestinal mucosa, and cells of the urinary bladder are in general more sensitive to this effect of Methotrexate. When cellular proliferation in malignant tissues is greater than in most normal tissues, Methotrexate may impair malignant growth without irreversible damage to normal tissues.[180]

The FDA also warns that methotrexate causes foetal death and/or congenital anomalies. It is therefore simply untrue to say that the drug only or essentially attacks the trophoblastic tissue. It attacks the entire embryo because an embryo is undergoing rapid growth. Cell replication is what an embryo does and by cell replication it remains alive. Methotrexate, by stopping cell replication, ends the life of the embryo. Except in the circumstances of freeze-drying during in vitro fertilization, an embryo that is not undergoing cell replication is a dead embryo.[181]

The trophoblast is a vital organ of the embryo and it too is undergoing cell division and so it too is destroyed by methotrexate along with every other part of the embryo. It is simply false to say that methotrexate is not a direct attack on the embryo.

Thus it would seem that the optimum management of ectopic pregnancy in monitored circumstances, with emergency services available, would be expectant management in the first instance until it is indicated that the condition will not naturally resolve and the mother's life may be at risk. Where medical opinion is that her life may be endangered by continuing to wait, then removal of the fallopian tube or the sealing of the woman's blood vessels that would cause haemorrhage and removal of the subsequently dead embryo would be permissible because neither are a direct or deliberate killing.

The use of methotrexate, however, would seem to be a direct assault on the embryo that causes the death of the embryo by interrupting cell division, that is, the living process. Methotrexate is effective because it destroys the embryo. The death of the embryo in that case is thus the means to resolving the condition.

---

180 Ibid.
181 Ibid.

10
Professional Conscience and Obstetrics and Gynaecology[182]

Obstetrics is second only to cosmetic surgery for the proportion of legal claims made against it, and obstetrics is the specialty most exposed to large claims.[183] Obstetricians are not likely to be more prone to negligence than any other medical specialty, so one can assume that the risk is related to the nature of the work itself.

Obstetrics and gynaecology is more likely than most specialties to involve differences of opinion about the morality of some of the procedures involved. It often finds itself in controversy. Partly that may be due to the intrinsic nature of a profession that often deals with two patients simultaneously. While what is good for mother is most often good for baby, there are circumstances in which the interests do not so exactly coincide and dilemmas arise. Partly the controversy may be due to the different values our pluralist society attaches to the importance of fertility and sexuality.

No-one in obstetrics and gynaecology is immune from having to make ethical decisions and thus having to take a stand on their own values with respect to what they are prepared to do.

Those decisions are in large part made according to the perception that the individual practitioner has a vocational role in medicine. The decision about who a doctor is, what the aims of the work are, and what makes a good doctor, shape the conscientious application of medical science.

---

182 Reproduced with permission after being published as Nicholas Tonti-Filippini "Professional Conscience", *Obstetrics and Gynaecology Magazine,* Vol 10, No 2, Winter 2008, pp. 27-8.
183 Insurance Statistics Australia Limited, *Medical Indemnity Report Executive Summary,* Medical Indemnity Insurers Association of Australia, 29 March 2004, p. 6.

Science does not shape conscience. The evidence does not determine the vocation but rather the vocation guides action in response to the evidence. Science cannot tell us what to do.

In the drafting of ethical guidelines, it has become the practice for Australia's National Health and Medical Research Council (NHMRC) first to identify the ethical values and principles to be applied. This is determined not by science, but by the moral sense of the community. The function of the Australian Health Ethics Committee (a committee of the NHMRC) with its diverse membership is to try to identify a consensus on those values.

A major value identified by this committee is respect for human beings, which is a recognition of their intrinsic value. In human research, this recognition includes abiding by the values of research merit and integrity, justice and beneficence. Respect also requires having due regard for the welfare, beliefs, perceptions, customs and cultural heritage, both individual and collective, of those involved in research.[184]

However, some see medicine as being less a professional vocation and more as an expertise, a morally neutral servant to the autonomy of the patient. The values to be applied are the patient's values; the doctor's values do not enter into it. That perception diminishes the dignity and integrity of the individual professional. "Professional" comes to mean the application of technical expertise, rather than professional judgement.

In this context of "deprofessionalising" the medical profession, there has been a push for what is called reproductive rights, the right to insist that a doctor provide reproductive medical services whatever the doctor's own personal views about the procedures involved.

Against such claims, in 2004, the NHMRC promulgated *Ethical Guidelines on the use of Assisted Reproductive Technology in Clinical Practice and Research*." The guidelines were reissued in 2007 with changes to accommodate the cloning legislation. Compliance by Australian IVF teams with the guidelines is secured by the terms of the funding agreements with the Commonwealth and by the administration of standards by the Reproductive Technology Accreditation Committee.

---

184 NHMRC, *National Statement on Ethical Conduct in Human Research*, Australian Government, 2007, Preamble.

The guidelines require that pre-implantation genetic diagnosis of embryos (PGD) must not be used for:

- prevention of conditions that do not seriously harm the person to be born;
- selection of the sex of an embryo except to reduce the risk of transmission of a serious genetic condition; or
- selection in favour of a genetic defect or disability in the person to be born.

This restriction may challenge those who uphold the notions of reproductive rights and reproductive freedom, especially those who are of the view that it is their right to choose the sex or other genetic features of their child.

IVF practitioners also raise questions about whether they can withhold IVF from a person who is, for instance, a convicted paedophile or for someone who already has children who have been taken into care.

The overall rationale adopted by the NHMRC for restricting choice in the use of reproductive technology is that "clinical decisions must respect, primarily, the interests and welfare of the persons who may be born, as well as the long-term health and psychosocial welfare of all participants, including gamete donors."[185]

The jurisprudential dialogue about reproductive rights occurs against the background of the legal tradition that the interests of the child are paramount. This principle found expression in the UN *Convention on the Rights of the Child*, which recognizes, amongst other matters, the rights of the child to an identity, nationality, family relations, and to personal relationships and direct contact with both parents. Family law too has been based on the principle that the interests of the child are paramount. Family law restricts parental choices and resolves conflicts in favour of the welfare of children.

The fact that there are conscientious decisions to be made by those who practice obstetrics and gynaecology raises questions about what happens when practitioners disagree on what is the right ethical decision.

---

[185] NHMRC, *Ethical Guidelines on the Use of Assisted Reproductive Technology in Clinical Practice and Research*, Australian Government, June 2007, p. 9.

The NHMRC, in several recent sets of guidelines, has indicated the need to respect conscientious objection. For instance, the guidelines on use of foetal tissue in research state:

> Those who conscientiously object to being involved in conducting research with separated foetuses or foetal tissue should not be compelled to participate, nor should they be put at a disadvantage because of their objection.[186]

Similar "no disadvantage" clauses can be found in guidelines on organ donation and brain death, assisted reproductive technology, the use of stem cells and medical research.

Finding oneself in a position in which one's own ethical values conflict with what is expected is not easy. Conscientious objection needs to be exercised responsibly so as not to put the patient in danger, and in a spirit of mutual respect for the consciences of others. The NHMRC notes that a person who exercises conscientious objection to participate in an activity ought not to undertake activities within the institution or directly involving the institution that might undermine confidence in other professionals within the institution.[187]

The exercise of conscientious objection also needs to be open to discussion so that the others can at least see that there is a rationale for the view even if they disagree. Part of the function of conscientious objection is to give witness to what one believes. That is an important part of what very often is a situation in which one is cooperating with others and that cooperation may be morally compromised if it implies an acceptance of what one sees as unethical practices. The explanation is needed for the sake of the person who wishes to withdraw and for the sake of others who need to understand that that is the case.

The idea of "secular neutrality" puts a person with ethical scruples at some kind of disadvantage. The freedom to act rationally, sensibly and

---

186 NHMRC, *National Statement on Ethical Conduct in Human Research*, Australian Government, 2007, n. 4.1.14.
187 NHMRC, *Organ and Tissue Donation after death: Guidelines for Ethical Practice for Health Professionals*, Australian Government, 2007, p. 20.

according to the evidence may be thought to be impeded by the person's ethical values.

It seems to me that we are seeing, in Australia, a very aggressive exclusionist form of secularism that views personal ethical values, particularly religious values, with arrogant intolerance and dismissiveness. This kind of secularist belief is characterised by attempts to exclude contributions to public discussion on the basis of a kind of bigotry that classifies the contributions of persons who have ethical scruples or who are religious in a nominalist way. Perhaps even more significantly, this kind of secularism undermines all those in the health professions who see themselves as more than just technically expert, those who see themselves as having a vocation to serve the good of their patients.

11
Amending the Abortion Law Reform Act 2008

11.1 Summary of the Problem

The Victorian *Abortion Law Reform Act* 2008 qualified the right to conscientious objection leaving many conscientious health practitioners in circumstances in which their conscientious practice is in breach of the law. That is having the tragic effect of forcing some practitioners out of some areas of health care practice, and young practitioners may not even be able to complete their training, because the new law overrides their conscientious practice to respect the life of both patients. They may be unable to meet employment or training requirements that they act in accordance with the law.

This is obviously discriminatory for those in our community who hold firm views on the right to life of the unborn. Some are, in effect, being barred from health care practice in Victoria. Some have already moved interstate to escape the effects of Victoria's law. At the same time it was not necessary for the law to be so rigid and exclusionary in this respect. Abortion is widely known to be available from a variety of centres in our community and no referral is needed for women to access those services. No women would be excluded from access to abortion by allowing doctors who conscientiously object to withdraw, provided that women are informed of the availability of abortion services.

There is a need to amend the Act in accordance with the principle of a right to freedom of conscience, thought and belief recognized in international law, and in accordance with the international and national codes of ethics.

11.2 Freedom of Conscience of Health Practitioners

The Medical Board of Australia which is responsible for registering medical practitioners and students has published *Good Medical Practice: A Code of Conduct for Doctors in Australia* which is used to guide the regulation of medical practice in Australia. The *Code* recognizes the right of medical practitioners to freedom of conscience, though and belief. The *Code* states:

> 2.4.6 Being aware of your right to not provide or directly participate in treatments to which you conscientiously object, informing your patients and, if relevant, colleagues, of your objection, and not using your objection to impede access to treatments that are legal.
>
> 2.4.7 Not allowing your moral or religious views to deny patients access to medical care, recognising that you are free to decline to personally provide or participate in that care.[188]

The National Health and Medical Research Council (NHMRC) has also recognized freedom of conscience in its guidelines:

> Conscientious objectors are not obliged to be involved in the procedures or programs to which they object. If any member of staff or student expresses a conscientious objection to the treatment of any individual patient or to any ART procedures conducted by the clinic, the clinic must allow him or her to withdraw from involvement in the procedure or program to which he or she objects. Clinics must also ensure that staff and students are not disadvantaged because of a conscientious objection.[189]

Both sets of guidelines are in accord with the World Medical Association meeting in Seoul in October 2008 which stated:

> The central element of professional autonomy and clinical independence is the assurance that individual physicians have the freedom to exercise professional judgment in the care and treatment of their patients without undue influence by outside parties or individuals

---

188 http://www.medicalboard.gov.au/Codes-and-Guidelines.aspx
189 NHMRC, "Ethical guidelines on the use of assisted reproductive technology in clinical practice and research", http://www.scribd.com/doc/6863092/nhmrc-art-ethics

The Australian Medical Association has stated the *Abortion Law Reform Act* 2008 (ALRA), "... infringes the rights of doctors with a conscientious objection by inserting an active compulsion for a doctor to refer to another doctor who they know does not have a conscientious objection."[190] This indicates that the peak body representing doctors in Australia sees the ALRA as infringing a hitherto accepted freedom of conscientious objection in medical practice in Australia.

Also the right to freedom of conscience is upheld by the Australian Nursing Federation and the Royal College of Nursing Australia.[191]

In Australia, however, no State or Territory has enacted legislation to protect freedom of conscience and the Commonwealth has not legislated on the matter despite being a signatory to the *International Covenant on Civil and Political Rights*, Article 18 of which states:

> Everyone shall have the right to freedom of thought, conscience and religion. This right shall include freedom to have or to adopt a religion or belief of his choice, and freedom, either individually or in community with others and in public or private, to manifest his religion or belief in worship, observance, practice and teaching.
>
> No one shall be subject to coercion which would impair his freedom to have or to adopt a religion or belief of his choice.
>
> Freedom to manifest one's religion or beliefs may be subject only to such limitations as are prescribed by law and are necessary to protect public safety, order, health, or morals or the fundamental rights and freedoms of others.

The Australian Constitution protects the freedom of conscience of people being employed by the Commonwealth, but does not protect the right more generally. Section 116 of the Constitution states:

> The Commonwealth shall not make any law for establishing

---

190 Victorian LA, *Hansard*, 9 September 2008, p. 3306.
191 Australian Nursing Federation, "Conscientious Objection", reviewed and re-endorsed in June 2011, http://www.anf.org.au/pdf/policies/P_Conscientious_Objection.pdf); Royal College of Nursing Australia, Conscientious Objection, 1998, currently under review http://www.rcna.org.au/_literature_30428/Conscientios_Objection_(1998)

any religion, or for imposing any religious observance, or for prohibiting the free exercise of any religion, and no religious test shall be required as a qualification for any office or public trust under the Commonwealth.

However that protection only exists for Commonwealth employees. There is in fact no legal protection for freedom of conscience for health practitioners generally.

In that legal environment on several occasions over the past thirty years, I have been approached by young medical practitioners who have found themselves in difficulty with a superior over conscientiously refusing to do a procedure. However, the situation always proved to be resolvable once we had arranged legal representation. The issue was not resolved by appealing to the law but to the general understanding that health professionals do have a moral right to freedom of conscience. Often the issue was more a matter of diplomacy, and sometimes the problem was more a question of the young practitioner being overzealous in being critical of the practice of others. Common sense prevailed.

We were able to depend on the fact that in Australian medical practice, freedom of conscience has long been upheld in medical practice, and recognized by senior members of the professions. The elements of conscientious objection usually include an understanding that a professional person may have a firm, fixed and sincere objection to carrying out a procedure because of deeply-held moral, ethical, or religious beliefs, and may on those grounds withdraw from providing a service. It is also generally recognized that the withdrawal is personal and not political, is to be expressed at the earliest opportunity that knowledge of the service arises, and withdrawal ought not to place other persons in jeopardy. As long as a young practitioner handled it diplomatically and gave adequate notice, it has in the past been manageable.

I fear now for the future, however, because the new abortion law has changed the expectation.

Recently, a graduate nurse applying for a position at a major public hospital was told that she would be required to assist with termination of pregnancy and that conscientious objection would not be permitted because of the new law.

A young doctor was called before the Medical Practitioners Board of Victoria because he had had some social media communications with other doctors in which he said his practice is not to refer for abortion. He also indicated an approach to such a request that might not have been ideal. A complaint was lodged with the regulator by those other doctors. My advice was that he should discuss with his lawyer admitting to error in relation to the way he indicated he responds to a request for abortion. Instead I suggested he should consider following the approach outlined by the Australian Bishops (see section 4.7) in which one seeks to listen to the patient and seeks to provide a less stressed opportunity for her to explore her deeply held values on the matter and make and decision that she can live with in the long term. The Bishops advise that by seeking to reduce pressure on her, supporting her own ability to think through the issues, she is more likely to make a decision in favour of her motherhood. That is a better alternative than trying to pressure her according to the practitioner's views and adding to the pressure on her and her sense of not being in control. If he were to indicate having reflected on it and adopted a more supportive and passive approach than he had indicated, that might be sufficient to meet that part of the complaint against him.

For the issue of having to inform the women of his conscientious objection and refer to someone who has no objection, the Board has sent him a paper advocating that doctors who have a conscientious objection should make that known to patients before they find themselves in the consultation room. That could be done with a pamphlet or notice made available by the receptionists at the time that bookings are made. On this issue the Board has since judged that the doctor was guilty of improper conduct for saying on social media that he would not refer and the Board acknowledged that the Victorian law was in conflict with their own *Code of Ethics*. In another State he would have behaved ethically according to the regulators' standards in other States.

When the new law was first proclaimed, Dr Mary Walsh, Dr Eamonn Mathieson, from the Catholic Doctors Association of Victoria, and I went to see the Medical Practitioners Board to discuss what to do. They supported the pamphlet approach saying that a patient who then requested a referral for abortion knowing that the doctor did not refer, would be likely to be seen as vexatious.

That advice does not sit well, because it may mean lost opportunities to actually be of assistance to women who may be caught in a pressured situation and need someone to provide them with the opportunity to discuss such a potentially traumatic decision.

Alternative legal advice we were offered was to not raise the issue of conscientious objection but to avoid referring on moral grounds alone. The law only requires informing the woman and referring if the objection is conscientious. That advice is untested and does not sit well with those who have moral and medical reservations.

Many pro-life doctors are simply choosing to provide their usual support and advice and take the risk of a complaint being made if they fail to inform about their conscientious practice and fail to refer. Other health professionals, such as nurses, pharmacists and psychologists, may find the situation even more difficult.

So what does the Act require?

11.3 The Abortion Law Reform Act 2008

In 2008, the Victorian Parliament passed the *Abortion Law Reform Act* 2008. The Act defined **abortion** to mean

> intentionally causing the termination of a woman's pregnancy by
> – using an instrument; or using a drug or a combination of drugs; or any other means.

This is a very broad definition that is not specific to ending the life of a foetus. It also includes treatment of ectopic pregnancy and the early induction of live birth. The legislation also made provision for nurses and pharmacists to conduct abortion medically. Having established wide parameters, the Act then included a section on conscientious objection, but imposed limits on the right to freedom of conscience. The Act has the following section:

> *8 Obligations of registered health practitioner who has conscientious objection*
>
> (1) If a woman requests a registered health practitioner to advise on a proposed abortion, or to perform, direct, authorise or supervise an abortion for that woman, and the practitioner has a conscientious objection to abortion, the practitioner must –
>
> (a) inform the woman that the practitioner has a conscientious objection to abortion; and
>
> (b) refer the woman to another registered health practitioner in the same regulated health profession who the practitioner knows does not have a conscientious objection to abortion.
>
> (2) Subsection (1) does not apply to a practitioner who is under a duty set out in subsection (3) or (4).
>
> (3) Despite any conscientious objection to abortion, a registered medical practitioner is under a duty to perform an abortion in an emergency where the abortion is necessary to preserve the life of the pregnant woman.
>
> (4) Despite any conscientious objection to abortion, a registered nurse is under a duty to assist a registered medical practitioner in performing an abortion in an emergency where the abortion is necessary to preserve the life of the pregnant woman.

The problem with section 8(1) is that a doctor who conscientiously believes that abortion is the destruction of a member of the human family will, as a matter of conscience, be likely to feel bound not to recommend abortion. Referral for a medical procedure is a recommendation of the procedure. The new law thus leaves many conscientious doctors in a situation of having to act in breach of Victorian state law, despite both the national regulator and the NHMRC recognising their right to freedom of conscience, and despite Australia having a commitment to protect them as a signatory to the ICCPR (referred to earlier).

The law in this respect is also impractical. It requires the practitioner to know the views of colleague on the issue of abortion. Most specialist gynaecologists would draw the line somewhere. For instance, few are willing to conduct abortions right up to term. Usually the precise conscientious views of gynaecologists and other doctors on the matter of abortion are not known to other doctors.

The implications for doctors who have a conscientious objection to abortion is that a patient, who was not referred to a doctor known not to have a conscientious objection, could lodge a complaint of misconduct to the regulator who might then bring a finding of misconduct. If the doctor held to his or her beliefs and refused to change his or her practice, that could have serious consequences for his or her right to practise medicine in Victoria. The medical insurers have also indicated that they will not indemnify doctors who are caught in this situation of acting in violation of the law.

This has very serious implications, especially for doctors in training and doctors at the start of their profession. The law threatens the traditional understanding that there is a right to freedom of conscience in the practice of medicine. As the law has effect on practice, those who do conscientiously object will find it difficult to complete their training in medicine and, if they do complete, they will find it difficult to find employment, given that their conscience obliges them to act in violation of the law. In time that will have a profound effect on the practice of medicine as those who are prolife will be forced out of medical practice.

Section 8(3) of the Act, also involves difficulties for conscientious medical practitioners. Where pregnancy risks the life of a woman, there are usually options that can be pursued to treat the condition, including sometimes options that may risk the life of the unborn child. The Act does not leave the doctor with that discretion, but instead specifies abortion.

Even more troubling, however, is the situation of nurses under section 8(4). They are obliged to assist a registered medical practitioner in performing an abortion in an emergency where the abortion is necessary to preserve the life of the pregnant woman. It needs to be born in mind that it could be considered such an emergency because the woman may consider suicide if the pregnancy is not ended. The provision means in practice that the judgement of the doctor overrides the judgement of the nurse, so that if the doctor considers it an emergency then the nurse must assist. There is no respect in this for the professional judgement and the professional conscience of nurses.

An example of the impact of this provision is the case of a graduate nurse, mentioned earlier, who applied for and was offered a position at a major public hospital in Melbourne was informed that she could not be given a position if she conscientiously objected to abortion because the law may require her to assist in abortions. Again that means that nurses who have conscientious views on abortion are being forced out of the profession.

The effect of these qualifications on conscientious objection in the Act are thus having a profound effect on who can practice medicine and nursing in Victoria. Similar effects may also be felt by psychologists and pharmacists who may have a role in the practice of abortion. Pharmacists may find themselves in difficulty, particularly, as no medical prescription is needed now for the morning after pill, one of the effects of which is to cause an embryo to be shed if fertilization has occurred. Pharmacists supply the morning after pill over the counter and not to do so and not to refer to another pharmacist places them in violation of the law. Psychologists may have a role in counselling in relation to abortion and they also may be required to refer against their firmly held moral beliefs.

11.4 Amending the Act

The *Abortion Law Reform Act* Section 8 does recognize the right to conscientiously object. The problem is the qualifications of the right. This is a separate issue from abortion. It does not limit a woman's access to abortion to uphold the right to conscientiously object. Abortion is available and known to be available from several centres in Melbourne, including some of the public hospitals, as well as well-known private abortion clinics. There is also no referral necessary to access abortion. A woman can simply attend one of the clinics.

This issue is whether the Victorian Parliament upholds the freedom of conscience, thought and belief recognized in international law and protected by both local and international professional codes of ethics. The situation created by the Act is an anomaly and could easily be repaired by amendment to section 8 of the Act. This is a basic issue of respect for human dignity that a person be free to act according to his or her own conscience. That is a separate issue from the legality or otherwise of abortion.

Amendment of the conscientious objection clause in the Act does however need to be carefully worded to reflect the need to balance the right to conscientiously object against the needs of a patient to know the availability of lawful services, and for the exercise of the right not to be overly disruptive in the provision of lawful services. If a practitioner is withdrawing for conscientious reasons, then the patient has a right to know that the service is available from other practitioners and an employer needs to be informed in reasonable time to be able to arrange others to provide the service and to organize rosters and the like.

It is also important that in protecting the right to conscientious objection, there is a no disadvantage clause for the person who objects; otherwise the right is not in fact protected. This is an important element in the NHMRC wording of its clause which states, "Clinics must also ensure that staff and students are not disadvantaged because of a conscientious objection".

Any amendment of the law needs to include the above elements.

Finally, there are circumstances in which pregnancy physically endangers the woman's life. Conscientious objection should not extend to not responding to the needs of a woman whose life is endangered. However, in the alternatives that they offer a woman in those circumstances, health practitioners need to be able to exercise their professional discretion and the law should not be prescriptive. These can be very difficult decisions in which to save the life of a woman, the unborn child's life may be endangered. Often what is called "double effect reasoning" is applied, which justifies such intervention. The Act currently prescribes abortion in sections 8(3) and 8(4) and the abortion is very widely defined in the Act. It would be better if the clause simply allowed the health practitioner to exercise discretion in relation to providing assistance necessary to protect the woman's life.

As a matter of political reality, it would also seem that an amendment would be likely to succeed if it did only what was necessary to protect freedom of conscience. Retaining the protection that section 8 currently affords for freedom of conscience would also seem to be important.

There is a need to amend the Act to remove the problems that it poses for freedom of conscience, but maintaining the balance needed for patients and health service employers who may be affected by the exercise of that right.

It would seem necessary that the law require that a health practitioner conscientiously objecting should

> (a) inform the woman that other practitioners may be prepared to provide the service that she has requested; and
>
> (b) notify an employer in a reasonably timely manner of his or her conscientious objection without the employer or the employer's agent causing disadvantage as a result of his or her conscientious objection.

Despite any conscientious objection to abortion, a registered health practitioner is under a duty to provide assistance necessary to preserve the life of the pregnant woman. It is important that conscientious objection not endanger the woman's life.

I was puzzled by the recent Irish case reportedly involving a woman dying because doctors would not assist after she had begun to miscarry. The reports were that she then developed septicaemia and died. The Church was blamed, but I could not see why they could not have intervened to treat the pathology, even if that indirectly resulted in earlier delivery of the child and his or her death. It all seemed very confused in the reporting.

It would be consistent with respect for freedom of conscience and the need to protect life to have a clause worded:

> Despite any conscientious objection to abortion, a registered health practitioner is under a duty to provide assistance necessary to preserve the life of the pregnant woman.

Sadly the Tasmanian Health Department has released a new Bill which is similar to the Victorian Act but goes further by imposing severe penalties on those who do not refer. In addition, counsellors, including volunteers, may also be heavily penalised if they do not refer. The offence would put at risk, not only pregnancy counsellors, but also ministers of religion, priests, rabbis, imams and pastoral workers.

12

Post Coital Intervention: "Emergency Contraception", "The Morning After Pill", or "Contragestion"[192]

12.1 From Fear of Pregnancy to Rape Crisis

In the practice of family medicine, women requesting what they usually call "the morning-after pill" often confront Catholic and pro-life physicians. This usually follows a broken or slipped condom or natural (unprotected) intercourse. The requests for post-coital intervention have arisen from concerted efforts to promote to young women the need to have post-coital hormonal intervention or "emergency contraception," as it is often called in such circumstances, to prevent pregnancy. Post-coital intervention is even made available without medical prescription in some jurisdictions, despite there being significant, relatively common medical contraindications and drug interactions.

A longer-standing problem has been the problem of rape crisis. Catholic rape crisis centres meeting the needs of women with dignity and compassion would seem to be an appropriate calling for Catholic health-care services. Yet in developed countries, there are few, if any, Catholic rape crisis centres. The obvious reason for Catholics to have withdrawn from that field is the lack of development of a morally acceptable alternative way of dealing with the risk of pregnancy following rape, in societies in which abortifacience is the recommended solution. Seemingly, Catholics and Catholic institutions wanting to abide by Church teaching have been frightened from the field.

---

192 This chapter was published as an article in *The National Catholic Bioethics Quarterly* 4.2 (2004): 275-288, and is reproduced here with permission. I was greatly assisted by Dr Mary Walsh who provided the case study from her own practice experience, reviewed the literature with me and edited the text.

12.2 Case Study

A patient, three months postpartum and breastfeeding, requested the "morning-after pill" (post-coital hormonal intervention to prevent ongoing pregnancy) after experiencing condom breakage on the previous evening. The birth of her child had occurred after she had had a similar event and been prescribed post-coital intervention which had failed.

It was unlikely that the previous night's event would result in pregnancy, given that she was breastfeeding, but she expressed a strong need for reassurance, her anxiety partly driven by the previous experience with combined condom and post-coital intervention failure.

Her circumstances led her general practitioner (GP) down an unexpected course. She decided to explore whether the patient's likely infertility could in fact be identified with certainty, thus avoiding the need for her concern and for any further action. The GP arranged for serum progesterone and oestrogen tests and contacted an endocrinologist whom she knew had a research interest in this area. He was able to inform her that the test results indicated that the patient was not in the ovulatory phase of her cycle, the oestrogen levels being far lower than would be the case if she were in a fertile phase, and the progesterone so low as to indicate that she was not immediately postovulatory. The GP was able to offer her the reassurance that there was little if any likelihood that she could become pregnant from the event of the broken condom.

This episode raises the question as to whether, on many of the occasions that the "morning-after pill" is requested, its use would needlessly expose women to its side-effects, discomfort, and disruption. There is the option of serum or urine ovarian hormone testing to determine whether the patient was in a fertile phase at the time of the incident. Luteinizing hormone tests might also be used but are much less informative and less reliable than testing progesterone levels (see discussion below).

In the discussions with endocrinologists that followed, it emerged that there are nonabortifacient alternatives in post-coital intervention. The use of oestrogen-only formulations to delay ovulation, well tried in the development of the oral contraceptive pill, would seem to be a morally acceptable defence against the pregnancy effect of rape. Unlike the combined progesterone-oestrogen formulation in the Yuzpe regimen, or the newer progesterone-only formulations (such as Postinor-2), a moderate dose of oestrogen would not disrupt the endometrium and potentially cause embryo loss (see discussion below).

12.3 A Common Problem

The requests for post-coital intervention often arise from condom mishaps. Catholic doctors find themselves embroiled in a mess largely made by government and other public health education efforts directed at young people and aimed at so-called "harm minimization," which largely avoid the central issue of avoiding the medical and moral personal disasters created by early sexual initiation and sex outside marriage.

Condoms are presented as the universal safety precaution. But even with perfect use to avoid pregnancy the medical evidence indicates a Pearl index for pregnancy for condoms between three and fifteen per hundred woman-years.[193]

Studies on perfect condom use are usually done on adults, there being ethical difficulties with undertaking such a study on teenagers. Consequently, it is much more difficult to obtain condom effectiveness figures for teenagers. Teenagers lack experience, may be more likely to be experimenting, and, often enough, change partners relatively frequently. One would expect condom efficacy in relation to pregnancy and disease to be different in teenagers.

In a major study on condom use by two hundred sexually active girls between the ages of 14-21, median 17 years, M. Christ *et al* found that a very high proportion reported problems with condoms in the past year, 3 per cent had experienced a condom breaking, 39.5 per cent had experienced a condom falling off, and 6 per cent had become pregnant with a condom. Eighty-five per cent reported negative experiences, including broken condoms or condoms falling off, pregnancy, condom painful or too tight, unpleasant smell, interrupted sex, and reduced sensation.[194]

---

[193] Willard Cates Jr., "Contraception, Unintended Pregnancies and Disease: Why Isn't a Simple Solution Possible?", *American Journal of Epidemiology*, 143.4 (1996); John Murtagh, *General Practice*, 2nd ed. (Melbourne: McGraw-Hill, 1998).

[194] Michael Christ, William V. Raszka Jr., and Christopher Dillon, "Prioritizing Education about Condom Use among Sexually Active Adolescent Females," *Adolescence* 33.132 (Winter 1998): 735–744.

Avoiding pregnancy and disease are justifiably a major source of worry for sexually active adolescents, but condoms do not alleviate that worry. Their experience with condoms often does not tally with the assurances that educators often give that condomised sex is safe. In general practice, girls often present distressed, requesting assistance after natural (unprotected) intercourse or after a condom problem has occurred.

12.4 Post-Coital Intervention

Post-coital intervention may be given as a double dose of one of the higher dose combined pills taken twelve hours apart, the so-called "Yuzpe regimen." It normally causes a shedding of the endometrium resulting in loss of the embryo if fertilization occurs in that cycle. The Yuzpe regimen may also suppress or delay ovulation. This latter contraceptive effect would, of course, be ineffective in preventing fertilization, if ovulation was occurring or had already occurred at the time of the intervention. In that case, the regimen's effect would be on nidation (implantation).[195]

It is unlikely that the Yuzpe regimen would cause changes to the cervical mucus sufficient to prevent sperm completely from reaching the fallopian tube. Even the normal natural rise in progesterone, which begins eight hours before ovulation, does not prevent residual channelling in the cervix, which is capable of allowing the passage of sperm on the third day after the rise in progesterone and the peak day of mucus.[196]

More commonly, a progesterone-only formulation (marketed as Postinor-2 in Australia) is being advocated for post-coital intervention. The manufacturer is vague about the method of action of the main

---

195 D.C. Stewart, "Contraception," in *Adolescent Medicine*, eds. A.D. Hofmann and D.E. Greydanus, 3rd ed. (Stamford, CT: Appleton & Lange, 1997), 566–588; G. Hewitt and B. Cromer, "Update on Adolescent Contraception," *Obstetrics and Gynecology Clinics of North America* 27. (March 2000): 143–162; American Academy of Pediatrics, Committee on Adolescence, "Contraception and Adolescents", *Pediatrics* 104.5 (November 1999): 1161–1166.
196 Evelyn L. Billings and John J. Billings, *Teaching the Billings Ovulation Method*, part 2, *Variations of the Cycle and Reproductive Health* (Melbourne: Ovulation Method Research and Reference Centre, 1997), 45, citing Erik Odeblad.

ingredient, levonorgestrel. There are three main possibilities:[197]

- altering the lining of the uterus so that the embryo, when it reaches the uterus at about six days old, cannot implant;
- preventing ovulation (likely to be less than a 33 per cent chance of preventing ovulation and may be as low as 19 per cent[198]);
- preventing the sperm from reaching the ovum by altering the production of mucus-carrying sperm in the cervix (the neck of the womb).

The first is not a contraceptive effect but an abortifacient effect. High doses of levonorgestrel have been shown by electron-microscope scanning of the endometrial surface to cause detectable changes affecting the receptivity of the endometrial surface.[199] The impact of those changes would be to prevent the implantation of the embryo, which takes place when the embryo has reached the stage at which differentiation of the cells into organs has just begun (at least 4-6 days old).

Preventing ovulation will not happen in most women following Postinor-2 use. The main ingredient in the combined contraceptive pill that prevents ovulation is oestrogen. Postinor-2 is progesterone only (levonorgestrel) and has a reduced effect on preventing ovulation.[200]

If preventing or delaying ovulation was all that was wanted, then a

---

197 See a review of the effects of oral contraceptive pills in Nicholas Tonti-Filippini, "The Pill: Abortifacient or Contraceptive? A Literature Review," *Linacre Quarterly* 62. (February 1995): 5–28.

198 I. Aref *et al*, "Effect of Minipills on Physiologic Responses of Human Cervical Mucus, Endometrium, and Ovary," *Journal of Fertility and Sterility*, 24.8 (August 1973): 578–583.

199 G. Ugocsai, M. Rózsa, and P. Ugocsai, "Scanning Electron Microscopic (SEM) Changes of the Endometrium in Women Taking High Doses of Levonorgestrel as Emergency Postcoital Contraception," *Contraception*, 66.6 (December 2002): 433–437.

200 Ibid. Note that there has been little research interest since early on in the oral contraceptive pill development in identifying the precise effects. The manufacturers have been content to be vague and not to distinguish between antinidation and contraceptive effects. The most recent product information simply states that the precise mechanism is unknown.

moderate dose of oestrogen is all that would be required. The ovulation-delaying effect of estradiol benzoate in oil was known as early as 1928 and well-known in the 1930s and '40s when it was used as a treatment for a variety of hormonal disorders. Its ovulation-delaying effect was a major focus in the early development of the contraceptive pill before the synthetic progesterones became available and Gregory Goodwin Pincus, Frank Colton, and others developed the combined pill. Estradiol benzoate reliably delayed ovulation, but an oestrogen-only pill was never marketed because many women would ovulate soon after the oestrogen was stopped at day twenty-one. It was only when the progesterone was added that ceasing the active pills at day twenty-one reliably produced bleeding rather than ovulation.[201] There is no evidence that oestrogen has abortifacient effects. The effect of oestrogen on the endometrium is to promote its development.

Taking oestrogen only would be likely to prevent pregnancy from occurring from an act the night before, provided that ovulation and fertilization had not already occurred.[202] To meet the needs of rape victims, there is a need for greater research on treatments that affect ovulation and sperm transport without affecting the endometrium. An oestrogen-only post-coital intervention would be less effective than the Yuzpe regime or the high dose of levonorgestrel, but only because it would not also be abortifacient. If the moral requirement were to limit intervention to contraception and not abortifacience then there would be no justification for taking either the combined or the progesterone-only formulations.

One of the acknowledged possible affects of levonorgestrel is a higher incidence of ectopic pregnancy, possibly due to its effect on the cilia in the fallopian tube, which are involved in the transit of the embryo.[203] This adds to the moral and medical concern about using it. Its use would be

---

201 This information was given to me by Emeritus Professor James B. Brown (endocrinology, University of Melbourne), who himself was involved in the work on the estrogens and had worked with Pinkus at that time. Conversation with author, March 5, 2004.
202 Professor James B. Brown, conversation with author, June 2002.
203 G. Sheffer-Mimouni *et al*, "Ectopic Pregnancies following Emergency Levonorgestrel Contraception," *Contraception*, 67.4 (April 2003): 267–269; D.A. Grimes and E.G. Raymond, "Emergency Contraception," *Annals of Internal Medicine*, 137.3 (August 6, 2002): 180–189.

irresponsible, potentially endangering the woman as well as the embryo. If it were not for the ideological commitment to abortion, there is no way that levonorgestrel would be medically permitted to be used post-coitally. It should be noted that there is no evidence available that oestrogen has an effect on the cilia and seemingly no reports of ectopic pregnancy associated with oestrogen use.

Preventing the sperm from reaching the ovum by altering the production of mucus-carrying sperm in the cervix is a known effect of progesterone if it is administered on a daily basis ahead of sexual intercourse. However, if intercourse happened the night before, it is a little late to try to prevent the passage of sperm if the woman is at a fertile time. The mucus channels that transport the sperm will already have been formed.[204] Sperm can be found within the fallopian tube within twenty minutes of sexual intercourse.

If the woman is in the period just prior to ovulation, some sperm may be stored in the crypts in the cervix.[205] One contraceptive possibility would be that the high levonorgestrel dose might trap those sperm by changing the character of the cervical mucus. However, a search of the literature yielded no publications to support that claim.

There has been some suggestion that levonorgestrel might affect the sperm itself. Some changes to straight-line velocity of sperm and to sperm-oocyte fusion have been observed in sperm treated with levonorgestrel but only at high concentration. W. Yeung *et al* conclude that these effects are not likely to contribute significantly to emergency contraception.[206]

There have also been suggestions that the effect on the cilia and contractions of the fallopian tube might so delay the transit of the embryo that, when it arrives at the endometrium, nidation cannot occur due to the later arrival of the blastocyst. I can find no publications or research finding that would support this suggestion.

---

204 Professor James Brown, conversation with author, 23 June 2002.
205 The function of the crypts and the cervical mucus have been well described by E. Odeblad *et al*, "The Dynamic Mosaic Model of the Human Ovulatory Cervical Mucus," *Proceedings of the Nordic Fertility Society* (Umea, Sweden, January 1978).
206 W.S.B. Yeung *et al*, "The Effects of Levonorgestrel on Various Sperm Functions," *Contraception* 66.6 (December 2002): 453-457.

From this it would appear that the abortifacient effect, destroying a six-day-old embryo, is the most likely effect of Postinor-2. The postfertilization effects thus have implications in such areas as informed consent, emergency department protocols, and conscience clauses.[207] This is especially significant for Catholic hospitals.

A Catholic, or at least pro-life, rape crisis centre ought not to include post-coital preparations containing only levonorgestrel as an option, given its abortifacient effects and the availability of other options that are not abortifacient or are at least less abortifacient. The Yuzpe regime is more likely to be contraceptive than the progesterone-only formulation, but only if administered prior to ovulation. At the time of ovulation or after ovulation, the effectiveness of the combined oestrogen and progesterone formulation relies on anti-nidation.

Since a woman is infertile most of the cycle, there is an issue whether post-coital intervention is in fact unnecessary. The Yuzpe regimen and the levonorgestrel alternative are not without significant medical side effects. They are certainly not recommended as a routine way of controlling fertility.

If it were possible to identify that:

a) an act of intercourse in the previous twenty-four hours could not have resulted in fertilization;
b) ovulation and hence possible fertilization might yet occur in the near future unless there is intervention; or
c) ovulation had already occurred and the ovum was already likely to have been exposed to sperm, and that fertilization, if it was to occur, had already occurred;

then this would seem to be useful information to determine whether any intervention is necessary and to allow the woman to make an informed moral choice based on identifying the morally significant aspects of the options made available to her in a society that accepts the practice of abortifacience.

---

207 C. Kahlenborn, J.B. Stanford and W.L. Larimore, "Postfertilization Effect of Hormonal Emergency Contraception," *Annals of Pharmacotherapy* 36.3 (March 2002): 465-470.

12.5 Identifying Fertile and Infertile Phases

The search for reliable methods of natural family planning has resulted in the capacity to identify the infertile and the possibly fertile phases of the cycle, and ovulation. A woman's own observation of the presence of mucus at the vulva, and the sensation it produces, allows her to recognize when she is infertile, when possibly fertile, and the occurrence of ovulation.

The phases of the cycle are also identifiable by testing for urine estrone glucuronide and urine pregnanediol glucuronide using the Brown monitor.[208] The Brown monitor was designed as a home kit. It is my understanding that it may not be so readily available in the United States and there has been some difficulty with the availability of the reagents since Prof Brown's death that is expected to be soon overcome when Prof Len Blackwell and Dr Andrew Thomas complete arrangements for commercial supply.

Serum testing of estradiol and progesterone also can be used to confirm the phases of a woman's cycle. In our experience, if the request is specified as urgent, a result can be obtained from a pathology laboratory within two to four hours.

Much of the literature on this topic tends to focus on testing for luteinizing hormone (LH). It should be noted that the progesterone test is far more reliable and much more informative. LH indicates only that the pituitary is sending it out to attempt to cause the follicle to rupture, and that may or may not be successful, and the ovary's response may or may not be delayed. There is ample evidence of luteinized unruptured follicles. When that happens, the woman does not ovulate then but may progress to ovulate at a later time when there is subsequent LH surge within that cycle. The progesterone level

---

208 J.B. Brown, "Timing of Ovulation," *Medical Journal of Australia* 2 (1977): 780–783; J.B. Brown *et al*, "New Assays for Identifying the Fertile Period," *International Journal of Gynaecology & Obstetrics* 1.suppl. (1989): 111–122; J.B. Brown, J. Holmes, and G. Barker, "Use of the Home Ovarian Monitor in Pregnancy Avoidance," *American Journal of Obstetrics and Gynecology* 165.6 (December 1991): 2008–2011; S.J. Thornton, R.J. Pepperell, and J.B. Brown, "Home Monitoring of Gonadotropin Ovulation Induction Using the Ovarian Monitor," *Fertility and Sterility* 54.6 (December 1990): 1076–82; L.F. Blackwell, J.B. Brown, and D.G. Cooke, "Definition of the Potentially Fertile Period from Urinary Steroid Excretion Rates: Part II: A Threshold Value for Pregnanediol Glucuronide as a Marker for the End of the Potentially Fertile Period in the Human Menstrual Cycle," *Steroids* 63.(January 1998): 5–13.

indicates the ovary's response to the LH surge and the precise timing of ovulation. Higher levels also conclusively indicate that the woman is in the postovulatory infertile phase. Relying on LH testing is a bit like asking parents what they told the child to do, rather than simply observing what the child is doing. The progesterone rise is a precise indicator of ovulation, the LH surge is an indication of the pituitary's attempt to cause ovulation.[209]

The oestrogen test is vital for precisely determining whether the woman has entered a potentially fertile phase. The progesterone test is vital for determining when ovulation occurs and the end of the potentially fertile phase.

It is our view that a Catholic rape crisis centre providing post-coital intervention would have an obligation to ensure that it had the capacity to undertake serum oestrogen and progesterone tests or urine estrone glucuronide and pregnanediol glucuronide tests, or at least to have rapid access to the tests by another agency.

Macroscopic analysis on internal examination can identify whether cervical mucus is present and whether it is of a consistency that indicates possible fertility. Low power microscopic analysis of the cervical mucus would confirm the mucus type,[210] but obtaining the sample (in a procedure similar to obtaining a sample for a Pap-smear test) does require experience.

Finally, ultrasound can be used to identify ovulation.

Working independently,

- Professor James Brown, charting the ovarian hormonal levels and correlating them with the women's charting of when intercourse occurred in relation to pregnancy occurring, established the relation between the ovarian and pituitary hormones and the different phases of the cycle.[211]
- Professor Erik Odeblad undertook biophysical assays of cervical mucus and identified the roles of the different types of cervical mucus in fertility and infertility.[212]

---

209 Professor James B. Brown, conversation with author, 5 March 2004.
210 Odeblad *et al*, "The Dynamic Mosaic Model."
211 See J.B. Brown in note 16 above.
212 Odeblad *et al*, "The Dynamic Mosaic Model."

- Drs. Evelyn and John Billings studied women's observations of their symptoms and correlating those charted observations of the mucus symptom with whether pregnancy resulted from sexual intercourse during the different phases of mucus symptom.[213] They devised a set of rules to avoid or achieve pregnancy on that empirical basis. According to the standards of evidence-based medicine, the Billings rules to avoid pregnancy have a method-related Pearl Index of 0–2.2 pregnancies per hundred woman-years in initiates.[214]

When these three areas of research were combined, they were mutually reaffirming, and each complemented the other in developing a full understanding of the relationship between the cervix, follicular development, and ovulation. Between them, the Billings, Brown, and Odeblad have reviewed hundreds of thousands of women's cycles. More than 750 cycles

---

[213] E.L. Billings, "The Simplicity of the Ovulation Method and Its Application in Various Circumstances," *Acta Europaea Fertilitatis* 22.(January–February 1991): 33–36; J.J. Billings, "The Validation of the Billings Ovulation Method by Laboratory Research and Field Trials," *Acta Europaea Fertilitatis* 22.(January–February 1991): 9–15; E.L. Billings and Ann Westmore, *The Billings Ovulation Method* (Melbourne: Anne O'Donovan P/L, 1998).

[214] The three major trials of the Billings Ovulation Method (BOM) (used to avoid pregnancy): a) World Health Organization (WHO) (1977–1981) Task Force on Methods for the Determination of the Fertile Period, Special Programme of Research, Development and Research Training in Human Reproduction. Multicenter–Auckland, Dublin, San Miguel, Bangalore and Manila. 869 women, 10,215 cycles of use, 2.2 method-related pregnancies per hundred woman-years in initiates (2.8 when initial phase excluded). "A Prospective Multicentre Trial of the Ovulation Method of Natural Family Planning: I. The Teaching Phase," *Fertility and Sterility* 36 (1981): 152ff; "A Prospective Multicentre Trial of the Ovulation Method of Natural Family Planning: II. The Effectiveness Phase," 36 (1981): 591ff. b) Indian Council of Medical Research Task Force on NFP (1995). States of Uttar Pradesh, Bihar, Rajasthan, Karnataka and Pondicherry. 2,059 women, 32,957 woman-months of use, 0.86 Method-related pregnancies per hundred woman-years in initiates. "Field Trial of Billings Ovulation Method of Natural Family Planning," *Contraception* 53.2 (February 1996): 69–74. c) Jiangsu Family Health Institute (1997). China. 1,235 women, 14,280 woman-months of use, No method-related pregnancies in initiates (5 user-related pregnancies). Shao Zhen Qian and De-Wei Zhang, "Evaluation of the Effectiveness of a Natural Fertility Regulation Program in China," *Bulletin of the Ovulation Method Research and Reference Centre* 24.4 (2000): 17–22.

have been monitored for ovarian hormone levels and contrasted with the women's charting of the mucus sensation at the vulva.

It is possible to offer to women who are in distress over an event that happened during the previous twenty-four hours, and which they fear may result in pregnancy, the possibility of identifying whether they are in fact infertile, or alternatively, whether they may conceive or may already have conceived.

Table 1, which is appended to the end of the chapter, was developed with assistance from Professor Brown, Dr John Billings, and Dr Evelyn Billings, describes the woman's cervical mucus symptoms and what might be found if an internal examination were to be done. An examination is often done for forensic purposes after rape. If a woman had been charting her symptoms, it would be unnecessary to undertake further examination or testing, but she might want further confirmation or, as is the norm unfortunately, she may be ignorant of her symptoms and how to interpret them.

Table 1 also shows serum estradiol and progesterone levels for each phase. Pathologists usually offer a service, including an after-hours service, for serum estradiol and progesterone testing. If marked "urgent," the result can be available in the same time that it takes to receive the results of early pregnancy tests (testing hCG), a matter of three or four hours.

Also shown in Table 1 are the urine estrone glucuronide and pregnanediol glucuronide ranges for the different phases of the cycle. If the woman, according to these indicators, falls into the areas of the preovulatory infertile phase or the luteal infertile phase, then she can be reassured that pregnancy is most unlikely from an event occurring during the previous twenty-four hours. It would be possible, if thought necessary, to add an ultrasound examination of the ovaries to gain further confirmation of the stage or absence of follicular development and whether or not ovulation was about to or had occurred recently, but either serum or urinary results would be sufficient.

From Table 1, it is evident that a woman who has a serum estradiol less than 440 pmol/L and serum progesterone less than 4.9 nmol/L, or a serum progesterone greater than 12 nmol/L, is in an infertile phase of her cycle. These figures are conservative, erring on the side of caution. There is a grey area when the progesterone is between 7 and 12 nmol/L which further research may narrow.

The symptoms of a woman who is charting would indicate whether she has ovulated. This information would more precisely identify the possibly fertile period. A woman who is charting adequately would not need confirmatory serum or urine testing. Though not trained to chart, a woman may nevertheless be able to provide some details of her cycle during the history-taking. The doctor may rely on this in conjunction with an examination and the blood or urine tests. A second blood or urine test taken a day later would also define more precisely the direction of the trend in serum or urine values, providing a basis for a more precise assessment. This is not necessary to identify whether a single act of sexual intercourse in the previous twenty-four hours may result in pregnancy, but it would provide more information for the woman and possibly greater reassurance.

It should also be confirmed with the woman that there were not earlier incidents by which she may have conceived.

A WHO study on identifying fertility by the mucus symptom showed that the probability of pregnancy in relation to the peak day (determined by the mucus symptom alone) was:

- if there is slippery mucus: 0.67 if intercourse occurred on peak day, 0.5 one day before peak day, 0.5 one to three days before peak day;
- if there is only sticky mucus, 0.5 on peak day, 0.4 one day after peak day, 0.2 two days after peak day, and 0.three days after peak day.

Outside the fertile period (commencement of mucus change to three days after peak day) the probability of pregnancy was 0.004.[215] The latter figure is especially significant for these purposes.

Most recently, D. Dunson *et al* studied the daily probability of intercourse resulting in pregnancy for each day of what they called the fertile window. Their study involved 782 healthy couples and 5,869 menstrual cycles. They

---

215 World Health Organization Task Force on Methods for the Determination of the Fertile Period, Special Programme of Research, Development and Research Training in Human Reproduction, "A Prospective Multicentre Trial of the Ovulation Method of Natural Family Planning: III. Characteristics of the Menstrual Cycle and of the Fertile Phase," *Fertility and Sterility* 40 (1983): 773–778.

used a rise in basal body temperature (BBT) (retrospectively) to recognize that ovulation had occurred. Nearly all pregnancies occurred within a six-day window, with peak fertility occurring two days before the day of temperature rise.[216]

The corresponding WHO data for the Billings Ovulation Method (above) indicate that the peak day as identified by the mucus symptom may be a slightly stronger indicator of peak fertility than the BBT rise minus two days, with a greater probability (0.67) of pregnancy resulting from intercourse on the peak day in the WHO study compared to probability (0.5) of pregnancy from intercourse two days before the BBT rise in the Dunson study for the most fertile age group, and lower probabilities for the older groups. However, there may be sampling differences.

Ovarian hormone testing gives a very accurate picture of what is happening in the woman's cycle. This is useful either to confirm the woman's own knowledge of her cycle, or in the absence of such knowledge, to determine whether or not she is at a potentially fertile phase of her cycle.

In the circumstance of rape, one would expect that it would be particularly reassuring for a woman who is in either of the infertile phases to be told that her cervix is closed with a G-mucus plug and that her vagina is naturally hostile to sperm. The information would also be reassuring for women following any unplanned exposure to the risk of pregnancy.

With this knowledge it becomes clear that one would have no need to use post-coital intervention during either of the infertile phases. Further, one can identify with some precision whether ovulation has occurred or is imminent, and thus, the time at which the contraceptive effect of the post-coital intervention would no longer be operable and the effect of preventing a birth would result from the abortifacient action of the post-coital intervention.

12.6 An Alternative to the Abortifacience

That leaves the period of possible fertility prior to ovulation. A double dose of a high-dose combined progesterone and oestrogen pill might not be the

---

[216] D.B. Dunson, B. Colombo, and D.D. Baird, "Changes with Age in the Level and Duration of the Menstrual Cycle," *Human Reproduction* 17.5 (May 2002): 1399–1403.

treatment of choice if the aim were only to achieve contraceptive cover for the previous evening's happening. It is relatively easy to delay or suppress ovulation beyond the stage at which intercourse in the previous twenty-four hours might result in pregnancy.

In my discussion with him, Professor Brown suggested that an obvious agent to use to delay ovulation (given the early research on the pill) would be a single, moderate dose of oestrogen only. This would be unlikely to cause harm to the pregnancy if ovulation had already occurred and would be unlikely to cause significant problems for the woman, especially if a natural oestrogen were used – though there needs to be some further exploration of this possibility and even a trial to see what dosage would be required. It should, however, be born in mind that there is a dearth of well-researched information about the effects of the existing post-coital interventions and their actions. More is known about the ovulation-delaying effects of a moderate dose of oestrogen, which were widely researched over an extensive period prior to the development of the combined pill, than about the dosage and pharmacological effects of a double dose of the combined pill repeated over two days, or of a large dose of a progesterone-only formulation.

12.7 Managing Pregnancy Scares

The information about identifying the phases of the woman's cycle is very useful for those who ask for the morning-after pill after a condom mishap or natural sexual intercourse. A first step in such cases is to attempt to exclude the possibility that the woman is already pregnant. Second, by taking a history and undertaking a clinical examination and, if necessary, testing the ovarian hormones (by blood test or by urine analysis), the doctor could tell her whether pregnancy from the recent event would be improbable (see table 1). Most of the time it is. The doctor could also tell her if pregnancy is possible on this occasion and, if so, discuss the implications with her at this early stage.

In most instances, knowing that pregnancy is improbable, the woman can choose to avoid the unpleasantness – the nausea, vomiting, severe abdominal pain and cramping, and heavy bleeding – of the post-coital intervention, and the moral and psychological issue in relation to having done something possibly abortifacient. By using knowledge of the ovulatory cycle, the woman can be freed of anxiety in many instances and perhaps learn something about her physiology and reproductive health—information which few women appear to have.[217]

In practice, it makes sense to offer women who request the "morning-after pill" the option of a serum test for oestrogen and progesterone levels and the possibility of being able to determine whether in fact pregnancy would be an improbable outcome without intervention. This option not only avoids the difficulties of the morning-after pill, it also assists the woman to better understand her own fertility and infertility.

A Catholic doctor may not formally cooperate in evil by prescribing contraception to prevent pregnancy, and especially not abortifacients. In the circumstances of a request for post-coital intervention, by taking steps to identify the likelihood of fertility or infertility, the doctor can narrow down the dilemma to a much smaller number of cases. In doing so, the doctor can develop a much better understanding of the woman and her needs and take the opportunity of the interaction to give her sound medical advice about the difficulties created by sexual intercourse outside of a relationship within which a child would be welcomed. This can be an exercise in much needed primary health care, especially in relation to the increasing incidence of sexually transmissible infection.

12.8 Rape Crisis

Providing care and support to those who have been raped is properly a function of Catholic health facilities. The medical component of that care needs to address the physical and mental trauma, and it needs to deal with the risks of pregnancy and of sexually transmissible disease.

In our societies where there are many immoral technological options that are lawfully offered, Catholic practitioners or facilities, for their own protection, need to make plain, publicly and on the occasion in which assistance is sought, that the service is conducted according to Catholic moral principles especially with respect to abortifacients, and that such services, though available elsewhere, will not be available from the facility.

---

217 D. Blake *et al*, "Fertility Awareness in Women Attending a Fertility Clinic," *Australian and New Zealand Journal of Obstetrics and Gynaecology* 37.3 (1997): 350.

Information is a particular need for a woman who has been raped. Offering the her pregnancy testing (testing for human chorionic gonadotrophin), in case she is already pregnant, and testing for ovarian hormone levels can provide her with valuable information. In particular, it would be reassuring for her to know, as would usually be the case, that she was at an infertile time, and the cervix was blocked with mucus that prevents sperm and diminishes the chances of sexually transmissible infection. Given that any technology can malfunction, it is important that she is also told the level of reliability of the tests offered.

It has long been accepted by orthodox Catholic moral theologians that it is legitimate in the circumstances of rape to attempt contraception as a defence against the effects of the aggressor, including the presence in her body of his sperm. The goods of the marriage relationship that are destroyed by contraception do not exist in the circumstances of rape.

However, once fertilization has occurred, then there is the matter of a new life having formed. By determining whether ovulation has yet occurred, it is possible to differentiate between contraception and abortifacience. A Catholic rape crisis facility could confidently reassure most that post-coital hormonal intervention is unnecessary, after determining this by testing the ovarian hormone levels and taking a history. If the woman's cycle is in a fertile phase approaching ovulation, Brown suggests that a moderate dose of an oestrogen-only formulation could be offered to delay ovulation beyond the capacity of the sperm to survive. Further research would determine with greater certainty the effectiveness of oestrogen in that application, using contemporary standards of analysis. At no stage of the cycle would it be morally appropriate to use a treatment that also contained progesterone, given the probability of its antinidation effect on the endometrium. The use of levonorgestrel as a post-coital intervention is never morally appropriate.

In rape crisis, the option of combining ovarian hormone testing, medical counselling and nonabortifacient contraceptive interventions would need to be integrated within complete professional support for a woman so violently used. It would also be important that the woman be informed that a Catholic or pro-life agency would manage her care differently from the way in which it may be managed elsewhere. A Catholic agency would do nothing that would endanger embryonic human life.

TABLE One: Determining whether pregnancy is unlikely when sexual intercourse has occurred in previous twenty-four hours

Menstrual Phase

Basic Infertile Pattern – Woman reporting dry sensation at vulva or unchanging discharge and no change yet this cycle. Clinical examination not necessary but if being done (for forensic purposes?), no strings of mucus should be seen macroscopically. Microscopic analysis of a sample taken from the cervix (by experienced doctor) would show G-type mucus.

Serum and Urine Confirmation:

Serum oestradiol < 440 pmol/L

Urine oestrone glucuronide less than 100 nmol/24hrs

Serum progesterone level < 4.9 nmol/L

Urine pregnanediol glucuronide < 4 micromol/24hrs

ADVISE PATIENT PREGNANCY MOST UNLIKELY IF INTERCOURSE <24HRS BEFORE

Possible Fertile Phase

Change at vulva to moist or slippery sensation. L and/or S-type mucus in cervix possibly with motile sperm

Serum oestradiol > 440 pmol/L Serum progesterone 0.5 - 4.9 nmol/L

Urine oestrone glucuronide >150 nmol/24hrs

Urine pregnanediol glucuronide < 7 micromol/24hrs

Peak Day - S, L and P Mucus on exam Very slippery sensation at vulva

Following three days after peak Dry sensation at vulva. G and some S mucus in cervix on clinical examination. Serum progesterone < 7 nmol/L

Luteal Phase

Dry or sticky sensation (not wet or slippery)

G-mucus in cervix

Serum progesterone > 12 nmol/L

Urine pregnanediol glucuronide > 12 micromol/24hrs

ADVISE PATIENT PREGNANCY MOST UNLIKELY IF INTERCOURSE <24HRS BEFORE

13
When Pregnancy is a Maternal Danger: The Lysaught Opinion

13.1 Introduction

Sometimes, particularly in early pregnancy, the circumstances are such that abortion is medically recommended to reduce the dangers for the mother of continued pregnancy when the pregnancy complicates the treatment of another life threatening condition. It may even be that the woman is advised that without abortion both she and the child are likely to die, and only by abortion can the mother be saved. This is sometimes called a "vital conflict."

The cases often described as necessitating abortion include: severe pre-eclampsia, acute leukaemia and some forms of cancer where the effects of the pregnancy on the maternal immune system hasten the development of a potentially fatal cancer in the mother. Finally, there are also cases involving arrested labour and the recommendation that craniotomy, which kills the child by dismembering his or her skull and brain, is warranted. Such cases may be more likely to occur in developing countries where there are fewer options.

This type of circumstance has led to significant disagreements and even, in one case, the local Bishop removing the Catholic status of a hospital. The rest of this article has been reproduced from an article which is expected to be published soon in the *National Catholic Bioethics Quarterly*.

The opinion given by M. Therese Lysaught on the St Joseph's Hospital,

Phoenix case[218] (see hospital letter below) and the recent articles about it by Magill[219], Rhonheimer[220], Cavanaugh[221] and Austriaco[222] highlight a new division within Catholic thinking and it is important that it is discussed at a deeper level. Ostensibly the division is about the nature of the moral act and how we are to characterize the object of the act in the context of double effect reasoning. Austriaco characterises that division as between a hylomorphic account and an intentional account of human action. However, underlying that distinction is a much more fundamental difference over what morality is for a Christian: what it means for the object of an act to be capable of being oriented towards God and whether our ultimate end is communion with God and the beatific vision, on the one hand, or integral human fulfilment, on the other.

This issue is complex. The Lysaught opinion invokes several different lines of argument to support the opinion, rather than one consistent argument. In referring to Germain Grisez and Martin Rhonhemier to support the view, Lysaught is in fact referring to two very different approaches. Further, there is an element of Lysaught's opinion that is separate from both the Grisez and Rhonheimer positions, when she claims that the nature of the procedure known as a Dilation and Currettage (D&C) can be described as merely a procedure to remove the placenta and therefore not a direct assault on the unborn child. This line of argument is irrelevant to the positions adopted by Rhonheimer and Grisez.

---

218 Lysaught, M. Therese, "Moral Analysis of a Procedure at Phoenix Hospital", *Origins*, 27 January 2011, Vol 40, No. 33.
219 Magill, Gerard, Quaestio Disputanta, "Threat of Imminent Death in Pregnancy: A role for Double Effect Reasoning", *Theological Studies*, Vol 72, 2011, pp. 848-878.
220 Rhonheimer, Martin, "Vital Conflicts, Direct Killing, and Justice: A Response to Rev Benedict Guevin and Other Critics" *National Catholic Bioethics Quarterly* Autumn 2011 pp. 519-540.
221 Thomas A. Cavanaugh, "Double-Effect Reasoning, Craniotomy, and Vital Conflicts" *National Catholic Bioethics Quarterly*, Autumn 2011, pp. 453-462
222 Austriaco, Nicanor Pier Giorgio OP, "Abortion in a Case of Pulmonary Arterial Hypertension: A Test for Two Rival Theories of Human Action", *National Catholic Bioethics Quarterly*, Autumn 2011, pp. 503-518.

After a long historical analysis that does not adequately account for the differences between what Austriaco refers to as the hylomorphic and intentional theses, Magill's argument is to support Lysaught in arguing that the placenta is an organ in common between the child and the mother and its removal is not a direct assault on the child.

Whatever one thinks of this case, whether the hospital acted correctly in supporting the intervention or whether Bishop Thomas Olmstead was correct in his action in rescinding the hospital's Catholic status, the point of interest is the arguments used by both sides to the discussion, because the analysis of the moral act involved has much broader implications than this case, or even just abortion. I am uncomfortable about drawing conclusions about what the hospital or the Bishop did, because I am not in their position and inevitably I do not have the facts as they were presented to them.

In defence of the Bishop's action, it should be noted that, in his statement, his concerns with the hospital had a history over a seven year period and his decision was not based on this case alone but on a number of concerns about practices at the hospital that appeared to conflict with the Ethical and Religious Directives of the United States Conference of Catholic Bishops. That said, however it is not the decision by the hospital or by the Bishop that are the topic of our discussion, but Lysaught's analysis. As I have indicated there are three quite different claims to be addressed in Lysaught's analysis:

- Rhonheimer's claim that in the circumstances in which without intervention both will die but that by intervening the mother could be saved, the double effect reasoning does not apply, because the act is straightforwardly an act of rescue of the mother - the baby cannot be saved so his or her death is not the result of the intervention - no evil is caused by the intervention in that case. For Rhonheimer, intentionally causing a physical evil is also a *moral* evil insofar as it violates justice. The baby would die anyway in the case of a vital conflict, so its death is not a violation of justice and hence not a moral evil.

- Grisez's analysis of the nature of the moral act in the case of craniotomy, in which he argues that dismembering the child in order to remove the child is not direct killing and whether that is a parallel to D&C in this case. Grisez's argument is based on an analysis of the intention which he argues is not killing, because the death of the child is not needed to save the mother. The limit of the intention is to narrow the baby's head, not to kill the child. Thus on Grisez's account there is no direct intention to kill.
- Lysaught's claim that a D&C is not a direct assault on the child but on the placenta, it being the placenta that is the source of the problems.

Each of these arguments is invoked in favour of the decision to intervene, though they are not in fact one argument but three separate arguments.

Finally, Lysaught has provided an analysis of the facts of the case that lead to the judgement that intervention in this way is the only option to save the life of the mother – either the surgeon intervenes or both mother and baby will die. We are not in possession of all the facts in this case, so we cannot know whether that was indeed the case. I am wary of being presented with a scenario that appears so cut and dried. That is not my experience of medicine. Further, the medical literature does give accounts of managing pregnancy until at least viability, in the circumstances of pulmonary hypertension, when the child can be delivered alive if the pregnancy is a risk to the mother.

In her analysis, Lysaught does not discuss any possibility of alternative management of the hypertension. The facts as presented by her indicate a 100% double mortality rate without intervention. Anyone addressing an issue such as this would need first to know what the alternatives to the proposed intervention might be. It would certainly not be a case of standing by and doing nothing. A recent review concluded:

> When evaluating primary pulmonary hypertension and pregnancy, early studies reported a maternal mortality rate as high as 50%. More recent studies report a maternal mortality of 30%. In this

article, cases of primary pulmonary hypertension undergoing pregnancy from 1978 to 2005 were reviewed, revealing a 22% maternal mortality for the total number of pregnancies.[223]

Termination of pregnancy is an option but the standard texts refer to managing the condition in women who do not wish to terminate.[224, 225] The Lysaught account indicating 100% mortality if the pregnancy continued, does not describe what was being done to manage the condition and why it was not possible to manage the mother's condition at least to get to the stage where the child could survive early delivery. That said, it is important to address her moral argumentation on the facts as she presents them. Exceptions in medicine are not unheard of.

13.2 Direct and Indirect Abortion

The matter that Lysaught takes up in her analysis as the central point of difference between the St Joseph's Hospital and Bishop Olmstead, is whether the intervention was a case of direct abortion. She implies that there is general acceptance that it would be wrong to perform a direct abortion. However in the statement issued it is not clear that the hospital invoked a claim that the abortion was indirect. The hospital's statement does not refer to the distinction:

> The announcement by Bishop Olmsted follows months of complex talks between the Phoenix Diocese, the hospital, and the hospital's parent company, Catholic Healthcare West. At issue is the life-saving care delivered to a pregnant patient in November 2009 at St. Joseph's. In that case, a decision was made to

---

223 E.J. Carro-Jiménez, J.E. López, "Primary pulmonary hypertension and pregnancy" *Bol Asoc Med P R*. 2005 Oct-Dec 97(4):328-33.

224 See for instance: Edmonds, Keith (Ed.) *Dewhurst's Textbook of Obstetrics and Gynaecology*, 7th Edition Wiley-Blackwell 2007; Michael A. Belfort, George R. Saade, Michael R. Foley, Jeffrey P. Phelan, Gary A. III Dildy, (Eds.) *Critical Care Obstetrics*, 5th Edition, Wiley-Blackwell 2010; David Vaughan, Neville Robinson, Nuala Lucas, Sabaratnam Arulkumaran, *Handbook of Obstetric High Dependency Care*, Wiley-Blackwell 2010.

225 P. Rachael James and CatherineNelson-Piercy, "Management of hypertension before, during, and after pregnancy" *Heart*. 2004 December; 90(12): 1499–1504.

terminate an 11-week pregnancy in order to save the mother's life. Consistent with our values of dignity and justice, if we are presented with a situation in which a pregnancy threatens a woman's life, our first priority is to save both patients. If that is not possible we will always save the life we can save, and that is what we did in this case," said Hunt. "We continue to stand by the decision, which was made in collaboration with the patient, her family, her caregivers, and our Ethics Committee. Morally, ethically, and legally we simply cannot stand by and let someone die whose life we might be able to save.[226]

On the basis of the hospital's statement, there is an obligation to intervene if it is necessary to save life: the character of the intervention is not the issue. However, Lysaught claims in her article that the hospital sought a determination on whether or not the intervention to address the placental tissue via a dilation and curettage would be morally appropriate according to Catholic teaching. She refers to their "understanding of the Catholic moral tradition" and that they had "determined that the intervention would not be considered a direct abortion".

It is important to separate the claim that a D&C to remove the placenta is not a direct abortion because it is an act directed at the placenta as the source of problems causing the condition in the mother, rather than a direct assault on the child, from a quite different claim being made in the Rhonheimer and Grisez positions. In their analysis of craniotomy they accept that what is a direct physical assault on the child is not an intentional assault on the child. Their arguments do not depend on the claim being made by Lysaught in relation to the D&C, that it is physically not a direct assault on the child.

About the issue of what counts as direct killing, there is something of an agreement that what constitutes direct killing cannot be described by the nature of the physical act alone. If I see someone plunge a knife into someone else's throat, resulting in death, that only describes the physical act. To form an assessment of the moral nature of their act, I would need to know what was in their mind. The person might, for instance, have been attempting a lifesaving procedure in the circumstances of a blocked trachea.

---

226 http://te-deum.blogspot.com/2010/12/bishop-olmsted-strips-st-josephs-of.html

A physical description of an act does not in itself permit moral assessment.

The above point about physicalism has been exploited by proportionalists[227] who have then sought to claim that one can only assess the moral nature of an act by taking into account all the consequences, and that the good consequences of an act may outweigh what they call the premoral evil of the act itself. That is not the position being adopted by Lysaught. Proportionalists usually reject the distinction between direct and indirect evil altogether. It serves little purpose when it is the overall consequences that determine the morality of the act.

The issue of the D&C and whether the placenta is or is not a vital organ of the foetus aside, what is at issue here are several different accounts of the moral act. Austriaco refers to a hylomorphic account which seems to reflect what has been the settled position in the tradition in relation to rejecting craniotomy, and an intentional account such as has been argued by Grisez, Finnis and Boyle. Austriaco places Rhonheimer's position in the same category as the latter intentional thesis. However, I do not think that is so and he himself rejects the claimed similarity between his position and the intentional thesis. Rhonheimer's position is that this is not a case of double effect reasoning at all because it is not a case of taking one life to save the life of another, such as in the standard indirect killing in self-defence scenario referred to by St Thomas. Rather, for Rhonheimer it is a case of vital conflict in which both will die if there is no intervention to save the only life that can be saved.

13.3 Rhonheimer and Vital Conflicts

Martin Rhonheimer resolves the craniotomy case in such a way that it is indeed helpful to the position adopted by St Joseph's Hospital, if one assumes that the case is a "vital conflict" involving a situation of certain death for both mother and child without intervention, and that only the mother's life could be saved by intervention that would end the life of the child. In a recent account of his position he writes:

> My argument is that in cases of real vital conflict a physician,

---

227 See my discussion of this in Nicholas Tonti-Filippini, *About Bioethics, Volume One, Philosophical ad Theologiael Approaches*, Connor Court, Melbourne, 2011, Chapter 3.5.

bound to save life, is in a situation in which there is no rational way out, because the choice of not removing the baby (by physically killing it) would lead to the immediate (though *a bit* less immediate) death of both the child and the mother. This for a doctor is a situation in which a deontological principle like "not doing harm" becomes counterintuitive, because it will lead to a result which is exactly the opposite of what the principle intends and what the medical profession obliges.[228]

Rhonheimer has referred to Lysaught's analysis in a recent defence of his view.[229] He claims that Lysaught seems to misunderstand, in an important respect, his view on the moral object. He writes that Lysaught distinguishes what he calls the basic intention included in the moral object from the exterior act, while according to Rhonheimer – and, in his understanding, Aquinas – the object precisely is the exterior act, insofar it presents itself to the will as a "good apprehended and ordered by reason".

Rhonheimer's argument is that in the circumstances in which both cannot survive, the choice of the death of the baby is objectively not possible.[230] Saving the baby is not possible. In that sense he argues that the choice to end the life of the baby is not on the table, so to speak, so it cannot be part of the intention in intervening to save the mother.

The case to which Rhonheimer applies this reasoning is not a case of pulmonary hypertension risking death of the mother and the child, but the case of craniotomy. The latter is not a problem that exists in modern obstetrics, but is claimed to have been a dilemma in the days prior to modern caesarean section. The scenario involves the child being too large for the woman's pelvis and thus lodging in the birth canal. Arrested labour would then result in the death of both unless there was intervention to crush the head of the child to permit birth to occur.

The craniotomy case has always puzzled me for reasons that are well

---

228 Private email correspondence December 2011
229 Martin Rhonheimer, "Vital Conflicts, Direct Killing, and Justice: A Response to Rev. Benedict Guevin and Other Critics", *National Catholic Bioethics Quarterly*, Vol. 11, No. 3, Autumn 2011, pp 519–540.
230 Ibid., pp. 534-5.

outlined in the article by Cavanaugh. I am also puzzled about how it ever came to be presented as a case of save the mother or both will die. Caesarean section has been with us for literally thousands of years – hence its name. Until relatively recently (the advent of antibiotics, aseptic technique, intrauterine stitching, transverse incision, blood transfusion), it had a high mortality rate for the mother. In the 1800s, maternal mortality following caesarean section may have been as high as 85%.[231] However there was also always the possibility of symphysiotomy[232] which involves severing the ligament that joins the two parts of the pelvis, thus increasing the diameter of the birth canal. That is still done as an option to Caesarean section in developing countries. In other words, the choice was always a choice between endangering the child or endangering the mother, never quite a vital conflict in the way in which it has been presented. They were choosing often between craniotomy which would kill the child, on the one hand, and, on the other, grave risk to the mother's life and health if they took one of the alternatives – caesarean section or symphysiotomy. It is thus puzzling how craniotomy ever came to be described as the only alternative to the death of both mother and child.

In a footnote to his recent article Rhonheimer comments on Lysaught's use of his treatment of craniotomy. He writes:

> [The] ... important feature of the case, and of my argument – that the exclusively life-saving intentionality depends on the objective constellation of the case and is not simply due to a (subjectively determined) shifting of intention – seems to me insufficiently emphasized (though neither is it denied) in a report drafted by M. Therese Lysaught from Marquette University that widely refers to my *Vital Conflicts* in assessing the so-called Phoenix case (M. Therese Lysaught, "Moral Analysis of Procedure at Phoenix Hospital," *Origins* 40.33 [January 27, 2011]: 537–549). The exact clinical facts

---

231 J.P. Boley, "The History of Cesarean Section", *Canadian Medical Association Journal*, Vol. 145, No. 4, 1991, pp. 319-322.
232 K. Bjorklund, "Minimally invasive surgery for obstructed labour: a review of symphysiotomy during the twentieth century (including 5000 cases)", *British Journal of Obstetrics and Gynaecology*, 2002 March; 109(3):236-48.

of the case are beyond my knowledge, so it is not possible for me to determine whether my argument really can be applied to it. Yet in her – somewhat unclear – account of what a moral object is, Lysaught in at least one crucial point seems to me to be mistaken. On page 542, column 3, she writes, "A proper description of the moral object, then, certainly includes the 'exterior act' – since it is a necessary part of the moral action as a whole – but it derives its properly moral content first and foremost from the proximate end deliberately chosen by the will." According to my understanding, however, it is wrong to distinguish the "proximate end" (deliberately chosen by the will) from the "exterior act" as if it were a formal part added to it; rather the object and thus the proximate end *is* precisely the exterior act, but as a "good understood and ordered by reason" (see note 23 above). The formal aspect of the object is not something *added* to the exterior act, but rather included in its rational comprehension and ordering. This is why the object can never be reduced to the "intention" as something distinct from the exterior act; the basic intentionality which is part of the object is part of reason's understanding and ordering of the exterior act. This is the crucial point."[233]

In this he is referring to a distinction that Lysaught made between the exterior act and the proximate end deliberately chosen. This is not a distinction that Rhonheimer makes. In fact in both his book and his recent defence of it he is at great pains to reject the notion that the intention alone determines the nature of the object of the act. In that way he distinguishes his position from that taken by Grisez and others. His position does not readily fit under the distinction that Austriaco makes between hylomorphic and intentional accounts of the moral act.

Nevertheless, Rhonheimer's position seems to me to be quite novel. He is in fact arguing that because the death of the child is not avoidable, the death of the child is not part of what can be willed and therefore the death of the child is "beside the intention" as Aquinas put it (*praeter intentionem*).[234] Aquinas does not argue that to intentionally kill an aggressor in self-defence

---

233 Ibid.
234 Aquinas, St Thomas, *Summa Theologiae*, II-II, 64, 7.

is permissible. Rather, he argues that in some cases the killing is beside the intention and, insofar as it is beside the intention, it does not morally specify the act. Likewise Rhonheimer is not arguing that killing in the case of a vital conflict (both will die without intervention but one can be saved with intervention) is similarly permissible, rather he is arguing that the death of the child is simply non-intentional because it is not chosen as a means: nature has already "decided"; no preferential choice against the survival of the child is done in favour of the mother's survival. Therefore, he argues, the killing does not specify the act morally.[235]

St Thomas's distinction that Lysaught refers to between the interior and the exterior act needs further analysis, but it is more relevant to the discussion of Grisez *et al* than to Rhonheimer's analysis, because Rhonhiemer does not in fact invoke the distinction in his analysis of vital conflicts. I will return to St Thomas and the distinction later.

The difficulty I have in attempting to apply Rhonheimer's analysis is that it seems to me to confuse a prognosis with a diagnosis. That someone will certainly die in the near future or even the very near future does not make my killing them any less a killing. It might be argued, as Rhonheimer argues, that I do not do the person a significant injustice in those circumstances. If they are about to die, my ending their life could be argued to be insignificant from the perspective of justice. He argues that a child, if he or she were competent, would willingly call for a craniotomy to be performed rather than a fruitless attempt at being born when the latter was impossible to achieve.[236] A crucial aspect of the craniotomy case for Rhonheimer is that the woman's life is threatened by the baby caught in the birth canal. The intervention is intended to save her life and the death of the baby will happen in any case so it is not part of what is intended. There is, he argues, no injustice to the child that would specify the act as morally evil.

But the issue is more complex than that. It certainly makes a great deal of difference to me, as the agent, if I kill someone who is about to die. That they die through causes I cannot prevent is very different from them dying at my hand. Justice is only part of the story. Saying that it may not be unjust,

---

235 Rhonheimer, email correspondence, December 2011.
236 Rhonheimer, Op Cit.

does not address the issue of intentional killing. That the person is to die anyway does not make my killing them less a killing, even if the outcome for them is the same, nor does it make my killing them less direct. Rhonheimer, however, is not arguing that the killing is indirect in these circumstances of inevitable death. Rather he is arguing that the death is not a result of the intervention at all because it was unavoidable. He argues that it is not an application of double effect reasoning.[237]

However, even accepting that craniotomy is a genuine case of vital conflict, the treatment of the moral issue by Rhonheimer seems inadequate because the concept of moral evil is too narrow, treating it as exhausted, in the case of killing, by the issue of justice. Justice in this case is narrowly construed to something of a head count of survivors rather than considering justice in terms of the choices actually being made and their meaning, especially in relation to the theological virtues. The use of justice in this way creates a sterility that avoids much of the meaning of killing and what I would refer to as a pre-emptive strike. That loss of meaning leaves no place for the theological virtues in assessing the object of the act. In the craniotomy case, the agent takes it on him or herself to produce the best consequences as a matter of justice, but in fact there is a point at which the agent assesses the situation and then plunges the instruments into the brain of the child to draw out the contents, rather like deflating a ball caught in a drain, in order to effect delivery. There is a sharp reality not only to causing the death in that way, but in also taking upon oneself the certainty of insisting that this is a vital conflict and without my intervention they will both die.

Relevant to this discussion is an earlier discussion between Rhonheimer and Servais Pinckaers on the nature of moral reasoning in *Veritatis Splendor*. Pinckaers has long been distinguished for his critique of the manualist tradition and what he calls the morality of obligation in place of the New Law. The morality of obligation, he claims, excludes the Decalogue and the Sermon on the Mount.[238] In particular, Pinckaers claims:

---

237 Ibid.
238 Servais Pinckaers, "The Return of the New Law to Moral Theology", in John Berkman and Titus Craig Steven, *The Pinckaers Reader: Renewing Thomistic Moral Theology* Catholic University of America Press, 2005, pp. 369-384.

The encyclical [*Veritatis Splendor*] introduces an important change in the interpretation of the Decalogue. The Ten Commandments are not reduced to a code of obligations imposed by God. Rather, they are presented as a gift of his wisdom and mercy, demanding a response of love. Since charity is grafted onto the natural love of what which we have just spoken, it remains the principle of the moral life, even before that a moral obligation. In other terms, the encyclical changes the cornerstone of moral life. Morality must be built upon the greatness of love rather than on a legalistic obedience, as was the case in the manuals of moral theology. It was left to spiritual theology to talk about the virtues growth and perfection.[239]

The authority for the claim about the encyclical is the passage that states:

The statement that "There is only one who is good" thus brings us back to the "first tablet" of the commandments, which calls us to acknowledge God as the one Lord of all and to worship him alone for his infinite holiness (cf. *Ex* 20:2-11). *The good is belonging to God, obeying him,* walking humbly with him in doing justice and in loving kindness (cf.*Mic* 6:8). In the morality of the commandments the fact that the people of Israel belongs to the Lord is made evident, because God alone is the One who is good. Such is the witness of Sacred Scripture, imbued in every one of its pages with a lively perception of God's absolute holiness: "Holy, holy, holy is the Lord of hosts" (*Is* 6:3).

But if God alone is the Good, no human effort, not even the most rigorous observance of the commandments, succeeds in "fulfilling" the Law, that is, acknowledging the Lord as God and rendering him the worship due to him alone (cf. *Mt* 4:10). *This "fulfilment" can come only from a gift of God:* the offer of a share in the divine Goodness revealed and communicated in Jesus, the one whom the rich young man addresses with the words "Good Teacher" (*Mk* 10:17; Lk 18:18). What the young man now perhaps only dimly perceives will in the end be fully revealed by Jesus himself in the invitation: "Come, follow me" (*Mt* 19:21).[240]

---

239 Servais Pinckaers, "Conscience and the Virtue of Prudence" in Berkman *et al*, op. cit. p. 346.
240 Pope John Paul II, *Veritatis Splendor*, n. 11.

The significance of this passage had been lost in my reading it until receiving Pinckaers' commentary. He connects it with the passage in *Gaudium et Spes:*

> Deep within his conscience man discovers a law which he himself is not laid upon himself that which you must obey. Its voice, ever calling him to long to do what is good and to avoid evil, tells him inwardly at the right moment: do this, shun that. For man has in his heart a law inscribed by God.[241]

I had followed the discussion in *Veritatis Splendor*, synderectically connecting the Decalogue with human goods, viz.,

> The different commandments of the Decalogue are really only so many reflections of the one commandment about the good of the person, at the level of the many different goods which characterize his identity as a spiritual and bodily being in relationship with God, with his neighbour and with the material world. As we read in the *Catechism of the Catholic Church,* "the Ten Commandments are part of God's Revelation. At the same time, they teach us man's true humanity. They shed light on the essential duties, and so indirectly on the fundamental rights, inherent in the nature of the human person".[22]
>
> The commandments of which Jesus reminds the young man are meant to safeguard *the good* of the person, the image of God, by protecting his *goods*. "You shall not murder; You shall not commit adultery; You shall not steal; You shall not bear false witness" are moral rules formulated in terms of prohibitions. These negative precepts express with particular force the ever urgent need to protect human life, the communion of persons in marriage, private property, truthfulness and people's good name.[242]

I had misunderstood this passage as allowing us to understand the commandments in terms of human goods interpreted in terms of integral social fulfilment and thus a law that had its own human autonomy. But the previous passage at n. 11, makes clear the central focus and dependency on acknowledging the Lord as God as the very core – the heart of the Law,

---

241 Second Vatican Council, *Gaudium et Spes*, n. 16.
242 *Veritatis Splendor*, with n. 13.

from which the particular precepts flow and towards which they are ordered, and that no human effort ends up fulfilling the law. This "fulfilment" can come only from a gift of God: the offer of a share in the divine Goodness revealed and communicated in Jesus.

That significantly changes the role of what has been understood as natural law in twentieth century casuistry, in giving direction to our understanding of the nature of the moral act. It is not enough that we provide moral analysis based upon human goods, intelligible as human goods only, rather than understanding the role and function of the New Law within our relationship to God that informs our relationship to neighbour.

By contrast, Ronheimer wishes to distinguish between the natural and the supernatural levels, between natural moral reason and the order of charity, or love. Within natural moral reason, he sees a place for a specifically philosophical discourse without which moral theology would not be able to identify intrinsically evil action. He sees how the New Law, the law of love of God, is the fulfilment or perfection of morality rather than intrinsic to it from the outset. He wishes to rediscover the specific ethical rationality of the moral virtues which is precisely that rationality, which is capable of then being elevated, affected, fulfilled and informed by charity or love.[243]

In other words, Rhonheimer postulates an intelligible human law that stands independently for the purpose of casuistry but which is elevated, fulfilled and informed by the love that is central to the New Law.

The article by Rhonheimer, and his commentary on Pinckaers, accurately identifies the point of difference, asserting a morality that is devoid of affectivity and the actual character of our relating to God and to each other as *imago dei* and what that demands. Rhonheimer seems to describe a morality that is open to God's grace and orientated towards fulfilment, but which is dependant on a prior morality developed at the level of reason and human relating, with God only becoming relevant at some later level of fulfilment of what is initially the result of human synderesis. He seems to propose a separation of the two levels of morality for the purpose of resolving the

---

[243] Martin Rhonheimer, "Christian Morality and Moral Reasonableness: Of What Is the Law of the Gospel of Fulfilment?", *Josephinum Journal of Theology*, volume 17, number two, 2010.

basic issue of casuistry, uncomplicated by Christian love and the demands of Scripture. The latter can be added in later, once the basic issues of justice between people have been resolved.

From my perspective, for which I draw support from Pinckaers, the fact remains that to give a Christian response, we cannot give an answer that is only at the level of the human and ignoring our ultimate end. Such an approach might help with discussion with non-believers, but it is not the complete answer to the morality of the object of an act. Further, I would argue that, as an approach, it is unrealistic because our culture and our very language of morality has a theological content. The division that Rhonheimer asserts does not exist in our experience. Considerations of justice are interrelated with considerations of love. A virtuous response will also be a loving response and not restricted to a narrowly human conception of justice alone. Our moral actions must be informed by the Beatitudes and by Jesus's treatment of the Decalogue.

Rhonheimer asserts that there are two levels which should be thought of as different sources, each with their proper and specific intelligibility, sources which in the end realize a mutual penetration and enrichment to form a new and unique moral spiritualism, the person in the image of Christ's. However, he claims that

> ... the moral rational requirements of the natural level, can never be deduced or inferred from the supernatural order of grace and charity. Just as in Christ the divine person assumed human nature. So these moral rational requirements must precisely be assumed, which is possible only if they possess a moral intelligibility that is proper and independent of the essential context of the new law we must therefore be aware of the danger of reducing morality to what is proper to the supernatural level.

This distinction between the natural law as a law of human nature is thus seemingly linked in Rhonheimer's mind to the human and divine natures of Christ. This then provides some link to what Austriaco referred to as the distinction between hylomorphic and intentional understandings of the nature of the moral act, even though, Rhonheimer's position is not strictly the intentional thesis of Grisez, Finnis and Boyle. Rhonheimer insists on a level of morality that is exclusively human with the Divine entering into consideration as an addition, but being nonetheless separate. That raises doubts about whether his approach is Nestorian.[244] When Christ as a man walked this earth and lived with the feet-on-the-ground detail of making decisions, He was also God and he never ceased to be both God and man. The New Law is not a specifically human law but a Divine law given to us and requiring from us a very full response to that Divine law with, of course, the grace to assist us do so.

Rhonheimer at least, seems to be alive to these issues in a way in which Grisez seems not to be, so the discussion has been fruitful. It is interesting that he finds solace in St Thomas and *Veritatis Splendor* n. 79, but that seems to be a highly strained reading of *VS* and not at all consistent with the role and function of the Decalogue which places God first in human relating. I find it fascinating not only that the first three commandments are about our relationship to God, but that our relationship to our parents comes ahead of killing. I do not find Rhonhemier's argument based on *VS* to be at all persuasive for that reason.

VS n. 79 states:

> The primary and decisive element for moral judgment is the object of the human act, which establishes whether it is *capable of being ordered to the good and to the ultimate end, which is God.* This capability is grasped by reason in the very being of man, considered in his integral truth, and therefore in his natural inclinations, his motivations and his finalities, which always have a spiritual dimension as well. It is precisely these which are the contents of the natural law and hence that ordered complex of "personal goods" which serve the "good of the person": the good which is the person himself and his perfection. These are the goods safeguarded by the commandments, which, according to Saint Thomas, contain the whole natural law.

---

244 Nestorianism refers to that view that Jesus did not just have a human and a divine nature, he was in fact two separate personalities, a human personality and a divine personality. It may be claiming too much to assert this belief on the part of Rhonheimer. I simply want to indicate that it is a risk of his position on separating the two levels of morality that he may be implying two personalities of Christ.

The passage cites St Thomas, *Summa Theologiae*, I-II, q. 100, a. 1 in which he says,

> It is therefore evident that since the moral precepts are about matters which concern good morals; and since good morals are those which are in accord with reason; and since also every judgment of human reason must needs be derived in some way from natural reason; it follows, of necessity, that all the moral precepts belong to the law of nature; but not all in the same way.

But this needs to be understood in the light of the following passage in the *Summa Theologiciae* where he says:

> But the community for which the Divine law is ordained, is that of men in relation to God, either in this life or in the life to come. And therefore the Divine law proposes precepts about all those matters whereby men are well ordered in their relations to God. Now man is united to God by his reason or mind, in which is God's image. Wherefore the Divine law proposes precepts about all those matters whereby human reason is well ordered. But this is effected by the acts of all the virtues: since the intellectual virtues set in good order the acts of the reason in themselves: while the moral virtues set in good order the acts of the reason in reference to the interior passions and exterior actions. It is therefore evident that the Divine law fittingly proposes precepts about the acts of all the virtues: yet so that certain matters, without which the order of virtue, which is the order of reason, cannot even exist, come under an obligation of precept; while other matters, which pertain to the well-being of perfect virtue, come under an admonition of counsel.[245]

Importantly St Thomas, in response to the objections that the law is not about all the acts of virtue but about justice alone, quoting Ambrose, asserts "a sin is a transgression of the Divine law, and a disobedience to the commandments of heaven. But there are sins contrary to all the acts of virtue. Therefore it belongs to Divine law to direct all the acts of virtue."[246]

---

245 St Thomas Aquinas, *Summa Theologiae*, I-II, q 100 art 2.
246 Ibid.

This is quite important to Rhonheimer's analysis of vital conflict in the craniotomy case in which he wishes to restrict the casuistry about killing to the virtue of justice alone. This seems to be explicitly excluded by St Thomas. There can be no ethico-philosophical discourse that is properly reflective of Christian morality but that is separate from moral theology. Nor can the New Law be held to be somehow dependant on this separate philosophical morality. The New Law, the law of love, that comes to us in the life, death and suffering of Christ is game changing, and much more demanding.

In the Phoenix case, the mother and her child are both at risk of dying. On the account given by Lysaught it is a 100% probability. That does not fit with my understanding of the management of pulmonary hypertension during pregnancy, but even if it were a true assessment of the odds, there is still a significant difference between killing the child in that expectation, and the child dying as a result of a disease process. Rhonheimer's argument, against the seemingly settled position of the Church on craniotomy, is unconvincing on this point precisely because he tries to narrow the consideration to a matter of justice narrowly construed and leaves out the significance of the child dying at the hand of the doctor and what that may mean for each of those directly involved, beginning with the choice that the mother makes in her request to the doctor. The difficult reality of the craniotomy case is in fact whether the woman would have her doctor make a choice between damage to her, including life risk, of caesarean section or the damage of symphysiotomy, on the one hand, or craniotomy resulting in the certain death of the child. With contemporary attitudes to pregnancy and the unborn, such choices are likely to protect the mother first with the child as patient coming second in the considerations. However, contemporary attitudes do not reflect what ought to be the witness of a Catholic hospital to respect the life of both and the obligation to recognize both patients. If a woman elected otherwise, then it would be a question of facilitating transfer to where she could have the obstetric management more consistent with her choosing. I discuss this option in the concluding section of this paper.

Lysaught, however, refers also to Grisez and his complex treatment of the moral act, which Austriaco has described as intentional rather than hylomorphic.

Grisez's Analysis

Before exploring Lysaught's use of Grisez, I think it is worth exploring the use of the distinction in St Thomas between the interior and the exterior act. In particular it is worth exploring the nature of the moral act in relation to our ultimate end. It is my view that Grisez's analysis of the moral act, and hence his casuistry, suffers from the position that he takes on the ultimate end in which he disagrees that the ultimate end of human acts is God alone.[247] In this Grisez not only disagrees with St Thomas, but he is also at odds with *Veritatis Splendor* firstly in terms of the nature of the Decalogue and secondly in terms of the specification of the nature of the object of the moral act.

In relation to the Decalogue and the Beatitudes, Pope John Paul II says:

> *The Beatitudes* are not specifically concerned with certain particular rules of behaviour. Rather, they speak of basic attitudes and dispositions in life and therefore they *do not coincide exactly with the commandments*. On the other hand, *there is no separation or opposition* between the Beatitudes and the commandments: both refer to the good, to eternal life. The Sermon on the Mount begins with the proclamation of the Beatitudes, but also refers to the commandments (cf. *Mt* 5:20-48). At the same time, the Sermon on the Mount demonstrates the openness of the commandments and their orientation towards the horizon of the perfection proper to the Beatitudes. These latter are above all *promises,* from which there also indirectly flow *normative indications* for the moral life. In their originality and profundity they are a sort of *self- portrait of Christ,* and for this very reason are *invitations to discipleship and to communion of life with Christ.*[248]

In relation to the object of the act the Pope stated:

---

247 Germain Grisez, "Natural Law, God, Religion, and Human Fulfillment", *American Journal of Jurisprudence,* 46 (2001) 3-36; Germain Grisez, "The Ultimate End of Human Beings: The Kingdon, not God Alone", *Theologiael Studies,* Vol 69 (2008) pp. 38-61.
248 Pope John Paul II, *Veritatis Splendor* n. 16.

The reason why a good intention is not itself sufficient, but a correct choice of actions is also needed, is that the human act depends on its object, whether that object is *capable or not of being ordered* to God, to the One who "alone is good", and thus brings about the perfection of the person. An act is therefore good if its object is in conformity with the good of the person with respect for the goods morally relevant for him. Christian ethics, which pays particular attention to the moral object, does not refuse to consider the inner "teleology" of acting, inasmuch as it is directed to promoting the true good of the person; but it recognizes that it is really pursued only when the essential elements of human nature are respected. The human act, good according to its object, is also *capable of being ordered* to its ultimate end. That same act then attains its ultimate and decisive perfection when the will *actually does order* it to God through charity. As the Patron of moral theologians and confessors teaches: "It is not enough to do good works; they need to be done well. For our works to be good and perfect, they must be done for the sole purpose of pleasing God."[249]

It is my contention that by not requiring the object of the act to be ordered by the will to God as an act of love, Grisez significantly shifts the grounds for determining the specification of the moral act and this has grave implications for his casuistry, particularly in relation to double effect reasoning. This is not to say that he adopts the position of the proportionalists in which the intended end can override evil in the object of the act if it is proportionate. Rather Grisez's position is due to the specification of the object itself and how the concept of direct intention is applied. If the specification is determined by the ultimate end, and the ultimate end is not God alone, but includes integral human fulfilment, then that changes the way in which the object is specified. He writes:

> Since the self-evident principles of practical reasoning direct us indiscriminately toward the well-being and flourishing of ourselves and everyone else, we reasonably take as our ultimate end an inclusive community of human persons along with other intelligent

---

249 *Veritatis Splendor*, n. 78.

creatures and God – insofar as we know other intelligent creatures and God and can somehow cooperate with them and/or act for their good.

... our ultimate end should include all the benefits that can be realized by protecting and promoting all the fundamental goods of persons in every way compatible with loving all of them and all aspects of their well-being and flourishing.[250]

An important aspect of Grisez's analysis of the ultimate end is that he claims that God alone is not sufficient, but that we must consider all the aspects of human fulfilment and not just our relationship to God. This is quite different from St Thomas's position in which God is the ultimate end, and love of neighbour (and thus the goods of human flourishing) is integral to that love of God. In Grisez's analysis, love of God is part of human fulfilment and not its sole end. Placing human fulfilment first in this way has consequences for specifying the nature of the object of the moral act because it affects the interior meaning of the act and hence the application of double effect reasoning. Instead of a participative theonomy[251], as proposed by Pope John Paul II in *Veritatis Splendor*, Grisez proposes anthropocentrism.

I shall argue that double effect reasoning in assessing the object of the act must not treat humanity as though we existed in isolation and did not depend on God, or that our good is not inextricably bound to our ultimate end of communion with him. It was significant that in the analysis of the Decalogue in the Sermon on the Mount, Jesus gave so much more meaning to them, such as, extending the fifth commandment to include anger, and the sixth commandment to include adultery of the heart. The New Law was a law of love and not just a law of obligation.[252] To follow Jesus demands so much more of us than the narrow treatment of the object of the act in terms of human fulfilment would suggest. The Theological virtues are relevant,

---

250 Grisez, op. cit., 2008 p. 55.
251 *Veritatis Splendor*, n. 41.
252 Servais Pinckaers, "The Return of the New Law to Moral Theology" in John Berkman and Craig Steven Titus, *The Pinckaers Reader: Renewing Thomistic Moral Theology,* Catholic University of America Press, 2005, pp. 369-384.

and not just the cardinal virtues (which are anthropocentric), because the ultimate end is God alone and our love for Him should inform every act.

Central to an analysis of the moral act is the concept of intention, which St Thomas is careful to explain, not in terms of the action itself, but in terms of the mind or will which moves to the end. The intention is an act of the will.[253] Second he argues that the will belongs to the intellect whose object is universal "being" and "truth". He describes the intellect as moving the will, presenting its object to it.[254]

In explaining what is specific to human actions, St Thomas accounts for free will as "the faculty and will of reason". Therefore those actions are properly called human which proceed from a deliberate will, and in the actions of man the object of the will is the end and the good. He concludes by claiming that all human actions must be for an end.[255]

Following Ambrose, he asserts that moral acts, properly speaking, receive their species from the end, for moral acts are the same as human acts.[256]

Finally he asserts that the ultimate end is God: "... we speak of man's last end as of the thing which is the end, thus all other things concur in man's last end, since God is the last end of man and of all other things."[257]

That analysis of intention and the intentional acts provides the basis for the distinction between interior and exterior acts. Referring to the above analysis he writes:

> Certain actions are called human, inasmuch as they are voluntary ... Now, in a voluntary action, there is a twofold action, viz. the interior action of the will, and the external action: and each of these actions has its object. The end is properly the object of the interior act of the will: while the object of the external action, is that on which the action is brought to bear. Therefore just as the external action takes its species from the object on which it bears;

---

253 *Summa Theologiae*, I-II, 12,1.
254 *Summa Theologiae* I-II, 9, 1.
255 *Summa Theologiae* I-II, 1, 1.
256 *Summa Theologiae*, I-II, 1, 3.
257 *Summa Theologiae*, I-II, 1, 8.

so the interior act of the will takes its species from the end, as from its own proper object.

Now that which is on the part of the will is formal in regard to that which is on the part of the external action: because the will uses the limbs to act as instruments; nor have external actions any measure of morality, save in so far as they are voluntary. Consequently the species of a human act is considered formally with regard to the end, but materially with regard to the object of the external action. Hence the Philosopher says (Ethic. v, 2) that "he who steals that he may commit adultery, is strictly speaking, more adulterer than thief".[258]

This paragraph is important for it qualifies the distinction between interior and exterior acts, referring to the species of the act as both formal and material. It would not be true to claim that the exterior act is irrelevant to the species of the act. The latter is the application of the distinction that Lysaught has made, claiming that the act can be determined by the interior act alone. That would suggest no morally significant relationship between the exterior act and the interior act. However, referring to the above passage, St Thomas has more to say about the specification of the act. He writes,

> ... a fourfold goodness may be considered in a human action. First, that which, as an action, it derives from its genus; because as much as it has of action and being so much has it of goodness, ... Secondly, it has goodness according to its species; which is derived from its suitable object. Thirdly, it has goodness from its circumstances, in respect, as it were, of its accidents. Fourthly, it has goodness from its end, to which it is compared as to the cause of its goodness.[259]

Later in the same article he writes,

> ... thus it may happen that an action which is good in its species or in its circumstances is ordained to an evil end, or vice versa. However, an action is not good simply, unless it is good in all those

---

258 *Summa Theologiae*, I-II, 18, 6.
259 Ibid., I-II, 18, 4.

ways: since "evil results from any single defect, but good from the complete cause," as Dionysius says (*Div. Nom.* iv).

The above references to St Thomas precede and are connected to what he says about double effect and the latter needs to be understood in the general context of his theory of the moral act. About double effect he says:

> It is written (Exodus 22:2): "If a thief be found breaking into a house or undermining it, and be wounded so as to die; he that slew him shall not be guilty of blood." Now it is much more lawful to defend one's life than one's house. Therefore neither is a man guilty of murder if he kill another in defense of his own life.
>
> … Nothing hinders one act from having two effects, only one of which is intended, while the other is beside the intention. Now moral acts take their species according to what is intended, and not according to what is beside the intention, since this is accidental … Accordingly the act of self-defense may have two effects, one is the saving of one's life, the other is the slaying of the aggressor. Therefore this act, since one's intention is to save one's own life, is not unlawful, seeing that it is natural to everything to keep itself in "being," as far as possible. And yet, though proceeding from a good intention, an act may be rendered unlawful, if it be out of proportion to the end. Wherefore if a man, in self-defense, uses more than necessary violence, it will be unlawful: whereas if he repel force with moderation his defense will be lawful, because according to the jurists … "it is lawful to repel force by force, provided one does not exceed the limits of a blameless defense." Nor is it necessary for salvation that a man omit the act of moderate self-defense in order to avoid killing the other man, since one is bound to take more care of one's own life than of another's. But as it is unlawful to take a man's life, except for the public authority acting for the common good, as stated above (Article 3), it is not lawful for a man to intend killing a man in self-defense, except for such as have public authority, who while intending to kill a man in self-defense, refer this to the public good, as in the case of a soldier fighting against the foe, and in the minister of the judge struggling with robbers, although even these sin if they be moved by private animosity.[260]

---

[260] *Summa Theologiae* II-II, q. 64, 7.

In *Quaestiones Quodlibetales* Aquinas writes that some kinds of human acts "have deformity inseparably annexed to them, such as fornication, adultery, and others of this sort."[261] Aquinas thus explicitly affirms that some actions are intrinsically evil, and corresponding to them are absolute moral norms.[262] In this Pope John Paul II would seem to have concurred when he wrote,

> If acts are intrinsically evil, a good intention or particular circumstances can diminish their evil, but they cannot remove it. They remain "irremediably" evil acts; *per se* and in themselves they are not capable of being ordered to God and to the good of the person. "As for acts which are themselves sins (*cum iam opera ipsa peccata sunt*), Saint Augustine writes, like theft, fornication, blasphemy, who would dare affirm that, by doing them for good motives (*causis bonis*), they would no longer be sins, or, what is even more absurd, that they would be sins that are justified?"[263]

He also writes in the same document,

> Reason attests that there are objects of the human act which are by their nature "incapable of being ordered" to God, because they radically contradict the good of the person made in his image. These are the acts which, in the Church's moral tradition, have been termed "intrinsically evil" (*intrinsece malum*): they are such *always and per se*, in other words, on account of their very object, and quite apart from the ulterior intentions of the one acting and the circumstances. Consequently, without in the least denying the influence on morality exercised by circumstances and especially by intentions, the Church teaches that "there exist acts which *per se* and in themselves, independently of circumstances, are always seriously wrong by reason of their object".[264]

What is important here is that the objects are incapable of being ordered

---

[261] "Quaedam enim sunt quae habent deformitatem inseparabiliter annexam, ut fornicatio, adulterium, et aliae huiusmodi, quae nullo modo bene fieri possunt." St. Thomas Aquinas, *Quaestiones Quodlibetales*, 9, q. 7, a. 2.
[262] Ibid.
[263] *Veritatis Splendor*, n. 81.
[264] Ibid., n. 80.

towards God, not because they are a destruction of human goods and thus hostile to integral human fulfilment, but rather because they radically contradict the good of the person made in his image. The consideration of one's neighbour stems from one's ordering towards God. The first part of the Decalogue importantly informs the second part.[265] Love of God informs love of neighbour. The function of our reason in seeking to assess the moral act begins with our love of God, with God alone as our ultimate end.

Grisez's analysis is complex, but if his intentionality thesis had succeeded, then it would seem to have had application to the Phoenix case. The issue centres upon an issue that was addressed by Pope John Paul II in *Veritatis Splendor* – the nature of what can be considered the object of a moral act and what makes that object good.

Lysaught has quoted Pope John Paul in the encyclical *Veritatis Splendor* and engaged the treatment of double effect reasoning offered by Grisez to interpret the encyclical. There are of course, many others who have taken a contrary view, and in quoting Rhonheimer and Grisez, there is a lack of balance, in that she has ignored the many criticisms of their views.

Grisez's argument is an application to the craniotomy case. He claims that craniotomy in the circumstances of arrested labour is not direct killing:

> In times past complications of delivery raised serious problems. Now where medical facilities are available such difficulties are rare, most difficult cases are prevented by timely surgery. However, if it were impossible to prevent the mother's death (or, worse, the death of both) except by cutting up and removing the child piecemeal, it seems to me that this death-dealing deed could be done without the killing itself coming within the scope of the intention. The very deed which deals death also (by hypothesis) initiates a unified and humanly indivisible physical human process which saves life.[266]

Originally Grisez's argument appears to have been based on an action

---

265 I am grateful to my colleague at the John Paul II Institute in Melbourne Adam Cooper for this insight, December 2011.
266 Germain Grisez, *Abortion: The myths, the realities, and the arguments*, New York: Corpus Books, 1970, p. 370.

theory that analyses an act as being an indivisible set of constituent parts.[267] In this case, according to Grisez, the surgeon performing craniotomy performs just one human act to save the life of the mother, but that act has a number of identifiable physical acts. He argued that it is only the human act, saving the life of the mother, that is subject to scrutiny. This chosen human act has an end, an intended end, namely, the preservation of the mother's life. The individual physical acts are not human acts and therefore do not fall under the scope of the intention. Therefore the act of dismembering the foetus is not a human act; rather it is part of the indivisible series of physical acts of saving the life of the mother. He held that it is therefore not a direct killing, because the death of the child is not required in order to save the life.[268]

On revisiting the issue, however, Finnis, Grisez and Boyle[269] appear to have repudiated that approach, but without changing their view about craniotomy. They say that the concept of indivisibility has not been used since 1970 and that it was a false step caused by the failure to appreciate the decisive significance of the perspective of the acting person.[270]

Grisez is a strong critic of proportionalism, but one could be forgiven for wondering how his original account of the indivisibility of the moral act essentially differs from Richard McCormick's claim that "an act cannot be classified morally simply by looking at its *material circa quam*, or at its object in a very narrow and restricted sense," and we must look at the intersubjectivity of the act in order to determine whether it is a moral evil.[271] More to the point, why is Grisez's current analysis of the subjectivity of the human act not open to the same criticism that he made of proportionalists: that it involves separating moral intent from psychological intent?

---

267 Jean Porter, "'Direct' and 'Indirect' in Grisez's Moral Theory", *Theological Studies*, Volume 57, 1996 p. 612.
268 Grisez, Ibid., pp. 333, 340, 341.
269 John M. Finnis, Germain G. Grisez. & Joseph M. Boyle, "'Direct' and 'Indirect': A Reply to Critics of Our Action Theory", *Thomist*, Volume 65, No. 1, 2001, pp. 1-44.
270 Ibid.
271 Richard McCormick, "Classification Through Dialogue", in Richard McCormick and Charles Curran, *The Historical Development of Moral Theology in the United States*, Paulist Press: New Jersey, 1999, pp.193-4.

A concern I have with the Finnis, Boyle and Grisez (FBG) analysis of the account of the moral act in *Veritatis Splendor* is that they seem to interpret the document in a way that provides a strained interpretation of both St Thomas and *Veritatis Splendor*. The latter states:

> By the object of a given moral act, one cannot mean a process or an event of the merely physical order, to be assessed on its ability to bring about a given state of affairs in the world.[272]

They say of this passage, referring to St Thomas, that the species of the moral act as good or bad is not in its species *in genere naturae* but in its species *in genere moris*. They argue that it is necessary to get beyond common sense accounts of what is being done and factors such as causal sequences, to which they give an unreflective priority over the perspective of the acting person.[273]

However, they seem to deny any role at all for the physical reality in determining the psychological reality. The issue is certainly to assess the act from the perspective of the acting person, but the latter cannot be completely unrelated to the reality of what he or she does. My concern is that in claiming that the narrowing of the child's head is the immediate object in order to save the life of the mother, the description omits a large part of what would be in the mind of the surgeon. "Narrowing the baby's head" is only one aspect of this and is not an adequate description of what the surgeon intends to do. Bear in mind what the surgeon does – he or she thrusts an instrument into the head of the child and evacuates the child's brain. Finnis *et al* assert that a surgeon performing craniotomy "resisting the undue influence of physical and causal factors that would dominate the perception of observers, could rightly say, "No way do I intend to kill the baby" and "It is no part of my purpose to kill the baby." They say that the killing in this case is not brought about as a chosen means and thus is not the immediate object in the sense defined in *Veritatis Splendor*.[274]

I cannot see that there can be a separation between the moral description

---

272 *Veritatis Splendor*, n. 78.
273 Finnis *et al*, op. cit., pp. 22-3.
274 Ibid, p. 23.

of the act and the clear psychological intent, which is to dismember the head in a way that is death dealing in itself, not as a side-effect. They argue that the death is not necessary and therefore is not intended. The doctor would do the same if the baby were already dead. But the fact that the death is not needed does not make the act any less an act that directly kills. There is a false distinction being made between moral and psychological intent. The major problem in the Finnis *et al* analysis is that they permit a moral narrative that is psychologically strained, so strained as to be totally implausible as a way in which anyone would actually reason. The acting person who reasoned like that could only be self-deceiving. The act of penetrating the head of the child and drawing out the contents cannot realistically be an act that is not perceived as an act of killing by the acting person. It so dramatically is an act of killing.

According to FGB, the morally relevant description of the act is narrowing the head of the child by dismembering it. That object they claim is to facilitate delivery and save the life of the mother. However the direct object is the dismembering, and that is synonymous with the death of the child. Note that Finnis *et al* are not claiming that the surgeon attempts forceps delivery and in so doing causes dismemberment. That would be quite different. They are proposing a separate procedure, the primary function of which is to dismember the head of the child. That would involve a very different set of instruments from those normally used to deliver a child.

This is not like St Thomas's example of seeking to stop a thief and the injury causing death. The dismemberment intends death. There is no other outcome possible.

There is a difference between this case and the types of cases for which double-effect reasoning ordinarily applies, where the death is clearly a side effect, such as bombing a military installation and killing citizens who happen to be in the vicinity, or removing a gravid cancerous uterus resulting in the loss of life of the child. In the case of dismembering a child to save the life of the mother, the death is integral to what is chosen rather than beside it. The death is synonymous with the act that is necessary to achieve the end of saving life. Someone who dismembers a child but describes their act according to the preferred consequence of saving life and not as a killing is deceiving themselves as to the nature of the act. A morally relevant feature is that the desired consequence is only part of the reality of what is deliberately chosen. To say that in dismembering the child, which is clearly the immediate object, I did not intend the death is just plainly untrue. This case, it seems to me, is quite unlike removing the gravid but cancerous uterus. In the latter case the act results in death, but the act is clearly separable from the death in that the latter is a side effect and therefore beside the intention. Death is not a side effect of dismembering a baby, it is the main event.

There is a difference between attempting to remove the child by forceps delivery and causing the child's death in the process, on the one hand, and, on the other hand, deliberately dismembering the child, as Grisez has described it, in order to achieve removal. The difference is between what is the immediate object and what is truly a side effect. Thus I can accept dismembering the head of the child (and death) if it happens as a side effect of attempts to remove, but not where the procedure in the first instance involves dismembering the head as a step on the way to removal.

I disagree with Finnis *et al* when, in response to Kevin Flannery, they say that the relevant description of the act of dismembering the head would not involve killing the baby. Psychologically, killing the baby would stand foremost as what the surgeon is doing in dismembering the head. On the other hand, if the surgeon attempted a forceps delivery in these circumstances and that resulted, or was likely or even certain to result, in dismemberment while trying to remove the child, that would be different from going in with a procedure to dismember the head of the child. The surgeon could consider the dismemberment to be a side effect of forceps delivery, but not if the dismemberment was the immediate goal of the procedure, presumably with instruments designed to dismember rather than forceps. In the latter case the dismemberment is a *pre-emptive strike* against the child in order to later effect delivery.

Finnis *et al* analyse a case that would seem to bear upon this problem. In their case E,[275] they refer to a farmer who castrates male calves in order to effect hormonal changes that will make them fatter and calmer. The authors say sterilizing is not a means or an end and hence is not part of the proposal to fatten the claves. The case, they argue, makes it clear that, depending on

---

275 Ibid.

what one proposes to do and what one only accepts as a side effect, one can be doing either of two acts different in kind even though everything about one's behaviour and the observable context is the same. The point seems to turn on their claim that sterilization is not essential to the goal of fattening the calves but is a side effect.

The removing of the testes, which is what the sterilization procedure involves, results in the loss of a source of hormones and that loss causes fattening and calmness. The loss of fertility is also an effect of the loss of the testes as they produce sperm. Finnis *et al* would claim that the loss of capacity to produce sperm (sterilization) is a side effect because it is not part of the proposal but foreseen or permitted. I struggle with this. I am unable to separate conceptually removing testes and removing the capacity to produce sperm. Generating sperm is what testes do. Psychologically it would seem to me that the procedure is to sterilize, because sterilizing causes fattening and calming. Unmanageable stallions are gelded for similar reasons. But the gelding could not be considered a side effect. Gelding is the event that usually produces the manageability and anyone who told a farmer that gelding was not sterilization would risk being laughed at or pitied.

Finnis *et al* argue that their account differs from previous accounts that have led the Magisterium to find teaching that supports craniotomy to be unsafe. The difference lies in their rejection of the position that they attribute to Henry Davis SJ and which appears in most accounts of double-effect reasoning:[276] that the good effect must follow at least as immediately and directly as the evil effect. It seems that this principle is an attempt to capture, in part, how it is that the evil in the act is indirect. It is a notion that extends beyond direct lines of causality; that is, the Davis principle does not claim that the impermissible evil is a means to the good, but rather that it precedes or is more immediate than the good.

This is, of course, the case with craniotomy. The dismembering and thus the death precede and are more immediate than the removal of the child that results in the saving of life. The latter is secondary to the procedure to dismember. Finnis *et al* argue that the traditional principle (the Davis

---

276 Ibid. pp. 19-20.

principle) is a mistake, referring to the soldier who throws himself on a grenade to save others. We applaud his heroism they argue, but his body being destroyed is more immediate than the grenade not doing injury, or as much injury, to his fellows.

The soldier's case is different from the craniotomy case both because it is his life and not someone else's that is lost if the grenade explodes, but also because the loss of life and the saving of life are in fact synonymous. His object is to shield the others, when he does so shield them he saves their lives when the grenade explodes and at the same time loses his. His life is not lost until the grenade explodes, and that is precisely when lives are saved. In the craniotomy case we have a dismembering of the child, and then the removal made possible by the dismembering and thus the resolution of the problem. It is a pre-emptive strike to effect removal.

As examples of this reasoning, Finnis *et al* then cite the mention in *Evangelium Vitae* of double-effect reasoning in relation to pain relief and refusal of burdensome life support where death is a side effect. *EV* says that in those cases the death is not willed or sought. But both of those cases are quite different from Finnis *et al's* account in which the evil is more immediate than the good. In the *EV* instances, the pain relief and the lessening of the burden of treatment are more immediate than the death. If in fact the death was expected to precede lessening of the burden or the relief of pain, then death would appear psychologically to be the immediate object (rather than the lessening of the burden). Rather than demonstrating their narrative of the moral act, the *EV* text would seem to indicate difference from it.

There is something of a connection between the Finnis *et al* account and proportionalism in that both seem to override the significance of direct killing. In Finnis *et al*, the moral narrative overrides the psychological narrative of direct killing. In the case of McCormick, the evil of direct killing is overridden by a commensurate reason. It seems to me that Finnis *et al's* account strengthens McCormick's position by substituting a moral narrative in place of the psychological narrative. In both narratives, what is psychologically direct killing is not considered to be morally relevant.

Importantly in referring to VS n. 78 and William Murphy's analysis of it, Lysaught has not referred to VS n. 79, which is a section that seems to have been designed to clarify the type of confusion that has been generated by the view taken by Grisez and others.

In n. 79, Pope John Paul II rejects as erroneous any theory

> ... which holds that it is impossible to qualify as morally evil according to its species – its 'object' – the deliberate choice of certain kinds of behaviour or specific acts, apart from a consideration of the intention for which the choice is made or the totality of the foreseeable consequences of that act for all persons concerned.[277]

The Pope then goes on in the next paragraph to say:

> The primary and decisive element for moral judgment is the object of the human act, which establishes whether it is *capable of being ordered to the good and to the ultimate end, which is God.*

In rejecting judging the morality of the object of an act by the totality of foreseeable consequences, the Pope seems to be rejecting proportionalism of the kind espoused by such writers as Richard McCormick. However, in rejecting judging the morality of the object of an act by its intention only, the Pope would seem to have been addressing the type of treatment of double effect reasoning espoused at that time by Grisez and others, in which they in effect separated moral intention from psychological intention.

Part of the reason for being able to classify the object in that way is Grisez's anthropocentrism. The question being asked is not whether this act is capable of being oriented towards God, (whether it expresses love for God), but whether it is consistent with, or aimed towards, integral human fulfilment. Significant in the analysis is that the case is presented as the child being unable to survive, whether or not there is intervention in this way. It is implied that nothing changes with respect to the integral fulfilment of the child, but it is possible by intervening to save the mother and act for the benefit of her integral fulfilment. Missing in that analysis is the meaning of the intervention in the context of the love of God and the ultimate aim of God alone. The Theological virtues of faith, hope and love imply a

---

277 Pope John Paul II, *Veritatis Splendor,* n. 79.

relationship to God in which we accept our inferiority as creatures and the source of all meaning in God alone.

When I reflect on these cases of what Rhonheimer calls "vital conflict", the very definition of vital conflict implies the agent assuming an assessment of the consequences that leaves no room for doubt about outcomes. That does not fit my experience of medicine in which there is a range of probabilities based on the different reported experiences and different treatment options employed. There is always some degree of uncertainty about diagnosis and, particularly about prognosis. Further, can I say that there is absolutely no place for providence? In the acting person (the mother or the surgeon) choosing an interpretation of likely events, the decision as the basis for acting is handled as of human relevance only. The analysis that Grisez offers is anthropocentric. The choice is an understandable choice, saving the only life that can be saved according to the advice, but is the decision to plunge an instrument into the child's brain and extract the contents one that is consistent with seeing the child as made in the image and likeness of God? Those are not questions that are posed in the FGB analysis which treats the matter as a matter of a type of natural law or practical reason that is anthropocentric and not focussed first and foremost and ultimately on God as the ultimate end.

Returning to the Lysaught analysis of the St Joseph's Hospital case, a crucial aspect of deciding what is the object of the act is what the acting person understands the act to be. To say that performing a D&C on a living unborn child is not abortion just flies in the face of the psychological reality. A surgeon in those circumstances is not likely to say that the procedure was aimed only at removing the placenta. This is a case of separating the moral intent from the reality of the psychological intent. The action of performing a D&C is to remove the contents of the uterus and if the child is alive that is considered by the Church to be an abortion. Prior to viability the child can only survive in the uterus of the mother.

The placenta is formed from tissue that is integral to the child, made from his or her tissue and begins its development in the formation of the blastocyst prior to implantation in the uterus. Genetically the cells of the placenta are the cells of the unborn child and prior to birth the placenta is in fact a vital organ of the unborn child providing the link between the circulation of the child and that of the mother.

There is a factual error in the Lysaught account in that respect. The removal of the placenta is not like the removal of a pregnant cancerous uterus. Rather it is an attack on a vital organ of the unborn child. To say that the intent is to remove the placenta that is causing problems for the mother is to obscure the psychological and factual reality. It is like saying that shooting a man in the lungs is not to directly intend killing him, because the intention was just to stop him breathing. One could well imagine a circumstance in which that was an issue, such as being trapped in a car trunk with him. The problem would be that that his breathing is using up the available oxygen. I could prolong the oxygen available until rescue became more likely by stopping him breathing. However, the reality is that stopping him breathing would be a direct killing.

Basically, in both the Grisez analysis of craniotomy and the Lysaught analysis of D&C in the circumstance of pulmonary arterial hypertension, I am disagreeing over the nature of the object of the act, because of the psychological reality of what is proposed, and how that reality relates to our ultimate end, God. It seems to me to be inappropriate for a Christian to undertake that analysis anthropocentrically rather than theologically. Within a complete Christian analysis of the psychological reality would be a beginning point in the relationship to God. For a Christian, love of neighbour as *imago dei* flows from love of God, it does not precede it.

Grisez has knowingly rejected St Thomas and, at least by implication, *Veritatis Splendor*. There has been no amendment of Grisez's position on anthropocentrism in the light of the "participative theonomy" presented in *Veritatis Splendor*. Whether Grisez *et al* are aware of the implications for their analysis of the moral act is not clear, but there would seem to have been reason for them to be concerned about the implications of the analysis of intention in *Veritatis Splendor* and the need to take into account what the Pope has said on the nature of the object of the act not only with respect to proportionalism, but also what Austriaco refers to as the intentional account. There is also need to consider that Grisez's acknowledgment that he differs from St Thomas on the nature of the ultimate end also has consequences for the nature of the moral act, and that difference with St Thomas is also a difference with *Veritatis Splendor*.

That is disappointing because their view does promote error with respect to the nature of the object of a moral act, such as the error made by Lysaught. A deliberate surgical assault on a vital organ of the unborn child involves an object that includes killing the child. That may be done for the good reason of saving the life of the mother, but it is direct killing and cannot be considered to be consistent with Catholic teaching, following the clarification by Pope John Paul II in *Veritatis Splendor*, and what had been the settled position on craniotomy – much earlier the Congregation for the Doctrine of the Faith addressed the question of craniotomy directly in 1884 saying that it was a direct killing of the innocent.[278]

This was seemingly reinforced by Pope Pius XI in 1930 when he taught in *Casti Connubii*:

> Upright and skillful doctors strive most praiseworthily to guard and preserve the lives of both mother and child; on the contrary, those show themselves most unworthy of the noble medical profession who encompass the death of one or the other, through a pretense at practicing medicine or through motives of misguided pity.

Grisez *et al* argued that his account differed from previous accounts that have led the Magisterium to find teaching that supports craniotomy to be unsafe. As discussed, one difference lay in their rejection of the position that they attribute to Henry Davis SJ and which appears in most traditional accounts of double-effect reasoning:[279] that the good effect must follow at least as immediately and directly as the evil effect.

This is an important aspect of the way in which a person would understand their own act. It is a highly strained interpretation of an act to say that the evil that one does that precedes a good achieved is not intended. Where there is such evil preceding the good, it is then not true to say that the act can be oriented towards God. The preceding evil is the psychological

---

278 John Connery, *Abortion: The Development of the Roman Catholic Perspective*, Chicago, Loyola University of Press, 1997, pp. 225-303.
279 Ibid., pp. 19-20.

intent and specifies the nature of the act, no matter the good that is sought.

The precise goal or purpose of *Veritatis Splendor* is to recall "certain fundamental truths of Catholic doctrine which, in the present circumstances, risk being distorted or denied."[280]

Pope John Paul II refers to "false solutions, linked in particular to an inadequate understanding of the object of moral action." He argues that such false solutions lead to a denial of the existence of "intrinsically evil acts." These last are particularly linked with certain "teleological ethical theories (proportionalism, consequentialism)."[281]

As mentioned above, Pope John Paul II rejects as erroneous any theory

> ... which holds that it is impossible to qualify as morally evil according to its species – its 'object' – the deliberate choice of certain kinds of behaviour or specific acts, apart from a consideration of the intention for which the choice is made or the totality of the foreseeable consequences of that act for all persons concerned.[282]

This is not the only place where the Pope made this point. In n. 72, for instance he says:

> The rational ordering of the human act to the good in its truth and the voluntary pursuit of that good, known by reason, constitute morality. Hence human activity cannot be judged as morally good merely because it is a means for attaining one or another of its goals, or simply because the subject's intention is good. Activity is morally good when it attests to and expresses the voluntary ordering of the person to his ultimate end and the conformity of a concrete action with the human good as it is acknowledged in its truth by reason. If the object of the concrete action is not in harmony with the true good of the person, the choice of that action makes our will and ourselves morally evil, thus putting us in conflict with our ultimate end, the supreme good, God himself.

---

280 Pope John Paul II, *Veritatis Splendor*, n. 4.
281 Ibid. n. 75.
282 Ibid. n. 79.

In my view this teaching not only excludes proportionalism, it also excludes Grisez *et al*'s separation of a moral narrative from the psychological narrative and their rejection of the time-honoured claim that in double-effect reasoning the evil must not be more immediate than the good sought. The latter, it seems to me, reflects accurately the psychological reality and the moral narrative cannot rightly be separated from the psychological reality. If I deliberately fatally dismember someone's head, I mean to kill them. Further a decision to act in that way raises questions about whether the object of an act can be characterised with respect to human fulfilment, rather than focussing first on our ultimate end, God alone, and thus immediately involving the theological virtues and the meaning of love of God as taking precedence over pursuing human fulfilment of ourselves or others.

This seems to me to indicate what may be underlying what Austriaco has called a distinction between a hylomorphic account of the moral act and the intentional thesis propounded by Finnis, Grisz and Boyle. This is whether the object of the act is to be assessed by reference to the good of life within integral human fulfilment and in a way that is separate from its meaning in relation to the New Law, the law of love. Does consideration of our ultimate end in communion with God change the way in which we see the acts that we perform, or is it just an add-on to synderesis with the latter being independently determinative of the nature of the moral act? Did Jesus significantly change our understanding of morality making it more demanding, the demands not only of justice, but also of love?

It seems to me that in their analysis of craniotomy, Finnis *et al* are seeking to construe the object by the intention to save life, ignoring the psychological reality of what the pre-emptive strike against the child actually means. The dismembering of the child's head is done in order to facilitate delivery. It is a separate and distinct assault on the child that causes the immediate death of the child. It is simply not good enough to say that it is simply making the child's head smaller. That is like saying, in the example I gave, that one only wanted to stop someone breathing. Having an intact head is essential to being alive, just as breathing is essential to being alive. It is simply false to say about either intervention that killing is not the immediate object.

Importantly the intentionality thesis does not require us to assess the decision involved in terms of the responsibility the doctor takes upon himself in deciding to act with lethal force. The death of the child is a result of a pre-emptive strike based on judgements that there will be disastrous consequences without that intervention. The very description of the case that demands certainty is in itself a counsel of despair. It seems not insignificant that a certainty has been claimed, for the death of both mother and child, that is not supported by the history of interventions in these circumstances. That is not my experience of medicine. To accept the logic: "crush the baby's head causing death or both will die" involves a confidence in human judgement that itself seem to offend against the Theological virtues.

The Pope reaffirmed that there exist "moral commandments … which prohibit always and without exception *intrinsically evil acts*."[283] But in understanding those commandments, it is not good enough just to relate them to protecting human goods understood only in terms of integral human fulfilment. As referred to above, Pope John Paul II explains the New Law in this respect: God alone is good, and the good is belonging to God, obeying him, walking humbly with him in doing justice and in loving kindness. He writes:

> *To ask about the good*, in fact, *ultimately means to turn towards God*, the fullness of goodness. Jesus shows that the young man's question is really a *religious question*, and that the goodness that attracts and at the same time obliges man has its source in God, and indeed is God himself. God alone is worthy of being loved "with all one's heart, and with all one's soul, and with all one's mind" (*Mt* 22:37). He is the source of man's happiness. Jesus brings the question about morally good action back to its religious foundations, to the acknowledgment of God, who alone is goodness, fullness of life, the final end of human activity, and perfect happiness.[284]

This seems to underlie the problems with Lysaught and her use of Germain Grisez's analysis of craniotomy.

The problem of the intentionality thesis and its basis in a difficulty

---

283 Ibid., n. 115.
284 *Veritatis Splendor*, n. 9.

concerning the anthropocentric identification of our ultimate end is not limited in its effect on causuistry to the case of craniotomy. Grisez's handling of at least two other matters would seem to indicate the same difficulty. In his handling of contraception, Grisez focuses on it being anti-life,[285] and in his handling of the issue of heterologous embryo transfer (HET) or so-called embryo adoption,[286] he again focuses on the protection of human life, and in both matters he places little emphasis on the *sacramentum* in marriage. If the ultimate end is God alone and our focus therefore is to be on love of God and through love of God, love of neighbour made in God's image and likeness, then the starting point for analysis should be the fact that marital intimacy is an expression of love, that is intended to be a witness to God's love in being both unifying and procreative. The starting point for both matters is thus not respect for life, though the latter is implied and included, but human love in God's image. The wrong of contraception is in its rendering marital intimacy to be something other than sacramental, something other than a witness to God's love.

Similarly, the morality of HET should also be explored in terms of the marriage covenant and whether the capacity to become pregnant and to bear a child is given exclusively to the marriage, thus prohibiting the wife from becoming pregnant other than through her husband. To describe the object of that act as life-saving rather than as becoming pregnant from outside marriage[287] is a similar misuse of the principle of double effect reasoning. The species of the object must be determined by whether it is capable of orientation towards God and that places love to the fore as determinative. The virtue of love is consistent with but more demanding than the virtue of justice because it demands that we be more like Christ and not just meet the obligations of justice.

Benedict XVI insisted on the role that the theological virtues play in

---

285 Germain Grisez *et al*, "'Every marital act ought to be open to new life': toward a clear understanding' in Ford, John C *et al*, *The Teaching of Humanae Vitae: A Defence* Ignatius Press: San Francisco, 1988, pp. 33-116.
286 Germain Grisez, *The Way of the Lord Jesus Vol 3, Difficult Moral Questions*, Franciscan Press: Illinois, 1997, pp 239-244.
287 This is claimed by William E. May in *Catholic Bioethics and the Gift of Human Life*, Our Sunday Visitor Inc:, Indiana, 2000, pp. 94-107.

Christian morality in his encyclicals *Deus Caritas Est, Spe Salvi* and *Caritas in Veritate*. As Cardinal Ratzinger, he also described as a fictional starting point the claim that it is possible to construct a rational philosophical picture of man intelligible to all and on which all men of goodwill can agree, "the actual Christian doctrines being added to this as a sort of crowning conclusion."[288]

In the same article, Ratzinger was highly critical of some Thomists, saying that it can hardly be disputed that as a consequence of the division between philosophy and theology established by the Thomists, a juxtaposition has gradually been established which no longer appears adequate. "There is, and must be, a human reason *in* faith, yet conversely, every human reason is conditioned by historical standpoint so that reason pure and simple does not exist."[289]

This may be the crux of the matter for both Rhonheimer and Grisez *et al*. If we admit the Sermon on the Mount into Christian morality, as we must if we are to be Christian, then it requires much more than can be determined anthropocentrically. As philosophers, we need God as the ultimate end, rather than integral human fulfilment, if we are going to account for a morality that adequately includes the theological virtues. To my mind, the proper exercise of moral philosophy is not a Cartesian or Kantian exercise in pure reason from purely logical beginnings, but rather the application of reason to the collection of assumptions that we inherit from our many different cultures, including the sources of Revelation. In that we can enter into a true partnership with theology, as required by *Gaudium et Spes* (n. 59) and by *Fides et Ratio* (n.77), because I am confident that Christian claims about what love is as gift of self, understood from the Christ event, can stand alongside alternatives robustly, and be readily sustained through the course of rigorous philosophical analysis. As Pope John Paul II expressed it, "Theology needs philosophy as a partner in dialogue in order to confirm the intelligibility and universal truth of its claims."[290] In my own experience

---

288 Joseph Ratzinger, "The Dignity of the Human Person", in Herbert Vorgrimler (ed) *Commentary on the Documents of Vatican II* Vol V (Burns & Oates: London, 1969), pp. 115-163.
289 Ibid.
290 Pope John Paul II, *Fides et Ratio* , n. 77.

chairing government public enquiries, presenting an overtly Christian view about relationships, between health professionals and patients and research participants, is much more persuasive than trying to present a natural law structure involving not violating basic human goods. Love makes sense of what otherwise appears to be arcane or merely dogmatic.

13.5 Conclusion

The issue in the St. Joseph's Hospital case is that they took it upon themselves to intervene in a way that caused the death of the child as a better alternative to risking the death of both through hypertension. In terms of calculation of consequences, it would have seemed better to intervene in favour of the higher probability of saving one life rather than losing both. As the hospital expressed it in their public statement, "... if we are presented with a situation in which a pregnancy threatens a woman's life, our first priority is to save both patients. If that is not possible we will always save the life we can save."

The latter statement would seem to take little account of the means used to achieve that end.

The St Joseph's Hospital case is not unique. On twelve occasions during my time as a hospital ethicist, I encountered the circumstances of a woman suffering from acute Leukaemia during pregnancy and being advised that termination of pregnancy was recommended. The reasoning was that if the woman was treated for the Leukaemia while pregnant she would probably miscarry and at a time when her blood platelets were at their lowest, and not only would the child die but she would also.

As a young hospital ethicist, I discussed the situation with the then President of the Australia and New Zealand Catholic Moral Theologians Association, the late Rev Dr William Daniel SJ. His advice was that one cannot "make a pre-emptive strike".

Of the twelve cases, eleven involved termination of pregnancy after transfer of the patient to a government hospital for "assessment and on-going management" in circumstances in which the Catholic hospital indicated that it could not be involved with an abortion. That raises some interesting questions about cooperation that were, in my opinion, well handled by the hospital. The hospital could not lawfully have prevented the woman from the transfer, and not facilitating it by making records available to the other hospital, etc., or not arranging ambulance transfer, would have amounted to an attempt to prevent. The doctors did not refer for abortion, they referred for "assessment and ongoing management". What happened at the other hospital was between the patient and the doctors there.

In one case, the patient elected to continue her pregnancy and to have management of her medical condition consistent with trying to save both her life and the life of her child. Against the estimated odds, she and the baby did both survive until the baby could be born. Both went home well, though she did die of an acute episode two years later. Her circumstances have made me very wary of what Rhonheimer calls "vital conflict" and pre-emptive strikes.

That also seemed to be the situation at the St Joseph's Hospital. They were intervening on the basis of probabilities to choose the more favourable probability of the mother surviving against the probability of both dying. The intention was undoubtedly good, but they engaged a means to achieve it that seems to be indistinguishable from direct killing, a pre-emptive strike. It is important to note that Rhonheimer has explicitly not endorsed this application of his view. I am not aware of any endorsement by Grisez either.

A difficulty I have with the handling of the craniotomy case, by Rhonheimer and Grisez, on which Lysaught relied, is that there is a world of difference between dismembering and thus causing the death of the child as a result of efforts to effect a forceps delivery, on the one hand, and, on the other, dismembering the child and thus causing its death in order to effect delivery. In the first case the dismembering and the death are genuinely a side effect. In the second they are a means to the end. The logic that allowed the dismembering as a means to the end in the craniotomy case becomes apparent when it is applied to abortion undertaken in order to reduce the risks to the life of the mother of a disease process. In the second instance, the logic permits a pre-emptive strike directly against the child. A pre-emptive strike is not part of the logic of self-defence within the Church's tradition. Importantly the logic that justifies the St Joseph's decision seems not to be based on morality as a participative theonomy based on our ultimate end being God alone, but a much more truncated and non-Thomistic notion of morality that is focussed anthropocentrically on human fulfilment.

In both the Rhonheimer thesis on vital conflicts and the Grisez intentionality thesis there is a narrowing of what can be considered within the scope of the object of the act. For Rhonheimer that means that the pre-emptive strike is not intended at all because the child's life cannot be saved and there is thus no injustice. Thus for him, the wrong of killing is limited to the extent to which it is unjust. In Grisez's analysis the object is assessed only in terms of the good of life understood in terms of integral social fulfilment, and not the more demanding scope of the theological virtues and their impact on giving witness to God's love and seeking communion with Him.

Servais Pianckers has convincingly demonstrated that the *Catechism* and *Veritatis Splendor* represent a significant enrichment of moral theology. *Veritatis Splendor* moves beyond synderesis to a broader understanding of a morality of love, still rigorously founded on protecting human development and flourishing, but doing so in a way that looks to the greater meaning of human acts as witness to God's love and dependant on goodness that is His alone. Moral theology should therefore be about our relationship to God first, and through that communion of love we are required to love our neighbour as *imago dei*. That profoundly effects how we must treat the anatomy of the moral act and double effect reasoning.

The St Joseph's Hospital public statement is distinctly lacking:

> Consistent with our values of dignity and justice, if we are presented with a situation in which a pregnancy threatens a woman's life, our first priority is to save both patients. If that is not possible we will always save the life we can save, and that is what we did in this case.

What is lacking is its dependency on our relationship to God. Christian morality is not just about human dignity and justice. God alone is good, and the good is belonging to God, obeying him, walking humbly with him in doing justice and in loving kindness (Micah 6:8). How we save life matters.

13.6 Like Cases

As I have discussed in reference to the St. Joseph's Hospital case and the craniotomy case, the conditions under which an intervention is a direct abortion, and even if it is indirect, whether it is permissible, given the relative risks to mother and child, are hotly debated. This leads to some resentment that the Church may be intervening in what is basically the woman's right to preserve her life. This may lead to reluctance on the part of Catholic ethicists and Bishops to give advice on such matters. My aim in including this chapter is to try to make the issues as clear as possible so that those women and their doctors who take a "two patients view" of pregnancy may explore what interventions remain consistent with respect for both mother and child. I know, from experience, how difficult that choice may be and do not wish to offer criticisms of those who made difficult choices.

Using the language of *Veritatis Splendor*, and not the FGB language, I take it that what is acceptable is where the act is not an intervention that directly results in the taking of a life but an act designed, in its immediate object to be life saving for the mother, and thus the death of the child is considered to be an indirect effect, and there is a favourable balance of probabilities given equal weight to respecting the lives of both mother and child. I argued that that way of thinking would rule out craniotomy for instance, or terminating a previable pregnancy in order to prevent severe pre-eclampsia. Those are two instances in which the intervention is direct in causing the death of the child and the benefit to the mother follows secondarily from the event that directly causes the death of the child. The intrinsic evil of direct abortion, in my view, cannot be outweighed by a favourable balance of probabilities.

There are, however, other ways of managing both of those situations but which involve greater risk for the mother.

The FGB analysis allows craniotomy and, presumably, abortion in the case of severe pre-eclampsia, though I have only seen them comment only in favour of craniotomy, and not abortion in the case of pre-eclampsia. Lysaught argued on the basis of Grisez's craniotomy analysis, and Rhonheimer's, in favour of abortion for severe pre-eclampsia.

There are treatments for pre-eclampsia, such as anti-hypertensives, and ways of giving greater support for her cardiac and lung function until viability is reached and the pregnancy can be terminated safely for both, though she still may die before that, and if she dies then so would the child, obviously. There is sometimes a period when the child is doubtfully viable, and that doubt may permit termination of pregnancy (induction of birth) if in an emergency the woman is at great risk, with the possible, even probable, death of the child still being considered indirect because he or she might have survived. The means of terminating pregnancy ought not, however, involve a direct assault on the child and must be restricted to bringing about birth only, as safely as possible for the mother and the child. There are prudential judgements to be made in that case about the relative risks to mother and child, taking into account that her death prior to birth may well result in the death of both.

In the case of arrested labour with the baby locked in the birth canal, which is not an issue in modern developed world circumstances where Caesarean section can be performed safely, there remains an issue in conditions where the surgical capacity does not exist. As we saw, in the nineteenth century, Caesarean section had an 85% maternal mortality rate, and that would be true still of some circumstances in developing countries where there is only relatively unskilled midwife assistance available. Nevertheless, in that case there is still an alternative to Caesarean section and craniotomy, and that is to sever the ligament that joins the two sides of the pelvis, a procedure called "symphisiotomy". That has greater long term problems for the woman, especially if the team lacks the surgical capacity to repair it, but it is a way of saving both lives in the immediate term.

In the case of acute Leukaemia, the maternal condition may be managed with a less aggressive form of chemotherapy and other supportive therapies, though the probability of maternal survival is much less than if the pregnancy was terminated. In the former case of the lesser therapies, there would still be a risk of causing miscarriage and haemorrhage and ultimately the death of both. So, in terms of numbers, abortion ends in the certain death of one, but the more conservative option potentially involves the death of both. However those deaths would be indirect, with everything, other than abortion, being done to save both lives.

In the case of aggressive tumours that are exacerbated by pregnancy and the complications to the maternal immune system, that too can be managed conservatively without abortion but with increased risk to the mother and also the possibility of causing a miscarriage, but again the deaths, if either or both happened, would be indirect.

The argument in Catholic circles is over the fact that direct abortion, in these cases, results in fewer deaths overall and on a vital conflict theory (Rhonheimer) or other moral act analysis (Grisez, Finnis and Boyle) that claims that the death of the child is indirect (GFB) or is simply not intended because inevitable (R). In secular circles, the argument is based on the contemporary view that the life of the child before birth counts for much less – a one patient rather than a two patient view.

A good pro-life doctor does not have direct abortion as an option. He or she will do everything possible to save both lives, other than direct abortion. There is always something that can be done to increase the chances of survival, including taking risks with either or both lives. That then involves some prudential judgements. Even so, it is the case that without the option of direct abortion, statistically, more women will die in relatively rare circumstances such as these, than would otherwise be the case. The decision to accept the probability of risk to herself in order to give her child a greater chance of survival is a choice that she may choose to make as a matter of love for her child and faith in God.

I might add that the recent Irish case seemed bizzare to me. I could not understand why they could not have acted to save her life without direct abortion, when the risks became so great. Why did they not manage the infection aggressively, even if it risked the life of the child? That would have been acceptable in terms of causing an indirect abortion, if the risks to her life and the child's life warranted it.

These decisions are difficult but to be made by the woman, in the first instance, and she has every right to seek alternative care in the event that those caring for her find that her preferred option would involve them in a conscientious objection. The difficult weighing of relative probabilities by those directly involved should not be a matter for the law, especially the clumsiness of criminal law.

14
Why Reject Contraception?

Contraception is intervention in the body of the woman or man or in the marriage act to suppress fertility.

Sometime that happens as a result of medical treatment for other purposes. For instance, a woman may have a cancer of the ovaries or the uterus and the treatment is to remove the tissue, resulting in infertility. Some women have dysmenorrhoea (very painful periods), which is usually treated with analgesics and anti-inflammatories but is sometimes treated with hormones that may affect fertility. Some doctors will prescribe the contraceptive pill for that purpose. It may not be the ideal treatment, especially for young women who are still developing, but it is a legitimate treatment. The pill is also taken for the whole cycle, when dysmenorrhoea is only for a few days of the cycle. Some will also prescribe the pill for some skin conditions, though there are alternatives.

Provided there is a legitimate reason for it, the Catholic Church accepts that the contraceptive pill may be used for other reasons, where the effect on fertility is considered a side effect and not the main reason for taking it, and there are no alternatives that are as effective.

The moral issue of contraception, however, arises within marriage when a couple choose to contraceive as a way of family planning.

The Catholic Church accepts that couples have a responsibility to regulate the size of their families and the spacing of births. However, the Church has not accepted the use of interventions in the body of the woman or the man, or in the marriage act itself, in order to achieve this end.

Instead, the Church has approved using knowledge of the natural cycle to determine whether or not to have sexual intimacy at a time when pregnancy is possible or likely.

Today the ability to identify the fertile and infertile parts of the cycle and when ovulation occurs is well developed and couples can readily access that information through established methods. The scientifically established methods include Sympto-Thermal, Billings, or Creighton. Each of these methods has an established reliability, published in reputable peer reviewed journals, that is on a par with the use of the low dose oral contraceptive pills and better than the results for barrier methods such as condoms, caps, diaphragms or intra-uterine devices.

The lesser popularity of fertility awareness methods in Western countries is not to do with its established effectiveness, but with perceptions of poor success and the fact that it requires abstinence if pregnancy is to be avoided. It has been the butt of "Vatican Roulette" humour that does not reflect the scientific reality. It is also sometimes claimed that women need regular cycles to use these methods. This may be true for methods that rely on calendar calculations, at least in so far as they can require extensive abstinence, but it is false for most contemporary methods because the latter rely not on calendar, but on charting signs and symptoms that accurately map the cycle and can identify the oestrogen rise associated with the start of possible fertility and the progesterone rise that marks ovulation. The infertile part of the cycle begins soon after, because eggs do not survive more than 24 hours.

The Church has always rejected contraception. It was rejected in Old Testament times and that rejection extended through the Early Fathers, such as St John Chrysostom and St Augustine, through the medievalists, such as St Albert the Great and St Thomas Aquinas, to the Popes of the modern era.

In a recent work on the encyclical *Humanae Vitae*, D. Vincent Twomey writes:

> For the spouses to take the initiative to exclude the possibility of new life is to act against the possibility inherent in that union of God's creative action; it is to act in contradiction with the image of the Triune God as reflected in the union of the spouses. In a word, it amounts to an attempt to exclude God from that human act where he is most present in the created order.[291]

---

[291] D. Vincent Twomey, *Moral Theology after Humane Vitae: Fundamental Issues in Moral Theort and Sexual Ethics* Four Courts Press/Dublin, 2010, p. 195.

Explaining the modern acceptance of contraception he speaks of the modern era placing trust in our relationship to material reality in which, through science, we have become maker and producer able to dominate and manipulate the natural world. Contraception and, to an extent, in vitro fertilization as discussed earlier represent our efforts to turn this capacity on ourselves, with the body becoming raw material to be shaped and used at will. Twomey argues that contraception is therefore inherently dualist, and morality becomes utility measured by outcomes, rather than by meaning and relationship with God.

Instead, he argues that in the Christian vision of man, we are not masters of the sources of life but ministers of the design established by the Creator. This is the view taken in *Humanae Vitae* (n.13) in which Pope Paul VI said:

> ... to experience the gift of married love while respecting the laws of conception is to acknowledge that one is not the master of the sources of life but rather the minister of the design established by the Creator. Just as man does not have unlimited dominion over his body in general, so also, and with more particular reason, he has no such dominion over his specifically sexual faculties, for these are concerned by their very nature with the generation of life, of which God is the source.

Twomey writes that mutual self-giving in marriage is self-surrender to each other, but also to God, respecting God's initiative in the woman's cycle to give life. The use of self-control through fertility awareness is in itself a virtue, whereas control by manipulation of the body is vicious.

Addressing this same issue, Pope John Paul II said that at the origin of every human person there is a creative act of God. No man comes into existence by chance; he is always the object of God's creative love. From this fundamental truth of faith and reason it follows that the procreative capacity, inscribed in human sexuality is - in its deepest truth – a cooperation with God's creative power. And it also follows that man and woman are not arbiters, are not the masters of this same capacity, called as they are, in it and through it, to be participants in God's creative decision.

The Pope went on to say:

When, therefore, through contraception, married couples remove from the exercise of their conjugal sexuality its potential procreative capacity, they claim a power which belongs solely to God: the power to decide in a final analysis the coming into existence of a human person. They assume the qualification of not being cooperators in God's creative power, but the ultimate depositaries of the source of human life. In this perspective, contraception is to be judged objectively so profoundly unlawful, as never to be, for any reason, justified. To think or to say the contrary is equal to maintaining that in human life, situations may arise in which it is lawful not to recognize God as God.[292]

The issue is complex because in part it depends on an exalted notion of Christian marriage. Pope Paul VI taught that husband and wife, through the mutual gift of themselves, which is specific and exclusive to them alone, develop that union of two persons in which they perfect one another, cooperating with God in the generation and rearing of new lives. This perfection, he said, stemmed from the fact that the marriage of those who have been baptized is invested with the dignity of a sacramental sign of grace, for it represents the union of Christ and His Church.[293]

In his explanation, Pope John Paul II in his *Theology of the Body* catechesis (see section 2.1) referred to the passage in St Matthew's Gospel in which Jesus refers to the Genesis account of the origin of marriage in the creation of men and women – both equal in God's image, with their relationship being the sign and symbol in the world of God's love, the love of God for all creation, the perfect and fruitful love between the persons of the Trinity, and the love that Jesus expressed at Gethsemane in accepting the Father's will, and subsequently on the Cross.

The sacramental significance of marriage, therefore, is that it is a sign and a witness to God's perfect, fruitful and self-giving love.

The difficulty with contraception is that it involves rejecting this sacramental role, with the couple rejecting their fruitfulness and thus no longer aspiring to make their love a perfect likeness to the Divine love. Pope

---

292 John Paul II, *L'Osservatore Romano*, 10 October 1983.
293 Pope Paul VI, *Humanae Vitae*, 1968 n. 9.

John Paul II, and Pope Benedict XVI after him, state that contraception "means negating the intimate truth of conjugal love, with which the divine gift (of life) is communicated."[294]

Pope John Paul refers to contraception as a falsification:

> When couples, by means of recourse to contraception, separate these two meanings that God the Creator has inscribed in the being of man and woman and in the dynamism of their sexual communion, they act as 'arbiters' of the Divine plan and they "manipulate" and degrade human sexuality – and with it themselves and their married partner – by altering its value of "total" self-giving. Thus the innate language that expresses the total reciprocal self-giving of husband and wife is overlaid, through contraception, by an objectively contradictory language, namely, that of not giving oneself totally to the other. This leads not only to a positive refusal to be open to life but also to a falsification of the inner truth of conjugal love, which is called upon to give itself in personal totality.[295]

To accept this thinking about the meaning of contraception within marriage, one first needs to accept what is a substantial development of doctrine about marriage.

The contemporary teaching has elevated the love between the spousal couple to the level that their sexual intimacy is the ongoing celebration of the sacrament. Through their love they seek their own perfection as a sign and symbol of God's love.

The change in doctrine no longer refers to the *debitum*, the duty of couples to have sex, referred to by earlier Popes such as Pope Pius XI and Pope Pius XII and by St Augustine. Nor does the new doctrine refer to any right to have sex. Gone also is the notion that one of the purposes of marriage is to quieten concupiscence or lust. Instead, Pope Paul VI explained married love as a fully human, fully free and total mutual gift of self that is also open to the possibility that God may endow the relationship with the gift of life.[296]

---

294 Benedict XVI, Interview on plane to Africa, AFP, 3 October 2008.
295 John Paul II, *Familiaris Consortio*, n. 32.
296 Pope Paul VI, *Humanae Vitae*, 1968, n. 9.

Husband and wife should not see each other as sex objects to be used for mutual sexual gratification. Instead their love expresses the deep meaning of being a sign and symbol of God's love by being a complete and mutual gift of self.

This echoed the teaching of Pope Pius XI when he wrote in 1930,

> For all men of every condition, in whatever honorable walk of life they may be, can and ought to imitate that most perfect example of holiness placed before man by God, namely Christ Our Lord, and by God's grace to arrive at the summit of perfection, as is proved by the example set us of many saints.
>
> This mutual moulding of husband and wife, this determined effort to perfect each other, can in a very real sense, as the Roman Catechism teaches, be said to be the chief reason and purpose of matrimony, provided matrimony be looked at not in the restricted sense as instituted for the proper conception and education of the child, but more widely as the blending of life as a whole and the mutual interchange and sharing thereof.[297]

In this the Popes have restored the earlier teaching of St Augustine and St Thomas that the marriage act has three purposes: the unity and fidelity (*Fides*) of the couple, their fruitfulness and openness to God's will in having children (*Proles*), and the sacramental nature of their love in being a sign and symbol of God's love (*Sacramentum*).

That their sexual intimacy is therefore holy takes on a much stronger meaning in its role within their relationship as a means by which they seek perfection in God's image. That notion of marriage which has its basis in Scripture thus provides a new and deeper understanding of the meaning of contraception. It is an intervention in the body or in the marriage act to reject God's cooperation and design to make the marriage act fruitful. The explicit purpose of contraception is to render unfruitful the expression of love that might otherwise have been fruitful. It is thus a rejection of God's design and a falsification of what the marriage act means.

In a way, a parallel can be drawn to chastity. The man who at the office

---

297 Pope Pius XI, *Casti Connubii*, 1930, n. 23-24.

party has a sexual relationship with a co-worker or with his boss, may say to his wife that this was important to protect his job prospects, which may have been damaged by rejection of the other. He may also say that it does not mean what his marriage means because it is only one act and the relationship will be thus passing. But no amount of persuasion on his part is likely to persuade her to accept that this was not a betrayal of the love and their commitment. His adultery will always be wrong no matter what good consequences it might produce.

In a similar way, contraception is an attack on the important meaning that a couple's marital love has in the context of their love for God with respect to the *imago dei*, and with respect to them being stewards of their bodies, not masters – co-operators with the divine plan. Essentially the body is the person, but contraception involves treating the body as an object and not a person.

On the other hand, a couple who genuinely love each other and wish to seek perfection in their imitation of Divine love can decide not to make love at times when their love-making may produce a child, at a time when having a child would involve significant hardship. There is no obligation to make love and it is not the only way in which they express love for each other. By abstaining, they express the virtue of temperance and chastity and can ensure that their love-making, when they do choose it, is completely intact, truly a total gift of self, and open to the divine plan for fertility. They have done nothing to interfere with its purpose and meaning.

This is what I have referred to as the sacramental meaning of the marital act. It links their love-making to their vocation to give witness to God's love, and to be open to the graces that belong to the sacrament of marriage. By their love they become closer to the Persons of the Holy Trinity.

For Mary and me this understanding of our love has been enormously enriching. We fail to be good lovers in many ways through human weakness, and suffer from the effects of sin in countless ways. But what is important is the aspiration that individually, the sacrament of marriage is how we are called to live as perfectly as we can in the image and likeness of the Holy Trinity and Their individual and collective love for each other and for all creation. As we have moved through the various phases of our relationship, including through the great joys and challenges of parenting, and through the losses occasioned by extended family deaths and through my illness, we have felt that we were called by God to give this witness as married persons and as parents. Not contraceiving has been a central aspect of our love, and finding other ways to express our love, when another child would have been too difficult, greatly enriched our relationship. We were fortunate that every one of our children was planned and deeply desired when on those occasions we decided to "leave it to God", thereby inviting Him to make us co-creators in the miracle of a new life.

Abstinence greatly enriched me, in particular. I cannot say that it was always easy. When one is deeply in love, one wants to express it in the most perfect way possible especially when sharing life with a beautiful woman who loves you and wants your love. However, fertility is not the only reason why couples abstain. There are so many other reasons that make sexual intimacy inappropriate, especially in the context of the demands that children make, particularly of their mother, who just wants a quiet embrace and sleep at the end of a physically very demanding day with young children. A woman's libido is often quite different from a man's, so much slower and so very fragile. In general for a woman, everything needs to be right with the world before she feels inclined to make love. For a man, everything is right with the world when he and his wife have just made love. A husband soon learns that he has a task in front of him to create the circumstances that are right for her. He needs to learn the ways in which she may feel loved, whether it is receiving gifts, or time to converse, or acts of service or homemaking or verbal expressions of his love for her, taking a greater share of the tasks associated with children. She needs to feel loved, supported and appreciated, and above all not taken for granted. She especially needs not to be tired or ill. The time of the cycle also affects her energy levels and her moods and libido and he needs to be aware of when she most needs his acts of affection and they may be times when for other reasons there can be no expectation of intimacy. He needs to show his love for her, pure and simple, not in expectation that he can buy her intimacy. He needs to show his unconditional love, and treat sexual intimacy as a wonderful surprise, a gift, when it happens that she wishes to be held in that very special embrace that celebrates the sacrament.

I thank God for Mary's love and understanding that so deepened my own understanding, and brought me ever closer to God through my love for her and through finding the image and likeness of God in her. Contraception would have so damaged us and I express the depth of my appreciation for those medical scientists, such as John and Evelyn Billings, who made living chastely easier and more certain, and gave us such a depth of understanding of the mystery of the hormonal highs and lows of a woman's cycle and the effect on creating the fertile window. Even if the science continues to develop after them, as is likely, the wisdom they brought to natural family planning and the affirmation of women's own observations will forever be hallmarks of this science. As a medical student, Mary had encountered the Sympto-Thermal Method. But it was attending a session at which I was speaking alongside John and Lyn, in 1985 at the Albury Hospital, that she realised that the Billings Method made that task of family planning so simple and gave women confidence in their observations without being prescriptive. Whatever a woman observed was happening with her symptoms could be interpreted and given meaning. To see Lyn and John in action together was inspiring.

In the subject I teach on Natural Family Planning, I have senior teachers from each of the methods teach. I advise students to choose one method and work with a teacher of that method, while acknowledging that all three are valid and effective.

There is a certain amount of territorial protectiveness between the three methods, which is very human. Having often sat through presentations from all three methods, I am convinced that at the same time, there are lessons that they could teach each other.

The Sympto-Thermal Method (STM) covers a broad range of options and observation of signs and symptoms. They critique the Billings Ovulation Method (BOM) for ignoring other relevant matters, especially the temperature change after ovulation. The BOM narrows the method down to the most informative and reliable symptom – the observable changes in the mucus symptom at the vulva associated with hormonal changes – but without ruling out the possible inclusion of other symptoms, if a woman finds them helpful. The BOM teachers critique STM for not teaching the mucus symptom adequately and the confusion that may be added by paying too much attention to "counting days" over being guided by symptoms. The use of the calendar calculations can also lead to much longer periods of abstinence, as the standard is the shortest and the longest cycle the woman has had. That may pose difficulties during weaning, after Pill use, during peri-menopause and illness, and if the woman does have or has had highly irregular cycles.

The BOM has no need for taking temperature when the progesterone rise after ovulation is reflected so clearly in the sudden drying up of the mucus symptom. This is explained by the role of the physiological phenomenon that is caused by the progesterone rise at ovulation. The phenomenon occurs in the "Pockets of Shaw" that release manganese into the vagina absorbing the moisture in the mucus and dramatically altering the vulval sensation from wet and slippery to sticky or dry. The temperature rise observation can also be confounded by other factors such as illness and fever or changed circumstances causing temperature alterations.

Finally, the BOM approach relies on vulval sensation and does not require the woman to undertake any kind of internal examination. The latter may confuse the vulval observation and may be an infection-risk if fingers are placed in the vagina, and particularly if the cervix is examined.

Historically, the third method, the Creighton or Naprotechnology approach, developed from the BOM but uses a much more standardised approach to classifying mucus, adding factors such as colour, consistency and stretchiness which involves a codified system of observation which is more prescriptive than an individual woman's own observations might have been. The extra detail is said to assist in medical diagnosis of pathologies. The Creighton Method (CM) is much more focused on using the method as a system of diagnosis, and is more directly linked to other forms of diagnosis such as ultrasound analysis, and to medical treatments. CM has developed the use of natural progesterone therapy where there is evidence of a poor *corpus luteum* after ovulation. The evidence suggests that the progesterone may prevent miscarriage.

The other methods can also use the information charted by the woman diagnostically. Where there is indication of a short Luteal Phase (after ovulation and before menstruation), Chlomid or the Gonadotropins may be used to improve ovulation, though there is a growing recognition of the use of natural progesterones. The latter are now also used by IVF clinics and are listed in Australia on the Pharmaceutical Benefits Scheme and eligible for government funding.

I suspect that in time, the differences between the three methods will become less significant, though I think competition prevents complacency and is not a bad thing.

The Billings had some reservations about the CM. First, the CM literature does not seemed to be informed about the Pockets of Shaw and their sudden effect on the mucus at the vulva that is so informative about determining that ovulation has indeed occurred. Misunderstanding that event or its absence could mislead a woman into thinking that ovulation might still happen or had already happened.

Second, the CM rules have the woman bearing down and wiping out the vagina to remove seminal fluid after intercourse. This is not likely to have a contraceptive effect because, if the woman is at a potentially fertile time, the sperm would already have entered the cervix and be beyond such attempts to remove semen. The vagina is a hostile place for sperm in any case, unlike the cervix which, during the possibly fertile time, will nourish the sperm and keep it alive for several days. The concern is the symbolism and emotional significance of the acts involved, as though they were a rejection of the husband's contribution. The aim of so doing is the removal of the seminal fluid to prevent confusing the observation of cervical mucus on the day after sexual intimacy. The rules of the two methods are thus different. In the days before the mucus change indicates the probable start of the fertile window, the so-called "early days", the BOM rules limit sexual intimacy to the evening of every second day – they call that the "Alternate Day Rule" or "Early Day Rule". The CM rules allow consecutive days to be used.

A third line of concern is what the Billings perceive is an over-complication of mucus observation and the need to actually examine the mucus rather than relying on the vulval sensation that is so important to the Billings charting.

The evidence suggests very little difference in success rates for either achieving or avoiding pregnancy. That is why I have my students taught all three methods and examined on all three with a separate section of the paper allocated to method specific questions. They need to know what method a client may be using and how that method works. They also need to know that there is no woman for whom natural family planning cannot work. The students are also advised that all three methods are scientifically valid, but that their clients should try to follow one method only, as the evidence for success rates does not involve combining methods.

The main point to make is that each of the methods provides an adequate way of managing family planning without needing contraceptive intervention. As discussed, the choice to deliberately contraceive is morally problematic because it is not consistent with the sacramental and vocational significance of marital sexual intimacy as a witness to God's love which is both unitive within the Trinity, and fruitful as the ongoing Creator of all creation. Contraceptive intervention treats the body of either partner or the marital act itself as a mere means to an end, rather than respecting the human body and the marital union itself as sacred because made in the image and likeness of the Triune God. The mutually loving sexual intimacy between husband and wife has a transcendental meaning as a witness to Divine love. This is the central principle of what is now known as the Theology of the Body (see Chapter Two).

15
Prevention of Sexually Transmissible Infection: Was the Catholic Church Wrong?

15.1 The Issue

In the 1980s, most Western governments adopted a policy on sexual transmission of HIV to promote abstinence, monogamy and safer sex.

The Catholic Church agreed with abstinence and monogamy, but not safer sex. The Church regarded the risk to life of an infected person having sex with a condom to be unacceptably high (given established failure rates) and the promotion of "safer sex' to be thus irresponsible. However, what came to be known misleadingly as "safe sex" has dominated government strategy as the promotion of condoms, allied to supply of clean needles for drug users. Governments have done little to promote the first two elements of the strategy.

The Catholic Church has also rejected so-called "safe injecting rooms." In July 2000, the Congregation for the Doctrine of the Faith advised the Sisters of Charity in Sydney to withdraw from the trial of a safe injecting room on the basis that participation would cause "scandal" in the broader community. Cardinal Ratzinger (later Pope Benedict XVI), then head of the Vatican's Congregation for the Doctrine of Faith, in a letter tabled in the NSW Parliament, is quoted as saying "these facilities encourage the abuse of and illegal trafficking in drugs, undermine respect for law, degrade social mores, and oftentimes represent the first step towards decriminalization of drugs."[298]

---

298 *Sydney Morning Herald*, 7 July 2000, p. 13.

The Catholic Church in Australia is a major provider of care for people with HIV through its hospitals, nursing home and hospices. The Church has supported sex education including:

- full information;
- emphasis on values;
- importance of sexual intimacy for three reasons:
  - total, fully human, free, faithful, secure, mutual gift of love that expresses unity of couple;
  - the possibility of new life;
  - witness to love that God has for people and love between persons of Holy Trinity.

Pope Benedict XVI spoke about HIV prevention during a flight to Africa in 2009:

> I would say that this problem of AIDS cannot be overcome merely with money, necessary though it is. If there is no human dimension, if Africans do not help [*by responsible behaviour*], the problem cannot be overcome by the distribution of prophylactics: on the contrary, they increase it. The solution must have two elements: firstly, bringing out the human dimension of sexuality, that is to say a spiritual and human renewal that would bring with it a new way of behaving towards others, and secondly, true friendship offered above all to those who are suffering, a willingness to make sacrifices and to practise self-denial, to be alongside the suffering. And so these are the factors that help and that lead to real progress: our twofold effort to renew humanity inwardly, to give spiritual and human strength for proper conduct towards our bodies and those of others, and this capacity to suffer with those who are suffering, to remain present in situations of trial. It seems to me that this is the proper response, and the Church does this, thereby offering an enormous and important contribution.[299]

---

299 Interview of the Holy Father Benedict XVI during his Flight to Africa, Tuesday, 17 March 2009. http://www.vatican.va/holy_father/benedict_xvi/speeches/2009/

15.2 Criticism of Church Policy

The Church has been criticized for causing deaths by failing to advocate condoms. *The Guardian's* Polly Toynbee, on the occasion of the death of John Paul II, called the Vatican, "a modern, potent force for cruelty and hypocrisy." Toynbee said with the "ban on condoms the church has caused the death of millions of Catholics and others in areas dominated by Catholic missionaries, in Africa and right across the world. In countries where 50 per cent are infected, millions of very young Aids orphans are today's immediate victims of the curia."

15.3 Does the data support the claim?

In Africa it is accepted that:

- HIV Transmission is largely a heterosexual problem.
- Risk of transmission *increased* by comparative higher rates of pre-existing inflammatory conditions, especially genito-urinary, due to
  - lack of clean water;
  - lack of treatment for infection;
  - inadequate nutrition;
  - poor health and hygiene;
  - lack of primary obstetric, gynaecological and perinatal care resulting in mother to baby transmission.[300]

A comparison of HIV rates with religion in Africa in 2009 shows lower HIV rates in relation to Catholic faith:

- Burundi, 62 per cent Catholic has a 3.3 per cent HIV infection rate.
- Angola, 38 per cent Catholic has 2.0 per cent HIV rate.
- Ghana, 63 per cent Christian and 33 per cent Catholic has 1.8 per cent HIV rate.

---

300 Melissa Pope, Asley T. Haase, "Transmission, acute HIV-infection and the quest for strategies to prevent infection", *Nature Medicine Review*, Volume 9, No. 7, July 2003, pp. 847-852.

- Nigeria, divided almost evenly between the strongly Muslim north and Christian and "animist" south, has 3.6 per cent HIV rate.
- Uganda, 33 per cent Catholic, maintains an abstinence and fidelity AIDS prevention programs and has 6.5 per cent HIV rate, significantly lower than it was.
- Of African countries with low Catholic populations, Botswana is typical with 24.8 per cent HIV infection, one of the highest in Africa, and 5 per cent of the total population Catholic.
- In 2003, Swaziland was shown to have a 25.9 per cent HIV infection rate and only 20 per cent Catholic population.[301]

CIA data indicates that Uganda provides the clearest example that the human immunodeficiency virus (HIV) is preventable if populations are mobilized to avoid risk. Despite limited resources, Uganda has shown a 70 per cent decline in HIV prevalence since the early 1990s, linked to a 60 per cent reduction in casual sex. The response in Uganda appears to be distinctively associated with communication about acquired immunodeficiency syndrome (AIDS) through social networks. Despite substantial condom use and promotion of biomedical approaches, other African countries have shown neither similar behavioural responses nor HIV prevalence declines of the same scale. The Ugandan success is equivalent to a vaccine of 80 per cent effectiveness. Its replication should require changes in global HIV/AIDS intervention policies and their evaluation.[302]

The Ugandan Health Ministry reported that epidemiological surveillance of HIV in Uganda has shown consistent decline in prevalence among antenatal and STD clients at sentinel sites. This is corroborated by parallel changes in sexual behaviour.[303]

---

301 https://www.cia.gov/library/publications/the-world-factbook/geos/by.html and https://www.cia.gov/library/publications/the-world-factbook/rankorder/2155rank.html
302 R.L. Stoneburner, D. Low-Beer, "Population-level HIV declines and behavioral risk avoidance in Uganda", *Science*, April 30; 304(5671):714-8, 2004.
303 W.L. Kirungi, J.B. Musinguzi, A. Opio, E. Madraa, *International Conference on AIDS*, 2002, July 7-12; 14: abstract no. WeOrC1269. STD/AIDS Control Programme, Ministry of Health, Kampala, Uganda.

The Guttmacher Institute, which is associated with International Planned Parenthood, reports that:

- HIV rates in Uganda declined during the late 1980s and early 1990s. The reduced levels of infection appear to have been sustained during the late 1990s.
- The proportion of women 15-17 who had ever had sex decreased from 50 per cent in 1988 to 46 per cent in 1995 and 34 per cent in 2000.
- There were also large declines in sexual experience among adolescent men between 1989 and 1995.
- Men and women of all ages were much less likely to have more than one sexual partner in a 12-month period in 1995 than in 1989. Among unmarried sexually active women, 15 per cent had more than one partner in 1995, compared with 3per cent in 1989; for unmarried men, the proportions were 26 per cent in 1995 and 59 per cent in 1989. The proportions continued to decline among unmarried women between 1995 and 2000.[304]

According to the WHO, since 1990 the adult incidence of HIV in Uganda has steadily declined from around 15% to around 5%.[305]

15.3.1 What Caused the HIV Decline in Uganda?

President Museveni encouraged input from numerous government ministries, NGOs and faith-based organisations. He relaxed controls on the media, and a diversity of prevention messages spread through Uganda's churches, schools and villages.[306]

This frank and honest discussion of the causes of HIV infection seems to have been a very important factor behind the changes in people's behaviour. Music and educational tours by popular musician Philly Lutaaya (who was the first prominent Ugandan to declare openly that he was HIV

---

304 http://www.guttmacher.org/pubs/summaries/exs_abc03.pdf
305 WHO Epidemiological Fact Sheet on HIV and AIDS Core data on Epidemiology and response http://apps.who.int/globalatlas/predefinedReports/EFS2008/full/EFS2008_UG.pdf
306 http://www.avert.org/aids-uganda.htm

positive) also spread understanding, compassion and respect for people living with HIV.[307]

15.3.2 What Happened in Uganda?

Much of the prevention work in Uganda occurred at grass-roots level. Many organizations were made up of people living with HIV educating their peers. These groups worked to break down the *stigma* associated with AIDS, and to encourage a frank and honest discussion of sexual subjects that had previously been taboo.[308]

The approach used in Uganda has been named the ABC approach – firstly, encouraging sexual *Abstinence* until marriage; secondly, advising those who are sexually active to *Be faithful* to one partner; and finally, urging *Condom use*, especially for those who have more than one sexual partner.[309]

15.3.3 Were Condoms the Solution in Uganda?

Condoms were not heavily promoted and distributed during the early years of the AIDS epidemic in Uganda, as the President felt that they offered false hope that the epidemic could be stopped without curbing multiple sexual partnerships. It was not until the mid-nineties that condoms were widely distributed. The number of condoms delivered and promoted by international groups rose from 1.5 million in 1992 to nearly 10 million in 1996.[310]

The momentum of condom distribution was lost in 2004 when the Ugandan government issued a nationwide recall of the condoms distributed free in health clinics, due to concerns about their quality. Millions of condoms were incinerated, and by mid-2005 there was said to be a severe scarcity of condoms in Uganda, made worse by new taxes that made the remaining stocks too expensive for many people to afford.[311]

Condoms were not the main element of the AIDS prevention message in the early years. President Museveni said, "We are being told that only a

---

307 Ibid.
308 Ibid.
309 Ibid.
310 Ibid.
311 http://www.avert.org/aids-uganda.htm

thin piece of rubber stands between us and the death of our Continent ... they (condoms) cannot become the main means of stemming the tide of AIDS." He emphasized that condoms should be used, "if you cannot manage A and B ... as a fallback position, as a means of last resort."[312]

After evaluating HIV prevention programs in Uganda, Senegal and Jamaica, one study reported surprise at finding evidence that declining HIV infection rates may be strongly linked to the involvement of faith-based organizations – in Uganda, this means Catholic, Muslim and Anglican. These organisations promoted abstinence and fidelity (approaches that have not been regarded as very effective by many working in AIDS prevention elsewhere).[313] There would seem to be a level of agreement that the decline of HIV in Uganda was not due to condoms but by efforts by both government and non-government agencies to seek to change behaviour.

15.4 HIV Prevention in Australia

In Australia by the end of 2000 there were:

- 8,810 AIDS cases and 6,174 deaths;
- 18,854 people diagnosed with HIV;
- 12,730 people living with HIV/AIDS.

In the prevention of sexually transmitted infections in Australia, the Government policy made the condom strategy central. The Government claims the success of Australia's policy has greatly limited the potential impact of HIV/AIDS, claiming that condoms have been repeatedly demonstrated to be the cheapest, most readily accessible, safe and practical way to prevent sexual transmission of HIV and some other STIs.[314]

However the incidence of HIV is increasing in Australia. The annual

---

312 President Museveni of Uganda, Interview with Jackie Judd, Kaiser Family Foundation, June 14, 2004.
313 E.C. Green, *The Impact of Religious Organizations in Promoting HIV/AIDS Prevention.* in *Challenges for the Church: AIDS, Malaria & TB.* 2001. Christian Connections for International Health, Arlington, VA.
314 http://www.health.gov.au/internet/main/Publishing.nsf/Content/3F25543027A17 8E9CA25710F0017AD3A/$File/hivaids_strategy.pdf

number of diagnoses of newly acquired HIV infection (infection within the previous 12 months) steadily increased from 1998 to 2003, from 151 to 277 diagnoses.[315]

Condoms have a significant failure rate in actual use. In one study involving 195 sexually active adolescent females attending a medical centre at an army base, the participants reported that

- 31% experienced a broken condom.
- For 39.5% the condom fell off.
- 6% became pregnant in the year.[316]

The failure rates for condoms vary from study to study. However the use of a condom results in:

- 10-18 pregnancies per hundred women years in actual use,[317] though with perfect use the rate is claimed to be as low as 2 per hundred women years[318];
- higher rates of pregnancies in youth;
- higher rates than for pregnancy of STI transmission from an infected person, because infection is always possible but pregnancy can happen in only 25 per cent of days in the cycle.

The studies with the longest follow-up time, consisting mainly of studies of partners of haemophiliac and transfusion patients, yielded an HIV incidence estimate of 5.75 (95 per cent C.I.: 3.16, 9.66) per 100 person-years. That represents an 80 per cent reduction in heterosexual HIV transmission[319]

---

315 http://www.health.gov.au/internet/main/Publishing.nsf/Content/3F25543027A17 8E9CA25710F0017AD3A/$File/hivaids_strategy.pdf

316 Christ, Michael, Raszke, William V, Dillon, Christopher A., "Prioritizing Education about Condom Use Among Sexually Activwe Adolescent Females", *Adolescence*, Vol 33, No. 132, Winter 1998.

317 Guttmacher Institute, "Choice of Contraceptives.", *The Medical Letter on Drugs and Therapeutics*, Volume 34, No 885, 1992, pp. 111–114.

318 R.A. Hatcher, J. Trussel, A.L. Nelson *et al*, *Contraceptive Technology* (19th ed.). New York: Ardent Media, 2007, http://www.contraceptivetechnology.com/table.html

319 S. Weller and K. Davis, "Condom effectiveness in reducing heterosexual HIV transmission" (*Cochrane Review*). In: *The Cochrane Library*, Issue 4, 2002.

from condom use. However, there is only a 50 per cent reduction in rates for genital herpes and genital warts virus because they spread from the whole genital area.[320]

In any given population, the long term results of a condom strategy will result in the same proportion of those using condoms becoming infected in the long term compared to those doing nothing to reduce the transmission of infection or pregnancy. The point is that if there is a significant failure rate, even though in the short term the infection and pregnancy rates may be slowed, in the long term a similar proportion expected to become infected or have an unplanned pregnancy.[321] Given that for pregnancy there are around twenty-five years of fertility for most women from the time they be become sexually active, and condoms have a contraceptive failure rate of around 3-15 per hundred women per year, an unplanned pregnancy while using condoms is very likely and the risk of disease transmission from an infected partner to be much higher.

Condom promotion to young people has been universal in Australia since 1984, through schools programs, public advertisements and community education and in higher education. It would have been very difficult for a young person not to have received the message that condoms are needed to protect against HIV/AIDS and other diseases.

15.5 Did STIs in young people fall?

HIV diagnoses in Australia did fall from the peak in 1985 and AIDS diagnoses also fell, though the latter is likely to be a result of the treatments for HIV that now prevent it from developing into AIDS. The annual number of AIDS diagnoses in Australia peaked at 954 cases in 1994 and dropped to 178 in 2001. This decline in incidence was due to a sharp drop in HIV incidence in the mid-1980s, and the effectiveness of combination antiretroviral therapy in delaying progression to AIDS in people whose HIV infection was diagnosed before AIDS diagnosis. The figure of concern, however, is a rising incidence of newly acquired HIV since 1997.[322]

---

320 Conversation with Melbourne Men's Health Clinic, October 2009.
321 Willard Gates Jnr., "Contraception, Unintended Pregnancies and Disease", *American Journal of Epidemiology*, Vol 143, No. 4, 1996, p. 317.
322 *notes.med.unsw.edu.au/nchecrweb.nsf/...4/.../ASRFigu.rescolour2009.ppt*

In the year finishing 31 December 2010, there were an accumulated 896 males and 150 females who had tested positive for newly acquired HIV, a total of 1,046. In the following year ending 31 December 2011, there were 994 males and 142 females who had newly acquired HIV, a total of 1,136 and 8.2 per cent increase,[323] reflecting an increasing trend since the year 2000.[324]

The incidence of Chlamydia, which is a major cause of infertility, has been rising steadily amongst young people (15-29),[325] despite the efforts to promote condoms and despite that Chlamydia is curable with antibiotics. In a study undertaken in participating health services, over a five year period in 2007-2011, the chlamydia positivity rate steadily increased among nearly all priority populations. In 2011, chlamydia positivity was highest among Aboriginal and Torres Strait Islander women (18.9%) followed by young heterosexual men (16.4%), Aboriginal and Torres Strait Islander men (15.9%) and young heterosexual women (15.5%) and lowest in men who have sex with men (7.9%) and female sex workers (6.2%).[326] The higher incidence in women generally may reflect its hidden nature, its lack of symptoms in women. The lower rate in female sex workers may reflect a standard practice of frequent testing and resultant successful treatment.

Gonorrhoea in Australia is similarly on the rise amongst young people reaching around 90 diagnoses per 100,000 in the 15-29 year age group in 2001.[327]

There is a very significant difference between the 15-29 age group and those over 39 for whom the rates of STIs drop to childhood levels.[328]

Genital Herpes is also a major public health concern in Australia, though it is not a notifiable disease and so data are not readily available. However a

---

323 Accessed 21/1/13 from http://www.kirby.unsw.edu.au/sites/hiv.cms.med.unsw.edu.au/files/hiv/resources/Apr2012-survrpt.pdf
324 Accessed 21/1/13 from: http://www.kirby.unsw.edu.au/sites/hiv.cms.med.unsw.edu.au/files/hiv/resources/2012AnnualSurvReport.pdf
325 Accessed October 2009 from *notes.med.unsw.edu.au/nchecrweb.nsf/...4/.../ASRFigu. rescolour2009.ppt*
326 Ibid.
327 Ibid.
328 Ibid.

stratified random sample of 4000 people was tested for the Herpes Simplex virus HSV-2, and 1000 for HSV-1, with sampling and weighting for various demographic factors.[329] The results indicted the following incidence of Genital Herpes :

- Australian adults 12 per cent;
- women 16 per cent;
- men 8 per cent;
- rural populations 9 per cent;
- metropolitan 13 per cent;
- Indigenous 18 per cent;
- non-Indigenous populations 12 per cent.

The virus associated with genital warts, the human papilloma virus (HPV), is also not a notifiable disease. However, according to Suzanne Garland, Director of Microbiology and Infectious Diseases at the Royal Women's Hospital in Melbourne, 1 in 2 Australian women aged 18 to 22 are carrying human papilloma virus but at 35, the risk is much lower at 1 in 10-20.[330]

To provide prevalence and risk factors for HPV in a female, sexually active, senior high school population in the Australian Capital Territory, a convenience sample of 161 females aged 16-19 years and attending a senior high school was evaluated. The prevalence of HPV DNA in this sample was 11.2 per cent.[331]

HPV affects mostly young people and the incidence is increasing despite education programs about modes of transmission and prophylaxis. It should be noted that HPV and Genital Herpes are as yet incurable, lifelong infections, and remain infectious lifelong, especially when flaring. There are now vaccines (such as Gardasil) for some types of HPV but not all and the long term efficacy of the vaccine is not yet known.

---

329 http://www.ncbi.nlm.nih.gov/pubmed/16581748
330 http://www.abc.net.au/rn/healthreport/stories/2006/1704762.htm
331 http://www.publish.csiro.au/paper/SH05047

15.6 The Education Issue

There is a variety of approaches to STI prevention education for young people, usually classified into:

- safe sex – condom and promotion;
- abstinence only;
- abstinence plus – abstain but use condoms if not;
- delay first intercourse programs – full information, including effects of early sexual initiation, plus behavioural program (including group CBT), some use pledge to delay (eg six months renewable).

The evidence however suggests that most sex education programs have little effect on behaviour. For an analysis of sex education programs see Chapter 23 in this volume.

16
The Oral Contraceptive Pill and Society: Fifty Years on

There are two areas in which the effects of the oral contraceptive pill (OCP) should be considered: the medical and relationship effects and the social and economic effects. As an ethicist, my interest is mostly in relation to the medical and relationship effects and I will return to those later.

16.1 Social and Economic Effects

On the economic front, economists Betsey Stevenson and Justin Wolfers undertook a review of the literature on women's well-being and reported that on economic indicators, women are better off than they were thirty-five years ago but on subjective measures of happiness and wellbeing they are less well-off, and they are also less happy than men:

> The lives of women in the United States have improved over the past 35 years by many objective measures, yet we show that measures of subjective well-being indicate that women's happiness has declined both absolutely and relative to men. This decline in relative wellbeing is found across various datasets, measures of subjective wellbeing, demographic groups, and industrialized countries. Relative declines in female happiness have eroded a gender gap in happiness in which women in the 1970s reported higher subjective well-being than did men. These declines have continued and a new gender gap is emerging—one with higher subjective well-being for men.[332]

---

[332] Betsey Stevenson and Justin Wolfers, "The Paradox of Declining Female Happiness", *American Economic Journal: Economic Policy*, Volume 1, No. 2, 2009, pp. 190-225 http://www.aeaweb.org/articles.php?doi=10.1257/pol.1.2.190

The period of their analysis roughly coincides with the advent of the OCP. There is no doubt that the OCP is associated with significant social change, with lower birth rates and a much higher engagement of women in the paid workforce and fewer women staying at home. The economy has changed such that housing affordability for a typical couple depends on her income. Salaries have not kept pace with housing costs or the extra cost of child care needed for them both to work.

Denver economist Timothy Reichert argues that the OCP has been a major factor in a decline in circumstances for women.[333]

Reichert argues that, prior to the pill, there was a single "mating market," populated by men and women in roughly equal numbers and who paired off in marriage. By lowering the cost of premarital and extramarital sex (pregnancy, shotgun marriage), contraception allowed a separate sex market (apart from prostitution) to form. That would not have affected either sex adversely if the numbers of men and women in both markets remained roughly equal, but they did not.

Because of limits to their fertility, women are inclined to move out of the sex market and into the marriage market earlier than men. This may make them relatively scarce in the former and abundant in the latter, able to negotiate better "deals" in the first but worse deals in the second where there is a scarcity of marriageable men.[334] Under these conditions, argues Reichert, men take more and more of the "gains from trade" and women take fewer and fewer. He comments:

> This produces a redistribution of bargaining power and, ultimately, of welfare from the later childrearing phases of a woman's lifetime toward the earlier, and in my view less important, phases. This redistribution has some very concrete, very undesirable consequences for women—and for the children that they bear.[335]

Reichert argues that this produces more divorce, an inflation of household costs, greater infidelity, and more abortion.[336] Women who delay

---

333 Timothy Reichert, "Bitter Pill", *First Things,* May 2010.
334 Ibid.
335 Ibid.
336 Ibid.

childbearing, for whatever reason, and there is a trend toward greater delay, are also more likely to suffer the sadness and emptiness of involuntary childlessness, whether or not they engage in reproductive technology

Striking "bad deals" in an imbalanced marriage market makes divorce more likely. Reduced commitment creates a "demand" for divorce even before the marriage begins (pre-nuptials). At the social level, women may allow the stigma of divorce to erode, and they support no-fault divorce laws. They compensate for these trends by developing relatively more market earning power, and invest less in family relationships, the moral formation of their children, and community activism. In doing so, they may become more like men, and the couples become less interesting to one another. "Sameness begets ennui, which begets divorce."[337] Mary (my wife), who runs a fertility assessment clinic (in her general practice), expresses surprise that many of the women whose charting she reviews have sexual intercourses so seldom.

As wealthier two-earner households bid up the price of homes, more women are forced into the labour market. With this comes a redistribution of welfare from younger to older generations, and from a family's younger, child-rearing years to its later childless years (when they could sell the $500,000 house). This redistribution "rests largely on the backs of the women in the labour force who support the higher housing cost and, ultimately, on the children who otherwise would have had the benefit of their mothers' time."[338]

This increases because the cost is lowered. Reichert argues that the sex market provides the opportunity, because married (successful, older) men are more attractive to younger women, than older women are to younger men. This, again, is to the detriment of women.[339]

Before the pill, the cost of an unwanted pregnancy was often borne by the man in the form of a shotgun wedding. Now it is more likely to be borne by the woman: contraception is her business and so therefore is the unintended pregnancy. If she keeps the baby, she forfeits opportunities in the labour market; if she has an abortion (which around one million women

---

337 Ibid.
338 Ibid.
339 Ibid.

in the US do each year), she usually pays the monetary cost and always the emotional costs.[340] Though it is important to acknowledge that the loss of his unborn child and the effect on his partner are not without emotional significance for men.

16.2 Medical and Relationship Effects

The OCP is a form of medication; all forms of medication have side effects and adverse events and the OCP is no exception. The fact that the OCP is likely to be used for long periods of a woman's life makes those effects even more significant.

However there is little medical protest or concern expressed about the effects of the OCP because the comparison is with unwanted or unplanned pregnancy. The benefits of the OCP are thought to outweigh vastly the negatives of unplanned pregnancy. The comparison is invalid. There are effective alternatives to the OCP that do not involve daily medication.

One of the surprising aspects of the medical assessment of the OCP is that there is seemingly no parallel with the concern about women taking hormone replacement therapy and the increased risks of breast cancer and heart disease. The hormones taken in the OCP are the same hormones. The dosage of oestrogen in the OCP is much lower than in HRT, but the dosage of progesterone is comparable. It is not surprising then that apart from the common side effects such as headache, breast pain, irregular vaginal bleeding or spotting, stomach/abdominal cramps, bloating, nausea and vomiting, depression, back pain, weight gain and hair loss, the OCP is also known for increasing the risks of serious illness including:

- 2-6 times the incidence of heart disease;
- 4-10 times the incidence of blood clots;
- 3-14 times the incidence of stroke;
- Slightly elevated risk of breast and uterine cancer.[341]

There is a huge market for the OCP, given that it is marketed to healthy and unhealthy women alike, and there are enormous corporate interests in

---

340 Ibid.
341 http://www.contracept.org/docs/Ogestrel-labeling.pdf

it. The same effort to market the OCP is not devoted to other ways of managing fertility. It comes as a surprise to many people, when they hear for the first time about fertility awareness methods, that the natural methods have very similar method-related pregnancy rates to the OCP.

A WHO trial of the Billings Ovulation Method in the late 1970s shows method related pregnancy rates of 2.2 per hundred women years in initiates and more recent studies by the Indian Medical Research Council and by the Jiangsu Family Health Institute in China showed method-related pregnancy rates of 0.68 PPHY and 0 PPHWY respectively.[342]

The fertility awareness methods rely on the fact that the rise in oestrogen that accompanies the maturation of the egg follicles in the ovary causes changes to the cervical mucus, which produces an observable change in sensation at the vulva that indicates the beginning of the fertile time prior to ovulation, and a sudden cessation of the symptom is caused by a rise in progesterone at ovulation. It is relatively simple for women who have learned fertility awareness to know whether or not they may be fertile. The WHO ranks the possibility of pregnancy occurring outside that fertile window, identified by changes in the cervical mucus, to be around 0.4 per cent.[343]

The comparison of side-effects and adverse reactions for the pill should not be between the OCP and pregnancy but between the OCP and

---

342 The three major independent trials of the BOM (used to avoid pregnancy):

a) WHO (1977-1981) Multi-centre – Auckland, Dublin, San Miguel, Bangalore and Manila. Published: *Fertility and Sterility*, 198, Volume 36, p. 152ff; 198, Volume 36, p.591ff. 869 women 10, 215 cycles of use 2.2 Method-related pregnancies per hundred women years in initiates (2.8 when initial phase excluded).

(b) Indian Council of Medical Research Task Force on NFP (1995) States of Uttar Pradesh, Bihar, Rajasthan, Karnataka and Pondicherry. Published: *Contraception 1996*, Volume 53, pp. 69-74; 2,059 women 32,957 woman months of use 0.86 Method related pregnancies per hundred women years in initiates.

(c) Jiangsu Family Health Institute, China (1997). Publication in English Translation: Shao Zhen QIAN, De-Wei ZHANG, "Evaluation of the effectiveness of a natural fertility regulation program in China", *Bulletin of the Ovulation Method Research and Reference Centre*, Volume 24, No. 4, pp 17-22, 2000. 1,235 women 14,280 women months of use, No method related pregnancies in initiates (5 user-related pregnancies).

343 WHO (1977-1981) Multi-centre – Auckland, Dublin, San Miguel, Bangalore and Manila, Fertility and Sterility 1981, Volume 36, pp. 152ff; 1981, Volume 36, p.591ff.

alternatives for managing fertility, which would include the barrier methods, the intra-uterine devices and the current fertility awareness methods.

The popularity of the OCP may be because it is more convenient not to have to worry about the fertile window and the possibility that for those days of the cycle, the woman may become pregnant. However I am not at all sure that women make that choice with full information. The fertility awareness methods do not produce a profit for anyone. It is information and not a product. There is no commercial interest in ensuring that women are well informed about their natural fertility.

Users of fertility awareness methods may be a select group but they have an extraordinarily low divorce rate, with studies showing results ranging from 0.2-5 per cent[344] compared to around 33 per cent of the Australian population who experience divorce, and one in four children of the latter experiencing the divorce of their parents.[345] It is also worth noting that though there are many possible variables, in the US, the divorce rate rose dramatically in parallel with the advent and rapid adoption of the OCP.[346]

The Australian Bureau of Statistics reports that dramatic shifts in social attitudes towards marriage, accompanied by significant changes in the divorce laws during the 1970s, resulted in a greater proportion of children experiencing parental divorce. That also parallels the introduction of the OCP in 1960-1. The *Family Law Act 1975* introduced a "no fault" approach which notably changed the divorce trend in Australia. After an initial spike in the divorce rate in 1976 following the change in legislation, the rate has remained relatively steady, albeit at a much higher level than prior to the legislative change. Based on the recent trend in divorce rates, it has been estimated that around one-third of marriages in Australia will end in divorce.[347]

---

344 Couple to Couple League International estimates based on its own studies and those completed by Nona Aguilar for her book, *No-Pill No-Risk Birth Control* (Rawson Wade).
345 http://www.abs.gov.au/AUSSTATS/abs@.nsf/Lookup/4102.0Main+Features40S ep+2010
346 Edward O. Laumann, John H. Gagnon, Robert T. Michael, and Stuart Michaels, *The Social Organization of Sexuality: Sexual Practices in the United States*, Chicago,. 1994.
347 http://www.abs.gov.au/AUSSTATS/abs@.nsf/Lookup/4102.0Main+Features40S ep+2010

Users of fertility awareness methods also are more likely to report having sexual intercourse more often than OCP users and being more satisfied with their relationships. That may, in part, be due to the impact of the OCP on suppressing libido.[348]

A recent report on fertility awareness methods summarizes the claims about the social benefits:

> Modern NFP [natural family planning] methods are associated with a lower incidence of induced abortion. They are also associated with a US divorce rate lower than that among the general US population. One nonrandomized survey found the ever-divorced rate among NFP users was 2 in 1000 if they had never used other forms of contraception. Four per cent of those who had used non-NFP types of contraception previously had been divorced. In the same year, 10.8 per cent of the general population identified themselves as presently divorced, with a divorce rate of 4 in 1000 per year. Catholics who do not use NFP have divorce rates similar to those of the general population, suggesting that religion alone does not account for this difference. The difference may be attributable to the methods or to selection bias, although neither has been clearly established.[349]

Wilson *et al* claimed that there is improved communication, and sexual interactions, deeper intimacy and respect for partners, and other aspects of psychosocial-spiritual well-being with use of natural family planning (NFP) methods.[350] The evidence in the Wilson study is limited by the fact that study was based on a single nonrandomized survey of NFP users. However the

---

348 Claudia Panzer *et al*, "Impact of Oral Contraceptives on Sex Hormone-Binding Globulin and Androgen Levels: A Retrospective Study in Women with Sexual Dysfunction", *Journal of Sexual Medicine*, 2006, Vol. 3, Issue 1, pp 104-113.
349 Stephen R. Pallone, MD and George R. Bergus, MD, "Fertility Awareness-Based Methods: Another Option for Family Planning", *Journal of the American Board of Family Medicine*, 2009, Volume 22 (2), pp 147-157. http://www.jabfm.org/cgi/content/full/22/2/147.
350 M.A. Wilson, "The practice of natural family planning versus the use of artificial birth control: family, sexual, and moral issues", *Catholic Social Science Review*, 2002; 7.

raw data are impressive. Several studies[351] into the effect of fertility awareness on relationships have tended to support the results that Wilson reported.

The point to be made is that an assessment of the medical and social effects of the OCP should take into account the alternatives. Women can have the social and economic gains of controlling their fertility without the medical effects of the OCP and without the apparent effects on relationships. The tragedy is that the commercial interests in keeping healthy women medicated have resulted in an imbalance in the provision of information about the OCP compared to the equally effective alternatives.

---

351 L.P. LaBarber, Psychosocial aspects of NFP instruction: a national survey. *Int Rev* 1990; 14: 34–53.; R. Fehring, D. Lawrence, C. Sauvage. Self-esteem, spiritual well-being, and intimacy: a comparison among couples using NFP and oral contraceptives. *Int Rev* 1989; 13: 227–36 ; L. VandeVusse, L. Hanson, R. Fehring, A. Newman, J. Fox. Couple's views of the effects of natural family planning on marital dynamics. *J Nurs Scholarsh* 2003; 35: 171–6.

17

Gender Reassignment and Catholic Schools[352]

17.1 Introduction

Recently, opinions were sought on the issue of a child in a Catholic school who was undergoing gender reassignment. A related issue has also arisen in relation to a teacher at a Catholic school advising that he was changing his gender, beginning by cross dressing.

There seems little doubt that the Catholic Church is likely to regard hormonal treatment and surgery to change gender characteristics as a mutilation of the body resulting in an unjustifiable loss of healthy function. However I am not aware of any official teaching on the subject other than teaching on the obligation to retain healthy bodily functions unless life is endangered and the functions are removed as a side effect of a treatment to save life. The *Catechism of the Catholic Church* states at n. 2297:

> Except when performed for strictly therapeutic medical reasons, directly intended *amputations*, *mutilations*, and *sterilizations* performed on innocent persons are against the moral law.

Well-respected theologians, Benedict Ashley and Kevin O'Rourke, in the fifth edition of their *Health Care Ethics: A Catholic Theological Analysis*[353] conclude that the good of the person cannot be achieved at the expense of the destruction of a basic human function, in this case the sterilization

---

[352] This chapter was published as Nicholas Tonti-Filippini, "Gender Reassignment and Catholic Schools", *National Catholic Bioethics Quarterly*, Volume 12, No. 1, Spring 2012, pp. 85-98, and is here reproduced with permission as published.

[353] Benedict Ashley and Kevin O'Rourke in the fifth edition of their *Health Care Ethics: A Catholic Theological Analysis*, Washington: Georgetown University Press, 2007, p. 111.

of the person, except to save the person's life. They add that the studies by no means give reassurance that sexual reassignment solves the problems of personality from which most people with gender identity disorder (GID) suffer. Those who support sexual reassignment point to the high suicide rates. Some claim that the suicide rate in this group may be as high as fifty per cent and that the treatment may therefore be seen as lifesaving.[354]

The issue in relation to whether to exclude a student or a teacher is complex. The moral situation for the Church requires clarification, if the legal exemptions under the equal opportunity law that apply to religious schools in many jurisdictions are to be applied to permit exclusion in this case. Presumably, if exclusion of a teacher were to occur, it would be on the grounds that the person was unable to give witness to the teaching of the Church: Their continued role on the staff may influence school children, and would thus affect the school's capacity to propagate the Church's teachings. Offence of religious sensibilities is also a legal ground for exemption from the equal opportunity provisions of most Australian State and Territory jurisdictions.

17.2 Disorders of sex development

There has been a tacit acceptance of medical interventions that seek to normalize the physical condition of children born with intersex disorders or disorders of sex development. Disorders of sex development include a group of conditions where there is a discrepancy between the external genitals and the internal genitals (the testes and ovaries).[355]

Disorders of sex development may have a genetic cause or they may be a result of problems that occur during development such as exposure to hormones before birth.

There are both male (46 chromosomes, XY) and female (46 chromosomes XX) sex development disorders in which the person has normal genes but a problem has developed in the expression of the genes such that a female has ovaries but external male genitalia or a male has external genitals that are

---

354 Ibid., p. 110.
355 Medline Encyclopedia, accessed at http://www.nlm.nih.gov/medlineplus/ency/article/001669.htm

incompletely formed, ambiguous, or clearly female and internally the testes may be normal, malformed, or absent.[356]

Some children are born with what is called true gonadal intersex disorder, in which they have both ovarian and testicular tissue. Genetically they may be normal or they may have an extra sex chromosome.[357]

There are many genetic disorders involving chromosome configurations other than simple 46, XX or 46, XY. These include 45, XO (only one X chromosome); and 47, XXY and 47, XXX (both with an extra sex chromosome, either an X or a Y). These disorders do not result in an intersex condition where there is discrepancy between internal and external genitalia. However, there may be problems with sex hormone levels, overall sexual development, and altered numbers of sex chromosomes.[358]

The symptoms associated with disorders of sex development will depend on the underlying cause, but may include:

- ambiguous genitalia at birth;
- micropenis;
- clitoromegaly (an enlarged clitoris);
- partial labial fusion;
- apparently undescended testes (which may turn out to be ovaries) in boys;
- labial or inguinal (groin) masses (which may turn out to be testes) in girls;
- hypospadias (the opening of the penis is somewhere other than at the tip; in females, the urethra [urine canal] opens into the vagina);
- otherwise unusual appearing genitalia at birth;
- electrolyte abnormalities;
- delayed or absent puberty;
- unexpected changes at puberty.[359]

---

356 Ibid.
357 Ibid.
358 Ibid.
359 Ibid.

In the past, the practice has been to intervene surgically to make the person definitely one sex or the other, depending on a judgement made as to which was dominant, though often the interventions seem to favour making the child female, this being easier to achieve in terms of appearance. Often people with sex development disorders are infertile.

In more recent times, there has been a tendency to delay intervening. Greater respect for the complexities of female sexual functioning has led medical experts to conclude that suboptimal female genitalia may not be inherently better than suboptimal male genitalia, even if the reconstruction is "easier." In addition, other factors may be more important in gender satisfaction than functioning external genitals. Chromosomal, neural, hormonal, psychological, and behavioural factors can all influence gender identity. Many experts now urge delaying definitive surgery for as long as it may be healthy to do so, and ideally involving the child in the gender decision.[360]

Delay in intervening may mean that the intervention happens to a child who is attending school. It may be difficult in some cases to explain the difference between the treatment of these conditions and what is popularly known as sex change hormonal treatment and surgery in the presence of what is known as gender dysphoria.

Ashley and O'Rourke claim that intersex conditions differ from Gender Identity Disorder (GID). In relation to intersex conditions they say that there is no objection to procedures to improve the normal appearance or function of sexually ambiguous children before puberty in accordance with the sex in which they are to be or have been raised. They say that the reasoning behind this traditional position is that a person must "live according to nature", insofar as this is humanly possible.[361]

Some people who have been treated as children for an intersex condition find that they identify with the opposite gender to the one to which they were assigned surgically as children. For example, a genetic male may have been assigned female gender based on the phenotypic appearance, despite

---

360 Ibid.
361 Ibid., p. 112.

having the opposite genotype. There would seem to be no ethical difficulty with later attempts to establish appearance and function consistent with the genotypic gender.

17.3 Gender Dysphoria.

The *Diagnostic and Statistics Manual of Mental Disorders* 4th Edition (DSM-IV) of the American Psychiatric Association describes gender dysphoria (Gender Identity Disorder or GID) as a persistent discomfort with gender role and identity, and distinguishes between GID and transvestic fetishism. The latter involves sexual arousal through cross-dressing. The former involves a strong and persistent cross-gender identification.[362]

GID occurs in children with the onset of cross-gender interests and activities usually between ages two and four years. Some parents report that their child has always had cross-gender interests. However, only a very small number of children with GID will continue to have symptoms that meet criteria for GID in later adolescence or adulthood.[363]

Commonly, treatment of GID in children and adolescents involves psychotherapy. Sexual reassignment surgery is not attempted. However in recent times there have been attempts to suppress the development of gender characteristics hormonally during puberty in adolescents with GID. There have been some controversial Family Court cases in which the Court has approved hormonal suppression.

The justification given for hormonal intervention for GID in adolescents has been the acknowledged high rates of self-harm and suicide.[364]

The DSM-IV reports that by late adolescence or adulthood, about three-quarters of boys who had a childhood history of GID report a homosexual or bisexual orientation, but without concurrent GID. Most of the remainder report a heterosexual orientation, also without concurrent GID.[365]

---

[362] American Psychiatric Association, *Diagnostic and Statistics Manual of Mental Disorders*, 4th Edition (2000). Accessed from http://www.psychiatryonline.com/resourceTOC.aspx?resourceID=1
[363] Ibid.
[364] Ibid.
[365] Ibid.

The corresponding percentages for sexual orientation in girls are not known. Some adolescents may develop a clearer cross-gender identification and request sex-reassignment surgery, or may continue in a chronic course of gender confusion or dysphoria.[366]

There are no recent epidemiological studies to provide data on prevalence of GID. Data from smaller countries in Europe with access to total population statistics and referrals suggest that roughly one per 30,000 adult males and one per 100,000 adult females seek sex-reassignment surgery.[367]

The accepted treatment of chronic GID in adults involves psychotherapy, which may result in recommendation for gender reassignment. When this occurs, a period of living as the other sex precedes hormonal treatment, cosmetic surgery and sexual reassignment surgery.[368]

With or without sexual reassignment surgery, there are very high levels of self-harm, suicide and unemployment in people with chronic GID that does not respond to psychotherapy. A proportion of those with GID spontaneously revert to normal gender identity.[369]

The National Health Service in the UK has recently declared that the condition was traditionally thought of as a purely psychiatric condition, which meant that its causes were considered to originate only within the mind. However, recent studies have challenged this, and suggested that gender dysphoria may have biological causes associated with the development of gender identity before birth. The claims are that gender dysphoria should be seen as a disorder of sex development during gestation and related to abnormal expression of the sex chromosomes, and that GID may be caused by hormones not working properly within the womb. The NHS concludes that more research needs to be done before the causes of gender dysphoria can be fully understood, but it is widely agreed that it can no longer be thought of as just a psychiatric condition.[370]

---

366 Ibid.
367 Ibid.
368 Ibid.
369 Ibid.
370 National Health Service (UK), *Causes of gender dysphoria*. Accessed 21/12/09 http://www.nhs.uk/Conditions/Gender-dysphoria/Pages/Causes.aspx

17.4 Is GID a Delusion?

In Schizophrenia, there may rarely be delusions of belonging to the other sex. However, insistence by a person with GID that he or she is of the other sex is not considered a delusion, because what is invariably meant is that the person feels like a member of the other sex rather than truly believes that he or she is a member of the other sex. In very rare cases, however, Schizophrenia and severe GID may coexist.[371]

A delusion is a fixed belief in something untrue. If GID were a delusion, then that would be ethically significant. Hormonal treatment and gender reassignment surgery would be the reinforcement of a delusion rather than the treatment of the underlying condition.

The existence of GID raises a number of questions including the very basic question:

What is gender? Is gender simply physiological or can it be seen as psychological and separable from the physiology? Is GID essentially dualistic in that it involves separating the psychology of gender from the physiology of the person?

In Australia, Justice Ormrod in *Corbett v. Corbett* (1970) held that three facts determine the sex of a person:

- the chromosomes (XY - male; XX - female);
- the gonads (testes/ovaries);
- the genitals (penis/clitoris, including internal sex organs)

This entirely physiological view of gender survived in Australia until 1988, when Justice Matthews in the New South Wales Court of Criminal Appeal in *R v Harris and McGuiness* (1988) held that Lee Harris, a post-operative male-to-female transgender person convicted of procuring "another" male person to commit an act of indecency, to be female for the purposes of criminal law. The judge's decision was based on the fact that the person's reconstructed genitalia was functionally female rather than male.[372]

Similar reasoning was used in Australia in *Secretary, Department of Social*

---

371 American Psychiatric Association, DSM-IV, Op Cit.
372 R *v Harris and McGuiness* (1988), 17 NSWLR, 158.

Security v HH. In this case, the Administrative Appeals Tribunal upheld a decision of the Social Security Appeals Tribunal that a male-to-female post-operative transgender person was a woman for the purposes of section 25(1) of the *Social Security Act 1947* (Commonwealth) and was therefore entitled to an age pension at sixty, rather than sixty-five. The judges referred to "psychological and anatomical harmony" in relation to the nature of the reconstructed genitalia.[373]

On 21 February 2003, the Full Court of the Family Court of Australia upheld a decision of Justice Chisholm in which he concluded that for the purpose of ascertaining the validity of a marriage under Australian law, the question whether a person is a man or a woman is to be determined as at the date of the marriage, not birth, and that in Australian law, specifically the law relating to marriage, the terms "man" and "woman" include transsexuals in accordance with their sexual reassignment.[374]

Thus the Australian Courts seem to agree with the American Psychiatric Association that GID is not a delusion, in that they accept that a person's gender can be changed by reassignment therapy. In fact, in the case just described, the Court took into account factors such as the person's life experiences, including the sex in which he or she is brought up and the person's attitude to it; the person's self-perception as a man or woman; the extent to which the person has functioned in society as a man or a woman; any hormonal, surgical or other medical sex reassignment treatments the person has undergone, and the consequences of such treatment; and the person's biological, psychological and physical characteristics at the time of the marriage, including (if they can be identified) any biological features of the person's brain that are associated with a particular sex.[375]

There have been some Australian cases involving children being treated for GID, *Re Alex: Hormonal Treatment for Gender Identity Dysphoria* (2004) ("*Re*

---

373 *Secretary, Department of Social Security v SRA* (1993), 118 ALR 467.
374 The Attorney-General for the Commonwealth & "Kevin and Jennifer" & Human Rights and Equal Opportunity Commission [2003] FamCA 94 (21 February 2003).
375 New South Wales Council for Civil Liberties, *Transexual Marriage in Australia*. Accessed from http://www.nswccl.org.au/unswccl/issues/transexual.php#StateOfLaw

Alex")[376] and *Re Brodie (Special Medical Procedure)* (2008).[377]

In the case of 12-year-old Brodie, born a female, the Family Court authorized her mother to consent to the administration of a gonadotrophin-releasing hormone analogue on a continuous basis, subject to the medical opinion of the child's treating specialists from time to time. The effect of the treatment would be to suspend the development of puberty indefinitely, but the Court was advised that the effect would be reversible. The Court also ordered that Brodie undergo regular psychotherapeutic counselling with a psychiatrist experienced in gender identity disorder cases, with a view (*inter alia*) to the child exploring any issues arising from the treatment, and to improving the child's general well-being. It is worth noting that Judge Carter was not satisfied that the treatment plan was a procedure "for the purpose of treating a bodily malfunction or disease," but nevertheless concluded that the present and future psychological benefit to the child, in being permitted to begin the treatment sought, outweighed the psychological risks to her in not receiving the treatment, and treatment was therefore in her best interests. He made that decision in the knowledge also that the treatment was the first stage of a package of interventions which would include irreversible interventions.[378]

In the case of Alex, a 13-year-old biological girl, Chief Justice Nicholson ruled that she was able to commence treatment for gender dysphoria. The child had always identified as a male, wore male clothes, used the male toilets and otherwise presented as a male. The Chief Justice found that the child was able to enrol at school using a male name, and commence administration of the oral contraceptive pill to stop menstruation immediately. He further ordered that the child, in consultation with the treating medical practitioners, could commence irreversible hormonal treatment at a later date but prior to Alex's 18th birthday. The proposed treatment would stimulate facial hair growth, masculinisation of the voice and physique, and lengthening of the clitoris.[379]

---

376 2004 Fam CA 297, "Re Alex".
377 http://www.austlii.edu.au/au/cases/cth/FamCA/2008/334.html
378 Ibid.
379 2004 Fam CA 297, "Re Alex".

In both cases, the Court relied on the uncontested evidence of doctors who are engaged in transsexual reassignment. In neither case did the Court seek opinions from what might be called mainstream psychiatry, which holds, with the American Psychiatric Association, that such treatments should not be administered to children.[380] In fact mainstream psychiatry recommends psychotherapy for GID in adults rather than sexual reassignment.[381] The British Psychological Society finds that counselling and supportive system establishment are thought to be the best approaches to treating this disorder.[382]

17.5 Is Gender Reassignment Corrective or Mutilating?

Mainstream psychiatric opinion holds that people who suffer from gender dysphoria are not delusional in the sense that they have a false belief. They acknowledge their biological gender determined by their genes, but they feel at a deep psychological level that they are the gender opposite to their biology. It is possible that there are biological causes for that feeling and that the condition is due to developmental abnormalities before birth. The evidence certainly suggests a very early onset.

The evidence also suggests that many will accept their biological gender, with some developing same-sex attraction and some being heterosexual. It is a minority in whom the condition continues into adulthood and remains fixed.

If a parallel is drawn between developmental sex disorders and chronic gender dysphoria, then the psychological condition might be considered in the same light as the failure to develop normal genitalia, ovaries or gonads. In the latter case, corrective medical intervention is accepted to establish as normal a condition as possible. Sex development disorders are thought to happen fairly early in the development of the embryo. Normally the Y-chromosome does not have effect until about the seventh week, when the testes develop and produce testosterone that then brings about male rather than female development.[383] Sex development disorders are thought

---

380 American Psychiatric Association, DSM-IV op. cit.
381 Ibid.
382 http://www.psychnet-uk.com/dsm_iv/gender_identity_disorder.htm
383 Ashley and O'Rourke, op. cit., p. 112.

to have their origin around that time and may be the result of environmental causes.

There may be a parallel between sex development disorders and GID, if in the case of GID it could be established that there were biological factors involved in the failure to develop normally psychologically in relation to gender.

That raises the issue of what might be considered corrective intervention in the case of gender dysphoria. The medical reality is that in a biological male, medicine has not been able to reconstruct the reproductive tract so that it can function as a female reproductive tract. At best, surgery can create a vagina that can function for the purposes of sexual intimacy but with no reproductive capacity. In a biological female, medicine can with some difficulty produce a pseudo-penis for the purpose of penetrative sexual intimacy but with no reproductive function. In both cases, the hormonal and cosmetic changes assist the person to assume the role and appearance of the opposite gender.

In both cases, the interventions would usually destroy what would otherwise have been healthy fertile reproductive systems. They are, in this respect, different from the interventions to treat the more conventionally recognized sex development disorders, where the person is often naturally infertile. The aim in the latter interventions is to restore as much normal function of one gender or the other as possible, given that gender is at least phenotypically and sometimes genotypically ambiguous.

The issue for the Church is how to give a teleological response to the circumstances of a person with gender dysphoria, who begins life as one gender and, due to causes that are not fully known, fails to develop psychologically in accordance with the biological gender. Increasingly, there seems to be support for the view that something happens to prevent normal development of psychological gender identity and that causation may be biological, but it might also be related to socialization and the nature of relationships with parents and others. Often a person with gender dysphoria will have a difficult relationship with the parent of their own biological gender, but it is unclear which comes first, the gender dysphoria or the difficult relationship.

Beyond congenital biological determinants, there are at least three well-published theories on gender development in children. The *biological theory* is based on evidence that high levels of the male hormone testosterone are associated with high levels of aggression in boys and tomboyishness in girls. *Social learning theory* proposes that gender typing is the result of a combination of observational learning and differential reinforcement. *Cognitive-Developmental theory* states that gender understanding follows a prescribed time line. The pattern put forth is that children recognize that they are either boys or girls by the age of two or three, followed shortly by recognition that gender is stable over time. By the age of six or seven, children understand that gender is also stable across situations.[384]

No matter what theory one adopts, for most children, whose sex and gendermap are congruent, this insight typically goes unnoticed. However, if there is a sex/gendermap incongruency, some children will be left perplexed about their gender status and begin a lifelong, often compulsive search for resolution of the discrepancy.[385]

Though it may have biological causal elements, the problem still seems to be a psychological one, and the treatments that seek instead to find a biological remedy in sexual reassignment would seem to be addressing the wrong problem, and by means that will destroy normal healthy reproductive functions. Because the Church regards the body as a unity of soul and body,[386] it regards gender also as a unity. Gender is not merely a psychological or social concept but is grounded in the physical reality of the body.

The Church therefore rejects the idea that gender can simply be chosen without regard to the biology. Pope Benedict expressed it in the following way:

> What is often expressed and understood by the term "gender" ultimately ends up being man's attempt at self-emancipation from creation and the Creator. Man wants to be his own master, and alone – always and exclusively – to determine everything that

---

[384] Anne Vitale, *Notes on Gender Identity Disorder*. Accesssed from http://webhome.idirect.com/~beech1/GENDERID.HTM
[385] Ibid.
[386] *Gaudium et Spes*, n. 14.

concerns him. Yet in this way he lives in opposition to the truth, in opposition to the Creator Spirit.[387]

If the evidence existed that showed that GID does have a biological cause, and is a developmental condition in much the same way as the developmental sex disorders are, the Church would still be unlikely to endorse gender reassignment surgery, firstly because the treatment should seek to restore normality and the abnormality would seem to be the psychological disorder, not the body itself. Radical treatment of the body to try to make the body congruent with the disorder would not seem appropriate, and the fact that the body seeks to revert to the phenotype associated with the genotype if hormonal treatment is stopped, that the treatment is more cosmetic than a real change, and that the evidence about its success as a treatment for the psychological disorder is equivocal, would be reasons why the Church would not support sexual reassignment. Second, the fact that the treatments destroy healthy functions would seem to exclude any possibility that the Church would support it. It is inconceivable that the Church could endorse the destruction of healthy biological functions, particularly when the Church attaches meaning to the gift of sexual intimacy in part because of the procreative meaning. It may be that, as part of instituting adequate psychological care, the Church might permit temporary measures to suspend puberty where its onset hindered treatment, but one would not envisage the Church endorsing the permanent loss of healthy functions.

The hormonal treatment alters some physiological characteristics, surgery can construct a sexually but not a reproductively functioning vagina or penis, and cosmetic surgery may alter appearance, allowing the person to adopt the role of the other gender more easily. The karyotype, however, remains unchanged and if the hormone treatments are stopped, it will reassert its dominance in the biology of the individual.

The reality is that physically a change from one gender to the other is

---

[387] Address of His Holiness Benedict XVI to the Members of the Roman Curia for the Traditional Exchange of Christmas Greetings, Clementine Hall, Monday, 22 December 2008. Accessed from http://www.vatican.va/holy_father/benedict_xvi/speeches/2008/december/documents/hf_ben-xvi_spe_20081222_curia-romana_en.html

not medically possible. What happens is, in fact, the destruction of normal healthy organs, leaving the person as essentially the gender of their birth and requiring constant hormonal interventions to try to suppress the natural tendency of the body to revert to gender type.

The proposal to undergo sexual reassignment would seem to conflict with the notion of gender expressed in the *Catholic Catechism*:

> God is love and in himself he lives a mystery of personal loving communion. Creating the human race in his own image ... God inscribed in the humanity of man and woman the *vocation*, and thus the capacity and responsibility, *of love* and communion.[388]
>
> God created man in his own image ... male and female he created them;" He blessed them and said, "Be fruitful and multiply;" "When God created man, he made him in the likeness of God. Male and female he created them, and he blessed them and named them Man when they were created.
>
> *Sexuality* affects all aspects of the human person in the unity of his body and soul. It especially concerns affectivity, the capacity to love and to procreate, and in a more general way the aptitude for forming bonds of communion with others.
>
> Everyone, man and woman, should acknowledge and accept his sexual *identity*. Physical, moral, and spiritual *difference* and *complementarity* are oriented toward the goods of marriage and the flourishing of family life. The harmony of the couple and of society depends in part on the way in which the complementarity, needs, and mutual support between the sexes are lived out.
>
> In creating men "male and female," God gives man and woman an equal personal dignity.[119] Man is a person, man and woman equally so, since both were created in the image and likeness of the personal God.[389]

and the *Catechism* defines sexuality, by referring to the depth of meaning of gender as encompassing not just biology but our innermost being:

> Sexuality, by means of which man and woman give themselves

---
388 *Catechism of the Catholic Church*, 2331-2334.
389 Ibid.

to one another through the acts which are proper and exclusive to spouses, is not something simply biological, but concerns the innermost being of the human person as such. It is realized in a truly human way only if it is an integral part of the love by which a man and woman commit themselves totally to one another until death.

> Tobias got out of bed and said to Sarah, "Sister, get up, and let us pray and implore our Lord that he grant us mercy and safety." So she got up, and they began to pray and implore that they might be kept safe. Tobias began by saying, "Blessed are you, O God of our fathers ... You made Adam, and for him you made his wife Eve as a helper and support. From the two of them the race of mankind has sprung. You said, 'It is not good that the man should be alone; let us make a helper for him like himself.' I now am taking this kinswoman of mine, not because of lust, but with sincerity. Grant that she and I may find mercy and that we may grow old together." And they both said, "Amen, Amen." Then they went to sleep for the night. [390]

and finally, in clause 372, the divine creation of gender:

> Man and woman were made "for each other" – not that God left them half-made and incomplete: he created them to be a communion of persons, in which each can be "helpmate" to the other, for they are equal as persons ("bone of my bones ...") and complementary as masculine and feminine. In marriage God unites them in such a way that, by forming "one flesh," they can transmit human life: "Be fruitful and multiply, and fill the earth." By transmitting human life to their descendants, man and woman as spouses and parents cooperate in a unique way in the Creator's work.[391]

The Church understands that each human being exists for a purpose and communion with God and the capacity to become a mother or a father are

---

390 Ibid., 2361.
391 Ibid., Clause 372

part of that vocation. The importance of procreation is expressed in the following way:

> By its very nature the institution of marriage and married love is ordered to the procreation and education of the offspring and it is in them that it finds its crowning glory.
>
> Children are the supreme gift of marriage and contribute greatly to the good of the parents themselves. God himself said: "It is not good that man should be alone," and "from the beginning [he] made them male and female;" wishing to associate them in a special way in his own creative work, God blessed man and woman with the words: "Be fruitful and multiply." Hence, true married love and the whole structure of family life which results from it, without diminishment of the other ends of marriage, are directed to disposing the spouses to cooperate valiantly with the love of the Creator and Saviour, who through them will increase and enrich his family from day to day.[392]

The Church thus regards gender as having a specific meaning that is determinative of vocation and is unchangeable. This is acknowledged particularly in the restriction of priesthood to men:

> Only a baptized man (*vir*) validly receives sacred ordination."[66] The Lord Jesus chose men (*viri*) to form the college of the twelve apostles, and the apostles did the same when they chose collaborators to succeed them in their ministry.[67] The college of bishops, with whom the priests are united in the priesthood, makes the college of the twelve an ever-present and ever-active reality until Christ's return. The Church recognizes herself to be bound by this choice made by the Lord himself. For this reason the ordination of women is not possible.[393]

17.6 A Teacher in a Catholic School

We now return to the cases with which this chapter on Gender Reassignment and Catholic Schools opened. The first case, as presented to me, involved a teacher who had been teaching at the school for some time and had

---

392 Ibid.,1652.
393 Ibid.,1577.

announced to the principal his intention to cross-dress and live as a woman as the first stage in progressing to hormonal treatment, cosmetic surgery and finally sexual reassignment surgery if the treating team agreed.

Legally, in most Western jurisdictions, a religious school may discriminate if it is necessary to do so to propagate religion that conforms to the doctrines of that religion, or to avoid injury to the religious susceptibilities of the adherents of that religion. The issue then, is whether it was necessary, for these reasons, to exclude a teacher who was cross dressing.

As in the Court cases cited above, the cross dressing cannot be considered on its own because it is intended as a first stage in a likely sequence of events culminating in sexual reassignment. In the case of GID, the cross dressing is an expression of the teacher's strong feeling that he is in fact a woman despite his biology.

For a teacher in a Catholic school to cross dress in the circumstances of GID and indicate that this is part of a process of gender change would contradict the teaching of the Church in relation to vocation, gender, sexuality, marriage and priesthood. His ability to give witness to the teaching of the Church would be severely compromised. Basically he would not be able to do his job in relation to propagating the faith.

Pastorally the circumstances would require very careful handling because the source of the problem is a recognized psychiatric condition with a high risk of suicide. It is important that any dealings with the man affirm his worth and dignity.

17.7 A Child in the Classroom

A school principal sought an opinion on the need to respond to an announcement made by the parent of a child, at a co-educational secondary school that the child, who was female, would soon undergo hormonal treatment as part of a process of gender reassignment.

The first concern is the wellbeing of the child in circumstances of a mental disorder that carries a significant risk of self-harm. There would be a need to seek advice from the child's psychiatrist concerning how best to respond to her individual circumstances. There are also difficult privacy issues during such a process.

The principal also has an obligation to all the children in the school, and one of the issues to be addressed is the impact that the child would have on others as she went through the process.

A major concern would be the impact on other children at a time when gender and gender orientation are matters about which there is often some uncertainty. There would also be concern about the impact on the ability of the faculty to give witness to Catholic teaching in the face of a public rebuttal of that teaching.

The principal would need to make a prudential decision, based on professional medical, psychological and pastoral advice about what may be expected to occur, as to whether the child could remain at the school, and take pastoral advice about how best to manage the circumstances. It is not impossible that the circumstances could be managed, but it would be very difficult.

The following is a draft letter to parents in a Catholic primary school that seeks to both preserve the privacy of the child and preserve a pastoral relationship with the child and his or her family, and at the same time act for the common good of the school community, including the school's obligation to give witness to the teachings of Christ and His Church.

If this was a case of gender dysphoria, then a court may have approved of the hormonal suppression of the development of puberty until the child reached an age to be considered competent to make her decisions about sexual reassignment surgery or hormonal treatment to produce features of normal sexual development in the opposite sex. The hormonal suppression of puberty might also happen in relation to an intersex condition.

In this draft approach, I have suggested that the specifics of the medical condition and treatments be kept private while outlining the various possibilities and Catholic teaching. The names and other identification are fictitious.

17.8 A Draft Letter to Parents[394]

Dear Parents,

I wish to inform you that an issue of some sensitivity has arisen and I seek your assistance and support for a decision that I have made as principal after seeking advice from the bishop and the Catholic Education Office.

Background

There is a range of relatively uncommon medical birth conditions known as *disorders of sexual development*. These conditions include children born either with an abnormal sex chromosome or with normal sex chromosomes but with abnormal expression of the sex chromosomes during development in the womb. Those conditions may result in a child with both ovaries and testes, or none, a child with both male and female genitalia, or none, or a child with inadequately formed genitalia.

It used to be the practice of paediatric surgeons to operate to make the child appear to be either male or female, often opting to make the child female, that being the easier course in relation to external appearance. Most children born with what are called "intersex conditions" will be infertile as adults. Sometimes, to establish an approximation of normal puberty, hormonal treatments may be required at that time. In more recent times, rather than make a mistake, the medical advice has been to wait until it is clearer whether the child would be more comfortable being one gender rather than the other. Parents may also opt for the child not to risk having surgery, leaving the child in an intersex state, at least until the child is mature enough to decide otherwise.

Disorders of gender development also include a psychological condition called "gender dysphoria" in which, usually from an early age, the child has a fixed and unchanging belief that he or she is of the gender opposite to his or her biological gender. There is some indication that there may be differences in brain structure that show brain similarities to the opposite sex, so gender dysphoria may not be entirely psychological. The Family Court has approved

---

[394] A version of this letter has been accepted for publication in the journal *Ethics and Medics*.

hormonal treatment to suspend the development of puberty in children with gender dysphoria. That may be done in order to assist psychiatric treatment, especially if the changes in puberty would cause significant distress. It may also facilitate later treatment for sexual reassignment when the child is mature enough to make a decision.

What is Gender?

In the understanding of the Church, gender is not elective, but is a biological reality that finds expression in the biological differences between men and women and in their capacity to be a mother or a father. The biological differences also have social, psychological and spiritual meaning and consequences. Those differences between men and women are the basis of the complementarity at all levels that makes marriage a possibility between a man and a woman. Though so different, they are equally made in the image and likeness of God, and, through their loving and intimate union, open to being blessed by God to become co-creators with Him in becoming parents.

Treatment

At the time of writing there was no explicit authoritative, publicly available Catholic teaching (such as by the Pope or the College of Bishops) on the treatment of disorders of sexual development. Applying Church teaching about the human body, love, sexual intimacy and marriage, theologians have generally favoured treatments of intersex conditions to make the child's condition more normal as either male or female. The Church has rejected treatments that would destroy healthy reproductive organs unless that was necessary to treat a condition that risked the life of the person. That would prohibit surgical procedures in a biologically normal person to reassign their gender by removing or reshaping healthy (potentially fertile) reproductive organs thus rendering the person infertile.

Our Circumstances

The parents of a child, who was originally enrolled and attended St. Raphael's School as a boy, have informed me that they would like their child to attend the school as a girl after the term holidays and she will dress in the girls' uniform and wishes to be treated as a girl by the school community. Obviously, this will not go without notice by other students. This is a complex matter and children will be naturally curious. However, as this is a medical matter, the child is entitled to privacy about such matters which will affect her now and later as an adult.

As the primary educators of your children, how your child is educated is your responsibility in the first instance, though in choosing a Catholic school you have elected to have your child educated in the Catholic faith in a partnership between you and the teachers. Because this is such a sensitive matter, we hope that you will anticipate and respond to your child's queries about this matter sensitively, on the basis of the information provided and try to discourage speculation, intrusive enquiries, or the formation of negative attitudes.

For our part, we will continue to deliver material about gender and sexuality that is age and maturity appropriate for your child and will keep you informed about the material to be used and the schedule of our well-established program in Christian sexuality according to the Diocesan Directives. You would have received the latter with the enrolment materials. I can make further copies available on request. We also comply with the new National Curriculum, but will add material required by our Catholic identity, as we always have done.

As you would be aware, many of the activities we schedule on sensitive matters are joint activities for you and your child, including take home work sheets that create what we hope will be teachable moments for you to respond, as you see fit, to the particular needs of your child, respecting his or her relative state of innocence. We also provide you with resources that may assist you with your child's learning.

The evidence suggests that the most important factor in your child's maturing toward being a healthy man or woman, who has successfully integrated his or her sexuality and sexual identity, and treats others respectfully, is the home context, and the health of your relationship as parents to your child. They learn first from you what it is to be a man or a woman, and about the unique love that may exist between a man and a woman, and the significance of sacramental marriage that makes a permanent commitment to give oneself completely to the other in imitation of God's love. We focus particularly on the love expressed by His Son for all of us while on earth, including accepting death on the Cross to redeem us from the effects of sin. We teach the children that love is giving oneself for the sake of the flourishing of the other, and as a witness to the Creator's love. In our experience, those who have themselves suffered from the tragic breakdown of their marriage want their children to aspire to and learn about the norms of Christian love, despite the parents' difficulties.

Our Response

Because of this unusual situation, we will begin next term with a focus on privacy about medical matters for all classes. For the age group with whom this child associates, Grade Four and the under ten sporting age groups, there will be a careful discussion about disorders of sexual development and their relative rarity, and we have re-scheduled our discussion about gender and puberty with a little more information than usual about the genetic, epigenetic and environmental factors that may influence gender development.

Note that, for those who may be concerned, we have checked the sporting records and have noted that on the basis of past performance there is no reason to think that this child will have an advantage over other girls. She is also a keen netballer and will be able to continue in the older age groups, under 12 and above, as a female when the competition rules require gender restrictions.

We have sought psychological and medical advice, including advice from this child's own doctor, about how best to manage these circumstances in her interests and the interests of each child in this community. With CEO and episcopal approval and legal advice, we decided to accept the change in enrolment status and we gave the child the option of either using the girls' toilet facilities or using the disabled toilet next to the staffroom. That will be a matter for the child and her parents depending on where she is most comfortable. Acting on medical and psychiatric advice, in all ways we will treat her as a girl. Hopefully, in time that will prove to be unremarkable.

Please feel free to discuss this matter with your child's classroom teacher, the school counsellor, the parish priest or with me. However, after much prayer and consultation, we have decided to do our best to respect this child's privacy about her medical matters, and to make the situation as normal and as informed in a general sense, as we can for her and for the whole community, as we would with any illness or disability. In fact, I have been guided by what we have done in the past to manage children with a range of disabilities, and am heartened by the sensible attitudes of the children, their acceptance, helpfulness, and tolerance of children with disabilities, and their efforts to be inclusive.

In adopting this course, we decided to continue to make quite clear our witness to Catholic teaching including a Scriptural and sacramental understanding of marriage and the importance of gender and chastity in the divine plan for us. There is to be no compromise of our faith identity.

If enough parents want it, I could schedule an information meeting of parents with some medical, educational and bioethical experts, if they are available. Please use the attached form to indicate your wishes in that respect. There is also some bioethical literature that may help and you might like to consult an article in a peer reviewed journal such as: **Tonti-Filippini, Nicholas, "Gender Reassignment and Catholic Schools",** *National Catholic Bioethics Quarterly,* **Volume 12, No. 1, Spring 2012, pp. 85-98.** The school secretary can arrange copies.

Conclusion

This is an unusual situation and I hope you will understand how difficult it has been to try to formulate an approach in the best interests of all the children at St. Raphael's. I am hopeful that, with the benefit of your good judgement, the basic goodness of children, the training and expertise of our staff, and divine grace, we will in fact enhance our education of your children in relation to disability and inclusiveness, and in relation to Christian sexuality, and better prepare them for the complexities that they will inevitability face as they develop, and as they more fully encounter, and engage with, our overly-sexualised culture.

Yours sincerely in Christ,
Ms. Bernadette Pruscino
Principal

18

Homophobia

18.1 Homophobic Harrassment

Many Western jurisdictions[395] have or are considering legislation that would make it an offence to make public statements in relation to sexual orientation that cause offence or injury, or that are considered to vilify people who are gay, lesbian, bisexual, or transsexual, or have an intersex condition (GLBTI). The offence is often described as homophobic harassment.

18.2 Effect on Free Speech and Religion

In relation to homophobia and mooted legislative change, freedom of speech and freedom of religion are a matter of grave concern, especially in relation to discussion of changes to the law in relation to exemptions to equal opportunity. That concern is immediate for Church organisations because the offence of homophobic harassment may be defined in terms that would include preaching or teaching sexual morality.

For instance, a Victorian government discussion paper entitled *With Respect* makes a case for amending Australian legislation to:

- address homophobic harassment against GLBTI people (Recommendation 10, pp. 33-6) and include the amendment in a separate part of the Act so that the section is not covered by the current exemptions under the Act, including the religious exemptions (Recommendation 11, p.36-7);
- ensure that the harassment provisions should operate as broadly

---

395 Including amendments to Canadian *Crimes Act (Hate Propaganda) Amendment Act* was signed into law on 29 April 2004; New Zealand *Bill of Rights Act*; South African Promotion of Equality and Prevention of Unfair Discrimination Act; UK Section 4 A of the *Public Order Act* 1986, which was inserted by section 154 of the Criminal Justice and Public Order Act 1994; *Prohibition of Incitement to Hatred Act.*

as possible and should not be confined to the areas of public life identified in Part 3 of the Equal Opportunity Act. The approaches warranting further consideration include:
- Applying the harassment provisions to public acts.
- Excluding private acts from the operation of the provisions.
- Limiting the operation of the provisions to circumstances where the harm done is reasonably foreseeable.
- Applying the provisions to harassment wherever it occurs. (Recommendation 12, pp. 37-42).
- Make it unlawful to harass another person on the basis of their sexual orientation or gender identity (Recommendation 13, p. 43-5).
- Define harassment as "conduct that offends, humiliates, intimidates, insults or ridicules another person," and so that other features of the definition include:
- That harassment be assessed against an objective standard, requiring that a reasonable person (having regard to all the circumstances including the history of discrimination or otherwise against persons of that sexual orientation or gender identity) would have anticipated that the other person would feel offended, humiliated, intimidated, insulted or ridiculed.
- That harassment be capable of being constituted by a single act (Recommendation 14, pp. 43-6).

Similar provisions have been proposed in most Western jurisdictions including the Exposure Draft of a Commonwealth Human Rights and Anti-Discrimination Bill 2012 which includes making unlawful merely causing offence in relation to matters that are subject to discrimination.

This approach is of concern to religious people and their organizations because most religions condemn behaviour that involves genital sexual intimacy between people of the same sex. It is customary for religious people to make a distinction between people and their behaviour, but it is also not uncommon for those lobbying for the rights of people described as gay, lesbian, bisexual, transgender and intersex not to distinguish between condemnation of certain acts and condemnation of the people who may be described in any of those ways and who may be thought to perform those acts. It is therefore to be expected that continuing to teach on the morality of the behaviours would cause GLBTI people to feel offended, humiliated, intimidated, insulted or ridiculed.

It would seem that what a preacher or a religious health educator might ordinarily say about sexual intimacy between people of the same sex, that is that such activities are immoral because unchaste, would qualify as harassment because a person who engaged in those activities might feel offended, humiliated, insulted or ridiculed. If the *With Respect* proposals were enacted, merely preaching from the Holy Scriptures on homosexuality could be treated as a hate crime.

One of the things the authors of *With Respect* decry is the fact that 35 per cent of Australians believed homosexuality was immoral (p. 13). Presuming that many of those who responded in that way were religious, the claim would not seem to distinguish the common religious belief that being homosexual is not in itself immoral, from the common religious belief that genital sexual intimacy between people of the same sex is immoral. The question does not distinguish and so the meaning of the answers is ambiguous.

The religious belief about such behaviour is related to the belief that sexual intimacy between people who are not married to each other is immoral. It would appear that the authors of *With Respect* do not make that distinction between the attribute or orientation and the behaviour.

The source given for the claim that 35 per cent of Australians believed homosexuality was immoral is a report by Flood and Hamilton,[396] who give their source as a large database compiled by Roy Morgan Research using self-completion interviews with 24,718 respondents aged 14 and over. The same data are referred to by Shirleene Robinson in *Homophobia: An Australian History*,[397] who says that the question survey respondents were asked was whether they agreed or disagreed with the statement "I believe

---

[396] M. Flood & C. Hamilton, *Mapping Homophobia in Australia*, The Australia Institute 2005. Accessed 9/2/10 from https://www.tai.org.au/documents/downloads/WP79.pdf

[397] Federation Press/Sydney 2009. Accessed 9/710 from http://books.google.com.au/books?id

that homosexuality is immoral." She regards this as a limited measure of homophobia and refers to further analysis of the same data that showed a marked gender difference, with 43 per cent of men and 27 per cent of women agreeing with the statement. She also cites other data[398] that show that male attitudes towards female homosexuality are much less negative. She postulates that the male response has something to do with masculine identity and the notion that gay men violate masculine identity, which is essentially heterosexual.

Australian respondents to the Roy Morgan survey were also asked whether they agreed or disagreed with the following statement: "Homosexual couples should be allowed to adopt children." Flood and Hamilton report that, as might be expected of those who believe that homosexuality is immoral, only seven per cent agreed with the statement. However even amongst those who did not agree that homosexuality is immoral, around half thought that gay couples should not be allowed to adopt children.[399] The latter negative judgement is thus separated in the minds of many from the morality of homosexuality. It might of course be a judgment about a child needing both a father and a mother, rather than negativity towards homosexuality per se.

Much of the literature refers to negative religious attitudes towards homosexuals, but in the material that I have accessed, the distinction between attitudes to the behaviour and attitudes to the person is not made. That raises a question about whether it would be practicable for a religious person to use the distinction as a defence against a charge of homophobic harassment. In the way in which the proposal has been worded, the test is not what the speaker meant by the words, but whether a reasonable person (having regard to all the circumstances including the history of discrimination or otherwise against persons of that sexual orientation or gender identity) would have anticipated that the other person would feel offended, humiliated, intimidated, insulted or ridiculed.

We might argue that the law should make a distinction between what

---

398 Gail Mason, *The Spectacle of Violence: Homophobia, gender and knowledge*, London: Routledge, 2002, pp.58-77.
399 M. Flood and C. Hamilton, *Mapping Homophobia in Australia*. The Australia Institute, 2005, p. 5.

is said about a person on the basis of a mere attribute, such as sexual orientation, and what might be said about particular behaviours. That is to say, religious people may well hold that it is unfair and unjust to speak badly of someone merely because of their sexual orientation, and even that the law should protect people who are GLBTI from being verbally abused for their orientation. The problem would seem to be that popular discourse does not make the distinction between such abuse of the *person* and what a religious person might say about the moral issue of *behaviour* that includes genital sexual intimacy between people of the same gender. The problem for religious people is the difficulty of reconciling in the public forum the two very different propositions that we hold:

- We deplore the treatment of homosexual persons as objects of violent malice in speech or in action and condemn it as a disregard for others which endangers the most fundamental principles of a healthy society, including the intrinsic dignity of each person, which must always be respected in word, in action and in law.[400]
- To choose someone of the same sex for one's sexual activity is immoral because it annuls the rich symbolism and meaning, not to mention the goals, of the Creator's sexual design, and homosexual activity is not a complementary union, able to transmit life; and so it thwarts the call to a life of that form of self-giving which the Gospel says is the essence of Christian living.[401]

---

[400] See for instance Congregation for the Doctrine of the Faith, *Letter To The Bishops Of The Catholic Church On The Pastoral Care Of Homosexual Persons 1986* n. 10. "It is deplorable that homosexual persons have been and are the object of violent malice in speech or in action. Such treatment deserves condemnation from the Church's pastors wherever it occurs. It reveals a kind of disregard for others which endangers the most fundamental principles of a healthy society. The intrinsic dignity of each person must always be respected in word, in action and in law."

[401] Ibid. n. 7, To choose someone of the same sex for one's sexual activity is to annul the rich symbolism and meaning, not to mention the goals, of the Creator's sexual design. Homosexual activity is not a complementary union, able to transmit life; and so it thwarts the call to a life of that form of self-giving which the Gospel says is the essence of Christian living. This does not mean that homosexual persons are not often generous and giving of themselves; but when they engage in homosexual activity they confirm within themselves a disordered sexual inclination which is essentially self-indulgent.

Religious people see no conflict between these propositions because we are used to discussing the morality of behaviours without condemning anyone. The Christian religion welcomes sinners and we do not exempt ourselves from being classed as sinners.[402] On the basis of Biblical teaching, we welcome the sinner, we stand ready to forgive the sinner, while condemning the sin. Others may find the approach difficult to understand and they may find it difficult to separate attitudes to sin from attitudes to the sinner.

The amendments to the law proposed in *With Respect*, by implication, may require us to give account of ourselves with respect to these two propositions. According to the first proposition, it may follow that we should support a law that protects homosexual and other persons from violent malice of speech or action directed towards them because of their orientation. According to the second, we should be free to express a moral view about unchaste activities. The immediate need therefore is to convince legislators that there is a distinction to be made that is not reflected in the way in which the legislative proposal is currently expressed in publications such as *With Respect*.

The proposed test of what constitutes "homophobic harrassment" is unjust, because it is not a test of the reasonableness of the anticipated response of the person that he or she would feel offended, humiliated, intimidated, insulted or ridiculed. If comment on the behaviour, but not the person, is anticipated by a reasonable person to be a cause of the other feeling in any of the ways listed, then that is sufficient to establish the offence, even if no such meaning was intended nor reasonably implied by what was said. As such, the creation of the offence would unjustly restrict free speech in relation to being able to discuss and draw moral conclusions about unchaste behaviour.

The *With Respect* proposal is too broad. It aims to protect people who are GLBTI from abuse, but its effect would be much broader than that because the test for such abuse would prohibit discussion of sexual morality, especially religious discussion of morality. The proposal endangers both freedom of speech and freedom of religion.

---

402 In using the language of "sin" and "sinner" we follow our Biblical tradition, without any desire to cause offence by the use of this language.

For religious people, sexual morality is primarily about chastity, which involves the successful integration of sexuality within the person and thus the inner unity of man in his bodily and spiritual being and thus involves beliefs about the way in which men and women are made. Religious people tend to believe that we exist for the purpose of our relationship to God. For religious people, therefore, sexuality has a purpose in the complete and lifelong mutual gift of a man and a woman. In other words, we are gendered for a reason.

To say as much as that, however, could be considered an offence of homophobic harassment under the recommendations in *With Respect*. If the proposal became law it would become an offence to preach or teach a biblical understanding of sexuality.

The proposal would severely restrict both freedom of expression and freedom of speech, such that discussion of the morality of certain acts could be considered an offence. Such a limitation would be unlikely to improve the status of people who are GLBTI, rather, if anything, it would be likely to foster resentment. Matters of morality are better conducted freely and without restraint so that irrationality can be exposed by that discussion. There may be a need to protect people who are GLBTI and other identifiable groups from those who would incite hatred against them, but this proposal goes much further than that.

A further danger in the phrasing of the offence is that it does not require any intent on the part of the perpetrator to cause harm. The test is whether a reasonable person would anticipate that another may be offended. If there is to be an offence of this nature, it needs to reflect the intention of the perpetrator and the test needs to be in relation to intentionally inciting hatred.

18.3 Should "Homophobic Harassment" Be an Offence?

There would seem to be little doubt that there is violence associated with negative attitudes to being GLBTI. The Australian Research Centre in Sex, Health & Society at La Trobe University undertook a telephone survey funded by the Victoria Law Foundation and managed through Gay and Lesbian Health Victoria (GLHV) with assistance from Victoria Police.

Recruitment to the survey was through emails publicising it, sent out through the GLBTI community and professional networks, Victoria Police Gay and Lesbian Advisory Unit, the Victorian Equal Opportunity and Human Rights Commission, domestic and family violence agencies and a number of government and non-government organisations. The survey was also publicised on Joy FM radio and 3CR in Melbourne and posted as a banner advertisement on Gaydar and Pinksofa from 23 November to 22 December 2007.

The methodology of the survey can be questioned, particularly as the sampling was not random but based largely on self-selection, and could have been biased towards those who have been abused and perhaps more inclined to respond to a survey request in relation to such violence. But while the results cannot be used to make predictions for the incidence of what the study calls heterosexist violence for the whole GLBTI community, the data obtained from the 390 respondents indicate that heterosexist violence against people who are GLBT exists in Victoria and is significant. Indeed, it appears to be a part of day-to-day lives of those who were interviewed. The findings included:

- Nearly one in seven GLBT respondents reported living in fear of heterosexist violence.
- Nearly 85 per cent of GLBT respondents had been subject to heterosexist violence or harassment in their lifetimes.
- Seven in ten GLBT respondents had been subject to heterosexist violence while alone in the past two years.
- Eight in ten GLBT respondents had experienced heterosexist violence as part of a *same sex couple* or *group* in the past two years.
- One in four GLBT respondents had been subject to physical violence or the threat of physical violence over the last two years.
- In 85 per cent of cases, violence and harassment were preceded or accompanied by heterosexist language.
- Approximately one in twenty GLBT respondents had been subject to sexual assault over the last two years.

Nearly half of reported incidents of heterosexist violence occurred in inner city Melbourne:

- 14 per cent was spread across rural and regional Victoria.
- One in three incidents of heterosexist violence occurred on the street.
- 13 per cent of violence against GLBT people occurred in their own home and 10 per cent at work.
- In 70 per cent of cases, the perpetrator was a stranger or had no prior relationship to the victim.
- 65 per cent of respondents reported that multiple offenders were involved.[403]

Most religious traditions condemn hatred and violence. We condemn violence, abuse and intimidation against people who are GLBTI. Every member of the human family has a right to feel and be safe within our community. Each has a right to be respected as a person. This was well expressed by the Lambeth Conference (1998) which stated that the Conference:

> recognizes that there are among us persons who experience themselves as having a homosexual orientation. Many of these are members of the Church and are seeking the pastoral care, moral direction of the Church, and God's transforming power for the living of their lives and the ordering of relationships. We commit ourselves to listen to the experience of homosexual persons and we wish to assure them that they are loved by God and that all baptised, believing and faithful persons, regardless of sexual orientation, are full members of the Body of Christ.[404]

Similarly, the Congregation for the Doctrine of the Faith (1986) affirmed:

---

[403] William Leonard, Anne Mitchell, Sunil Patel, Christopher Fox, *Coming Forward: The under reporting of heterosexist violence and same sex partner abuse in Victoria* Australian Research Centre in Sex, Health & Society, La Trobe University December 2008 Accessed 16/2/10 from http://www.glhv.org.au/files/ComingForwardReport.pdf

[404] Accessed 21/1/13 from http://www.lambethconference.org/resolutions/1998/ 1998-1-10.cfm

It is deplorable that homosexual persons have been and are the object of violent malice in speech or in action. Such treatment deserves condemnation from the Church's pastors wherever it occurs. It reveals a kind of disregard for others which endangers the most fundamental principles of a healthy society. The intrinsic dignity of each person must always be respected in word, in action and in law

The public policy issue is how to educate our community better so that the matter of a person's sexual orientation, sexuality or gender is not cause for the kind of intolerance, rejection and negativity that underlies such violence.

Creating a homophobic offence as proposed by the *With Respect* and many others would seem to be too strong a measure, particularly as it would restrict the free discussion that is necessary to achieve that greater understanding and tolerance. It may be more likely to increase resentment than create understanding and tolerance.

The term "homophobia" suggests that the cause of the problem is fear.[405] Fear and anxiety may be an element but other acknowledged elements are disgust.[406] Neither motive accounts for the position taken by the Churches, which is to welcome people who are GLBTI, treat then with the respect for their dignity that is due to every member of the human family, and call on all our people to minister pastorally and sensitively to all irrespective of sexual orientation and to condemn irrational fear of or disgust for homosexuals. That view is consistent with teaching according to a religious understanding of sexuality and chastity that rejects sexual acts between people of the same sex as incompatible with Scripture and with a purposeful understanding of sexuality.

---

405 Carolyn J. Douglas, Concetta M. Kalman, and Thomas P. Kalman, "Homophobia Among Physicians and Nurses: An Empirical Study", *Hospital and Community Psychiatry*, Volume 36, December 1985, pp. 1309-1311; C.W. Blackwell, "Registered Nurses' Attitudes Toward the Protection of Gays and Lesbians in the Workplace", *Journal of Transcultural Nursing*, Volume 19, No. 4, 1 October 2008, pp. 347-353; Harry Brod and Michael Kaufman, *Theorizing Masculinity*, Sage Publications, 1994.

406 University of Arkansas, *Daily Headlines*. "Disgust not fear drives homophobia, say UA psychologists" (7 June 2002).

While from the religious perspective, homosexual activity is seen as annulling the goals, symbolism and meaning of the Creator's sexual design, it is a mistake to claim that the Church's teaching about the significance of sexual intimacy justifies intolerance, malice or violence or to claim that it is motivated by fear or by disgust.

The definition of "homophobic harassment" proposed in *With Respect* makes no distinction between intolerance and malice on the one hand, and, on the other, a religious belief in the revealed design of the Creator for human sexuality. While this belief may cause another to feel offended, humiliated, intimidated, insulted or ridiculed, that is not the outcome desired in teaching what is firmly believed to be a religious truth. The creation of the offence would cause great disharmony, and the enforcement of such a law could create martyrs, and even greater division between religious people and people who are GLBTI.[407]

---

[407] I express my gratitude to the members of the Ad Hoc Interfaith Committee on Social Issues, of which I am a member, for their assistance in revising the material in this chapter, much of which was used in a submission to government, though I take responsibility for any errors that the chapter contains. Working in an interfaith context has been informative and delightful, even if at times challenging , and I am most grateful for the tolerant treatment I have always received from the other members.

19
Same Sex Attraction

19.1 Not a Choice

So much happens in discovering our sexuality. We learn to recognize and integrate our feelings and emotions so that they serve our intelligence and our wills rather than dominate us. Feelings and emotions are important; often they are what gets us out of bed in the morning. Our problem is to make sense of them and to direct them so that they are a positive force for good, for love.

For a significant proportion of young men and women, the mystery of sexuality is more of a challenge because they find they are attracted to someone of the same gender. It is not likely to be a choice. It is something that happens.

19.2 A Vocation to Love

The Christian vocation is to love God and neighbour. Much of our literature is about what that love means. In His life, suffering and death on the cross, Jesus gave love a particular meaning, as a complete gift of self to another for the sake of the other. Love serves the development and flourishing of the other.

We speak of many different types of love: love of country, love of one's profession, love between friends, love of work, spousal love, love between parents and children, love between family members, brotherly and sisterly love, love of neighbour and love of God. Jesus loves us all without distinction and without demanding love in return. However he also wished to be loved – at Gethsemane he asked his apostles to stay awake with him, when he healed the lepers he wanted them to return to thank him. He also had a particular friendship with each of his disciples, so evident in the calling of Peter and Andrew. He asked Peter three times, "Do you love me?". Jesus loved his disciples.

As Christians we are called to love in all these ways: to love our neighbour without distinction, to want to be loved, and to give our love and loyalty to our friends.

19.3 Discovering Gender

As human beings we are a unity of body and soul in this life and in the next life. We are bodies, and we give and receive love, as bodies. For most, one of our earliest discoveries as children was the relationship to our mothers and our fathers. We tend to associate those relationships with activities and ways of being that were either male or female in the way in which our mothers and fathers expressed their gender differences.

A little later, we became more conscious of our own gender and were able to relate that gender to either our father or our mother. Gender assumed a significance for us that was largely social, because the full biological reality of gender had not yet developed.

By the time of adolescence, we had become aware of the biological significance of the capacity to be a mother or father and the intimacy that makes that possible. At that time, the concept of chastity had meaning for us, even if we did not use that word. "Chastity" means the *integration* of a person's sexuality into their personal identity.

19.4 Integration of Sexuality

The successful integration of sexuality within the person means achieving an inner unity of our bodily and spiritual being. It means being at peace with our own identity as a man or as a woman, and comfortable with being able to relate responsibly to others, men or women.

The divine gift of our sexuality means that we are not just spiritual beings, but belong to the biological world as potentially mothers or fathers. In the biological world we inhabit as adults, we ordinarily have the complementary capacity to achieve the *one flesh* integration of a man and a woman that may result in parenthood. Parents share with God in the creation of new life, and, in that creative love, give witness to God's love for all of us.

19.5 Witness to God's Love

In giving themselves completely in love and receiving the other completely in love, spouses give full expression to being made in the image and likeness of God – imitating the love of the Persons of the Trinity for each other, and the love of the Persons of the Trinity for us.

Marriage has three purposes: the *unity* of their mutual love, the openness to the *gift of life* in having and nurturing children, and in the expression of those two purposes, its *sacramental* meaning and vocation to be a witness to God's love which is both unitive and fruitful. Marriage is a sanctifying reality: spouses help each other to be holy, to be Christlike.

We were created man and woman, with the differences that we have, that allow us to be a mother or a father and, in the bodily unity of spousal love, to give witness to God's love for us. Jesus refers to himself as a bridegroom and the Church as his bride. Spousal love thus has a deep significance because it gives expression to being made in the image and likeness of God. However, our ultimate vocation is union with God – the God of love did not marry and he told us that in heaven there is neither husband nor wife.

> But Jesus answered them, "You are wrong, because you know neither the Scriptures nor the power of God. For in the resurrection they neither marry nor are given in marriage, but are like angels in heaven. And as for the resurrection of the dead, have you not read what was said to you by God: 'I am the God of Abraham, and the God of Isaac, and the God of Jacob'? He is not God of the dead, but of the living." And when the crowd heard it, they were astonished at his teaching.[408]

19.6 Jesus Calls Us

Forty-three per cent of Australian adults are not, in fact, married. The average for time spent in a never married state for males is 45 years. Most people therefore have other ways of expressing their vocation to love. Being same sex attracted does not change that vocation. As discussed earlier, the sacrament of marriage is not possible for someone who is exclusively same sex attracted, but marriage is not the only way to give ourselves in love.

---

408 *Matthew* 22: 29-33

We are all called to love as Jesus loved, and his particular love for his disciples is an important aspect of His love. His loyalty and friendship were not the same as marital love. They did not have the purposes that we recognize in marital love. But they were love nonetheless. He wanted what was best for them.

Wanting what is best for a friend, and wanting to share activities with them, are part of being Christian. Being same sex attracted does not alter that love; it does mean however that we have to integrate that attraction into who we are. However, we should always live in a way that truly respects and wants the good of the other person. Sexual intimacy outside marriage means acting contrary to the divine plan for sexual intimacy.

Most people experience sexual desire that they should not express, such as for someone to whom they are not married, or, even within marriage, at a time when the other is not responsive, or when for a serious reason it would not be wise to cause a pregnancy. Also within marriage, not every sexual act is acceptable as an expression of complementary self-giving and two-in-oneness. Integrating our sexuality means accepting the feelings and emotions that we have, but guiding and directing them so that they are for good rather than for harm. Many of us fail to serve that vocation, but God still calls us; and his forgiveness depends only on us asking. His love transforms us. His love gives us strength.

19.7 Giving Ourselves in Love

Being sexually attracted to someone other than a spouse, including same sex attraction, is not in itself evil. The issue is in how we integrate our sexuality – there are so many important ways of giving oneself in love, of living for others as Jesus did.

Sexuality is strongly linked to our vocation as Christians to love God and neighbour. But sexual intimacy outside of marriage lacks elements that would make it part of the calling to be a Christian. Sexual intimacy between same sex partners cannot express the complementary, two-in-one flesh self-giving of marital intimacy. It is a meeting of sameness rather than the complementarity and fruitfulness that is the design plan for sexuality.

However, we are all called to give ourselves in love. We are all called to integrate our sexuality by accepting the divine plan, and being at peace with the reality of being a man or a woman in our friendships and other responses. By mastering our sexuality we become more like Jesus, more of a gift to others and to our community, seeking to serve rather than to use. Jesus with his disciples, with the woman at the well, healing the sick, and finally on the Cross so as to redeem all creation, showed us how to love.

The intimacy between husband and wife is a way of expressing love and it is blessed by the possibility of being fruitful. But it is not the only way in which we are called to love others, as Jesus exemplified in his love for his friends, the disciples, the women he encountered, and for his mother and step-father, and for his father in heaven. Jesus, as a man, provides the supreme example for human love. Those who are same sex attracted are no less called to love as Jesus loved. They are, however, not called to express their love in sexual intimacy.

20
Marriage is More than Romance

20.1 Redefining Marriage

We all have friends or family who are gay or lesbians ... these are people we know and love and are part of our families. The Rudd Government's removal of laws that discriminated against them was most significant in ending inequality in the law.

> Now though we face something very different: the redefinition of marriage to exclude the words "a man and a woman" from what marriage means.

20.2 Biological Marriage

What is at stake in this redefinition is the biological reality of the two in one flesh union between a man and a woman, and its importance to children. Biological marriage establishes rights and duties in relation to children because the couple is bound to each other and to the child at every level: genetic, gestational, nurturing, social, physical and spiritual. Biological marriage is not just a relationship of mutual benefit to the spouses, rather the love is by design fruitful and outreaching, potentially involving mutual and unilateral obligations of motherhood and fatherhood that have a biological origin.

That is why the law provides for the celebration of biological marriage involving gender difference, and recognizes the uniquely generative power of the union between man and woman. It is much more than romance. The couple's relationship is open to being extended to include children who come into existence as an equal third party to the union, an embodiment of the couples love for each other, and thus as a permanent sign of their love for each other. As a consequence, marriage confers security and identity on the children who result from the biological union and the unconditional obligations of being mother and father at all levels – genetically, gestationally, socially, physically and spiritually. The possibility of children is the crowning glory of biological marriage.

The biological parents of a child are in fact irreplaceable. A step-parent never has exactly the same status because their relationship is always overshadowed by the reality of the existence of a natural, biological parent. The search for identity of, and access to, natural parents, by donor offspring is testament to the importance of biological parenthood. The major difference between biological parenting and step-parenting is that biological parenthood is much more than a choice.

20.3 Removing Motherhood and Fatherhood

The proposed removal of the union of a man and a woman and the consequent exclusion of gender from the documentation, goes hand in hand with State laws in relation to the status of children in which the word "mother" has been retained for the woman giving birth, but the words "father" and "husband" have been removed in those states that have legislated to allow same sex parenting and surrogacy. Instead of husbands and fathers, there are now simply parents or substitute parents. A child in a surrogacy arrangement also has no legally recognized mother under the agreements, once they are in force, with her role being taken by parent one or parent two, or a substitute parent or parents. Professor Tom Frame of Charles Sturt University, in evidence to the Senate Select Committee in the Marriage Equality Bill 2012 on 4 May 2012 said:

> Given that children raised by a married same-sex couple will not be nurtured by both their parents – indeed, the child will have at least three parents – the committee needs to consider this potential consequence of amending the Marriage Act. That a same-sex couple will be married – and marriage is understood to be the pairing of two people to the exclusion of all others – the capacity of a donor, for instance, to be involved in the nurture of a child will inevitably be affected.

It is ironic, when we are aware of how much children have suffered from absent fathers, that the proposed law is no longer to honour the role of biological parents, especially fathers, but also mothers. This process of redefinition would, in fact, be a cause of great injustice to children, denying them their right to know, to have access to, and be nurtured by their biological mother and father - rights recognized by international law.

Recently and widely reported at the time, a New South Wales Court removed a child from her mildly disabled mother.

> The mother did not lose her child because she was an incompetent or abusive mother. Indeed, the reports from the paediatrician, the psychologist and the family support worker presented in court all acknowledged her love, dedication and capability. The mother has a mild intellectual disability and she lost her child because it was determined that the elderly relatives of her estranged partner – who had challenged for custody of her daughter – would make better parents. Now the mother has access to her daughter only on alternate weekends and for part of school holidays – a decision which she cannot appeal and about which she must remain publicly silent. Her advisers believed they could not resist a decision in favour of her former partner's family and accepted a consent order – there can be no legal challenge to that order. Their decision was based on potential legal liability and restrictions on the role of a litigation guardian, an appointee whose job is to "stand in the shoes" of a disabled person during court proceedings.[409]

What is extraordinary in this case is that the Court seems to have acted in a way that most find counter-intuitive, by overriding the natural relationship between a child and her natural mother. On this logic, any parent and her or his natural child could have that parenthood, and the natural rights and obligations that exist, stripped from them and the child on the basis that someone else is better resourced and perhaps better able to act as the child's parent. Somehow the natural rights and obligations have been dismissed. We are now in danger of creating another Stolen Generation.

---

409 Accessed 21/1/13 from http://www.daru.org.au/resource/a-child-taken-a-mother-grieves

20.4 Same Sex Unions and Step-children

In a same sex union in which there are children, the child is always a step-child of at least one of them. There are a large number of studies on types of parenting, including some fourth level studies or reviews of the range of available well-constructed studies. There is almost no material available on parenting by two men, but there is some material about parenting of young children by two women. If they are in a stable relationship, then the research tends to indicate that there is not an immediate disadvantage for a *young* child being brought up by two mothers rather than by a mother and a father. However, tragically, the weight of evidence also indicates that, especially at adolescent level, step-children are at greater risk cognitively, emotionally and in relation to social problems. When the structural factors are taken into account, a child living with stable biological parents is likely to do better than a step-child within a secure parental relationship to a parent and step-parent. The absence of the biological parent matters.

Since a child in a same sex situation will always be a step-child, of one of the parties at least, as adolescents, they suffer the same disadvantages of lacking a direct relationship to at least one natural parent. When one of the biological parents is not resident and not taking a nurturing and authoritative role in the child's life, the child suffers, especially as an adolescent, when the unusual origin is likely to be known and meaningful and a part of the young person's identity. Further, the difficulties often extend into adulthood. The literature suggests that the involvement of natural parents in at least supervising or assisting with homework and other activities is crucial. See chapter 23.

Because the evidence indicates that the problem of being a step child is not resolved by living with married parents rather than de facto parents, there is also little evidence to support the idea that "gay marriage" would benefit children, because the child will always be a stepchild in those circumstances.

20.5 Role of the State and Marriage

The State has a role in biological marriage, for the sake of any child who results, to protect the child's security, identity and right to have access to, and be nurtured by his or her natural mother and father. Those rights are protected to some extent by honouring marriage between the child's biological mother and father, and are recognized in the ICCPR and the CRC.

On the other hand, the State has no reason to intrude upon same sex unions. A same sex relationship is incapable of generating children. Where children exist in a same sex household, they always have a step-father or stepmother. What we know of step-child situations indicates that step-children living in a blended family with the biological children of their stepmother tend to suffer disadvantage compared to her natural children. Biological motherhood in terms of genetics and having given birth to the child really matters, as does losing that relationship.

To cope with Assisted Reproductive Technology, we have enacted other laws to define the status and identity of step-children and step-parents, now known in some State laws as "parent one" or "parent two", or "substitute parent", but a same sex relationship is not the source of the child. That happens from outside the same sex union. When we form families that deny a child knowledge of, and access and nurturing by, both natural parents we do disadvantage them at least as adults. The information about the comparative higher rates of adjustment problems for children who have a step-parent and no such access to the missing natural parents, whether the circumstances are through adoption or through ART arrangements, including using donors or surrogacy arrangements, is undeniable.[410]

The issue is the importance of honouring and protecting a child's origin in the relationship between his or her biological mother and father – the complementary relationship in which a child usually originates, is carried in the womb and is nurtured by a mother and father. The strength of the unilateral obligations of parenthood is in the relationship being genetic,

---

410 Patricia Harper and Jan Aitken, *Child is not the cure for infertility: Workshop on Infertility: a report of proceedings of a national workshop held in September, 1981/* jointly sponsored by the Institute of Family Studies and the Citizens' Welfare Service of Victoria Australian Government 1981. Also available online: http://trove.nla.gov.au/work/25848469?select edversion=NBD2203650; See also Kay S. Hymowitz. "The Incredible Shrinking Father" *City Journal*, Spring 2007. Accessed 23/1/13 from www.city-journal.org/html/17_2_artificial_insemination.html; Ivan S. Netto and Nilesh Shah, "Psychological support for fathers of artificial insemination donor children", *Indian J Psychiatry*. 2010 Jul-Sep; 52(3): 282–283.

gestational and social, and the child coming to be as an expression of their union, as an embodiment of their love and thus as an equal third party to their love. Anything else is a substitute for the reality of that bond between a child and his or her natural mother and father. Substitute parenthood is a choice, not a natural, biological reality.

It is often a great sadness for same sex couples that their union is not, and can never be, biological marriage. A same sex union lacks some essential attributes of marriage in the design of marriage being for the love to reach out at all levels to include the child who results. Same sex relations lack that biological connectedness to the child and the inherent rights and responsibilities that flow from it.

20.6 Conscientious Objection

Marriage is not just about romance and the love between two people. If the law changes to make legal marriage just about romance, as the proposed redefinition would do, then that will create a moral problem for both ministers of religion, and couples who believe in the biological marriage status quo. Conscientious ministers of religion would have to address the issue of whether we should adopt the European situation, in which religious marriage and legal marriage have separate ceremonies, and dual registration for each, and withdraw from the legal role.

For couples in a biological marriage, there will be the issue of whether they should conscientiously avoid having their marriages legally registered because the law would no longer recognize their reality.

20.7 Marriage is about Sexual Intimacy

The proposal to redefine marriage to include people of the same gender also prompts the question: *why just those people?* Why not include any two persons who want their relationship of co-dependency to be socially, legally recognized? Why should a mother and daughter, two siblings, or an uncle and nephew living together in a relationship in which they care for one another on a more or less permanent basis, not also be included within the definition?

The reason is that support for recognition of gay 'marriage' is not just about recognising interdependency and commitment. The legal change would confer legitimacy on sexual relations between people of the same sex – sexual relations that are not designed to be biologically complementary or fruitful. If this were not the case, the argument would be much broader than just same sex relationships, but would be inclusive of any relationship of co-dependency and mutual love.

The claim that same sex relationships "involve the same love" is often made in this context. To not legally recognize gay 'marriage' is held to be a continued social rejection of the claim to legitimacy of sexual relations between people of the same sex. The marriage issue is thus not so much about a gain in rights, but a gain in social recognition of sexual intimacy between people of the same sex. The purpose is to claim the honour and dignity that is merited by marriage for sexual intimacy between people of the same gender,

20.8 Same Sex Unions are not Marriage

Unfortunately, gay marriage is biologically (and according to God's design) an impossibility, and changing the law would rob us of the institution of marriage. It would make marriage no longer recognized for what it is, as a love that goes beyond romance at all levels, to establish the unilateral bonds of the project of being mother and father together, and being bound to each other by that shared biological relationship to the child, thus protecting the child's identity, security, lineage, nurturing and familial connectedness. Marriage would be about romance only rather than family formation.

21
Masturbation and Pornography

There is little doubt that young people are likely to masturbate as part of exploring their bodies and learning about themselves. The American Psychiatric Association in their diagnostic manual record that at about age three years, children begin to focus much more on their genital regions. Whereas toddlers were interested in looking at and exploring their bodies and genital apparatus (which served the purpose of their constructing a gender identity), young children seek sensual pleasure by manipulating their penile or clitoral area. Children discover masturbation in the natural process of exploring their genital regions.[411]

For adolescents it may happen, initially at least, accidently. For some, it may also happen associated with dreaming and males may wake in an aroused state or after ejaculating. Such events are not chosen and are hence not a moral issue. The Church acknowledges that immaturity is often a factor:

> Psychology helps one to see how the immaturity of adolescence (which can sometimes persist after that age), psychological imbalance or habit can influence behavior, diminishing the deliberate character of the act and bringing about a situation whereby subjectively there may not always be serious fault.[412]

Masturbation can develop as a behavioural problem. Such behaviour, and other compulsive behaviours, can be signs of an emotional problem. As

---

[411] American Psychiatric Association, *Diagnostic and Statistical Manual of Mental Disorders* (fourth edition, text revision). Washington, DC 2000.

[412] Sacred Congregation for the Doctrine of the Faith, *Persona Humana*, Declaration On Certain Questions Concerning Sexual Ethics, Vatican City. 1975, n IX.

such, that may need to be addressed by a mental health specialist. As with any "nervous habit," it is more helpful to consider the causes of compulsive behaviour, rather than try to repress masturbation.[413,414] There is discussion between professionals and other interested parties as to the existence, and validity of the concept, of sexual addiction.[415] Compulsive masturbation is regarded as one of the symptoms of sexual addiction by proponents of that concept.[416,417]

Masturbation otherwise, however, is a conscious choice. It is this that the Church advises involves a grave moral disorder.

> The deliberate use of the sexual faculty outside normal conjugal relations essentially contradicts the finality of the faculty. For it lacks the sexual relationship called for by the moral order, namely the relationship which realizes "the full sense of mutual self-giving and human procreation in the context of true love."[418] All deliberate exercise of sexuality must be reserved to this regular relationship.[419]

In a culture that has become sexualised, this teaching may seem, to many, to be anachronistic. Masturbation, they may say, causes no harm and is a natural release of sexual tension, and it is pleasurable. They may even

---

413 Childrens Medical Office of North Andover, P.C., "Masturbation in Early Childhood", http://www.chmed.com/mod.php?mod=userpage&menu=1907&page_id=142&PHPSESSID=a76dc0f6fb1882506f5666b63fb98062

414 Patricia Fawver (01/10/2006). The Sexual Health Network. http://www.sexualhealth.com/question/read/love-relationships/sexual-addiction-compulsion/11608/

415 D.A. Kingston and P. Firestone, "Problematic hypersexuality: A review of conceptualization and diagnosis", *Sexual Addiction and Compulsivity*, Volume 15, 2008, pp. 284-310.

416 BBC Relationships: Addicted to sex http://www.bbc.co.uk/health/physical_health/sexual_health/probs_sexaddiction.shtml

417 P. Briken, N. Habermann, W. Berner, A. Hill, "Diagnosis and Treatment of Sexual Addiction: A Survey among German Sex Therapists", *Sexual Addiction & Compulsivity* Volume 14,, 2007, pp. 131–145.

418 Congregation for the Doctrine of the Faith, "*Gaudium et Spes*," 5AAS 58 (1966), p. 1072.

419 Sacred Congregation for the Doctrine of the Faith, *Persona Humana, Declaration On Certain Questions Concerning Sexual Ethics*, Vatican City, 1975, n IX.

argue that, within marriage, masturbation serves to balance the differences between sexual drives of the two partners. Outside marriage, they may point to its role in relieving sexual tension and thus avoiding the pressure or the temptation for otherwise sinful sexual encounters.

The issue for the Church, however, is to teach the ideal of chastity, the integration of a person's sexuality. The teaching is founded on the reality that sexuality is a divine gift and has a purpose in the divine plan for us, which includes the expression of unifying, mutual love between spouses, the possibility of sharing with God in the creation of new life, and in that creative love giving witness to God's love for all of us. We were created man and woman, with the differences that we have that allow us to be a mother or a father and in the unity of spousal love to give witness to God's love for us. Jesus refers to himself as a bridegroom and the Church as his bride. Spousal love thus has a deep significance because it gives expression to being made in the image and likeness of God.

Chastity is very important to the Church because God has given sexuality such importance. For the secular world "chastity" means "abstaining from extra-marital or from all sexual intercourse,"[420] but for the Church it means much more. The Church defines it as the successful integration of sexuality within the person and thus the inner unity of man in his bodily and spiritual being. Sexuality, in which man's belonging to the bodily world is expressed, becomes personal and truly human when it is integrated into the relationship of one person to another, in the complete and lifelong mutual gift of a man and a woman. The virtue of chastity therefore involves the *integrity* of the person and the *integrality* of the gift.[421]

The terms "integration" and "integrality" are technical theological terms. By "integration of sexuality" the Church means the unity and wholeness of the person in which the gifts of love and of life retain their full meaning. Because we love God, we seek to act in ways that express both love for God and love of neighbour. We want all our actions to be true. Male masturbation usually involves a choice to pretend that one is making love to someone. Often the pretence is about someone the man knows, or perhaps

---

420 *Oxford English Dictionary.*
421 *Catechism of the Catholic Church*, St Paul Publications, 2000.

an image from a magazine or the internet. So it is saying something false. Masturbation is therefore false because it is definitely not an expression of love, and it implies an exploitative concept of the other person, as a mere sex object, rather than a person to be loved and respected.

Instead of a person mastering their sexual desires and instincts and redirecting them so that they are true and genuinely express love, masturbation may develop as a habit in which another or others have a false and exploited place within the fantasy.

Within marriage, masturbation involves using one's sexual capacity not to express love but in a solitary act. The total gift of oneself in marriage becomes fragmented and no longer a gift that is *integral* to, a part of, the relationship. The gift of sexuality in marriage belongs to the other but in masturbation it is used for a purpose that does not involve the other, except in fantasy, and does not express the unity of the couple. It undermines the two-in-one-flesh nature of the marital act.

This has great spiritual significance because it involves a rejection of God's plan for our sexuality to give love and life through love for someone else.

Masturbation is thus a falsification of the inner truth of conjugal love: the expression of the integrity of self in our love-giving and life-giving power. Male auto-eroticism is a bit like a postman throwing the mail into a drain, instead of delivering it as he is meant to do.[422]

Within marriage, masturbation is a decision to make the marriage and the spouses less than ideal, to make of themselves less than reason would have them be. It involves a loss of virtue because it is a less loving option that rejects temperance and chastity – the integration of our sexuality in all its meanings. It falsifies the unitive dimension of sexuality because marital unity is the mutual willing of the flourishing of the other including development of virtue and of communion with God.

The use of pornography is not without consequences. There is a process of desensitisation that occurs. Psychologists who work with sexual disorders speak of the effect of pornography on relationships and the fact that a man

---

422 This was how my father explained it to me.

may lose the capacity to be aroused by an ordinary relationship, and may make demands that his spouse finds uncomfortable, distressing or degrading. Doctors also report that there is a growing demand for plastic surgery of genitalia, labiaplasty particularly, to make the woman's genitalia resemble the airbrushed images shown in pornography. It is sad that a woman would feel driven to alter her healthy body in that way to conform to false imagery. The obvious problem with pornography is that it is not about love but about self-gratification, and the "other" is depicted as an object for that purpose.

22
The Catholic Church and Paedophilia

22.1 Introduction

In Australia, the management by Catholic Church leaders of complaints they received alleging sexual abuse of children is divided between the current era beginning in 1996, when formal policies were adopted and made public, and the period of the twentieth century before that, including complaints involving alleged victims, or their families who are still alive. In the current era, the policies, *Towards Healing* and the *Melbourne Response*, have been transparent and publicly available.

At the time of writing, there were enquiries in the Victorian Parliament, and terms of reference had been announced, by the Prime Minister, for a Commonwealth Royal Commission into sexual abuse of children by both government and non-government agencies. The Catholic Church and its policies have figured prominently in the need for those enquiries. There had also been an enquiry instigated by the Catholic dioceses of Sydney, Armidale and Parramatta into the management of a particular case and a report by Mr Tony Whitlam QC.

22.2 The Incidence of Paedophilia in Clergy and Religious

The current clerical paedophilia crisis affecting the Catholic Church in Australia is a surprise only in that it seems to have taken so long for the extent and gravity of events to have become public knowledge.

That there are priests who abused prepubescent or adolescent children is to be expected. They are prone to the same human frailties as the members of any other professional group. It has been claimed that, in the US, the evidence indicates that paedophilia (sexual attraction to prepubescent children) affects 0.3% of the entire population of clergy which is lower than the average for males, and homosexual attraction to adolescent boys affects around 2% of clergy, about the same proportion that affects married males.[423]

However, a report commissioned by the US Catholic Bishops in 2002,[424] for the period 1950-2002, produced some disturbing results:

- 195 dioceses and 140 religious communities were surveyed; seven of the dioceses and 30 of the communities did not respond to the survey.
- From the responses, a total of 4,392 priests, deacons and religious were identified to have been accused of such offenses.
- They represented 3-6% of priests in the dioceses and 1-3% in the communities. The overall percentage of accused in terms of all priests and religious in the US was 4%.
- 75% of the alleged incidents took place between 1960-1984.
- A report to the police resulted in an investigation in almost all cases. 384 of the 4,392 were criminally charged. Overall only 8.7% of those accused ended up being charged.
- Of the 384 charged, 252 were convicted – a 66% conviction rate. Some of them had more than one conviction on different counts. Those convicted represented only 5.7% of the total that had been accused.
- As of 2002 (before all the massive costs since then imposed by subsequent court rulings), the cost to the dioceses and communities between 1950-2002 was estimated at about $573 million – $501 million for victim compensation and treatment, and the rest for priest treatment and legal fees.[425]

It has been claimed that the incidence of priests abusing their office in these ways would seem to be no greater than for doctors abusing their patients, lawyers abusing their clients, or teachers abusing their students.[426]

---

423 http://catholiceducation.org/articles/facts/fm0011.html
424 http://www.catholicbishops.org/nrb/johnjaystudy/index.htm
425 Ibid.
426 http://catholiceducation.org/articles/facts/fm0011.html

The main difference may be that the community expects a higher standard of morality for clergy, and sexual crimes by clergy involves both hypocrisy and offence against their high office. Further, sexual crimes against children are grave criminal offences and are seen to be particularly heinous.

However, it is very disturbing that in my home city of Melbourne, in evidence to the Victorian Parliamentary Enquiry, Professor Des Cahill, of RMIT University, reported that 14 of 378 priests graduating from Corpus Christi, the diocesan seminary, between 1940 and 1966 were convicted of child sexual abuse, and Church authorities had admitted that another four who had died were also abusers, a rate of 4.76 per cent.[427] I have since confirmed the likelihood that these numbers are correct with some priests who were training for the priesthood during that period, but I am not free to name them. If the American data, showing only 5.7% of those accused were later convicted, were indicative of the fate of complaints here, then the proportion of priests in Melbourne about whom complaints had been made would be impossibly high, given that 4.76 per cent were convicted. If the data were indicative of a very high proportion of priests being the subject of complaints, that might explain why there appears to have been little response to complaints. There would simply have been too many of them. Professor Cahill told the Victorian Parliamentary Enquiry, "I remain comfortable with that figure and the incidence is much higher than in the general population and much higher than for any other professional group."

I must also say that the Archbishop of Melbourne from 1974 until 1996, the late Archbishop Sir Frank Little, was a personal friend of my family and to me, a caller at our home when we lived in the same suburb, and he often sought my advice on matters to do with bioethics. I have the highest regard for him and for his intentions, though readily admit, on this issue, he may not have been well advised and would have been affected by the mistaken assumptions and misleading expert advice of that earlier time.

It is difficult to know what to make of the American data and the low proportion of complaints that result in conviction and the extraordinarily high proportion of priests who have been convicted in Melbourne, and

---

427 Melbourne *Age*, 23 October 2012, http://www.theage.com.au/victoria/one-in-20-priests-an-abuser-inquiry-told-20121022-2816q.html

whether that indicates a very high proportion of priests against whom complaints have been made here.

It seems significant that, in the US, the rate of offending amongst diocesan clergy seems to be roughly double that of offending by those in religious life. That might have something to do with selection and formation. It might also be something to do with greater surveillance when living in a religious community.

22.3 Formation

There are questions about whether the high proportion of convicted offenders in Melbourne is related to systemic issues in selection and formation. However, the public concern would seem to have focussed more on the way in which the Church authorities have responded to complaints and proven offences, especially where victims were underage and there was a reasonable suspicion of activity that was criminal in nature.

In relation to formation, I asked questions of some of those who were trained at the diocesan seminary at Werribee, during the period in question, about conditions in the seminary. One priest told me that the Jesuit community responsible for their formation retired to their own community in the evenings and left the seminarians to themselves. Two priests said words to the effect that some of those who were later convicted were considered a little strange or eccentric, and some were known by their peers to have had other problems, such as alcoholism. Some had clearly identified their homosexual orientation to their peers and the former tended to form their own sub-group. A senior priest was responsible for the formation of the seminarians. The priests I spoke to questioned the quality of the spiritual direction that they experienced.

The selection and spiritual direction of candidates for the priesthood and religious life have been subjected to intense scrutiny since the 1980s, when the problem first began to come to notice both in the Church and publicly. It is not a matter about which I have expertise, though I have had some involvement in addressing some related ethical questions and I have at times been asked to lecture to seminarians on sexuality and bioethics. However, I am puzzled why the Theology of the Body and the related topics of affectivity and Trinitarian anthropology, at the time of writing, do not seem to be taught with any degree of enthusiasm in theology programs attended by seminarians, and the teaching they receive about marriage and sexuality and about Bioethics does not seem to have been affected by those reforms that were discussed in Chapter 2. The result is that an opportunity for a strong theological formation in sexuality, relating the vocation to celibacy or to married life to Christ and the common vocation of a Christian to seek communion with God by making a gift of oneself, seems to be being missed.

In my view, the seminarians could be better prepared to respond to the modern realties and the challenges of the sexualisation of our secular culture. Our own students at the Institute are, in my view, well-formed and informed, in general, and we have a good record of a proportion of our students choosing to enter priesthood or religious life (as well as others choosing to marry). In my view, much more could be done to develop a mature, theologically and scientifically informed approach to sexuality in our seminarians, that encourages them to integrate their sexual identity into their personal identity as a Christian called to communion with Christ. In that way they would be encouraged to genuinely celebrate their own choice of celibacy, positively, as a witness to the Kingdom and a way of upholding the values and attitudes that see marriage as a witness to divine love.

22.4 Misprision

Returning to the era before 1996, the concern that has been expressed by many victims, and those who support them, includes the claim that the Church authorities have been reluctant to report sexual crimes involving underage victims to the police or child welfare authorities, that they have encouraged secrecy, including offering settlements that required confidentiality, that they have not always acknowledged the gravity of the harm done, or ensured adequate treatment of complainants, and that they have not always removed the perpetrators from office, and, as a result, the latter have been able to reoffend.

Lay Catholics know that priests are as frail as the rest of us when it comes to committing sin, and we would be naïve if we thought that there would not be a proportion of those in the priesthood likely to commit many of the same sins in the various categories as in the general male community. The Catholic community often seems to be willing to forgive the sins of our pastors. It is not uncommon for parish communities to support their priests, even when their past sins are public knowledge.

What is difficult for lay Catholics to accept is that conduct that amounts to a serious crime against a child would not be reported by Church authorities to the police so that justice may be done. This neglect is contrary to current official Vatican policy, which is that civil law concerning reporting of crimes to the appropriate authorities should always be followed.[428] It is also the case that Church officials or their agents, lack the investigative and forensic capacities of the police and the ability to compel witnesses. A Church led or appointed enquiry may be less likely to be able to reach a definite conclusion about what may have occurred.

In many jurisdictions, professions such as doctors, social workers and teachers are in mandated professions and required by law to report that a child is at risk, but priests (and bishops) are not a mandated profession. The obligation to report crime for those not mandated to do so may be a moral and social obligation but, apart from some recent changes to the law in some jurisdictions, it appears not to be a legal obligation, except that if one helps to hide a crime then that may be considered to be an offence of aiding and abetting. Relevant to the issue of reporting obligations for clergy, including bishops, is that in many jurisdictions there is legal protection for the secrecy of the confessional. However Church authorities, in an administrative position with respect to someone suspected of abuse, are advised not to hear their confession precisely because that could generate a conflict.

The confession issue is a bit of a red herring, because

- The type of information made available usually lacks the specific detail required to identify offender, victim, and time and place because confessions do not need that degree of precision.
- Paedophiles and their victims seldom confess to a priest as

---

[428] Motu Proprio *Sacramentorum sanctitatis tutela* (MP SST) of 30 April 2001, "Guide to Understanding Basic CDF Procedures concerning Sexual Abuse Allegations" http://www.vatican.va/resources/resources_guide-CDF-procedures_en.html

it is a very secretive matter and victims are usually fearful of disclosure, especially given the influence of perpetrators.

- In confession, Catholics believe that the priest acts in the person of Christ and the nature of the Sacrament prohibits disclosure in order to preserve the Sacrament – disclosure merits severe penalties within the Church – and the obligation to preserve secrecy is not optional and priests would not comply with a law that was not consistent with their Sacramental role.
- In confession, the priest can prevail on the penitent (victim or perpetrator) to go to the police or other authorities, and that opportunity may be lost if people lost confidence in the Sacrament – the priest can also make notifying the police a condition of absolution on the part of the perpetrator.

As far as I am aware, until relatively recently, no Church authority in Australia had been charged with aiding and abetting crime for not reporting criminal sexual offences against children, despite credible complaints and even sometimes admission of guilt by perpetrators. There may have been a common law offence of misprision that applied, but the only cases of action for alleged misprision, in Australia, are very recent. So in the past, the question of Church authorities reporting crime would seem to have been a matter of a failure to meet a moral and social responsibility rather than a legal issue. That situation is now changing. It is also expected that the Victorian parliamentary enquiry and the Commonwealth Commission may make recommendations for further changes to the law with respect to obligations to report a reasonable suspicion that a crime has been committed against a child. They may also make recommendations for legislative change to make Church authorities and the Church as an institution able to be held responsible for the past actions of individual Church leaders.

Leaving aside the obligation to report a crime, there is concern about the ways in which these matters were managed, particularly with respect to priests known or strongly suspected to have committed crimes against children, and those with unresolved complaints against them, being appointed or re-appointed to circumstances where they had opportunity to re-offend. There is concern about what would seem, in some cases, to have been a failure to protect children, including a failure to warn others in authority about the risk.

The contemporary official Vatican policy is that, during the preliminary stage, a Bishop can act to protect children by restricting the activities of any priest in his diocese. According to the policy, this is part of the Bishop's ordinary authority, which he is encouraged to exercise to whatever extent is necessary to assure that children do not come to harm, and this power can be exercised at the Bishop's discretion before, during and after any canonical proceeding.[429]

The policy has been criticised because it permits, but does not require, a Bishop to suspend or remove the priest while the allegation is investigated.

The Church's own law, canon law, also prescribed a process by which a bishop can appoint a tribunal to investigate and make findings about a matter that might lead to loss of clerical status. There is a question over whether, before 1996, bishops appropriately availed themselves of that capacity when they should have done so.

In dealing with the Ireland situation, Pope Benedict XVI said that the Irish Bishops had failed, at times grievously, to apply the long-established norms of canon law to the crime of child abuse, and serious mistakes and grave errors of judgment were made, and failures of leadership occurred:

> It cannot be denied that some of you and your predecessors failed, at times grievously, to apply the long-established norms of canon law to the crime of child abuse. Serious mistakes were made in responding to allegations. I recognize how difficult it was to grasp the extent and complexity of the problem, to obtain reliable information and to make the right decisions in the light of conflicting expert advice. Nevertheless, it must be admitted that grave errors of judgement were made and failures of leadership occurred. All this has seriously undermined your credibility and effectiveness.[430]

---

[429] Motu Proprio *Sacramentorum sanctitatis tutela* (MP SST) of 30 April 2001, "Guide to Understanding Basic CDF Procedures concerning Sexual Abuse Allegations" http://www.vatican.va/resources/resources_guide-CDF-procedures_en.html

[430] http://www.vatican.va/holy_father/benedict_xvi/letters/2010/documents/hf_ben-xvi_let_20100319_church-ireland_en.html

The Pope also asked them to co-operate with the civil authorities.[431] In his pastoral letter to the Catholics of Ireland (19 March 2010) he also said:

> The program of renewal proposed by the Second Vatican Council was sometimes misinterpreted and indeed, in the light of the profound social changes that were taking place, it was far from easy to know how best to implement it. In particular, there was a well-intentioned but misguided tendency to avoid penal approaches to canonically irregular situations. It is in this overall context that we must try to understand the disturbing problem of child sexual abuse, which has contributed in no small measure to the weakening of faith and the loss of respect for the Church and her teachings.[432]

The Pope has acknowledged the wrongs, and repeatedly apologized and asked forgiveness on behalf of the Church for its own failures in responding to the child abuse by clergy.[433] In recent years there has been a great deal of re-writing of policy by bishops' conferences and the establishment of better mechanisms for investigating and responding to complaints. We can therefore expect the future to be different.

22.5 The Puzzle about Managing Suspicion of Serious Crime

There remains a puzzle, however, over how it was that, in the past, known offenders, or those who were reasonably suspected of grave offences against children, were not at least suspended indefinitely, or removed from the priesthood or religious life. In some instances, even convicted paedophiles, after serving their term in gaol, have been admitted, as religious, back into their religious communities, and presumably a position of trust and respect, even if restricted from contact with children. There was an ABC TV report recently of one such person being described in an official newsletter as a "Patrician Treasure". There is a need for the Church to explain its failure to adequately protect children and to meet the needs, of those who have been abused, to have their claims against perpetrators validated by the Church authority. The defence offered for having the man return to his religious

---
431 Ibid.
432 Ibid.
433 Ibid.

community was that the Patrician Brothers took responsibility for him and ensuring that he did not re-offend. The description of him as a "treasure" was said to be an editorial mistake.[434]

In the past, the response to offences against children appears to have been dealt with in a spirit of providing pastoral care to perpetrators and to victims and treating the wrong as a mental and, or spiritual disorder requiring treatment and spiritual rehabilitation. The response appears to be more fitting for a judgment that the perpetrators were good men who had erred on an occasion out of human weakness. That they were in fact criminals who should be punished and the community protected from them, and that they were more likely to be multiple offenders living a life of deception, would not seem to have informed the management of suspected offenders.

It is unfair to say that secrecy was preserved solely in order to protect the Church, because at that time it was generally accepted that confidentiality was in the interests of the victims. The change in psychiatric opinion to an understanding that promotes the need for admission and recognition of the harm done is more recent. If one compares the *Diagnostic and Statistical Manual of Mental Disorders* of 1980 (the DSM-III) with the DSM-IV of 1994, one of the major changes is in relation to the inclusion of childhood sexual abuse as one of the diagnostic criteria for mental disorders, especially borderline personality disorders. The latter were not even listed in the DSMIII. The DSM IV had the following new entry:

> Numerous studies have shown a strong correlation between child abuse, especially child sexual abuse, and development of BPD [Borderline Personality Disorder]. Many individuals with BPD report to have had a history of abuse and neglect as young children. Patients with BPD have been found to be significantly more likely to report having been verbally, emotionally, physically or sexually abused by caregivers of either gender. There has also been a high incidence of reported incest and loss of caregivers in early childhood for people with borderline personality disorder.

---

434 ABC TV *Lateline*, 26 November 2012, http://www.abc.net.au/news/2012-11-26/patrician-head-discusses-convicted-brother/4393614

They were also much more likely to report having caregivers (of both genders) deny the validity of their thoughts and feelings. They were also reported to have failed to provide needed protection, and neglected their child's physical care. Parents (of both sexes) were typically reported to have withdrawn from the child emotionally, and to have treated the child inconsistently.

Additionally, women with BPD who reported a previous history of neglect by a female caregiver and abuse by a male caregiver were consequently at significantly higher risk of claiming sexual abuse by a noncaregiver (not a parent). It has been suggested that children who experience chronic early maltreatment and attachment difficulties may go on to develop borderline personality disorder.[435]

The great harm done by sexual abuse and, more to the point, the need to acknowledge the abuse in order to adequately treat it, is something that has emerged within psychiatry. It would thus be unfair to blame those in authority in the Church, prior to the current era, for not understanding the importance of acknowledging the abuse and validating the feelings of the abused person. It would appear that the Church was simply in-line with the thinking of the time in not adequately understanding the needs of people who were abused as children.

22.6 Ignorance about Paedophilia

In relation to the perpetrators, there appears to have been a general ignorance about paedophilia and recidivism and about the inability to treat it. It would appear that the responses of Church authorities were often based on the idea that successful treatment of the offender was possible. Presumably they were given that advice by experts in the field. It would help the community to better understand the responses of the Church authorities if the advice they received were to be made public. There was also a belief that the children were better off if less were made of the abuse, and parents, doctors and even police seemed to act upon that assumption. There were no specialist units in police forces with the expertise to deal with this issue and to manage alleged victims well. So the Church authorities would have made assumptions and received advice about both the victims and the perpetrators that were quite

---

[435] Accessed 16/1/13 from http://www.borderlinepersonalitytoday.com/main/dsmiv.htm

different from current expert advice, and, if they had gone to the police, there was no guarantee that the victims would have been well managed.

The current thinking on the perpetrators is quite different and is summarised in the following paragraph from the US:

> Pedophilia, the sexual attraction to children who have not yet reached puberty, remains a vexing challenge for clinicians and public officials. Classified as a paraphilia, an abnormal sexual behavior, researchers have found no effective treatment. Like other sexual orientations, pedophilia is unlikely to change. The goal of treatment, therefore, is to prevent someone from acting on pedophile urges – either by decreasing sexual arousal around children or increasing the ability to manage that arousal. But neither is as effective for reducing harm as preventing access to children, or providing close supervision.[436]

That paedophilia is an orientation that is not to be cured or treated was not understood or at least not well understood. The emphasis on the primary means of preventing harm being to prevent access to children or to provide close supervision is also a significant development.

There have thus been considerable changes in the psychiatric understanding of paedophilia. The proposed US criteria for diagnosing paedophilia, now to be called Pedohebephilic Disorder [including Pedophelic Disorder (sexually attracted to children under 11) or Hebephelic Disorder (sexually attracted to children between 11 and 14)] in the new DSM-5 are:

> A. The person is equally or more attracted sexually to children under the age of 15 than to physically mature adults, as indicated by self-report, laboratory testing, or behaviour.
>
> B. The person is distressed or impaired by these attractions, or the person has sought sexual stimulation from children under 15 on three or more separate occasions.

---

436 Harvard Mental Health Letter July 2010, "Pessimism About Pedophilia" accessed 16/1/13 from http://www.health.harvard.edu/newsletters/Harvard_Mental_Health_Letter/2010/July/pessimism-about-pedophilia

C. The person is at least age 16 years and at least 5 years older than the child or children in Criterion A.

Specify if:

- Sexually Attracted to Children Younger than 11 (Pedophilic Type).
- Sexually Attracted to Children Age 11–14 (Hebephilic Type).
- Sexually Attracted to Both (Pedohebephilic Type).
- Specify if:
- Sexually Attracted to Males.
- Sexually Attracted to Females.
- Sexually Attracted to Both.[437]

The significant changes to the diagnosis of paedophilia are that

- the new diagnostic criteria include not just acts but also the attraction itself where the latter either causes distress or impairment to the person or the person seeks sexual stimulation from children;
- identification may be by self-report, laboratory testing or behaviour; and
- there is a distinction between attraction to pubescent and prebuscent children.

There is now a much greater consciousness of paedophilia with specialist units being set up in most police forces to investigate and prosecute it, and, in most Western jurisdictions, the law in recent times also makes possessing child pornography a criminal offence. There is now a much greater understanding of the condition and the need to protect children from those identified as paedophiles. Offences of this nature against children are much more likely to be prosecuted, though the proportion of complaints that

---

437 Ray Blanchard, "The DSM Diagnostic Criteria for Pedophilia", *Arch Sex Behav* DOI 10.1007/s10508-009-9536-0, 16 September 2009. Accessed 16/1/13 from http://www.dsm5.org/Documents/Sex%20and%20GID%20Lit%20Reviews/Paraphilias/DSMV.PEDO.pdf

result in successful prosecution still appears to be low. It is often a difficult offence to prosecute because victims tend not to come forward until much later, when it may be difficult to obtain evidence. Of course, the diagnosis is much wider than the legal offence, because it covers the attraction or orientation. It is only an offence when the attraction leads to behaviour involving children, including possessing child pornography.

22.7 Church Authorities Not Alone

As a matter of history, the Church authorities were not alone in not notifying the civil authorities when there was a reasonable suspicion or knowledge of sexual offences against a child. It appears that most organizations lacked the capacity to deal with this issue adequately, including not only private and State organizations that had the care of children, but also the armed forces which recruited pubescent children. The latter seemingly did not provide the protection, supervision and avenues for complaint that are now thought to be essential wherever there are underage persons or persons who are otherwise vulnerable. Organizations in general were ill-equipped to deal with the problem. Like the Church, most were also naïve about the risks and the need to provide supervision. Most organizations and children in their care were easy prey for those paedophiles who had developed a deceptive lifestyle around their criminal activities. Children who had disabilities may have been especially vulnerable.

The latter is is no more evident than in the recent revelations about BBC legend Jimmy Savile. According to the BBC, the earliest recorded Savile offence was in 1955 with the most recent in 2009. His offending was most frequent during the period 1966-1976 when he was between 40 and 50 years old. Reports of his offences at the BBC spanned more than 40 years, from 1965-2006 and there were 174 known female victims and 40 males, with most being under 15. Many of his offences took place in hospitals and mental health facilities.[438]

22.8 A Grave Misjudgement

A spirit of therapy rather than punishment, the perceived needs of victims and their families for privacy and confidentiality, the lack of appreciation

---

438 http://www.bbc.co.uk/news/uk-20984284

of the gravity of the harm to the victims, and ignorance about the harmful psychological effect of not validating a complaint, might account for the failure to report crime and to seek justice in that respect. However it can only be considered now as a grave misjudgement.

Amongst other matters related to the investigation and punishment of serious crime and the protection of children, the misjudgement concerns the needs of victims and their families to have their complaint validated and to see that justice was done. They have a legitimate grievance that before the current era, there appears to have been a failure to recognize and take account of the harm done. There also seems to have been a policy of pursuing settlements that included confidentiality clauses. It is difficult to explain the latter except as a design to protect either the Church, or institution, or the alleged perpetrator from the harm that might be done by further disclosure of the matter. There was no other reason to establish such an obligation. Whether or not it was in the interests of the victim to disclose the abuse should always have rested with the victim and his or her family. If anything, the pressure should have been towards disclosure in order to be able to better protect others. To my knowledge, the policies in place now do not include confidentiality clauses and I would expect the practice to have ceased altogether. The idea that a settlement buys silence does not serve the legal or the therapeutic interests of victims, and it certainly does not serve the interests of the community if it means that the perpetrator can continue to abuse others.

The misjudgement was also about the nature of the perpetrators and the tragic reality that a perpetrator, in this respect, seldom had only a solitary victim. In fact, in some instances, it would appear that perpetrators had lived a life of deception and may have joined the priesthood for the opportunities that it afforded. The high probability of recidivism and the inability to "cure" paedophilia are also a matter of more recent knowledge, certainly post 1990-1994, as indicated earlier. To the credit of the Church authorities, the policies changes soon after the medical advice changed, so that by 1996 the approach had completely changed.

Finally, the misjudgement was in relation to the effect of gross immorality on the office of the priesthood. The therapeutic approach would seem to have missed the significance of the grave harm done to victims and the heinous nature of an offence against a child which could only have been addressed by severe penalties for the perpetrators. The failure to remove them from office, or at least suspend them, also damaged the office of priesthood and has continuing effects on both laity and on other clergy. That a perpetrator of such a grave offence, and such a misuse of the office, could be permitted to continue in office is a grave scandal.

22.9 Parallels

There are some parallels also to another issue. The Church authorities have had to deal with the circumstances of priests or male religious in the Catholic Church who have formed relationships with adult women. Sometimes there are children from the relationship. In the past, the main aim of intervention was to give priority to rescuing the vocation. That involved securing a commitment not to have contact with the family, the woman and the children, with the diocese or the religious order then taking financial responsibility for the man's alimony obligations and putting in place financial support for the woman and any children of the relationship.

That policy raises questions about the man's responsibilities to the child as the child's father, responsibilities not exhausted by providing financial support. Given the attitude of the Church towards parenthood, it appears to be hypocrisy to handle the matter by requiring, or even permitting, him not to fulfil his obligations as a father. The child also has rights under international law "to know and be cared for by his or her parents" and "to maintain personal relations and direct contact with both parents on a regular basis", and both parents have obligations to nurture the child.[439] The Convention on the Rights of the Child was ratified by the Vatican in 1990 and, in June 2009, Pope Benedict XVI issued a telegram, signed by Cardinal Secretary of State Tarcisio Bertone, saying there was an "urgent need" for the United Nations Convention on the Rights of the Child "to be implemented to the full."[440]

---

439 United Nations *International Covenant on the Rights of the* Child 1990 Art. 7, Art. 9, and Art. 18.
440 http://www.lifesitenews.com/news/archive//ldn/2009/jun/09061210

The approach that placed the vocation to the priesthood and to celibacy ahead of the rights of the child, and the obligations of a father, is deeply troubling. It also gives rise to a question about whether, in the management of allegations of sexual abuse of children, there was a similar concern to protect the vocation of the alleged perpetrator, and, to some extent, the investment the diocese or the religious order had made in training and supporting him. That seems a shocking thing to say, because the idea that a bishop or superior might want to retain a man in the priesthood or religious life after his having committed a serious crime of that nature, if a crime had indeed been committed, seems utterly contradictory. However, the question does need to be asked whether preserving the vocation was part of the motivation for the manner in which complaints were managed.

22.10 The Historical Obligation to Try and Punish a Serious Crime

The failure to report crime, the secrecy and the adoption of a therapeutic approach, can to some extent be explained by the general lack of knowledge of the time about the grave harm done, the belief that it was a curable condition, and lack of understanding about the high risk of recidivism. The failure to impose penalties, however, is more difficult to explain. That sexual offences against children are serious crimes is not new to the Church. Pope Pius V's Constitution of 30 August 1568 designates priestly abuse (sodomy) of children as 'horrendum illud scelus' – that horrendous crime![441] There was also a ruling by the 3rd Lateran Council in 1179 on violations of the clerical state requiring those who committed sodomy to be dismissed from the clerical state:

> 11. Clerics in holy orders, who in open concubinage keep their mistresses in their houses, should either cast them out and live continently or be deprived of ecclesiastical office and benefice. Let all who are found guilty of that unnatural vice for which the wrath of God came down upon the sons of disobedience and destroyed the five cities with fire, if they are clerics be expelled

---

441 Constitution *Horrendum illud scelus*, 30 August 1568, in *Bullarium Romanum*, Rome: Typographia Reverendae Camerae Apostolicae, Mainardi, 1738, chap. 3, p. 33 English translation accessed 14/1/13 from http://www.traditioninaction.org/religious/n009rp_HomosexualPriests.htm

from the clergy or confined in monasteries to do penance; if they are laymen they are to incur excommunication and be completely separated from the society of the faithful. If any cleric without clear and necessary cause presumes to frequent convents of nuns, let the bishop keep him away; and if he does not stop, let him be ineligible for an ecclesiastical benefice.[442]

This removal of clerical state for the offence of sodomy, in the Middle Ages, would probably have exposed the perpetrator to capital punishment by the civil authority for such an offence. Presumably even more so if the offence were against a child.

The Cluniac (10th Century) and Gregorian (11th Century) reforms were in part to address sexual abuse issues by clergy and in the monasteries.[443]

This is thus not a new problem for the Church: there have clearly been episodes in the Church when widespread sexual offences by clergy had to be dealt with specifically. That there should be severe penalties for sexual offences against children is long-standing in the Church. It is thus puzzling why it was that, in the period between 1950 and 1996, it appears that some Church authorities, at least, did not think it appropriate to ensure that those who had committed serious criminal offences crimes against children should be prosecuted and punished. There appears to have been little commitment to informing the civil authorities of a reasonable suspicion, or even where there was certain knowledge, of a serious criminal offence against a child. The burden of reporting crime seems to have been left to the victims and their families. At the same time, the Church authorities had no capacity to impose penalties themselves, nor, as was mentioned earlier, the powers of the police and the courts to investigate, gather evidence or compel witnesses. The most that they could do was to remove perpetrators from office and withdraw priestly faculties, and even that could be canonically difficult given the lack of investigative powers to establish wrongdoing in the face of denial. There have been cases of priests successfully appealing to Rome

---

442 http://www.papalencyclicals.net/Councils/ecum11.htm
443 John Howe, *Church Reform and Social Change in Eleventh-Century Italy: Dominic of Sora and His Patrons* (The Middle Ages Series), University of Pennsylvania Press, 1997, pp. 149-159.

against a local removal or suspension of their faculties in the absence of concrete evidence.

The public apologies have tended to be non-specific. Perhaps they need to address each of these aspects of the misjudgements. There is certainly a need for those who were involved to explain the advice they received and why they did what they did.

22.11 The Obligation to Protect Children

There has been a complete change of sensitivity within the Church. It would now seem that we can be confident that those who have been found to have committed offences of this nature are not left in positions where they can re-offend. Nevertheless, there remains an issue concerning the social obligation to report crime, or reasonable suspicion of crime, to the civil authorities so that justice is done and can be seen to be done. The circumstance in which the victim and his or her family do not report the allegation to the police appears to remain a difficulty.

As discussed earlier, because this is not the first time in history in which the Church has been riven by scandal of this nature, we can expect that the Church will survive the present difficulties, but there is an opportunity to limit the extent of the harm done by the scandals, by the nature of the response and the restoration of confidence.

The outstanding issue for Church authorities is that some victims and their families do not want action by the civil authorities. As noted above, the problem then is that an internal investigation lacks the powers and the capacity of the police and the judiciary, with respect to obtaining evidence and acting upon it. There is thus good reason to support making reporting, by those in authority in the Church, mandatory. The other side of the argument, however, is whether such a requirement would inhibit the reporting of offences by victims and their families.

There are also difficulties when a complaint is made and investigated by the police, but no charges are laid, or charges are laid but no conviction results, through lack of evidence. The Church may then have the matter investigated internally.

One of the oddities of a matter being handled internally, in those circumstances, is that a finding may be made in favour of a victim on the balance of probabilities and compensation paid, but there may not be sufficient evidence to provide cause to punish or at least remove the offender from office. There are issues of justice involved for both victim and perpetrator when an accusation is made and, with only a small proportion of complaints resulting in successful prosecution, the complaint is not proven. That raises a question about how the bishop or the religious superior should act in that case when an accusation is not sustained, but it is not disproven either.

When an accusation is made, the alleged perpetrator is likely to stand down, or be stood down, while the matter is investigated but what should happen when, as is often the case, the matter is not resolved either way? Is this a case in which someone remains innocent until proven guilty and so they are to be returned to office when the case lapses? Is it prudent for the person in authority to return a man to office when uncertainty remains? What is just for both the alleged perpetrator and the alleged victim? What is prudent in terms of protecting other children, if some suspicion remains? Is the practice of returning the alleged perpetrator to office, but restricting and monitoring their activity so that they do not have unsupervised contact with children, the solution? If a man remains a member of a religious community, or retains his faculties as a priest, is it realistic that he can be prevented from reoffending, especially as others may be unaware of the restrictions and the history, and still treat him with respect and trust? Also deception is commonly a significant aspect of paedophilia and it may be difficult to enforce the restrictions. Finally, does his retaining that position scandalise the complainants and their families because, despite his past actions for which they have been compensated, as far as they are concerned he still holds a respected and trusted office?

After the victims themselves and their families, those most harmed by what has occurred are the vast majority of priests who lead good and holy lives of great sacrifice and devotion. They benefit most from the adoption of rigorous approaches to those who have abused their office. However they can also become the victims of the change in sensitivity because now an allegation, whether or not it is well-founded, is likely to bring immediate suspension from public ministry for an indefinite time. Such allegations are often difficult to prove or disprove and, in the meantime, during the prolonged investigative process which, as is often the outcome, may ultimately not end in resolution, both alleged victim and accused remain in a state of limbo.

I have seen this happen to a priest who was accused of improper sexual conduct against adults, not criminal matters, nor even matters for police investigation. When nothing was found against him after repeated investigation by a variety of Church agencies, and evidence was also obtained to the contrary, he was still unable to clear his name through the lack of the Church processes to act, as a police and a court investigation might, in gathering and presenting the evidence. He even lost his job, when his suspension lasted more than a year, which might be interpreted by the public as a finding of guilt. He has therefore resorted to taking defamation action against the media and the reporters in order to seek a court judgement in his favour exonerating him.

Nevertheless, where children or vulnerable people are involved, I would suggest that the primary obligation is the protection of potential victims from what is grievous harm. There is also an obligation to the alleged victim because we now know that not being believed, if someone has been harmed this way, compounds the psychological harm done. That would seem to require that justice for the alleged perpetrator, who may have been falsely accused, may need to be sacrificed, if significant doubt remains about what occurred. There may be circumstances in which an innocent man cannot be returned to office because of the perceived risk. I say this while knowing how an innocent person might suffer from a false allegation.

22.12 The Future

Now and in the future, it is likely that priests and male religious will take care not to allow themselves to be in a position which might give rise to suspicion. That is sad because it prevents much innocent contact between them and children. But those are now the circumstances in which we live. They are not alone. I recall being advised, as an academic starting to teach at university, not to allow a student of any age or gender to be in my office with the door shut and never to accompany a student alone outside hours.

A concern I have is that loss of confidence on the part of bishops and their priests will cause them to take a low public profile. I have heard of priests being advised by their bishop not to be seen in public, such as on public transport or attending a sporting event or the theatre, wearing clothes that identify their priestly status, for fear of being spat on or otherwise badly treated. That is very sad, but perhaps even more a matter of concern is if bishops and other Catholic religious leaders choose to remain silent on other public issues because of the adverse publicity on this issue.

In my view, in addition to admitting our faults and expressing our sorrow, it is only holiness, and genuine witness to holiness, that will overcome the damage done by the scandals. At this difficult time, I feel it is most important for Catholics, especially Catholic laypeople, to increase their efforts to give that witness. We especially need to give witness to the importance of chastity and its meaning within our vocation to seek communion with Christ. The Theology of the Body reforms have a vital role in providing meaning where so much harm has been done to the Catholic brand.

The cooperation with civil authorities that Pope Benedict urged the Irish bishops to take[444] would seem to be advice that would best be taken generally. There would seem to be a need, for those appointed to manage responses to allegations against clergy by Church authorities, to cooperate closely with the civil authorities in order to expedite effective resolution as quickly as possible for the sake of all concerned. In this case, justice deferred is justice denied for all.

22.13 Response to the Commission

The response of the Australian Bishops Conference to the appointment of the Royal Commission was to support it and to express a desire to openly embrace and co-operate with its work. The President of the Bishops Conference, Archbishop Denis Hart, recently announced a council to assist the Royal Commission.[445]

---

444 http://www.vatican.va/holy_father/benedict_xvi/letters/2010/documents/hf_ben-xvi_let_20100319_church-ireland_en.html

445 Media Release, Announcement of Chair & CEO of the Catholic Church Council for the Royal Commission, 12 December 2012. Accessed 14/1/13 from http://www.catholic.org.au/

The Truth, Justice and Healing Council fully supports the Royal Commission and will do everything within its power to cooperate with it and its exploration of truth for everyone who has been affected by the tragedy of child abuse by:

- identifying systematic institutional failures that have impeded the protection of children;
- promoting lasting healing for the survivors of previous abuse;
- identifying all necessary measures to prevent abuse of children in the future.[446]

My major concern with the enquiries, including the Royal Commission, is that I fear they will not reveal what needs to be revealed. At some stage, the public will reach saturation with the stories of children having been abused, including abuse within indigenous communities. Each story is so horrifying and the sheer volume of complaints leads us as a community to ask questions about those decisions that did not punish offences and permitted re-offending.

The identification of perpetrators, at least those still alive, is a task for police, not for a commission, and I doubt the Commission will be very helpful in that respect, although it does have the function of preparing prosecution briefs for the police. The Commission will no doubt address the systemic issues, how organisations should act to protect children and to respond to complaints, and issues such as mandatory reporting for clergy.

What is likely to be missing, however, is the second-tier of those in authority who in the past made poor decisions; not reporting to police, not removing known or reasonably suspected perpetrators from ministry or other positions, causing their transfer to other parishes or schools, or not warning other bishops or religious leaders into whose jurisdiction they were moved, even when there was evidence of possible, probable or even acknowledged criminal behaviour. Those people who were responsible for those decisions have every reason to avoid the enquiries, or to avoid answering questions if they are called. Why should they expose themselves to civil litigation, even, if not, criminal prosecution? Why would they not withhold material if they can lawfully do so?

---

446 Ibid.

However, it would certainly help to clear the air if they offered explanations of what they did and the advice on which they acted. As I have suggested, it would seem that the mistakes made, according to contemporary understanding, might be explained if we were to know the assumptions on which the decisions were based, including the authority, and his or her advisers, not understanding recidivism and paedophilia, and that paedophilia is not a treatable condition, and not understanding the extent and nature of the harm done to victims and their need to have their complaints validated. Were they given advice that perpetrators had been "cured" after having been sent for spiritual renewal, or at least like a recovering alcoholic, not cured but not likely to reoffend?

I suspect that the only way that these enquiries will uncover significant material of that nature, is if something like the South African Truth and Reconciliation Commission were to be achieved. The latter indemnified those who made truthful admissions as to their wrongdoing, against civil or criminal proceedings. That is what we may need. There are some people in the Church who were in significant positions of responsibility prior to 1996, when the current policies were put in place, and it is probable they are still in high positions.

22.14 Current Thinking

At the time of writing, I am confident in the current policy in Melbourne, the so-called *"Melbourne Response"*. I would prefer that the national policy, *Towards Healing*, did not ever involve someone who has been abused by the clergy needing to front another member of the clergy, or a religious, carrying out the investigation or offering pastoral or other support. That must be very difficult for those who have reason to mistrust the clergy. There is also something of a conflict of interest in having priests and religious involved, because the community they belong to as priests and religious is quite small, and they are usually well known to each other. There is a danger of an internal group acting protectively towards colleagues – "there but for the Grace of God go I".

The *Melbourne Response* handed the issue across to professional lay-people including non-Catholics. I do not accept the criticism of the *Melbourne Response* that they have not referred to the police. The reason for that is that the *Melbourne Response* does not enquire into anything that is the subject of an on-going police enquiry. The rationale for the *Melbourne Response* was to try to assist those people who had either had their matters dealt with by the police, or for whom there was either insufficient evidence, or an unwillingness to deal with the police. The purpose was to assist those who had fallen through the cracks of the government response and to take responsibility for providing them with support, counselling and, in many cases, compensation. Had there been a requirement that those involved in the *Melbourne Response* mandatory report, that would have made it easier, and I support that possibility. Without mandatorily reporting, it is very difficult to know how to deal with a complainant who will not go to the police, despite being urged to do so.

I applaud the establishment by the Bishops of a council to assist the Royal Commission and that it is chaired and resourced by expert lay people. However, as well as providing information about what happened in an open and transparent way, it is of major importance to defend the Church's approach to sexuality and the universal vocation to chastity. The Theology of the Body was never so needed and it is well-equipped to do it. At our Institute we find that our subject on that topic is enormously popular with young people. It offers them something that was otherwise lacking in their Catholic education. As I discussed in Chapter 2, it is such a powerful and positive message for good, and it is based on Holy Scripture and essentially Christocentric. This is not a time for a pure reason approach to natural law, but instead to appeal directly to the holiness of the vocation of a Christian, called to communion with Christ and giving practical witness to Divine love, to agape and eros, as embodied human beings who are happy to love and to be loved as sexual beings. An important aspect of the Theology of the Body is the work being done on affectivity, and coming to terms with our emotional experiences, and the need to redirect them towards virtue, and through virtue to the good of the person. The Theology of the Body has so much more to offer than other contemporary approaches including new natural law. See the discussion in chapters 2 and 13.

22.15 A Third Tier?

Concerning the work of the appointment by the Bishops of the new Council, in relation to the secrecy about what I have called the "second-tier", the Catholic and wider communities have no way of distinguishing between people in authority who were merely ill-informed, or ill-advised or perhaps not competent to deal with this type of situation, or even unable to believe such evil in their contemporaries, as distinct from those who were part of paedophile rings, actively grooming people and sending them on to their partners in crime, and themselves thus involved in the criminal behaviour. Whether that third tier of complicity in criminal behaviour existed in the Church may never be known. It has been alleged by some, though the main allegation, of which I am aware, relates to the grooming and exploitation of young seminarians by older homosexual priests. I find that very disturbing.

22.16 Issues in Clerical Formation and Professional Development

The final issue to be considered is whether the manner of selection and formation of priests and religious took men when they were too young, and was somehow responsible for them being paedophiles and behaving as they later did. There are, of course, two aspects to someone abusing children. They are sexually attracted to children and they must choose to act on that attraction, despite the nature of the evil and the harm to the child. It is difficult to see how a formation in a seminary or religious congregation can be attributed with both making someone attracted to children and willing to do such evil.

There was a practice, long since abandoned, of young men entering religious life quite early as adolescents in their mid-teens, and commonly candidates for the priesthood entered the seminary straight from school at aged 17-18. It is possible that the kind of life that they joined and the absence of normal relationships with women and their families, including their fathers as well as their mothers, from that young age, in some way prevented some of them from maturing normally. However, I have not seen any kind of developmental theory that suggests that paedophilia might be the result.

Bishop Geoffrey Robinson (retired, Archdiocese of Sydney) has been very critical of the manner in which these issues have been handled. I have reservations about many of the suggestions he has made. However, I am interested in what he says about priestly formation. He writes:

Over several decades there has been a strong move towards greater professionalism in most fields of human activity, but priests and religious have limped a long way behind. Their attitude has been one symptom of the idea of being above other human beings and so not needing the assistance and controls that others do.

In the light of all that has happened, there is a crying need that priests and religious should rapidly catch up with the wider society in this field of being truly professional in all they do. Among the elements that need serious and immediate consideration are:

- better selection processes of candidates, with a selection panel wider than just clerics, and with full use of a psychological assessment;
- a training that places as much emphasis on human development as on religious and priestly development, for you simply cannot have a good priest who is not first a good human being;
- a proper professional appraisal every five or six years, with the community participating in commenting on all aspects of the work of the priest or religious, including any signs of harmful or dangerous activity;
- a spiritual director;
- a supervisor with whom priests or religious can discuss their work and how they have dealt with problematic situations;
- in-service training, with promotion or renewal of an appointment (for instance, as parish priest) dependent on regular attendance;
- a code of conduct that sets out expected and acceptable modes of conduct in various circumstances;
- a form of dress (such as a distinctive tie) that serves to identify the priest or religious but is in conformity with modern usage and does not serve to stress their "otherness" from ordinary people;
- attention to living conditions such that a healthy emotional life is facilitated.

A further consideration needs to be added. It is not healthy that any group of people should believe that they have a job for life no matter what they do. The Code of Canon Law makes provision for the removal of a parish priest when his ministry "has for some reason become harmful or at least ineffective, even though this occurs without any serious fault on his part." In the same way, there needs to be provision for the removal from priesthood or religious life altogether of the person who, even without fault, has shown a radical unsuitability for that life.[447]

In relation to the above, it would seem appropriate that for a priest to remain in each of the forms of ministry for which he is ordained, he should be subject to the same requirements for professional development in each of those areas as any other professional who is engaged in counselling. It is also important that anyone engaging in counselling should have the opportunity to de-brief to someone who acts as a mentor or supervisor. This is important to prevent burn-out, if nothing else, and is normal for clinical psychologists and social workers.

The formation of the person as a committed celibate has different burdens at different times of life: the young celibate may feel most greatly the loss of intimacy and may have much in common with those who remain single for lack of a suitable partner; the middle-aged celibate may feel most the loss of parenting and the joys and challenges of parenting, and in many ways have much in common with infertile couples; the older celibate may feel the loss of companionship and have much in common with those who have been divorced or widowed. These are all causes for grieving. The depth and strength of the vocation may need to adapt to the changing nature of the challenges during life's journey.

However, underlying that sense of loss and grief, needs to be a strong sense of what it is to be a "eunuch for the sake of the kingdom" (Matthew 19:12). It seems to be of greatest importance contemporarily that the Theology of the Body, with its focus on male and female embodiment, affectivity and complementarity in relation to vocation and sacramentality, be a significant part of both formation for chastity and the on-going renewal of our priests and religious.

In relation to mentoring within the formation period, I have wondered

---

[447] http://www.abc.net.au/religion/articles/2012/11/13/3632146.htm

what happens when others in formation have reservations about those with whom they live and also about the quality and structure of spiritual direction. There does need to be some monitoring of the development of individuals in formation to become committed celibates.

Second, a spiritual director ought not be someone in an administrative position, and the choice should be by mutual agreement of the candidate and the spiritual director, and should be without implications for the candidate administratively, other than that he must be seeing one. It does need to be a relationship in which the candidate has absolute confidence.

I wondered also whether there is a place for married persons to be available for spiritual direction. When my wife and I presented talks to seminarians, we have occasionally been surprised by the naïveté of the questions, and sometimes the oddness of the underlying presumptions, and that was in an open forum, not a private conversation.

On other occasions, in bioethics discussion, I have been dismayed by some of the presumptions expressed by clergy about married life that assumed what I would consider a lack of chastity in married life to be normal. It is significant that what was known as the "debitum", and the inclusion of "quieting concupiscence" as a purpose for marital intimacy, have not appeared in Church documents since 1930.[448] I presume that this is an effect of the Second Vatican Council's teaching on marriage and it is an obvious exclusion in relation to the Catechesis on the Theology of the Body and the emphasis on the sacramentality of marital intimacy as a witness to God's love. Often comments by clergy imply values that would not be consistent with a sacramental understanding of marital intimacy.

This is related to claims that there is a causal connection between celibacy in the priesthood and religious life and paedophilia. Given the medical understanding of paedophilia discussed above, one would not want to wish on his wife and children, a man who could not control his sexual behaviour. Marriage would be the last place for a paedophile, especially if he had sought sexual relations with an underage person, but even if he were just in the category of distressed or dysfunctional as a result of being sexually attracted

---

448 Pius XI, *Casti Connubii*, n.57.

to persons underage.

As discussed earlier, there may be a causal connection in the opposite direction in that knowing he is a paedophile either actively, or in the sense of being attracted only, may be a reason for a man to seek priesthood or religious life for the cover it gives for being a celibate and the opportunities afforded for a trusted role in which he can access children.

Reading some of the evidence of witnesses to the Melbourne parliamentary enquiry, I have wondered whether the sexual determinism that pervaded the thinking explained in the Kinsey Report,[449] and appears to be endemic in our culture, may have extended its influence to some priests and religious, leading them to believe that they had little control over their sexual desires, and causing them to act out in the way one paedophile Salesian religious was reported as saying "God made us this way and it's his fault."[450] However, if that was so, it was the opposite of what the Church teaches about free will and individual responsibility.

Perhaps those who have been convicted of these awful offences will be able to explain why they did as they did. However, I suspect that the priesthood and religious life were a convenience and not a cause. In a naïve Church community, the trust in which they were held was too easily exploited and their brothers in the priesthood and religious life too willing to disbelieve the victims, or too willing to forgive what was a heinous crime against a child. We have learned, but at a terrible price for the many victims and their families.

Formation, monitoring, mentoring and on-going professional development are important at all stages of life. A married man or a member of a religious community is likely to get feedback, but is there adequate feedback for a diocesan priest living alone? Was his original formation adequate and is he receiving on-going formation appropriate to where he is on the journey?

There is no doubt that since 1996 much has been done not only to review

---

[449] Alfred Kinsey, *Sexual Behavior in the Human Male*, Saunder,s 1948.
[450] Mark Russell, 'No noise, no talking': priest plied boys with 'acrid-tasting' Milo, *Melbourne Age*, 15 November 2012, http://www.theage.com.au/victoria/no-noise-no-talking-priest-plied-boys-with-acridtastingmilo-20121114 9bqp.html#ixzz2KNcvEv00

policies in relation to complaints, but also in relation to the selection and formation of priests and religious. It is now not the norm for men to enter seminaries straight from school. Candidates for the priesthood are much more likely to have significant life experience and to have lived as celibates within the community and without the protections afforded by the seminary or religious life.

I still would like to see better formation in sexuality and in the related bioethical issues. There is a need to ensure that the reforms generated by the Second Vatican Council in relation to marriage and sexuality and the resultant development of the Catechesis on the Theology of the Body inform their formation and equip them for dealing with our overly sexualised culture.

23
Sex Education and the National Curriculum[451]

23.1 The National Curriculum

Sex education is now included in the Australian National Curriculum in the area of Health and Physical Education. That is of concern because it does not necessarily place education in sexuality in an area where there is the capacity to develop the attitudes, skills and behaviours necessary for a safe and smooth transition from childhood to adulthood. The literature in this area strongly acknowledges the need for values education, but will that best be delivered by teachers whose primary interest may be in Health Science or in Physical Education? Are there other areas of the curriculum where teachers are better prepared to assist students to learn the important values that should guide sexual relationships?

One of the stated purposes of the National Curriculum for the area of Health and Physical Education[452] is that it

> ... offers experiential learning, with a curriculum that is relevant, engaging, contemporary, physically active, enjoyable and developmentally appropriate. In Health and Physical Education students develop the knowledge, understanding and skills to support them to be resilient, to develop a strong sense of self, to build and

---

[451] I am grateful for some research contributed to this chapter by Dr Helen McConnell who undertook a literature survey.
[452] Australian Curriculum and Assessment Authority *Draft Shape of the Australian Curriculum: Health and Physical Education* March 2012 Accessed 10/12/2012 from http://www.acara.edu.au/verve/_resources/DRAFT_Shape_of_the_Australian_Curriculum-HPE-FINAL.pdf

maintain satisfying relationships, to make health-enhancing decisions in relation to their health and physical activity participation, and to develop health literacy competencies in order to enhance their own and others' health and wellbeing. As students mature, learning how to address issues such as personal transitions, safety, healthy eating, substance use, and mental and sexual health are critical to maintaining and promoting the health of young Australians.[453]

There are questions to be asked as to whether placing sexuality in this area is just a matter of finding a convenient place for it, or whether serious consideration as been given to placing it with those best equipped to assist young people.

The proposed aims and content of the education in sexuality component of the National Curriculum are broad enough to allow religious schools to conduct appropriate programs and to do so in a way that recognizes each child's parents as the primary educators of their children in these areas.

The placement in the area of Health and Physical Education does, however, raise the need for a religious school to seek to coordinate what happens in this area of curriculum with other areas, including education in faith and religion. It would make sense that if the sensitive matters are being raised in the Health Science class or by the Physical Education teacher, that other teachers are aware. The Social Science teacher may be able to discuss some significant dimensions of human relating, and the Religious Education teacher may seek to raise related matters that link faith and responsible conduct in relationships, including the relationship between sexual behaviour and the possible generation of new life, and responsibility for consequences and for protecting others. The faith dimension also provides meaning that encourages young people to see their bodies and their capacity for sexual intimacy as a divine gift and sacred in its purposes.

Parents need to be aware of timing of programs in sex and relationship education so that they can be appropriately involved in their contribution to the education partnership when their children are engaged with these topics. Seeing the parents as a significant resource and developing curricula that encourage young people to seek information from parents, thus

---

453 Ibid., p. 3.

providing opportunities for parents, is obviously advantageous for the child's development.

Pastoral care and chaplaincy may also need to be aware of increased need for counselling at the time of sensitive matters being raised in education classes involving sexuality and relationship, and the types of issues that may arise may need coping strategies.

This need for a broad multi-disciplinary approach is acknowledged in the National Curriculum:

> It is acknowledged also that the Health and Physical Education curriculum will draw on its multi-disciplinary base with students learning to question the social, cultural and political factors that influence health and well-being. In doing so students will explore matters such as inclusiveness, power inequalities, taken-for-granted assumptions, diversity and social justice, and develop strategies to improve their own and others' health and wellbeing.[454]

The National Curriculum also proposes that

> 21. Through the study of Health and Physical Education young people will learn that a range of factors influence health and physical activity values, behaviours and actions. These factors include individual, interpersonal, organisational, community, environmental and policy influences. When considering and analysing the influence of these factors on wellbeing, the curriculum should support students to understand that health practices and physical activity participation are, in part, socially constructed.[455]

This makes it clear that the resources needed extend well beyond those involved in Health Sciences and Physical Education.

Programs need to be related to the maturity of the children and to respect the ages of innocence. Some matters may be inappropriate for a classroom in which the children, though of similar age, are at very different stages of maturity. Children have a right not to be embarrassed and the context of

---

454 Ibid., p. 5.
455 Ibid., p. 8.

introducing information needs to consider that. Sometimes it may be better that the decision about when, and at what level of specificity, to introduce a topic to a child may be best left to the parents, as the people who usually best know their own child and his or her state of sexual and emotional maturity. Some material is not suited to the broad range of students in a classroom or to the classroom context, which may be embarrassing. Some content may be better delivered on a one on one, or smaller group, basis or given to parents to introduce to the child when the child is ready. Normally discussion with a natural parent involves a strong commitment on the part of the parent in the child's best interests and is unlikely to be exploitative. The evidence for the effect of a good relationship with a natural parent on delaying sexual initiation and thus associated risk is strong (see later discussion). Formal curricula could seek to encourage those relationships with safe, likely to be well meaning adults, such as natural parents.

In this chapter, I explore the evidence for factors that influence the sexual conduct of young people. What predisposes a young person to delay sexual initiation? What causes a young person to have multiple sexual partners? What influences a young person in regard to the types of relationships that he or she forms and whether they are exploitative or expose them or their partners to risks of unplanned pregnancy and possibly abortion, or sexually transmissible infection? What are the trends in Australia and how do they compare with trends elsewhere? Does sex education change anything in that respect?

In relation to the National Curriculum, we are discussing formal education. Is that where sex education is most likely to occur, or do young people learn the knowledge, attitudes, behaviours and skills involved elsewhere? How effective is formal sex education compared to the influence of peers, parents and family, other adults and the various forms of media to which they are exposed, both professional and social? What role does exposure to violent and or erotic pornography play? There are different types of formal sex education. What does the evidence show in relation to relative effectiveness? How should we assess the effectiveness of sex education programs?

These are questions that are obviously important for parents, for those teachers they engage to educate their children, and those designing curricula.

There is acknowledgement in the National Curriculum that formal education in this area is of limited capacity and cannot be the complete answer to the problem of seeking to encourage young people to behave well in relation to their sexuality:

> 14. For some years, there has been increasing pressure for the Health and Physical Education curriculum to be the 'cure-all' for a range of public health concerns about children and young people. It should be recognized that although the curriculum will support the development of the knowledge, understanding and skills students need to make healthier and safer choices, it cannot be expected that the curriculum will 'fix' all of the social problems and other issues that may contribute to young people's health and wellbeing.[456]

The role of spiritual wellbeing is acknowledged in the section on Asian culture. It is a little surprising that spiritual values are not more universally acknowledged in the curriculum aims and purposes. The evidence suggests that young people who are engaged in formal religious activities are much less likely to be early sexual initiates. (This is discussed in detail later). In relation to Asian culture the document states:

> Students of Health and Physical Education will also learn about the important and varied roles that movement activities play in the culture and beliefs of Asian peoples, reinforcing how physical activities are culturally significant and valued differently. Students will participate in a range of activities that are traditional across Asian cultures and explore the link between spirituality and physical wellbeing and the concept of exercising the mind-body-spirit connection through physical activity.[457]

In the Asian context the curriculum also acknowledged the role of families:

> The Australian Curriculum: Health and Physical Education enables students to explore and appreciate the diversity of ethnic backgrounds, cultures and traditions within the nations of the Asian region. In Health and Physical Education, students develop communication and interpersonal skills that reflect cultural

---
456 Ibid.
457 Ibid., p.22.

understanding, building awareness of and respect for the diverse range of beliefs and customs that play an important role in Asian communities. While exploring the role of family and community in the lives of all young people, students will have opportunities to develop an understanding of the nature of family structures within different cultures, including Asian cultures, and investigate the important role family plays in the lives of young people.[458]

Why only Asian families? The evidence indicates the beneficial effects of the role of parents in sex education, particularly their own example in their relationships, but also in the way in which they seek to pass on values, attitudes and beliefs, is significant in all families.

At Years 7–8 (typically 12–14 years of age) the National Curriculum will require that

> 82. Students in Years 7 and 8 will critically reflect on factors that influence their perception of themselves and their capacity to be resilient. Students will propose practical actions they can take to develop a sense of control over their future, such as personal goal-setting, optimistic thinking styles, early help-seeking strategies and positive self-talk.
>
> 83. Students need opportunities to practise using creative and collaborative processes to work within a group or team to communicate effectively, solve problems, resolve conflicts and make decisions in movement and social contexts.
>
> 84. Students further develop their understanding of the physical, social, emotional and intellectual changes associated with moving through puberty and adolescence and develop effective self-management strategies to deal with these changes. Students also need to be able to recognize sexual feelings and evaluate behavioural expectations for different social situations. Students need to develop the knowledge, understanding and skills to recognize instances of discrimination and harassment and act responsibly to support their own rights and feelings and those of others.[459]

---

458 Ibid.
459 Ibid., p.14.

It is appropriate that the National Curriculum thus acknowledges the wide scope of learning in relation to sex and relationship education and the importance of the contexts in which young people find themselves. The evidence discussed later on the beneficial effect on delaying sexual initiation that participation in a youth group may have, or similar benefits from a child having an acknowledged area of success in his or her life, or similar benefits from participation in organized religious activities, are matters that are highly relevant to decisions to shape or encourage a young person's activities.

In the Years 9-10 (14-16 years of age), the National Curriculum directs:

> 96. Students will investigate a range of health issues relevant to young people including mental health, sexual health, healthy eating, personal safety, body image and behaviours associated with substance use. As they do so, students will develop knowledge, understanding and skills (such as early help seeking strategies, assertive behaviours, conflict resolution, emergency care and first aid management skills) to appropriately respond to a range of situations where their own or others' wellbeing may be at risk.[460]

It is important to bear in mind the interconnectedness of some of these issues. Later, I will discuss the connection between the speed and frequency of relationships and their breakdown amongst young people in this age group, and the increased danger of suicide and self-harm, when that happens.

The document also demonstrates how wide-ranging the curriculum and the expertise required needs to be when it states for those at year 9-10 level:

> 99. Students need opportunities to explore the nature and benefits of meaningful relationships, and to develop skills to manage a range of relationships as they change over time. Students develop the knowledge, understanding and skills to analyse how a range of socio-cultural and personal factors influence sexuality, sexual attitudes and behaviour. They also develop an understanding of the role that empathy, ethical decision-making and personal safety play in maintaining positive relationships, and learn the skills they need to be proactive in dealing with a range of relationships.[461]

---

460 Ibid., p.16.
461 Ibid.

The inclusion of sex education in the National Curriculum is no doubt a matter of concern to parents and the organizations that take an interest in the development of well-being of young people. The Churches would be included amongst those, especially those in Catholic schools who have responsibility as education providers for implementing the National Curriculum in this respect. However, inclusion of sex and relationship education in the National Curriculum need not be seen as a bad thing, even though it may be considered unfortunate that it has been placed in just the one area of Health and Physical Education. That does not mean that we cannot ensure that there is coordination with other areas that are relevant and possess significant expertise. I would suggest that what is needed is for schools to appoint someone to coordinate education in sexuality, as it is defined by the curriculum across the relevant key learning areas, and not just in Health and Physical Education. This was in fact the conclusion drawn in 2002 by the Catholic Archdiocese of Melbourne when it issued its *Directives for Christian Education in Sexuality*.[462]

In a religious school, there is an obvious need for those engaged in Religious Education to be aware of the material to be used and to be involved in the curriculum design so that material used does not provide contradictory value messages. How the empirical material relating to sexuality, relationships, health and well-being is presented is important and can create opportunities for discussion of the ethical, relational and spiritual dimensions. More importantly, a religious school is likely to recognize that parents are the primary educators of their children, especially in this area. It is important that the schools seek to engage the parents in the decisions about curriculum design and how to protect the ages of innocence and avoid embarrassing young people in the classroom. There are so many different teaching and learning strategies that can be applied to assist parents in this task. It is also important to be aware of the multitude of factors that influence young people in relation to the way in which they conduct their relationships and to acknowledge that formal sex education is not the most significant influence. In fact, the evidence suggests that most formal sex education programs have little influence on attitudes, the acquisition of knowledge and skills, and change in behaviour in relation to the sexual conduct of young people.

---

[462] Catholic Archdiocese of Melbourne, *Directives for Education in Sexuality*, East Melbourne, Catholic Education Office, 2002.

This chapter reports the results of a literature survey on the effectiveness of sex education I undertook with a research assistant, Dr Helen McConnell, for whose assistance I am very grateful. The chapter concludes that much education in sexuality focuses on avoiding unplanned pregnancy and preventing sexually transmissible disease. As a matter of pedagogy, there is little evidence that reciting the facts about harmful consequences and presenting a smorgasbord of sexual choices has a positive effect on the behaviour of teenagers in this matter. It may be that they attach much greater importance to identity issues, forming relationships, and peer opinion than to sober messages about their health. There is also little to indicate that public-health education messages are effective. Education in sexuality is much more complex because it deals with matters involving sexual identity, personal relationships, and personal morality. The literature is pointing very strongly to the importance of addressing the context of young people as being more significant in relation to avoiding risk behaviour. By context, I mean factors such as their relationships to both natural parents, home life, whether parents disapprove of early sexual initiation, participation in youth groups and in religious activity, and academic, sporting and other achievements.

I argue that in approaching education in sexuality, one ought to address the matter of what the *needs* of the target group are, what *objectives* may be drawn from those needs, what *methods* might be employed to meet those needs including who should be involved, and finally how to *evaluate* what is done in a way that respects privacy.

On the basis of the little evidence available, I speculate about the criteria that effective sex education would need to meet. The view taken here is that there is little point in preaching sexual taboos if you have not already established a context which upholds some more fundamental notions about the importance of being human, about making genuinely free choices that foster personal growth and development, and about respecting the human body and gender identity as a man or as a woman.

According to this view if you want to do sex education effectively, then do not start with sex education (in the usual sense of what is meant). Rather, you start with matters to do with healthy living and behavioural notions related to identity as man or as woman, family relationships, friendship, self-worth, and the worth of other persons. That then gives a context to matters that are causative in relation to behaviour, particularly in establishing behaviour that through being respectful of the person, including his or her body, is genuinely protective of the person and his or her physical and mental health. This view is that the appropriate educational sequence is: understand, appreciate, protect.

It should be noted that this approach seems to be entirely consistent with the National Curriculum, though much will depend on what material is developed and whether it comprehensively reflects the National Curriculum in that respect. What no-one should want is a so-called "values-free approach" to education in sexuality. All young people need an approach that aims to be protective and to guide them in the formation of good relationships. That means relationships that are genuinely loving, and that, before becoming sexually initiated, they wait until they are sufficiently mature and committed for the relationship to be a lasting one and they are able and willing to share responsibility for the consequences. Often the emphasis is on prophylaxis against pregnancy and sexually transmissible infection, but the much more serious danger may be the emotional and even mental health effects of becoming sexually involved in a state of immaturity. The youth suicide and self-harm rates are testimony to that, especially the association that has been made between relationship breakdown and suicide and self-harm. But even in relation to spread of sexually transmissible infection, the biggest factor is obviously multiple sexual partners, and that is most likely with early sexual initiation and immaturity. Younger people who are sexually active are more likely to have multiple sexual relationships.

For this chapter, as mentioned earlier, an extensive literature review was undertaken to see what the evidence is for effective sex education. Of course, judging the effectiveness of sex education needs first a coherent understanding of what the needs are.

Though the needs are often portrayed simply in terms of preventing pregnancy and infectious disease, delaying sexual initiation is also a relevant factor for both. In addition, the sexual well-being of young people relates to a much wider range of matters including avoiding other harms such as risk of emotional harm, self-harm and suicide, risks to emerging gender identity, and risk of premature exposure to adult concepts and loss of childhood innocence. There is also a range of positive matters to do with the need for personal affirmation of young people and their self-confidence in matters such as gender identity, the acquired ability to make free and reasoned choices about sexual (and other) conduct, and enjoying good relating as a man or a woman and good dating. However, the available research seems to be more or less limited to factors related to protective behaviours in relation to sexually transmissible infection and pregnancy rates. There is also limited data on delaying sexual initiation.

23.2 Literature Review

23.2.1 Introduction

During the past several decades, adolescent sexual and reproductive health has attracted special attention from international governments and researchers in the developed countries. To date, sexually transmitted infections (STIs), especially HIV, and teenage pregnancy remain a considerable moral and economic problem for modern society.

Historically there has been an increase in sexual encounters at a younger age since the so-called "sexual revolution" of the 1960s. Adolescent sexual activity has resulted in increased occurrence of sexually transmitted infections[463] and teenage pregnancy.[464] These consequences of the "sexual revolution" gave an impulse to the creation of a number of national strategies and frameworks which determine the key principles of sexual education in public and private schools.[465] Sadly, in Australia we have continued to see increased rates of early sexual initiation, STIs and teenage pregnancy.

23.2.2 National Strategies and Programs in Australia and U.S.A.

In relation to reducing sexually transmissible infection there are the:

---

463 Department of Health and Ageing, Commonwealth of Australia, *National Sexually Transmissible Infections Strategy 2005–2008*, http://www.vicaids.asn.au/contentfilesuploaded/STI_strategy.pdf.

464 Douglas Kirby, "Reflections on Two Decades of Research on Teen Sexual Behaviour and Pregnancy," *Journal of School Health*, 69.3 (1999): 89–94.

465 A. Mindel and S. Kippax, "A National Sexually Transmitted Infections Strategy: The Need for an All-Embracing Approach," *The Medical Journal of Australia*, 183.10 (2005): 502–503.

- Sixth National HIV Strategy.
- National Hepatitis B Strategy.
- Second National Sexually Transmissible Infections Strategy.
- Third National Hepatitis C Strategy.
- Third National Aboriginal and Torres Strait Islander Blood Borne Viruses and Sexually Transmissible Infections Strategy.[466]

The first Australian National Sexually Transmissible Infections Strategy 2005–2008 was released by the Federal Department of Health and Ageing in 2005. Some states and territories employ their own guidelines, for example, in Victoria, *A Statement on Health and Physical Education for Australian Schools*[467] and as we have seen, there has been a significant development in relation to incorporating sex and relationship education in the National Curriculum. In Queensland *The Strategic Policy Framework for Children's and Young People's Health* has been implemented.[468]

In the State of Victoria there is a government program for sex education in schools called, "Catching on everywhere: sexuality education program development for Victorian schools".[469] It refers to "Whole school learning in sexuality education" which it describes as aiming to

- Provide P–12 sexuality education.
- Ensure the education is comprehensive, e.g. includes a focus on:
    - family
    - puberty and healthy development
    - the reproductive cycle
    - abstinence safer sex and STI prevention
    - pregnancy prevention
    - gender identity

---

466 Australian Government Department of Health and Ageing, *Sixth National HIV Strategy 2010–2013*, Australian Government, Canberra 2010, p. 2.
467 Curriculum Corporation, Carlton, Victoria, 1994.
468 Queensland Government, 2002.
469 http://www.eduweb.vic.gov.au/edulibrary/public/teachlearn/student/coeverywherept2.pdf

- relationships
- decision making
- same-sex attraction
- sexual safety
- values
- fertility protection.

- Ensure the education is covered across a range of domains e.g. H&PE, English.
- Interpersonal Development, Science.
- Utilise curriculum resources, e.g. Catching On resources.
- Ensure materials are readily available, e.g. library, classrooms, appropriate websites.
- Ensure all learning is respectful of diversity.
- Assess and report student achievement against the Victorian Essential Learning Standards.

Again, there is no reason why religious schools cannot work with this framework. The challenge is to ensure that good materials are used that are consistent with the religious and faith development of the young person. Much of what is suggested is about harm minimization and prophylaxis rather than seeking to delay sexual initiation and addressing the issue of having multiple sexual partners.

In the U.S.A., an organization called SIECUS (the Sexuality Information and Education Council of the United States) was established in 1964. In the last four decades, SIECUS has provided various sexual education programs and technical assistance to partner organizations around the world.[470]

In the U.S.A. there is also the National Campaign to Prevent Teen Pregnancy. The campaign was founded in 1996. The campaign aims to:

- Strengthen a culture of *personal responsibility* regarding sex, getting pregnant, and bringing children into the world, as well as strengthening the practice of always using contraception when you aren't ready to have a child.

---

470 SIECUS, 1999, http://www.siecus.org.

- Support *responsible policies* that will increase the use of contraception, particularly by those who cannot afford it and by those at greatest risk for having an unplanned pregnancy.
- Provide *more education* to teens, parents, and young adults in their 20s that encourages them to take sex and pregnancy seriously, stresses personal responsibility and respectful relationships, and includes extensive information about contraception.[471]

In the US, about three in ten teens become pregnant by age 20, the rates in the United States are still the highest among fully industrialized nations, and, after 15 years of continuous decline, the US teen birth rate is now on the rise. At present, about half of pregnancies are unplanned.[472]

23.2.3 The Main Directions of the Research

The entirety of research in the area of teenage sexual education could be usefully divided into three directions: first, the rate of actual spread of STIs and HIV/AIDS among young people as an indicator of the effectiveness of sexual education; second, the incidence of pregnancy in teenagers who receive modern sexual education, and, third, analysis of available curricula for sexual education in schools.

Aside from the published statistical reports and national surveys commissioned by government, the above three indicators offer an important indirect measure of efficiency of sexual education.

Note that early sexual initiation rates are not usually considered in relation to sex education. The fact that this is obviously relevant, but is not included, may indicate an ideological position in favour of a liberal approach, but it may also indicate a reticence to gather data on such a private matter. However, at a population level there are studies available that indicate the general trends in relation to early sexual initiation.

23.2.4 Sexually Transmitted Diseases and Sexual Education

If left untreated, nearly all STIs eventually result in severe, long-term physical consequences. For instance, a chlamydial infection in females often ascends to

---

471 http://www.thenationalcampaign.org/about-us/default.aspx
472 Ibid.

the fallopian tubes, where it causes inflammation and potential infertility and ectopic pregnancy. In males, chlamydia may cause epididymitis and ensuing sterility.[473]

STIs have been increasing significantly in many developed countries in the last several decades. The following examples are derived from recently collected Australian data. The incidence of Chlamydia trachomatis in young people aged 12-24 years increased more than threefold from 98 to 338 cases per 100,000 of population between 1991 and 2001. A similar tendency is found among young people of the same age diagnosed with gonococcal infection. Incidence of gonorrhoea increased by 150 percent between 1991 to 2001, from 47 to 72 per 100,000 of population.[474]

The median age of initiation of sexual intercourse in Australia is reportedly 17 years of age.[475]

In Australia, La Trobe University has been regularly reporting a study on the sexual activity of young people at year 10 (15-16 years old) and year 12 (17-18 years old).[476] In relation to behaviour, the study reported:

- The majority of students (78%) have experienced some form of sexual activity.
- Over one quarter of year 10 students and just over half of year 12 students had experienced sexual intercourse.
- The proportion of students who had experienced sexual intercourse has increased between 2002 and 2008 surveys. In 2002 35% of students reported having sexual intercourse with

---

473 S.R. Skinner and M. Hickey, "Current Priorities for Adolescent Sexual and Reproductive Health in Australia," *The Medical Journal of Australia*, 179 (2003): 158–161.
474 Australian Institute of Health and Welfare (AIHW), "Australian Young People: Their Health and Wellbeing 2003," *Canberra: Australian Institute of Health and Welfare* (cat. n. PHE50); M. Chen and B. Donovan, "Chlamydia Trachomatis Infection in Australia: Epidemiology and Clinical Implication," *Sexual Health*, 1 (2004): 189–196.
475 Department of Education and Early Childhood Development 2008, *The state of Victoria's young people*, Department of Education and Early Childhood Development and Department of Planning and Community Development, Melbourne.
476 A. Smith, P. Agius, A. Mitchell, C. Barrett, M. Pitts, 2009. *Secondary Students and Sexual Health*, 2008, Monograph Series No. 70, Melbourne: Australian Research Centre in Sex, Health & Society, La Trobe University.

this proportion increasing to 40% in 2008.
- Student condom use has remained stable between 2002 and 2008 surveys. In 2008 most students (69%) reported using a condom the last time they had sex and half the sample of sexually active students always used a condom when they had sex in the previous year.
- A considerable proportion of sexually active students have sex with three or more people in a year, and this proportion had increased significantly in 2008. Between 2002 and 2008 surveys the proportion of students reporting three or more sexual partners increased from 20% to 30%.
- Just under half the students surveyed had experienced oral sex.
- Although most of those students reported having oral sex with one partner in the previous year, a considerable proportion (28%) had oral sex with three or more people. This proportion had increased appreciably since the 2002 study (19%).
- For young women, experience of unwanted sex has increased significantly between 2002 and 2008 surveys. In 2002 28% of young women reported ever having unwanted sex and in 2008 this figure had increased to 38%.
- Almost 1 in 10 students surveyed reported their most recent sexual encounter was with someone of the same sex. For young men, the likelihood of having a same sex encounter at the most recent sexual experience had increased from 2% in 2002 to 8% in 2008.
- Most students report positive feelings after having sex, however for young women there is some evidence of a decline in more positive feelings between 2002 and 2008 surveys.
- Between 2002 and 2008, there has been an increase in student confidence with respect to talking with their parents about sex and sexual health related matters.
- Fewer students in the 2008 survey reported using no contraception the last time they had sex.

- Use of the birth control pill (37% vs. 50%) and morning after pill (4% vs. 8%) increased between 2002 and 2008.[477]

The study also reported on knowledge matters. Some significant matters were that

> The overwhelming majority of students knew that both men (91%) and women (90%) could still pass on a sexually transmissible infection without having any obvious symptoms, and a larger majority also knew that HIV was an infection not confined to gay men and injecting drug users only (84%). Fewer students were aware that always using condoms does not offer complete protection from all STIs (76%), that apart from HIV not all STIs could be cured (60%), that cold sores and genital herpes can be caused by the same virus (60%), that chlamydia can lead to sterility amongst women (55%), that oral sex can transmit gonorrhoea (55%) and that genital warts are spread by skin to skin contact not simply through having intercourse (54%). A minority of students were aware that chlamydia affects both men and women (47%) and that once a person has genital herpes they will always have the virus (47%).[478]

The increase in oral sex, so-called 'outercourse', and related promiscuity would seem to be based on the belief that it is safe. That may be related to the above levels of false beliefs in relation to sexually transmissible infection. There has been significant promotion of oral sex in magazines that are aimed at teenage girls.

In the United States, federal surveys for the Department of Health and Human Services have found a decline in sexual activity among adolescents 15 to 19 years of age during the last decade.[479] Nevertheless, overall rates of STIs in the United States are among the highest in the industrialized world. Every year, approximately three million sexually active adolescents acquire

---

477 Quoted directly from the study summary, Ibid.
478 Ibid.
479 J.C. Amba et al, "Fertility, Family Planning and Women's Health: New Data from the 1995 National Survey on Family Growth, National Centre for Health Statistics," *Vital Health Statistics*, 23 (1997): 1–114.

STIs.[480] A recent population-based study found that 4.7 percent of young women and 3.7 percent of young men in the United States are infected by Chlamydia trachomatis.[481]

In recent research conducted in this area, many authors utilize the wide spread of STIs as indirect evidence of ineffectiveness of different approaches in sexual education.

An analysis of published studies utilizing data from six surveys on sexual behaviour and surveillance of STIs in the date range from 1970s to 2001 was conducted by A.E. Biddlecom in the United States. The results showed that incidence rates for gonorrhoea among adolescents declined in the last decade (1990s), notwithstanding the increased proportion of teenagers who have had sexual intercourse. In conclusion, the author emphasized that data sources were difficult to compare over most main indicators.[482]

Interestingly, according to the National Longitudinal Study of Adolescent Health in the U.S., younger individuals at first intercourse were associated with higher odds of STIs in comparison to older ages. However, both groups exhibited similar propensity for contracting STIs in later teenage years.[483]

It was proved that biological factors, health care, and social relationships contribute to the risk of contracting STIs.[484] There is no doubt that parents

---

480 L.C. Cooper, N.L. Leland, and G. Alexander, "Effect of Maternal Age on Birth Outcomes Among Young Adolescents," *Social Biology*, 42 (1995): 22-35.
481 W.C. Miller, C.A. Ford, and M. Morris, "Prevalence of Chlamydial and Gonococcal Infection Among Young Adults in the United States," *Journal of American Medical Association*, 291 (2004): 2229–2236.
482 A.E. Biddlecom, "Trends in Sexual Behaviours and Infections Among Young People in the United States," *Sexually Transmitted Infections*, 80 suppl. 2 (2004): 74-79.
483 C.E. Kaestle *et al*, "Young Age at First Intercourse and Sexually Transmitted Infections in Adolescent and Young Adults," *American Journal of Epidemiology*, 161.8 (2005): 774-780.
484 J. Ellen, S. Aral & L. Madger, 1998, "Do Differences in Sexual Behaviours Account for the Ratial/Ethnic Differences in Adolescents Self-Reported History of a Sexually Transmitted Disease?", *Sexually Transmitted Diseases*, vol. 25, pp. 125-129. Cf. H.R. Harrison, M. Costin, and J.B. Meder, "Cervical Chlamydia Trachomatis Infection in University Women: Relationship to History, Contraception, Ectopy and Cervicitis," *American Journal of Obstetric Gynecology*, 153 (1985): 244–251; Aral (1998).

and the school play a significant role in adolescent life. For instance, as is discussed later, studies have revealed that adolescent girls who perceived that their parents disapproved of their sexual intercourse were less infected by STIs. In addition, post-secondary school teenagers with better academic performance in school were less likely to have acquired STIs in six years time than those with lower academic grades. Consequently, the adolescents' academic success and parental disapproval of sexual intercourse could diminish risk of acquiring STIs, particularly in girls.[485]

23.2.5 Teenage Pregnancy and Sexual Education

Adolescent pregnancy, as mentioned earlier, could also serve as one indication of effectiveness of sexual education. According to the Australian Institute of Health and Welfare, Australia's adolescent birth rate for females aged 15-19 years declined from 55 per 1,000 of population in 1971 to 20 per 1,000 of population in 1988 and has remained fairly stable since that time.[486] Australian indications are significantly lower than in the U.S. at 87 per 1,000 of population.[487]

Accurate statistics on the number of pregnancy terminations are difficult to obtain since both the Medicare data and National Hospital Morbidity Database are combined to provide statistical figures. In 2003, 13,855 women aged up to nineteen years had induced termination of pregnancy. This group represents 16.5 percent of the total number of all performed abortions in Australia.[488] It also ought to be noted that abortions achieved early by chemical means, using the morning-after pill, and, even later, agents such as RU486 (mifepristone), are usually not recorded as pregnancies or terminations of pregnancy. The morning after pill, contragestion or emergency contraception has a variety of actions. If taken before ovulation it may prevent fertilization, but if taken at the time of or after fertilization,

---

485 C.A. Ford *et al*, "Predicting Adolescents' Longitudinal Risk for Sexually Transmitted Infection," *Archive of Pediatric and Adolescent Medicine*, 159 (2005): 657–664.
486 AIHW, "Australian Young People."
487 S. As-Sanie, A. Gantt, and M. Rosental, "Pregnancy Prevention in Adolescents," *American Family Physician*, 70.8 (2004): 1517-1523.
488 N. Grayson, J. Hargreaves, and E.A. Sullivan, "Use of Routinely Collected National Data Sets for Reporting on Induced Abortion in Australia," *AIHW National Perinatal Statistics*, 17 (2005): 34.

then its effect is likely to be abortifacient. Of course, much of the time it is taken unnecessarily because the woman is not within the fertile window. These matters were discussed in chapter 10.

An interesting investigation was performed in the United States by R. Barbieri.[489] The author examined the relationship between population density and the percentage of teenagers who electively terminated their pregnancy. Positive correlation between population density and percentage of adolescent termination of pregnancy was found. In particular, in areas of low population density teenagers preferred to give birth.

Consequences of teenage pregnancy are quite serious. Many studies demonstrate that teenage pregnancy and teenage maternity have a negative effect on the social and psychological adaptation of young women in modern society. This situation affects young mothers through often unstable family relationships and financial disadvantage,[490] low self-esteem, and postpartum depression.[491] Further, low interest in education and, dislike of school, are associated with subsequent risk of adolescent pregnancy.[492]

C. Seamark and D. Pereira-Gray performed a study which confirmed the hypothesis that pregnant teenagers are more likely to come from families with mothers who themselves had experienced adolescent pregnancy than their counterparts who did not become pregnant at that age.[493] This issue was addressed in the popular film "Looking for Alibrandi".

---

489 R.L. Barbieri, "Population Density and Teen Pregnancy," *Obstetrics & Gynecology*, 104.4 (2004): 741–744.
490 S. Dyson and A. Mitchell, "Sex Education and Unintended Pregnancy: Are We Seeing the Results?", *Australian Health Review*, 29.2 (2005): 135-139.
491 K.D. Wagner *et al*, "Attributional Style and Depression in Pregnant Teenagers," *American Journal of Psychiatry*, 155.9 (1998): 1227-1233; B. Barnet *et al*, "Association Between Postpartum Substance Use and Depressive Symptoms, Stress and Social Support in Adolescent Mothers," *Pediatrics*, 96.4 (1995): 659-666.
492 C.P. Bonell *et al*, "Effect of Social Exclusion on the Risk of Teenage Pregnancy: Development of Hypotheses Using Baseline Data from a Randomised Trial of Sex Education," *Journal of Epidemiology & Community Health*, 57.11 (2003): 871-876.
493 C.J. Seamark and D.J. Pereira-Gray, "Like Mother, Like Daughter: A General Practice Study of Maternal Influences on Teenage Pregnancy," *British Journal of General Practice*, 47 (1997): 175-176.

Children of adolescent mothers are at risk of pre-term birth, and developing future behavioural disorders.[494] It should be underlined that prematurity is the greatest single cause of underdevelopment of infant's internal organs and death after delivery.

The fathers in teenage pregnancy also undergo psychological stress. J. Quinlivan and J. Condon from Melbourne University examined anxiety and depression in fathers in the setting of teenage pregnancy.[495] The authors performed a cross-sectional cohort study comparing fathers in the setting of teenage (main) and non-teenage groups. It was shown that significantly more fathers from the main group have exhibited psychological symptomatology and required assistance services along with teenage mothers.

The widely accepted findings of the above studies serve to demonstrate the seriousness of consequences of teenage pregnancy upon young people and have been generally relied on in the state and national educational programs in Australia and other countries.

Effectiveness of sexual education is examined by analysis of curricula, involvement of participations in programs, timing of sex education, and impact of different external factors on adolescent sexual attitudes and behaviour. Interestingly, results and conclusions of studies in this specific area appear to differ significantly.

R. Lederman *et al* studied effectiveness of participation in a sex-education program by both school students and their parents.[496] It was found that this "tandem" offers a promising approach to effective education about HIV and teenage pregnancy. In a different study, P. Borgia *et al* assert that the sole apparent benefit of the peer-led intervention, compared to the education programs delivered by teachers, was a greater improvement in knowledge of HIV.[497]

---

494 M.C. Jolly *et al*, "Obstetric Risks of Pregnancy in Women Less Than 18 Years Old," *Obstetric Gynecology*, 96 (2000): 962-966.
495 J.A. Quinlivan and J. Condon, "Anxiety and Depression in Fathers in Teenage Pregnancy," *Australian and New Zealand Journal of Psychiatry*, 30.10 (2005): 915-920.
496 R.P. Lederman, W. Chan, and C. Roberts-Gray, "Sexual Risk Attitudes and Intentions of Youth Age 12–14 Years: Survey Comparisons of Parent-Teen Prevention and Control Groups," *Behavioural Medicine*, 29.4 (2004): 155-163.
497 P. Borgia *et al*, "Is Peer Education the Best Approach for HIV Prevention in Schools? Finding From a Randomised Controlled Trial," *Journal of Adolescent Health* 36.6 (2005): 508–516.

The analysis based on qualitative data from four primary Australian schools performed by J. Milton revealed that both mothers and teachers had difficulties discussing the sexuality issues with primary school students owing to their insufficient prior training.[498] C. Somers and M. Eaves examined the hypothesis of probable harm of earlier sex education in a school in the U.S.A.[499] The subjects in the study were 158 adolescents. The authors showed that sex education at a younger age could be beneficial, provided that topics and their interpretation are relevant to the specific age group.

The sources of sex education, and their impact on adolescent sexual behaviour, are very important in the technological era. In the present time, alternative origins of information can be more authoritative than parents' opinion. In the past, sexual education has been provided as a formal school program. Nevertheless, children obtained sexual knowledge informally from peers, books, movies, TV programs, etc.

Modern technologies provide opportunities for obtaining a wide variety of relevant information by users. In the last several years directed research has been performed in this area. G. Goldman identified and selected relevant websites, which were presented for sexual education in children and preschoolers.[500] In the following year, the author introduced a comprehensive investigation considering the role of parents in sexual education today. It was underlined that learning should be actively shared by parents and children together. Computer-educated parents are seen to be more authoritative by children and thus are able to improve quality of their sexual education.[501] Conversely, research performed by C. Somers

---

498 J. Milton, "Sexuality Education and Primary School: Experiences and Practices of Mothers and Teachers in Four Sydney School," *ACHPER Healthy Lifestyle Journal* 51.4 (2004): 18-25.
499 C.L. Somers and M.W. Eaves, "Is Earlier Sex Education Harmful? An Analysis of the Timing of School-Based Sex Education and Adolescent Behaviours," *Research in Education* 67 (2002): 23-32.
500 J.D.G. Goldman, "Sexuality Education for Children and Pre-Schoolers in the Information Age," *Children Australia* 28.1 (2003): 17-23.
501 J.D.G. Goldman and G. Bradley. "Sexuality information for older people in the technological age", *Australian Journal of Primary Health*, 2004; 10: 96–103; J.D.G. Goldman, "An exploration in Health Education of an integrated theoretical basis for Sexuality Education pedagogies for young people", *Health Education Research*, Vol. 26, no. 3 2011, 526–541.

and A. Surman has shown that earlier learning in school is more important for adolescents than other sources of sex education such as peers, media, and other adults.[502]

The impact of the media on adolescent sexual behaviours has been examined in the U.S. by S. Escobar-Chaves *et al*.[503] The research was carried out by systematic review of the relevant biomedical and social-science literature and other sources on the sexual content of various mass media, published in English between 1983-2004. The effect of media issues on adolescent sexual behaviour was also imported into consideration.

The authors compared a group of American adolescents with a representative group of adolescents from other post-industrial English-speaking countries. They concluded that television was the only medium watched by teenagers with ongoing assessment of its sexual content. Other media were not considered in the basic investigations. Only 12 of 2522 research-related documents (less than 1 percent) involved media and their youth-addressed effect.[504]

The majority of studies were limited by express cross-sectional and sampling patterns and small sample size. Many crucial questions regarding the long-term effectiveness of various social-cultural technological and media approaches were not considered by the authors. In the concluding recommendations the authors showed concern over the development of adequate and comprehensive research methodologies and measures. Escobar-Chaves *et al* finally conclude by noting that the long-term studies should be the method of choice.[505]

The influence of religiousness on the sexual attitudes and behaviour of adolescents has been under consideration by a wide range of researchers. The problems, which authors cover in their examinations, could be characterised by the following examples.

---

502 C.L. Somers and A.T. Surman, "Sources and Timing of Sex Education: Relation with American Adolescent Sexual Attitudes and Behaviour," *Educational Review*, 57.1 (2005): 37-54.
503 S.L. Escobar-Chaves *et al*, "Impact of the Media on Adolescent Sexual Attitudes and Behaviours," *Pediatrics*, 116.1 suppl. S (2005): 303-326.
504 Ibid.
505 Ibid.

S. Rostosky *et al* completed a multifactorial analysis of studies published between 1980 and 2001 aimed at understanding the role and influence of religiousness of adolescents in relation to their sexual attitude and behaviour.[506] The authors collected and examined approximately fifty studies, selected according to the authors' criteria. It was found that the vast majority of studies have used cross-sectional designs whereby crucial developmental changes in religious attitude, beliefs, and behaviour of participants could not be adequately described. Nevertheless, the results indicate that religious beliefs and practice delay the sexual debut of teenage girls. In conclusion the authors recommend improvement to examinations in this sub-field though utilisation of large-scale longitudinal study, which should ideally include the interaction of different systems.

A second group of researchers examined the connection between religious affiliation and frequency of attendance at religious services at age 14 years against a range of sexual behaviour among women aged 15-24. Indications included age at first intercourse; contraception used, timing of birth, and the number of sexual partners. The researches exploited national representative data. Multivariate analysis verified that frequent attendance at religious services at age 14 years continues to have a strong delaying effect on the timing of first intercourse. Albeit in conclusion, the authors accentuated that the survey data and small sample size prevented them from gaining a complete understanding of associations between religious affiliation and reproductive behaviour.[507]

Among a number of approaches to sexual-education study, the abstinence-only program (abstinence until marriage) is central. Today this mode of education is widespread in schools and is advocated by its proponents as unambiguously safe and effective. However, the last assertion is often questioned. According to the American Academy of Pediatrics, abstinence-only education programs have not demonstrated successful

---

506 S.C. Rostosky, B.L. Wilcox, and B.A. Randall, "The Impact of Religiosity on Adolescent Sexual Behaviour: A Review of Evidence," *Journal of Adolescent Research* 19.6 (2004): 677-696.
507 R.K. Jones, J.E. Darroch, and S. Singh, "Religious Differentials in the Sexual and Reproductive Behaviour of Young Women in the United States," *Journal of Adolescent Health* 36.4 (2005): 279-288.

outcomes with regard to delayed initiation of sexual activity and decreased STIs among adolescents.[508]

The same opinion is expressed by Steven D. Pinkerton, who asserts abstinence almost certainly has a failure rate.[509] His simulation studies suggest that abstinence appears to be about as good as condoms for the prevention of STIs. Prior to Pinkerton, a systematic review performed by A. DiCenso *et al* allowed the authors to isolate a finding that primary prevention strategies, including abstinence-only, did not delay the initiation of sexual intercourse or reduce the number of pregnancies in adolescents.[510]

On the other hand, the assertion of total ineffectiveness of abstinence-only programs appears to be at least inaccurate. The distinction between abstinence as an individual choice and abstinence induced by public intervention is not examined, albeit it is a crucial factor in its own right.

Logically, as a personal choice, abstinence is clearly 100 percent effective in avoiding STIs and pregnancy. Conversely, abstinence-only approaches by public intervention may, and do, provoke intrinsic protest in adolescents. J. Fortenberry supposes that, as a public-health intervention used at a population level, abstinence approaches almost certainly will have a failure rate, even if successful in a larger sense.[511]

P. Goodson *et al* studied how program directors and instructors define the term "abstinence."[512] Interviews were conducted with twenty-nine program staff (ten directors and nineteen instructors) from a sample of a federally funded abstinence-only-until-marriage program. The results indicated substantial variability in the definition offered by the subjects. The authors

---

508 J.F. Hagan *et al*, "Sexuality Educational for Children and Adolescent," *Pediatrics* 108.2 (2001): 498-502.
509 Steven D. Pinkerton (2005).
510 A. DiCenso *et al*, "Interventions to Reduce Unintended Pregnancies Among Adolescents: Systematic Review of Randomised Controlled Trials," *British Medical Journal* 324 (2002): 1426-1433.
511 J.D. Fortenberry, "The Limits of Abstinence-Only in Preventing Sexually Transmitted Infections," *Journal of Adolescent Health*, 36 (2005): 269-270.
512 P. Goodson *et al*, "Defining Abstinence: View of Directors, Instructors and Participants in Abstinence-Only-Until-Marriage Programs in Texas," *The Journal of School Health*, 73.3 (2003): 91-95.

concluded that this created difficulties in the development of the program as well as in evaluation of its effectiveness. There are obviously issues in relation to whether abstinence includes oral sexual intercourse in the way in which young people respond to surveys. The latter applies not only to young people – one only has to consider President Clinton's denial of having had a sexual relationship with Monica Lewinski and what he might have meant by that in the light of later evidence.[513]

23.2.7 Methodology of Research

The question of *methodology* utilized in studies of effectiveness of sexual education should be taken into consideration. As was mentioned above, the results of examinations can differ vastly. It is reasonable to assume that the cause could be hidden in the different approaches of each investigating author or group.

There are two types of epidemiological investigations: experimental studies and observational studies. The former includes randomised control studies in which similar individuals at the beginning are randomly allocated to two or more treatment groups, treated, and analysed; and the outcomes for each group are then compared after sufficient follow-up time. In an observational study, the allocation or assignment of factors is outside the control of the investigator, and the combinations are self-selected.

For example, qualitative evaluation was used in studies seeking to determine the views of parents, teachers, and school counsellors about a) contraception, b) the usefulness of peer mentors in sexual education, and c) the association between sexual activity among urban adolescent girls and the four select measures of psychological adaptation.[514]

---

513 Jeane Macintosh, "Monica Lewinsky set to reveal Bill Clinton's sex secrets in tell-all", *New York Post*, 20 September 2012.
514 J. Milton and L. Berne, "Condom and Contraceptive Availability for Young People: Do Australian Teachers, Parents and School Counsellors Support Access in School Settings?" *ACHPER Healthy Lifestyle Journal*, 51.1 (2004): 7-11; S. Yoo *et al*, "A Qualitative Evaluation of the Students of Service (SOS) Program for Sexual Abstinence in Louisiana," *Journal of School Health*, 74.8 (2004): 329-334; A. Martin *et al*, "Early to Bed: A Study of Adaptation Among Sexually Active Urban Adolescent Girls Younger Than Age Sixteen," *Journal of American Academy of Child & Adolescent Psychiatry*, 44.4 (2005): 358-367.

It should be noted, published observation studies are appreciably greater in volume then randomised control trials. G. Guyatt *et al* performed a systematic review comparing the results of randomised trials with observation studies of interventions seeking to prevent adolescent pregnancy.[515] The authors found that the difference between the results of these types of studies were statistically significant in two out of eight outcomes. Observational studies exhibited greater reliance on estimates in assessing effectiveness of sex-education programs compared to randomised trials of adolescent pregnancy.

Besides objective difference in the results of observation there are methodological limitations of studies. For instance, some of the articles dealing with the effectiveness of education programs have been published in the format of a narrative review.[516] Further, the outcome data can be collected using improper questionnaires,[517] or insufficient cohort of participators.[518] Jadar *et al* established methodological procedure important for the development and validation of any health measurement.[519] In particular, Jadar's group argued that the quality of clinical trials should be assessed by blinded raters to limit the risk of bias in meta-analyses and produced their own guidelines for assessment. The guidelines incorporate randomisation, double blinding (usually utilized in clinical treatment), and withdrawals and dropouts.

T. Furukawa *et al*, in analysing the sources of bias in diagnostic accuracy studies pays attention to the "gold" or reference standard, used in medical

---

515 G.H. Guyatt *et al*, "Randomised Trial Versus Observational Studies in Adolescent Pregnancy Prevention," *Journal of Clinical Epidemiology*, 53.2 (2000): 167-174.

516 A. Visser and P. Van Bilsen, "Effectiveness of Sex Education Provided to Adolescent," *Patient Education and Counseling* 23 (1994): 147-160; C. Jacobs and E. Wolf, "School Sexuality and Adolescent Risk-Taking Behaviour," *Journal of School Health*, 65 (1995): 91-95.

517 K.K. Coyle *et al*, "Draw the Line/Respect the Line: A Randomised Trial of a Middle School Intervention to Reduce Sexual Risk Behaviours," *Research and Practice*, 94.5 (2004): 843-851.

518 J.D. Woody, A.D. Randall and H.J. D'Souza, "Mothers' Efforts Toward Their Children's Sex Education: An Exploratory Study," *Journal of Family Studies*, 11.1 (2005): 83-87.

519 Jadar *et al* (1999) cf. D.L. Streiner, G.R. Norman, *Health Measurement Scales: a practical guide to their development and use*, Oxford University Press, 2008.

trials.[520] A hypothetical ideal of "gold" standard test has sensitivity and specificity of 100 percent. Unfortunately, the authors discuss utilisation of this test only for diagnostic purposes. A further significant limitation upon any given study is the time and funding constrains.[521]

23.2.8 What Should Be Done for Improvement of the Research?

It should be noted that quality of research has improved simultaneously with the understanding of the importance of utilization of adequate methodologies for investigations. Nevertheless, sometimes the conclusions as to the effectiveness of education are contradictory and difficult to interpret. Accordingly, the quality of research may be ameliorated by adopting varying approaches.

The utilization of reliable primary data is the basic requirement for achieving trustworthy results. It has been suggested that use of thoroughly designed questionnaires is preferred to the use of reports prepared ad hoc by individual participants.[522] Randomized control trials are deemed to be a method of choice for test of interventions in sex-education programs. Observational studies, both longitudinal and cross-sectional are recommended for use only in the situations where randomized control studies are not available as a first alternative.[523]

A major disadvantage for authors of meta-analyses and systematic reviews is that the assessment of the quality of their investigations depends on the information available in the collected reports.[524] Sometimes, the inappropriate description of methodology of trial could create an impression of deficiency of data, where this may not be the case.[525]

---

520 T.A. Furukawa and G.H. Guyatt, "Sources of Bias in Diagnostic Accuracy Studies and the Diagnostic Process," *Canadian Medical Association Journal* 174.4 (2006): 481-482.
521 K.L. Wilson et al, "A Review of 21 Curricula for Abstinence-Only-Until-Marriage Programs," *Journal of School Health* 75.3 (2005): 90-98.
522 N.D. Brener et al, "Reliability of the Youth Risk Behaviour Survey Questionnaire," *American Journal of Epidemiology* 141 (1995): 575-580.
523 Guyatt et al, 2000.
524 M. Silva, "The Effectiveness of School-Based Sex Education Programs in the Promotion of Abstinent Behaviour: A Meta-Analysis," *Health Education Research, Theory & Practice* 17.4 (2002): 471-481.
525 A.S. Detsky et al, "Incorporating Variations in the Quality of Individual Randomised Trial into Meta-Analysis," *Journal of Clinical Epidemiology*, 45 (1992): 255-265.

23.2.9 Types of Programs for Young People: Do They Work?

It is possible to categorise programs roughly as

- safe sex/condom promotion to prevent STIs (often including promotion of contraception also);
- abstinence only;
- abstinence plus – abstain, but use condoms if not;
- delay first intercourse programs – full information including prophylaxis and contraception but also including effects of early sexual initiation, plus behavioural program (including group CBT), some use pledge to delay (e.g., six months renewable).

Another factor to be assessed is the involvement of parents in school curricula. As we discussed earlier, the limited research available on parent participation in school-based programs is very positive.

A concern I have about promoting so-called "safe sex" is that it gives young people the impression that using condoms makes sexual intimacy safe. It may make sexual intimacy safer in relation to infection and pregnancy, but it certainly does not make sexual intimacy completely safe in that respect, nor does such promotion address the wider issues such as risk of emotional harm, self-harm, and suicide, risks to emerging gender identity, and risk of premature exposure to adult concepts and loss of childhood innocence. Such programs also do not address positively the need for personal affirmation of young people and their self-confidence in matters such as gender identity, the acquired ability to make free and reasoned choices about sexual (and other) conduct, and enjoying good relating as a man or a woman and good dating.

Condoms are not even safe in relation to pregnancy and infection. They have a Pearl index of 3-15 pregnancies per hundred women years. The rates are higher in youth, and the rate of STI transmission from infected persons is higher again than the pregnancy rate. Condoms reduce chances of sexually transmissible disease, with the heterosexual HIV transmission rate reduced by 80 percent,[526] but only 50 percent reduction in rates for genital herpes and genital warts viruses, because they are spread from the genital area.

---

[526] S. Weller and K. Davis, "Condom Effectiveness in Reducing Heterosexual HIV Transmission (Cochrane Review)," *The Cochrane Library* 4 (2002).

Since 1984, condom promotion to young people has been universal in Australia in schools, public advertisements, community education, and higher education. But the take-up and continuance rates are mixed. A basic question to ask is whether STIs in young people fell. In fact, rates for the common STIs such as chlamydia, genital herpes, and the human papilloma virus are increasing in young people.

Overall, the assessment of prevention programs for youth is not very encouraging. A review commissioned by the World Health Organization indicated dismal results for sex-education programs.[527] A. Grunseit *et al* reviewed 47 studies (published between 1974 and 1995) that evaluated sexuality-education interventions implemented in various countries. All studies addressed the behavioural impact of programs. Twenty-five reported that education neither increased nor decreased sexual activity and attendant rates of pregnancy and STIs; 17 reported that education delayed the onset of sexual activity, reduced the number of sexual partners, or reduced unplanned pregnancy and STI rates; and three found increases in sexual behaviour associated with education (one of these was an abstinence-only program, one had potentially significant selection bias, and one reported correlational results, which do not imply causality).[528]

My view based, on reviewing the research, is that programs, like the "safe sex" programs that focus on avoiding or minimising harm, have not been shown to be effective. Similarly there is little evidence that abstinence-only programs are effective. However, programs that present the facts *and* have values and behavioural components, like the pledge or delay-first-intercourse programs, have been shown to have some success. This fits with the evidence that it is the young person's context that is more important than what they may receive in formal sex education programs. The pledge or delay programs address the context, as they are based on a commitment to peers.

The pledge or delay-sexual-intercourse programs are an interesting and

---

527 A. Grunseit *et al*, "Sexuality Education and Young People's Sexual Behaviour: A Review of Studies," *Journal of Adolescent Research* 12 (1997): 421-453.
528 Ibid.

very positive phenomenon according to the evidence. These programs have

- Full information about risks and prevention, and a behavioural component (e.g., group CBT) addressing factors that lead to early sexual initiation.
- Short term focus (e.g., six-month pledge) that gives renewable protection, delays risk, and encourages more considered sexual decisions.

They are thought to be more realistic than abstinence-only programs but may have more social and behavioural content than most sex-education programs.

There is much evidence that the pledge or delay-first-intercourse programs have had some success. Michael Resnick *et al*, using a longitudinal study, showed that the effects of a virginity pledge in reducing sexual activity were statistically significant at the 99.9 percent confidence level.[529]

Andrew Doniger showed that "Not Me, Not Now," an abstinence-oriented, adolescent pregnancy prevention communications program produced both shifts in attitudes and a decline in sexual activity rate over the intervention period that were statistically significant at the 95 percent confidence level.[530] The difference in the rate of decline in adolescent pregnancy in Monroe County, when compared to other geographic areas, was statistically significant at the 95 to 99 percent confidence levels.

Elaine Borawski *et al* showed similar results for delay-first-intercourse programs.[531]

---

[529] Michael Resnick *et al*, "Protecting Adolescents from Harm: Findings From the National Longitudinal Study on Adolescent Health," *Journal of the American Medical Association* 278 (10 September 1997): 823-832.

[530] Andrew S. Doniger, "Impact Evaluation of the 'Not Me, Not Now' Abstinence-Oriented, Adolescent Pregnancy Prevention Communications Program, Monroe County, New York," *Journal of Health Communications* 6 (2001): 45-60.

[531] Elaine Borawski *et al*, "Evaluation of the Teen Pregnancy Prevention Programs Funded Through the Wellness Block Grant (1999-2000)," Center for Health Promotion Research, Department of Epidemiology and Biostatistics, Case Western Reserve University, School of Medicine (23 March 2001).

Peter Bearman and Hanna Bruckner. showed that the effects of a virginity pledge were shown to be statistically significant at the 95 percent confidence level.[532]

In a six-month follow up for Intercourse Delay Program, Stephen Jorgensen *et al* showed that the effects of the program in reducing the rate of onset of sexual activity were statistically significant at the 94.9 percent confidence level.[533] The effects of the program on specific areas of knowledge were significant at the 95 percent confidence level and above.

The quantity of sexual education programs and analyses of their effectiveness has increased significantly in the last several decades. Western society has increasingly turned to resolving the problems of adolescent sexuality and the associated increase in STIs. Teenage pregnancy and its social consequences have also drawn public attention. The investigation of improvements in teenage sexual health may potentially play a crucial role in defining the problem of effectiveness of programs and approaches. Quality research is the way to improve sexual education of adolescents whereupon a healthier society can be maintained.

However, the focus seems to have been on evidence in relation to factors that lead to avoiding teenage pregnancy and sexually transmissible infection, and has included, to a limited extent, a focus on factors that delay sexual initiation or "debut." It is not at all clear that that focus reflects the actual needs that young people have in relation to education in sexuality. What is needed is research firstly on what those needs are. From that research, it would be possible to draft education objectives based on those needs and then to develop and evaluate the effectiveness of various methods aimed at meeting those objectives.

---

532 Peter S. Bearman and Hanna Bruckner, "Promising the Future: Virginity Pledges and First Intercourse," *American Journal of Sociology* 106.4 (January 2001): 861, 862.
533 Stephen R. Jorgensen, Vicki Potts, and Brian Camp, "Project Taking Charge: Six-Month Follow-Up of a Pregnancy Prevention Program for Early Adolescents," *Family Relations* 42.4 (October 1993): 401-406.

23.3 Education in Sexuality: Needs, Objectives, and Methods

23.3.1 The Goals of Education in Sexuality

The review of the literature would seem to indicate that effective sex education is holistic, containing information, values, and behavioural components. I would suggest that, in fact, education about sexual intimacy is a small component of sexuality education. A basic question to ask is: what are the goals of sexuality education? But before that question can be answered, there is the prior question: what are the needs of the target groups?

The reality is that, though we may to a large extent understand the biology, human sexuality is a mystery emotionally, cognitively, and spiritually. It is a mystery that unfolds throughout life. The differences between men and women are a part of that mystery and constitute the phenomenon of complementarity. Being man or woman is part of our identity, and our sexuality affects all aspects of being an individual who is, at one and the same time, both a bodily and a spiritual being. Sexuality especially concerns affectivity, the capacity to love and to procreate, and in a more general way, the capacity to form bonds of communion with others.

Education in sexuality thus begins with the first relationships that a child forms with his or her parents and siblings. There a child normally feels secure, is recognized and loved, and learns to become a lover, one who gives of himself or herself to others. In the first instance, guidance in human sexuality thus happens by the example of the parents and their love for each other and the creation of an environment of respect for the human person and individual dignity.

Sex-education programs therefore are an adjunct to a process that is already well-established by the time a child begins formal education. There are of course numerous other influences that are formative of a child's capacity to relate and to enter into communion with others. They include:

- Peers
- Television
- Movies

- Internet (chat and downloading)
- Computer games
- Magazines
- Newspapers
- Books
- Busybodies

An obvious need in education in sexuality is to respect the dignity of the individual who is the focus of the education. Crucial to that is to ensure that content is age appropriate, appropriate to the level of maturity of the child. Looked at from that perspective, much of the education that comes from "other" sources is not respectful of the dignity of the child, for it is designed to serve other goals. It is also not controllable. Much of the need for education in sexuality is thus remedial or preventative, a response to content that is of an exploitative nature.

While sex-education programs are invariably directed to adolescents, the foundations for a well-adjusted individual are laid much earlier than that. Along the way one hopes that a child's education in sexuality would have:

- fostered positive self-image and self-esteem;
- formed confidence in his or her gender identity (male or female);
- protected innocence;
- responded encouragingly to curiosity;
- provided a home environment in which he or she can appreciate parents' love for each other and thus has good behavioural models for the way in which men and women relate to each other;
- established the capacity in knowledge, values, skills, and behaviour to understand, appreciate, and protect his or her health, including fertility, and to develop friendships and to respect the dignity of others;
- assisted the child to regard sexual intimacy as purposeful, significant, and powerful in its capacity to express and receive love, but also vulnerable and needing to be protected and reserved for those committed circumstances in which it is an expression of love rather than of use.

These then are some general goals for sex education. However they do to an extent represent an idealistic view. The reality for many children is not so positive. A reason for the focus on sex education is the fact that, as a community and as parents and teachers, we often fail our children. One of the greatest fears every parent has is that a child will be so maladjusted and so unhappy as to commit self-harm. The evidence about the causes of self-harm and of suicide is compelling. We know that there are strong associations between social factors and self-harm and suicide.

The National Health and Medical Research Council review of youth suicide identified major social factors in relation to youth suicide including: low socioeconomic status, poor educational achievement, parental separation or divorce, parental psychopathology, family history of suicidal behaviour, parental discord, childhood abuse, and poor parental care. Other factors include mental illness, sexual orientation, interpersonal losses or conflicts, legal or disciplinary crises, other life events, and unemployment.[534]

The goals of education in sexuality are inseparable from the general goals that parents have for their children, for them to be secure, happy, well-adjusted, and developing as persons in truth and love toward greater freedom. Education in sexuality is a part of seeking happiness and fulfillment, and it is obviously subject to whatever conclusions have been drawn about what constitutes happiness and fulfilment.

Christian values are important to education in sexuality because Christianity portrays sexual intimacy positively, as an opportunity to develop in the image and likeness of God. Christian values recognize that human beings find fulfilment in outreach to others. Marriage is a gift of self to one's spouse and that gift of love may become the gift of a child as an embodiment of that loving union. Marriage is thus a God-like role being a *self-sacrifice*, giving oneself as Christ gave himself to all mankind, *covenantal* as God's relationship to us is covenantal, and *creative* in giving and nurturing life, so that those children develop in love and truth as free individuals in the way in which the creator made us free. The religious values exclude notions

---

[534] National Health and Medical Research Council, *National Youth Suicide Prevention Strategy. Setting the Evidence-Based Research Agenda for Australia: A Literature Review* (1999), http://www.nhmrc.gov.au/publications/synopses/mh12syn.htm

of use and exploitation and replace them with notions of loving and giving. Central to that divine imagery is the notion of a community of persons, the community of persons of the Trinity, the community of persons of a marriage, the community of persons of one's family, and the local and wider communities.

But whether or not one takes a religious view, one can recognize the importance to human fulfillment of developing human virtues. The human virtues are the acquired personal attributes necessary to develop as a human being. Human beings are social beings and dependant on their relationship to others. The premise of a Christian concept of virtue is the notion that individual human development is important. The core virtues are about being able to discern what is good for human development and to choose how to achieve it (Wisdom), about recognizing the needs of others and acting justly towards them (Justice), about having the strength (Courage) in the face of difficulties to pursue goodness, and about achieving self-mastery of the will over one's instincts (Temperance). These virtues are said to be core, firstly because they are common to all reasoned approaches to morality; secondly, because they are essential to good community life; and thirdly, because, if one pauses to reflect on them, one can see that the complete absence of any one of them would in fact constitute a mental illness!

These virtues are also essential to being a good lover. To be able to give oneself to another, one needs to be able to discern goodness so that one can serve the other by pursuing what is good for their development and for one's own development. To love someone, one also must be just towards them. Giving oneself in love also requires a great deal of courage, because love makes us vulnerable and more easily hurt. Finally, and very importantly, giving oneself in love is a reasoned choice in which one masters one's own instincts and redirects one's drives for the sake of the other. Classically this aspect of loving is known as chastity.

Chastity is the successful integration of sexuality within the person. To be a good lover, one must first have mastered one's sexual instincts and directed them towards the unified goodness of one's entire person as a physical, emotional, intelligent, and spiritual being. Only then is one able to make a complete gift of oneself to another. Chastity is important for it allows the bodily aspects of sexuality to become personal, and truly human, by being integrated into the relationship of one person to another, in the complete and lifelong mutual gift of a man and a woman. In this way, the sexual joining of a man and a woman is expressive of their personhood at all levels and not just at the biological level, because it is giving rather than using. The virtues make it possible for a person to be at ease with himself or herself, to achieve self-mastery, and to experience joy in leading a morally good life. Goodness becomes that person's normal practice, and he or she is fully free because not impeded by vice. A vice is a disposition toward practices that impede, obstruct, or destroy human development.

Therefore, a central objective of education in sexuality is to guide young people to be good lovers. To be good lovers they need to acquire the core virtues, and chastity is an element of those core virtues. This is not, of course, an isolated goal. The evidence would suggest that abstinence-only programs are ineffective. More than that, we would suggest that they do the child or the young person a disservice because the virtues are aspects of human development that are interrelated.

The problem of imbalance in sex education would seem to arise in sex education being something of a remedy for failures in education, or a response to the age inappropriate and exploitative education that is the effect of the media. The task, I would suggest, is a much broader task and begins the moment, as an infant, a child starts to relate to others. The task is to guide a person toward an appreciation of the goodness of human existence and human development, toward a desire to know the truth (including self-knowledge), a lively interest in and awareness of the needs of others, and a desire for self-mastery. This is basically what sex education is about, and we do a child a disservice if we focus only on one aspect. Education forms a person in knowledge, skills, attitudes, and behaviours. Education in sexuality ought to address each of those components.

23.3.2 Partners in Sex Education

Obviously parents have the primary role in the broad notion of education in sexuality presented here. They form the child's first relationships, and they usually provide the first example to the child of manhood and womanhood and of a giving relationship between a man and a woman. Their love for the child and for each other is thus formative.

The role of parents is, in a strong sense, God-like, initiating life, providing the environment for the new life, and nurturing directed towards the child ultimately gaining the freedom that comes from knowledge, acquiring skills and behaviours, learning to value, and deciding to act in ways that foster human development. Their love for the child gives them the natural authority to lead in the development of their child. The parents' role is so primary that any other person intervening should be seen as partners with the parents rather than as independent of them. In that respect, our view is that those conducting education in sexuality should first seek that partnership with the parents and work through the content of proposed programs with them, seeking their approval, collaboration, and support. It follows, then, that schools and public education programs should see themselves as primarily supportive of the parents' role. As professional educators, teachers have access to resources and new developments in teaching methodology which help to inform behaviour and values. By working closely with the parents, teachers can assist them in their task.

Crucial to good programs is the assessment of need, so as to determine what is age appropriate for children at the level they are and given the exposure they have to events inside and outside the home. Parents are crucial to that assessment as they are likely to know their individual child and his or her circumstances better than anyone else. Respecting the age of innocence and allowing children to be children is important and a child's right.

That said, parents may find educating their children in sexuality a difficult and embarrassing task. In our experience, parents often turn to the school to provide resources and support in this respect. Teachers and schools can assist by imparting knowledge and up-to-date resources suitable for parents to use.

Public educators, including those considering a state-wide or national program such as the National Curriculum's entry into sex education, would be well advised to address their material to parents for them to use with their children. In my experience, one of the most effective forms of education is the worksheet designed for children and parents to work with together.

If material is provided to parents, they, then, can decide when particular material is suitable for their child and introduce it in the safety and security of the parent-child relationship. Also, if teachers require children and parents to work together in the completion of a task, they are in fact reinforcing a key aspect of the child's context which will serve to be more protective in relation to reducing the likelihood of early sexual initiation.

23.3.3 Foundations of Education in Sexuality

In my view, the foundation of an education in sexuality is the notion that our sexuality reflects our capacity to give and be given love, and to give life, and the primary value is the worth and dignity of each member of the human family. Also foundational is the reality that sexuality involves the whole person and that respecting human dignity means both respecting a person as a body and as a chooser.

For that reason, sexuality should occur across the key learning areas and not be seen as the prerogative of any particular area. It is a grave mistake to see sexuality education as a matter of health-science alone or of physical education or of social science and history or of religious studies. Each has a part to play in the development of the child. Adequate education in sexuality is not fragmented. The biology of reproduction, for example, and matters of reproductive health, ought not be taught without reflecting on human love and supportive relationships.

That points to the need for adapting the National Curriculum so that education in sexuality within a school is formally coordinated across the key learning areas. Information should be appropriate to the different phases of a child's development and delivered in a context in which the child feels comfortable and not embarrassed. Sensitivity should be shown towards those aspects of sexuality that are best treated individually. Dependence on the role of parents, in that respect, is important for they normally provide a relationship of friendship and trust. The intimate details of sexual union are never matters for classroom discussion.

Presentation of material of an erotic or arousing nature to children or young people is exploitative. No one should ever be invited, let alone obliged, to act in a way that could offend against modesty or against his or her own sense of delicacy or privacy.

Educators in this area need to be particularly sensitive to the cultural and family environment in which a child lives. At the same time, it would be a mistake for educators to endorse an exploitative cultural or family situation.

23.3.4 Methods of Education in Sexuality

Applying the National Curriculum, schools, parents and religious organizations need to ensure that education in sexuality warrants the attention of our best minds in teaching and learning methodology. Creativity and innovation should be encouraged, but supported by sound research and comprehensively evaluated to ensure that it is meeting the broad goals of education in sexuality. However, it is important that that creativity not breach fundamental principles in relation to what is age appropriate and respectful of the age of innocence and what is respectful of human dignity and the love-giving and life-giving meaning of sexuality. Interventions that promote an irresponsible or recreational attitude to sex, or treat it at the level only of a bodily function, are not only not helpful, but are dangerous to the emotional, physical, and spiritual well-being of young people.

As has been shown by the research review, there is no evidence to show that so-called "safe sex" programs are effective when they do not also teach the dignity of the human person and the meaning of sexuality. While hygiene concerning bodily fluids should be taught at an appropriately earlier age, the sexual transmission of disease needs to be handled sensitively and accurate medical information provided. It should be introduced with care only at an appropriate age and discussed in the context of the meaning of sexuality and a holistic understanding of the human person and human relationships. Sexuality programs need to be integrated so that they encompass the development of the whole person.

23.4 Ethics and the Evaluation of Effectiveness of Education in Sexuality

Systematically gathering information about children or young people is research and raises a number of important issues including:

a) Whether they are in a dependent relationship (teacher-student, for instance) and thus not entirely free in their participation.

b) Confidentiality.

c) Suggestive effects of raising sensitive topics with children.

In Australia, there are national guidelines on the ethics of human research. The *National Statement on Ethical Conduct in Human Research*[535] has been published by the National Health and Medical Research Council and endorsed by the Australian Vice Chancellors Committee and the Australian Research Council. The Statement should govern the conduct of research on the effectiveness of education in sexuality.

Of particular note is the fact that if teenagers are asked about their sexual (or other behaviour) they may disclose information about crimes such as sexual or violent abuse or illegal drug taking. Under state law that information may not be held confidential by those in mandated professions, but is required, under the mandatory reporting provisions, to be reported. If one is asking questions in those areas then, under our law, one may not guarantee anonymity. The individuals remain re-identifiable usually, in any case, if the information is of an intimate or descriptive nature.

Basically anyone conducting such research would be well-advised to seek approval for a formal protocol from:

1. An NHMRC-registered human research ethics committee.
2. The school principal and the education authority (or the leadership of the youth group to whom the program is being delivered).
3. The parents of each child.

The protocol would need to include the plain-language statement to parents. It would need not only to specify anonymity and confidentiality, but also the conditions under which disclosure would be made, such as if a young person were discovered to be at risk of abuse, or other matters of a criminal nature. The plain-language statement would also need to specify how the information was to be handled, the purposes for which it would be used, how long and how it would be stored, what efforts would be made to de-identity it and how re-identification would be prevented, who would have access to it, and how statistical data gathered from the information would be used, especially information that related to a particular group.

---

535 http://www.nhmrc.gov.au/guidelines/publications/e72

23.5 What Works in Sex Education?

With the National Curriculum requiring schools to include education in sexuality, it is important that this be done effectively.

In the United States, most of the factors associated with a delay in sexual intercourse appear to be contextual or sociodemographic and not easily amenable to intervention, including:

- two-parent households, which account for only 18 per cent of early sexual initiates;
- higher socio-economic background;
- better school performance;
- greater religiosity, especially regular participation;
- suicidal thoughts absent;
- felt that adults cared;
- parents with high expectations.[536]

As mentioned earlier, in a study by La Trobe University, Melbourne, one of the results of most concern was the high instance of young people reporting having sex against their will, affecting 39% of young women in year 12, and 34% in year 10.[537] This should be something that is addressed in sex education both in terms of potential perpetrators and victims. However, this has seemingly not been included as a factor in sex and relationship education, or at least not effectively.

Another La Trobe University study[538] concluded that though social and

---

[536] Christina Lammers, Marjorie Ireland, Michael Resnick, Robert Blum, "Influence on Adolescents' Decision to Postpone Onset of Sexual Intercourse: A Survival Analysis of Virginity Among Youths Aged 13 to 18 Years", *Journal of Adolescent Health*, Volume 26, 2000, pp. 42-48.
[537] La Trobe University Australian Research Centre in Health and Society Secondary Students and Sexual Health 2008 http://www.latrobe.edu.au/arcshs/download_reports.html#young_people
[538] Murray Couch, Gary W. Dowsett, Sophie Dutertre, Deborah Keys, Marian K. Pitts, "Looking for more: A review of social and contextual factors affecting young people's sexual health" http://www.latrobe.edu.au/arcshs/assets/downloads/reports/looking_for_more.pdf

contextual factors (like religion) play a major role in delaying sexual initiation, most approaches adhere to a psychosocial and behavioural approach to sexual health issues, despite the increasing recognition of the importance of social context.

The study also concluded that social and contextual factors influencing vulnerability are very often one and the same for HIV/STI infection, unwanted pregnancy and sexual harm, though sometimes to varying degrees. Second, the factors that impact upon young people are almost always the same factors that impact on adults. All are made vulnerable by cultural and economic inequality and social upheaval, for example. The study concluded that for young people, vulnerability may be exacerbated by cultural views of them as immature, irresponsible and not ready for sex, and by the legal and policy restrictions particular to young people that are based upon these assumptions. These cultural understandings and restrictions reflect the relative powerlessness of young people, and the younger they are the less power they wield. In a way this also relates to some extent to the matter of unwanted sex.

Skeeran, in the UK, attempted to pin down the association between religious affiliation and sexual activity by setting up research that differentiated between several different aspects of religious connection of British Christians. The study found that current attendance at religious services was a more important factor than religious upbringing; that is, those young people who were active in a church were less likely to have sex than those who were not, regardless of religious upbringing.[539]

Cheesbrough *et al* in New Zealand and a study undertaken in Washington found that church involvement delayed initial intercourse in some groups,

---

539 P. Sheeran *et al*, "Religiosity and Adolescents' Premarital Sexual Attitudes and Behaviour: An Empirical Study of Conceptual Issues", *European Journal of Social Psychology*, Volume 23, No. 1, 1993, pp. 39-52, 246.

but individuals in these groups were more likely to have unprotected sex when sexual debut did occur.[540]

Considering the effect of Islam on sexual behaviour, Obermeyer describes how demographic and socioeconomic transformations are bringing changes to sexual experience in Morocco. The conditions, before and after the changes, demonstrate discrepancies between Islamic doctrine and its application. In the past there had been interplay among several forces: a relatively permissive Islamic tradition, an inegalitarian system restricting women's autonomy, and the privileging of male satisfaction. The changes have altered the frequency and quality of interactions between men and women and the realities of the marriage market, and contributed to the emergence of a youth culture attuned to the global as well as local sensitivities.[541]

In general, it is clear that religion, especially active engagement in Christian faith, reduces the likelihood of early sexual initiation and hence sexually transmissible infection and unplanned pregnancy. Condoms reduce the rate of infection but they are not fail-safe. They slow down the rate of infection, but as shown earlier in chapter 15, slowing down the rate may still see the same proportion of people at risk infected in the long term, given a reliance on condoms over a lifetime of sexual activity.

In answer to the question: "What works in delaying sexual initiation and reducing STIs and pregnancy rates in young people?" we can answer that it is the context that is most important, including factors to do with home life such as

- Two parent households.
- Girls relating to their natural father.
- Higher socio-economic status.

---

540 S. Cheesbrough, R. Ingham and D. Massey, *Reducing the rate of teenage conceptions: A review of the international evidence on preventing and reducing teenage conceptions: The United States, Canada, Australia and New Zealand*, Health Education Authority, 1999; "Sexual Behavior [Journal Summary, ReCAPP]", in *Keeping the Faith: The Role of Religion and Faith Communities in Preventing Teen Pregnancy*, National Campaign to Prevent Teen Pregnancy, Editor, 2001: Washington, DC, Chapter 2, p. 245.

541 C.M. Obermeyer, "Sexuality in Morocco: Changing context and contested domain" *Culture, Health & Sexuality*, Volume 2, No 3, 2000, pp. 239-254.

- Better performance academically, sport or other.
- Belonging to youth group.
- Greater religiosity, especially regular participation.
- Absence of suicidal thoughts or self.
- Felt that some adult cares.
- Parents with high expectations "in something".
- Parents who disapprove of early sexual initiation.

As far as formal education goes teachers might profitably develop activities that relate to the home or other context, such as peer groups. Developing projects that involve parents, or other significant adults, might help to improve or reinforce a more effective home context. Context aside, programs that are likely to be effective would contain:

- Full information about risks and prevention and a behavioural component (e.g., group CBT) addressing factors that lead to early sexual initiation.
- A short term focus (e.g., six month pledge) which gives renewable protection, delays risk and encourages more considered sexual decisions.
- Address behavioural elements to provide skills to manage situations that may occur and encourage self-confidence and empower young people.

The latter is important in relation to the high, and in fact growing, incidence of young people reporting unwanted sexual intimacy. It is also important to address the question of healthy relationships and the matter of domination or abuse of power. It seems significant, that the matter of equality, and its opposite in domination and possessiveness, is explained in the Theology of the Body (see Chapter 2) in relation to sin. Christ's teaching, life, suffering and death redeemed us from the effects of sin, and in the place of sin is love, the kind of love that, through giving oneself, restores the equality between men and women – equal respect for their inherent human dignity, each made in the image and likeness of God.

The La Trobe study also shows that alcohol and drug use plays a part in unwanted sexual intimacy. Drug education is relevant to relationship education. Peer groups that adopt healthy attitudes and reinforce responsible conduct are important. To have friends who are positive influences for better health practices is important and a matter to be discussed as young people reach ages where they may be at risk. Again what is at stake is dignity and love, including a love that respects the human body and seeks to protect its development and flourishing.

Earlier in the discussion of abortion, I pondered the lack of curricula activities to address the circumstance of a young person who discovers that she is pregnant, or a young man who discovers his partner is pregnant. The emphasis in current programs is on avoiding that situation rather than coping with it well when it happens. The reality is that, if young people are sexually active, then, despite prophylaxis, a proportion will have that experience and so they need to be prepared for it. There would seem to be a place at appropriate stages of maturity to develop activities that role play coping with the types of situation that are not improbable.

I am convinced that the Theology of the Body provides a rich vein of affective and anthropological material that addresses positively, in a very personalist way, the challenge of our secularized culture. That is, it focuses particularly on matters of emotional development and personal identity that are so important to young people in their relationships. The immediate need is to develop curriculum materials that bring the Theology of the Body into the classroom, and the youth group, and which inform the education of parents and those adults to whom young people relate. Teachers can do so much to help to develop those relationships by setting tasks that call upon the resources of the parents and other significant adults in the life of the young person. Parishes can do so much to establish youth groups of different kinds so as to appeal to the different personalities, but based on material that gives practical focus to the Theology of the Body. We should not be frightened to introduce young people to Christ as a mentor and friend and to explore his relationships with his own Holy Family, his mother and stepfather, and the drama of their early survival, with the elders in the Temple, with the woman at the well and the woman caught in adultery, with Mary Magdelene, and with his own apostles and disciples in the different phases of His mission before and after His death.

Recently, Mary and I attended a dying friend, but no ordinary friend, none other than Dr Evelyn (Lyn) Billings. On seeing us she scolded us for not having seen more of her and Dr John Billings in recent years. John died a few years ago.

Lyn was struggling with aphasia complaining that she was having trouble with lucidity. However, though losing the thread occasionally as she struggled for a word, her meaning could not have been clearer, with the words often coming in a rush before becoming stuck. We felt much loved and inspired by her love for us. In all her difficulty and her knowing that death was near, she continued to smile. Despite her frailty and one-sided paralysis, and the gaps in speech, it was still the Lyn of old. I felt as though she was about to offer one of her trade mark sponge cakes. She joked about dying not being much fun. On one occasion struggling for a word, she said she was stuck, and then completed what she had to say by saying instead that she was "stuck in love". This followed talk of the many difficulties of the organization but the fact that it was love, human and divine, that saw the work survive.

Rev Dr Frank Harman, who did so much to establish our Institute before his death, and who was my mentor for many crucial years, including when I married, would refer to the story of Mary's pregnancy with Jesus and betrothal to Joseph as explaining so much of what a young person needs to know about sexuality. Both what Mary experienced and the Incarnation, are so important for understanding our sexuality, especially male chastity. Here was Jesus, who was like us in his human nature, and conducted friendships with women, as well as men, and loved us all. At the same time, he saw in married love a potent analogy for God's love, both Agape and Eros. His was a wonderful acceptance of sexual intimacy as capable of giving perfect witness to divine love, the love between God and us, but also the love between the persons of the Holy Trinity: Father, Son and Spirit. His was also a wonderful witness to the connection between respect for marriage and for celibacy as both involve the same complete gift of self of love – both are nuptial. There we have the central importance of the two vocations of marriage and of celibacy. Each in its own way is a witness to God's love and a pathway to communion with Him. These two sacraments are so important for understanding human sexuality. When we love, we develop in the divine likeness and our love brings us closer in communion not just with each other, but through our love for each other to God.

I can make no greater compliment to my wife Mary than to say that in her love for me, and in returning her love, I have been brought closer to God. We are weak and frail and prone to error and my illness makes ordinary activity so difficult, but my feebleness and our mistakes make the power of divine love burn ever more strongly within us as we seek the infinite strength of His love, knowing that only through His grace is anything possible. In responding to the challenge of the National Curriculum, the *Theology of the Body* has so much to offer.

24
Mothers, Grandmothers and Others: Some Reflections

For reasons explained in the Preface and the Introduction, this chapter is something of an autobiographical account of my cultural background, an afterword that is relevant to understanding why I have approached these topics as I have.

In my own mother, Coralie, I not only had someone who loved me and my siblings, without qualification or reservation, I also had the example of her love for my father, Michelangelo. A child is extraordinarily privileged in being such a close observer of love. My parents' relationship fascinated me. They had their difficulties and differences, their tensions and anxieties. Often in the naïveté of a child, I experienced their differences as insuperable and wondered about whether they would separate, especially in the middle of some major stress between them, and their struggle to parent ten children in necessarily straightened economic circumstances. There were no shortages of such occasions.

As a child I sided with my mother, usually seeing her view and agreeing with it. It was only later that I understood my father better and his motivations. As one tends to, I remain critical of both my parents and hope that in my own adult life I have learned enough to make better choices. But it is a significant challenge. They were very special people who tried so hard to live a life informed by the life and teachings of Jesus, and as members of the community of His faithful, the Church. That meant living a life of selfless love. As children, their love for us was a constant certainty, even though we might not always have welcomed, or even fully understood, the ways in which they chose to express it.

For my parents, the truth was in Jesus Christ, in the mystery of the incarnate Word. They saw in Christ, God revealing Himself to us and revealing the truth of God's love for us, and the truth about ourselves, that we are made to be like God and to be lovers. God loves us and wants to be loved by us. They lived the central Christological teaching of the Second Vatican Council long before it was proclaimed in *Gaudium et Spes*, n. 22. For them, the sacraments were central, especially the sacrament of the Eucharist. In the Eucharist, Christ was truly present and that meant everything.

How they came to their faith is, of course, not one story but two. Around the time of the Second World War beginning, when they met in the Catholic youth movement known as the Grail, they were well formed in their faith. The Grail was a spiritual, cultural and social movement of women grounded in Christian faith and seeking to respond to the challenge of the Gospel in today's world and in their own lives. Called by spiritual values, the Grail, led originally in Melbourne by Dutch women, envisions a world of peace, justice and renewal of the earth, brought about by women working together as catalysts for change. In the 1940s it was a movement well ahead of its time. Young men did not belong, but were invited to attend many of the Grail activities.

Perhaps my father was more advanced in his life of faith. He had certainly had to cope, at the age of fourteen, with the death through illness of his father, Count Ercole Tonti-Filippini, and not long after, the loss of his grandmother, who had played an important role in his childhood, as his parents were so often on tour with the opera. He was, from the time of his father's death, a daily communicant as much as he was able to be so. A keen yachtsman and competitive fencer, he was recruited into the Australian Army while an engineering student at the University of Melbourne. They married during the Second World War, when he was 22, just two days after my mother's 21st birthday in 1941. In later life, his fencing mask became part of his outfit for managing swarming bees!

His father, Count Ercole Tonti-Filippini, came to Australia first in 1912 with the Gonzales Opera Company performing Italian Grand Opera. In 1914 he settled here and met and later married my grandmother, Anne (Nancy) McParland, who was an Irish Australian, but later known, because of her marriage, as Contessa Filippini, and to us as Nonna. Because of his early death, we only know him through her and our parents' memories, in newspaper cuttings, Nonna's autobiography *Nancy Take the Stick*, and the occasional historical account, such as Frank Clune's *Try Anything Once*, where he mentions being a member of their company, or the book *Per l'Australia* by Julia Churcher and published by the Italian Historical Society that devotes a page to my grandfather, and a photo of him in a role from the opera *Pagliacci (The Clowns)*.

Ercole was a baritone and had a voice reportedly of great power. It was said that he had a party trick in which he would flick a crystal glass to make it ring, and then sing the note shattering the glass, proving both his perfect pitch and the power of his voice. My father would say, cynically, that it was all in the flick.

Nonna and Ercole must have been an interesting couple. He was critical of her singing. She was an opera singer, but he only reluctantly allowed her onstage, preferring her as conductor, and managing other parts of the production and direction. Nevertheless, she had an incredibly powerful voice. Close to ninety years old, she sang when Mary and I were married, in 1985. She died in 1987. It was during the signing of the register. The bridal party with the several priests on the altar had moved into the sacristy, where the register was kept. While there, we heard her begin the *Ave Maria*. Justin, my brother was accompanying her on the organ unrehearsed and not with the right arrangement for accompaniment, so at one point he stopped and simply left her to carry on solo. The *Ave Maria* (Hail Mary) is a strong prayer of supplication and, when understood, is highly emotional.

Suddenly everyone who was with us in the sacristy left, in order to better see and hear what was going on. It was the most arresting performance I have heard of that prayer, sung with great passion and depth of emotion. At that time, her ordinary speaking voice was affected by her asthma and aging, and reduced to a croak, but, when singing, the frailty disappeared into a voice of expressive power, though unable to sustain the notes for long. It was the voice of a much younger woman, rather like recordings I have heard of Maria Callas, fraught with emotion and literally drilling in its intensity and an expression that compellingly gave voice to her devotion to the Blessed

Mother. Apart from more personal matters and Mary's loveliness, obviously, Nonna's singing is the most memorable event for me of that day. Shattering crystal might not have been impossible.

Going to a sung Mass with Nonna was always an experience, because she would not hesitate to give the congregation the full benefit of her operatic strength, and she never failed to give the words an intonation that conveyed their affectivity. Her liturgical singing was always a theological revelation, so full of meaning. We lost so much with the dumbing down of liturgy after the Second Vatican Council. We need to see good music and good lyrics, especially, restored. Dr. Percy Jones was a family friend and in a very short time produced the arrangements in the vernacular used by many Australian congregations. Those bland arrangements and the introduction of happy, clappy popular guitar songs in place of our sacred music robbed our liturgy of much of its beauty and meaning. I support the introduction of the vernacular and less mystical rubrics, when so many people were unable to read Latin, and I am not opposed to guitars in Church, but I wish the changes had happened in a way that had retained the beauty that had been a universal aspect of Catholic liturgy. I choke each Holy Week in my own parish when what used to be sung *a capella* and solemnly is now guitar accompanied, and with some translations that completely lose the meaning. I recently asked an elderly choir member how she felt singing: "And the old shall be terminated" in place of "Ancient types have long departed". I am in favour of the greater dignity of the recent translation revisions, returning us to something closer to the Latin and to Scriptural accuracy. I just wish we had better modern hymns and arrangements.

But returning to family matters, I have Ercole's portrait on my study wall. He was an interesting character. He had the courage to immigrate, and then to establish an opera company, the Italo-South Australian Opera Company that toured Australia, including the major metropolitan theatres, such as the Regent in Melbourne, but also outback Australia. Performing grand opera to audiences in places such as Winton and Longreach, took some doing. I have been to some of the places where they performed in what were basically tin sheds. In some of the places they went in outback Queensland, there were substantial Italian communities amongst the cane cutters, but not all.

They were very well loved. My mother's parents used to talk about going to see "the little Count". They were loved for bringing grand opera to Australia, and were reportedly the first company to do so.

Nonna was always a grand lady and, even in old age, the central focus of any company in which she found herself. She commanded attention. The story that Nonna tells of her romance with Ercole was that she was a student of his, and then one day, when he was demonstrating the performance of an aria to her, she realised that he was singing the song, not for her, but to her. I suspect that, as a music graduate, she had become his student because attracted to him in the first place. But it was a grand story. They soon joined together in opera, and she became an opera singer and later the first woman to conduct the Sydney Symphony Orchestra. She had been educated by the Sisters of Charity at St Vincent's, Potts Point, NSW, and later at the University of Sydney, graduating from there in music. St Vincent's recently contacted me about honouring her with a plaque in their new performing arts building, a matter I have not yet pursued as it would require a decision by the wider family and financial support.

My father, Michelangelo, and his sister Josephine were often left to be cared for by their Irish grandmother, Nonna's mother, who lived with the family and maintained the household when their parents were on tour. So they had more an Irish upbringing than an Italian one. I remember talking to my father, asking him why he was not fluent in Italian, though he understood it, and he said, "Well, I spoke more Irish at home, than I spoke Italian." They were often apart from their parents and my father went to boarding school, St Patrick's, Ballarat, and later Xavier in Kew. My Aunt Jo was educated by the Presentation sisters in Melbourne. I think it was a difficult time for the children, especially with their parents on tour and then their father dying so early. After Ercole's death, Nonna supported the family through teaching singing in the Catholic schools throughout Melbourne. I have often met elderly people who remember the Contessa from their schooldays.

According to Nonna's autobiography, when her mother came to Australia as an Irish immigrant, a priest had recommended Mary MacKillop to her. She was a single woman, school teacher and musician. She subsequently lived with Mary MacKillop and her Josephite Sisters before deciding that the convent was not really for her.

Always gracious, always interested in each person, Nonna was renowned for her hospitality. Right to the end, almost, she was going to films and shows so that she could talk about whatever was current. She did not succumb as many old people do, to living in the past. My father died of cancer and during his illness he developed immune suppression from the treatment and then pneumonia. It was the height of the AIDS scare in the 1980s when we had no treatments to prevent HIV becoming AIDS and immune compromise was a common result. Nonna shocked us by asking whether her son had AIDS, which of course he did not. She was well up with the events of the day and would talk freely about what was happening in the world. She did have some short term memory loss towards the end, but she had strategies for dealing with it. One was that she kept close to hand a very small, barely noticeable pad on which she would write *aide memoirs* during a conversation, especially anything that she did not immediately understand or had not heard properly, but also matters that she wanted to discuss further when the conversation flow would permit.

A second strategy was that, when in a group, she would ask a young person to sit beside her. As the conversation progressed in the lively way it does in big families, she would then tell her, 'Remember that. I want to talk about that,' relying on the young person to raise matters that had been passed over, when the occasion allowed it. In that way she did not spoil the flow of the conversation, but could nonetheless take it to where she wanted to go.

When I first became involved in public life, Nonna took me aside and explained a strategy that gave some indication of why she was always so well liked. It is not something that I have had the patience to emulate. After a social event, she would sit down and make a list of the people she had met and write notes on the conversations that she had had with them. The notes were then used when she was due to meet the same people again. She would have recorded information about people and their families and concerns, and she would refresh her memory so that the information would become her small talk, impressing people about how much she cared that she would remember their issues, family illnesses and the like, no matter how long it had been. She was not a gossip. The information was kept and used for their benefit. Nonna was not a gossip because she was too interested in ideas to be bothered, and she tended to think the best of people. There is good reason for the love and admiration that she attracted.

There are various accounts of my grandparents' travels bringing Italian opera to Australia and New Zealand. In his *Try Anything Once*, Frank Clune talks about them always lacking money. That seems to have been the case. There are newspaper accounts of a court case here in Melbourne where they were sued by a theatre agent for fees and so on. They won that case. But there always seems to have been great difficulty financing the operas. At that time, there was no government support or corporate patronage. So they were hiring local singers, stage crews and venues to perform grand opera. They even performed *Aida*, which is huge cast. We still have parts of some of the stage costumes. Ercole was not a great financial manager, so the burden seemed to fall on Nonna.

Doing that and then travelling around, by train obviously, all over the country, it must have been extremely hard. They were both teaching singing in order to pay their way. And so they would teach for a time in a place until they had enough money to hire a cast and venue, and put on a performance. They were hard days for Nonna. She often depended on her friends to provide them with capital to fund an opera venture. One of the great sadnesses was the loss of grandfather Ercole's marked up music scores when Melbourne's Allans Music Store burned down, the fire consuming their singing studios located on a floor above the store.

I have struggled to fully comprehend the outback opera touring. However, I understand that to make it financial and physically viable, the couple and their company might limit the performance to just the arias and with limited stage props to create atmosphere, thus avoiding the need for a large cast and all the rest of the retinue and staging. In Nonna's much sanitised autobiography, there are still interesting stories, such as when, as a group mainly of Italians, they arrived in a country town, and people reacted in a xenophobic way. They laughed about it, but still obviously felt the hurt. They were highly educated people, but treated on a par with the less well-educated Italian cane-cutters who were clearly discriminated against.

There is one story in her book about the tenor, Balbone, who was a difficult man and may have suffered from some form of mental illness, later suiciding.

He was also very flamboyant. When he ate he had a habit of tucking the serviette into his collar. There was a moment when in indignation a waitress suddenly piped up, "The dago's going to blow his nose", as though they were animals in a freak show. I think they suffered a lot from the attitudes of the time. Those attitudes still existed in country Victoria where I attended school in the 1960s and 70s and encountered the same xenophobia that expected that all that I did would be weird and probably not hygienic.

We pride ourselves on our multiculturalism in Australia, but it is really only in more recent times that Italians and Greeks have been tolerated. There always was intolerance towards the latest arrivals, such as there is now to the Sudanese and other Africans, who are our newest and are obviously identifiable. Hurtful things are said about them, without much appreciation of their culture, nor understanding of what they have been through, what it is to have lived as a child in refugee camps and to have witnessed violence and self-harm, and even rape and torture, and to have lived under the lawlessness of warlords and without a reliable police force or judiciary. That may mean that they are more likely to distrust police, not being used to police representing justice and fairness.

Ercole came to Australia just before the First World War, but had Argentinian nationality, even though he was Italian born of Italian parents. He had lived with his maternal uncle and aunt in Buenos Aires since being orphaned at the age of four. The main Italian and Greek migrations came much later, after the Second World War, but at the time of the First World War, little would have been understood culturally about an Italian born Argentinian. The Gonzales Opera singers were a rarity in Australia in the time that they were here before, during and after the First World War.

After being born Ercole Filippini in Italy, in 1885, his parents took him with them to visit his maternal uncle and aunt in Argentina. The family story has it that his parents were killed in a train crash, and being four years old at the time, he was subsequently brought up in Argentina by his maternal uncle and aunt. Later he was to become a Bocce champion for which we hold some of his medals. The title of Count belonged to his uncle, until Ercole started to make a name for himself in opera, winning La Scala, Milan, where he was principal baritone for the La Scala Opera Company. His uncle, being childless, relinquished the title in Ercole's favour, and the latter became Count Ercole Tonti-Filippini, with the Tonti name carrying the title since an ancestor was given it by the Borghese Pope Paul V in 1608 when he became Cardinal Michelangelo Tonti, Archbishop of Barletto. My brother, Count Michael Francis, has possession of the intact documentation of the lineage complete from then to this generation. Barletto was a town in southern Italy, where a church was dedicated to S. Maria di Nazareth in memory of an archbishop of Nazareth in Palestine who sought refuge in Barletta. Cardinal Tonti bought the Nazreno palace in 1622, the year of his death, with the purpose of bequeathing it to a new college for the poor to be managed by the Piarists, then favoured by Pope Gregory XV.

Founded in the 16th century, the main occupation of the Piarist fathers was teaching children and youth, the primary goal being to provide free education for poor children. It is interesting that the contemporary family interest in education has a long history. The palace remains now as a school. I maintain contact with our Italian relatives who now live in Firenze and have the name Leonardi. The daughter of the household, Elisabetta, and her husband, both doctors, work with refugees on the Thai border. Our son, John, was fortunate to find her at home in Firenze recently and to be welcomed at her family home and taken to dinner by her. Elisabetta's father, Claudio, and her grandmother maintained correspondence with us, and at one time as an academic he accessed the Vatican records of the family and sent us a copy of material he had found. The unusual Italian name, Tonti, had its origins much earlier in the thirteenth century. The family name had been *Spada*, but dropped by a rebellious son who adopted the name *Tonti* instead, before establishing his own reputation under that name with the family later elevated to the nobility as described above.

According to the family stories, Ercole probably did not help his own inculturation in Australia because, though he knew English, he refused to speak a language that ended words so often with consonants. He thought that would spoil his singing voice and the gloriously expressive Italian vowels. My father, then 14, told of travelling with his dying father on a Melbourne tram in 1933. The count had peripheral neuropathy and his unsteadiness made other passengers regard him as drunk and treat him accordingly. It would have been humiliating. Drunkenness tends to be anathema to Italians, a matter of great shame. I have some empathy for his condition, now suffering from peripheral neuropathy myself. If you cannot feel your lower legs and feet, you are at the mercy of surface irregularities, being unable to sense and adjust to them, and a moving floor, such as in a tram, is very difficult. Also it is difficult to hold on to anything, lacking sensation in one's hands. Without the sensation, one forgets to hold on. I have swallowed my pride and use a stick outside the home.

When Ercole died on 15 March 1934 at St Vincent's Hospital, at the age of 49, he left Nonna a widow with two children and in a precarious financial position, as he had been ill for some time. She recalls hearing him calling for her as she entered St Vincent's Hospital, where he was dying, "Nensi, Nensi, Nensi…" Nensi was his name for her, "Nancy" being a version of her formal name "Anne". Nonna soon established herself in a number of less exotic but important roles as a singing teacher and choir mistress. She conducted the choir at St Patrick's Cathedral here in Melbourne, appointed by Archbishop Daniel Mannix. During a Eucharistic Congress in Perth she also conducted a one thousand voiced choir made up of school choirs

However, when the Vienna Boys' Choir were stranded here in Melbourne at the outbreak of World War II and when their adult members and leaders were incarcerated as enemy aliens, Mannix took them in, found them billets and sacked his choir and the choir mistress, replacing them with the boys. The St Patrick's Cathedral Choir has been all male since, which I think is a shame. I do not think that young boys can understand or express the affectivity needed, and I prefer an adult mixed choir. The pure tones of a boy soprano have an early attraction that soon palls in the singer's inability to understand and give life to adult meaning. I can say that with some authority having been a boy soprano in the Bendigo Cathedral choir and then having progressed, as my voice gradually changed, from singing with the sopranos, then the altos, then joining the male tenors, and finally becoming a bass. Perhaps because of the constant singing, my voice never "broke" as such, it just became deeper. I remember once in a school choir having to drop an octave below what had been my fellow sopranos. Usually that meant dismissal. But having been a soloist, I was retained by the choir mistress who had me learn a tenor line and then partnered me in a duet with the principal, Fr Jack O'Keefe, a more frightening experience for a 12-year-old.

On the music side of things, there is a family story of my cousin, the well-known singer/songwriter and multiple *Aria Award* winner, Paul Kelly, talking to Nonna, about his music. Nonna was explaining *Bel Canto*, the method of singing that she and our grandfather had used. As I understand it from Nonna in the few instructions she gave me, *Bel Canto* basically means that you keep the same beautiful quality, the same tone, resonance and timbre, right through the range. So there's no gap in the range, it is seamless. It also goes with not sliding to a note or "glissing" which some singers use rather than having the sense of pitch to be able to jump directly as written from one note to another anywhere in the range. To learn *Bel Canto*, she said to first identify a note in your range where you are happiest with the tone, resonance and timbre, then seek to make every note in your range sound like that. It sounds simple but it is not always easily done. Many opera singers have a significantly different sound between their lower and upper registers and there is often a sense of disquiet in an audience waiting for that change as the singer moves through the register, and frequently disappointment that one part of the register is not as good as another.

The point about singing *Bel Canto* is to gain the control and fluidity of voice to provide an instrument that is capable of subtle expression of affectivity. There should be no sound differences other than those that the singer intends for the purpose of expression of meaning. The human voice is so much more meaningful than any other instrument. To do that well, the voice production irons out the kinks across the range so that the changes of tone and modulation are deliberate and expressive, not caused by factors beyond the singer's control. Important also in *Bel Canto* is not to overproduce. Some voices are so overproduced that the vowel sounds blend into one another and the words are indistinguishable. The great Dame Joan Sutherland had that fault later in her career, and Dame Kiri Te Kanawa is such a contrast in being able to be understood. Of the two, I much prefer the latter, though Sutherland's voice had a steely quality that was unsurpassed.

According to the story that Nonna told, she was talking to Paul about this, and Paul turned to her and said, "Well, I don't really sing like that. In my singing you have to shout a bit, you know, in order to be heard." He was trying to explain to her that very often he was singing in pubs and bars and so on. Our daughter Claire has experienced that. Usually the conversation does not stop simply because there is a singer! In those venues it does not seem to matter who you are. People are out for a good night and the singer must compete with their evening conversation, dating, and so on. So you really have to command an audience by sheer volume. Trying to sing *Bel Canto* in those circumstances, would be a bit silly. These days, of course, Paul commands a listening audience and he has developed greater subtlety, not only musically, but also because he is older and has more interesting things to say. There are clever layers of meaning in his lyrics.

Both my grandmothers were diligent in remembering our individual birthdays despite the large number of surviving grandchildren they both had (27 and 17 respectively). There was always a birthday card with some money in it from each of them. At the age of 21, I received a card from my mother's mother, Iris, that she had posted on the day she had her fatal fall on the post office steps. She died before I received it.

Nonna was a wonderful and very intelligent correspondent and I often wrote to her about my studies or about events in my life. Right up until the last few weeks before she died she was still writing. I was able to use her as a sounding board for essays in philosophy and often used a letter written to her as a way of overcoming writer's block. Somehow it was much easier to explain concepts and my take on a matter to her and, then, having done so for that very sympathetic audience, to convert the letter into an essay for my lecturer.

In many ways, though I was closer to my mother's mother, born Iris Mumford (nee Williams) of a Welsh protestant father (Williams) and an Irish Catholic mother (nee Rae). With my brother Damian, I spent many school holidays staying with her and my grandfather, Roy Mumford, who had converted to Catholicism from being an Anglican before marrying, perhaps to marry, my grandmother. His family strongly disapproved of the conversion and the match and his family remained estranged until much later. Also he, as the family member who drew the short straw to run the family business and not volunteer for the First World War, bought out their shares of the family business, JC Mumford and Co., from his brothers who did go to war. That may have added to the sense of estrangement. They had returned "shell-shocked", what is now known as "Post-traumatic Stress Disorder, but not well understood then."

My grandmother, Iris, would tell us the story of seeing Roy for the first time when they travelled home on a tram through the Kew cutting. She said she especially noted his very large hands. She, herself, was a tiny person under five feet, with "the legs of a sparrow". I have a lovely photograph of them in middle age at my mother's wedding. From under a hat of flowers, she is smiling directly, prettily and obviously very self-consciously straight down the lens. He on the other hand is looking across and down at her with a strong expression of what looks like joy and admiration. I love that photo but have never had the courage to copy him with respect to Mary, modern photographers want down the lens wide smiles. Iris and Roy's love and respect for each other and their shared humour and willing conversation are strong impressions. After he suffered a devastating heart attack and was left bed-ridden and with limited speech and cognitive function, she nursed him for several years at their home where he died. She was wonderfully devoted and missed him greatly from thereon.

My grandmother did not drive and was a keen walker. Almost every day she scheduled a long afternoon walk and that would often be after having walked to and from the shops in the morning to do the daily grocery shopping. Those long walks were spent in conversation with her, mostly about what we would see on the walks as she was a keen botanist, but often about what she had been reading, which included her travel books and some women's magazines. I have many fond memories of those conversations and learning what would please her. She was a fan of H.V. Morton, G.K. Chesterton and C.S. Lewis and would quote things they had written. My grandfather shared those writers, but his book shelves also contained Agatha Christie and P.G. Wodehouse, which we were allowed to access, and he also subscribed to some Marian religious journals. I used to enter the competitions on the children's pages with his encouragement and won a few book prizes for my efforts. They were both devoted to the Blessed Mother and when with them, we said the rosary at bedtime and followed by a litany of prayers for family members, for the pope, bishops and clergy, the "dear sisters" and the "poor brothers" in religious life, and our politicians, "so much in need of enlightenment and divine grace".

My grandmother was always ready to accept a compliment about her appearance and as a child I soon learned to do so. I was fascinated by the way her hair would change colour and by her nightly beautification rituals. She used to spend a time slapping her face at night, which we could hear, and the smell of Pond's Cold Cream is something I forever associate with her night time ritual - that and the lavender that was kept with her handkerchiefs. She loved hats and would remake the hats she bought from the Bourke and Collins Street boutiques, replacing the artificial flowers on them with the real thing. She always owned a red woollen overcoat and pretty umbrellas. On Sundays and visiting friends she always wore a tailored suit, but her ordinary day dress was a frock. I never saw her in trousers, even when she was gardening, which was one of her passions. Her gardens had many small pathways leading to and from grottos, which she would furnish with a seat and a religious statue. She loved shopping, and I recall many train trips to the city with her and the delight of afternoon tea at Georges, an upmarket department store.

Our conversations, though, were wide ranging and she was not above mentioning things that Damian and I could not have understood then, for our later reference. For instance, I recall her saying on one occasion, "Bad girls do not have babies". I do not know what had prompted her saying so to two children. It must have been some event I did not understand well enough for it to have made sufficient impression on me at the time to be recalled now, perhaps some celebrity gossip from a magazine. However, it could only have been later that I would have understood what she meant. So many of her sayings stay with me, many of them being similarly pithy in capturing her wisdom. We called her the French "Ma Mere", as early on she was too proud to be called "Grandmother" or "Granny". My mother always used the German word "Mutter" for her mother.

My grandmother would often talk about her childhood during a time of great sectarian bigotry and what it meant to be Catholic and have a Protestant father. I remember her quoting her father saying to her mother. "That Church of yours even invades the marriage bed!" Again this would have been well above my head, but stored away for a time when I did understand what it meant, and I suspect that was what she intended. I recall one of her stories when, as a teenager, she had borrowed her father's umbrella, an item that he had brought with him from Wales and distinguished by its triple row of spokes. On her way home from Mass the umbrella had been irreparably blown inside out in a high wind and destroyed. Her mother, fearful of his reaction, had already claimed responsibility for the damage, unbeknown to my grandmother, who herself confessed to him having borrowed the umbrella without his permission. She said he responded, "You Catholics, you go to Mass and come home telling lies."

She and my grandfather, Roy, had a clear division of labour. Inside the home she was mistress of the household and her word was law, and as children we knew that we would have him to reckon with if we did not do exactly as she said. But he managed matters outside the home and drove the car. She would refer to men as "drones in the hive". I remember a conversation in which she was shocked to find that my mother intended to make her own decision about which political party she would support at an election, and it was likely to be different from my father's intention. My grandmother's view was that such matters were a male prerogative and a wife should vote to suit the husband's business!

Despite such attitudes that saw a division of roles that perhaps suggested a perception of different intellectual aptitudes, my relationships to my grandmothers and my mother were such that I never had any doubt about the intellectual equality of men and women. They were strong-minded women who had informed opinions on intellectual matters and read if not widely, at least deeply, and kept up with political events.

My grandfather once told me that in Australia one should vote to ensure the State and Federal governments were not of the same party and praised the way that the Senate was elected so that often the party in power federally did not dominate the Senate as well. In any conversation between my parents or involving my grandparents, there was absolutely no question that ideas had merit of their own and who had brought an idea to the conversation was not determinative. As a child I was accustomed to hearing and following adult discussions in which women played a strong intellectual and well-read role. My older sister's passionate engagement in current issues was also influential. Six years younger than her, I disagreed with her at my peril.

The gender roles of the past reflected an era in which men were breadwinners and women managed the household. In some ways they were much gentler times when a single income was sufficient to sustain the lifestyle that was expected, including payment of the mortgage. Married women were expected not to have paid employment, but were expected to have significant unpaid roles. Now it is the case that one salary is not likely to be sufficient. That has not reduced the demand on women in relation to managing households and other unpaid roles, apparently. Often, paid employment seems merely to have been added to their unpaid roles. Men have been slow to share the domestic load. Consequently, I doubt that women or their children are better off, even though women have better opportunities for careers. In many ways my maternal grandmother's lifestyle was enviable. Though responsible for managing the household, she had time to read widely and to pursue her artistic pursuits as a painter, and met regularly with her circle of friends. They would discuss the books they were reading and occasionally play cards.

On the other hand, my father's mother would have suffered greatly, as a single mother for the latter part of his childhood, from the disparity that existed then between male and female incomes for the same work.

My mother was straight out of a convent school, Genezzano, where her father had kept her for an extra year after she had matriculated, presumably because he judged her to be too immature. That year was spent mostly on her own with an aristocratic elderly German nun, Mother Mary Philomena Beck, learning a variety of languages and history. This was 1939 and a time of great turmoil internationally. Strange for an Australian girl to have had a German teacher at that time and one who taught her racial and religious tolerance, the dignity and essential equality of all members of the human family, and a balanced view of history, at a time when fascism and communism were rampant. Throughout her life, my mother has been a monarchist and I wondered how much that was influenced by being taught by someone who claimed to be a relative of the Kaiser. It might also have had some bearing on her being attracted by my father and his family history of an Italian aristocratic title, eventually struck down as they all were during the Mussolini period.

My oldest brother was born during the war and soon after they married. He died at two weeks. In those days post-partum women stayed in hospital for a couple of weeks. My mother still grieves over Christopher and resents the way it was handled. She says that she was unaware that the child was ill before he died and she did not see him after death. She was simply told that he had died. Discharged from hospital, she guessed the day of the funeral when the family members had left the house and two of her mother's friends arrived to sit with her. She heard later that my father had carried the child's coffin on his own. Her father had made the funeral and burial arrangements and my mother resented also that he gave the documentation for the gravesite to her mother-in-law, Nonna. They were very different times for the way in which grief was buried and for the way in which the affairs of a young couple in their early twenties could be managed by their parents. The way it was all managed seems so incomprehensible and so cruel now. Later, my grandfather also paid the deposit on the first houses for each of his children, bringing them into the arrangements only when it was time to arrange a mortgage and their signatures were required on the documentation. He was a businessman and seemed to presume that it was his role to handle such matters.

After the war, my parents rebelled against what they saw as the materialism of the alternative ideologies that dominated the period of the war and the pre-war period. They joined a group of students from the University of Melbourne (the only Victorian university at that time) who, under the charismatic leadership of an older man, (he was in his thirties), Ray Triardo, were experimenting with a Catholic commune at Whitlands, in the hills near Benalla and Wangaratta, famous for the outlaw, (Harry) Power's Lookout. The story of Whitlands is told by David Carvalho in his Master's thesis, *A High Society: A Radical attempt at Society reform at the Catholic Rural Commune "Whitlands, 1941-51"*, a copy of which is held in Melbourne by the National Library of Australia.

My parents were the only married couple at Whitlands and many of the others had taken at least temporary vows of celibacy. The experiment was largely funded by my mother's parents who themselves bought a house nearby and moved there in retirement. As a sociology student, I took an interest in reading about similar communities, what we would now call "covenant communities". My guess is that this one was doomed to fail mostly because it was based around the charismatic leadership of Triardo and he did not ever propose a rule that could be recognized by the church authorities as acceptable. Such communities survive if they can articulate a rule that is liveable because it protects each individual. Triado's efforts to draft a rule were not democratic and were not met with ecclesial support despite his appealing directly to Rome over the head of the local Bishop. I understand that my parents were instrumental in the break-up of the community, taking their concerns to Bishop Stewart of Sandhurst and to Archbishop Daniel Mannix, who had previously given permission for Fr John Heffey to live with the community as their chaplain. Fr Heffey was later associated with other Catholic communities.

My parents eventually had left the community by 1950 when my older sister was born, but not before two of my brothers were born there. My mother told many stories about Whitlands, often nostalgically, especially music and singing round the fire, and theological and social debate. The values that took my parents there continued to form their lives thereafter. They lived community life very strongly wherever they were, always making a strong contribution to parish life and to the wider community, but at the same time holding themselves aloof from the materialism of our culture and other aspects that were contrary to their beliefs. They would talk about being "in the culture but not of it". As children we were always aware of the culture wars, both within the Church, and between the Church and our increasingly secularised society in Australia.

However, there were lasting sadnesses and resentments also about Whitlands. One story that is relevant to this book concerns my mother's account of giving birth to her third and fourth children "on the mountain" as she described Whitlands. Apparently, Triardo had decreed that the women of the community were to observe the birth. This was without having consulted my mother who had views about her privacy, naturally, and long before the contemporary practice in which husbands are expected to be present during birth. As it happened, her father arranged for an obstetrician and a midwife to be staying with the community when the child was due, and the obstetrician, Dr Stan Ingwersen, ensured her privacy and that there was no-one to observe their management of the birth.

My childhood memories are replete with many of my mother's stories of the time spent at Whitlands. Her feelings were obviously mixed. She was proud of their having made the decision to go there when my father was demobilised from the Australian Army Reserve Corps after the Second World War ended. During the war, for which he had volunteered as a university student studying civil engineering, he was based at Darwin airport when the airport was bombed by the Japanese forces. My mother did her best as a young bride to follow the army and to be close to where he was based, living for a time in Townsville when he was located there. They used to breach the censorship rules with their own code in which they would drop letters slightly below the line to provide a hidden message that the censors failed to identify. Apparently this was easier for my father whose writing was more irregular in any case. In those days, letters would often have sections cut out with a blade if they were judged to contain classified information.

As a child growing up, I had little understanding of their relationship. When I look back on it, I can see that despite the tensions, there was great love. By contemporary standards, my father behaved badly towards her. Like many of his generation, he was sexist. Decision-making for them involved my mother campaigning for what she wanted, nagging might be more accurate, until my father would make a unilateral decision for which he would then be blamed for not having done exactly as she wanted.

My father made some decisions that seemed odd, in retrospect. At a time when they had seven children already, he chose to buy a vintage British sports car, a Bristol coupe. It was a most beautiful car, with its leather and wood interior, its British racing green livery, a powerful engine said to be built for aircraft during the war, and its curvaceous, aerodynamically designed lines for maximum road holding capacity at high speed. Today, when I see one, which is a rare experience, I still get a buzz of excitement. It was a most exciting car for a child and he tended to drive it to its limits at a time when there was no maximum speed limit on the open road. As children we used to encourage him to race others, making gestures out of the back window indicating a challenge to the car behind. At least that is what I believed a two fingered gesture meant at that time of childhood innocence. In any case, the gesture would often result in the driver behind overtaking. The car was totally impractical for the number of children, though well-suited for racing, with wonderful cornering capacities.

My siblings have a variety of views about my parents and do not necessarily share mine or even my recollections. That is, as one would expect. There were 10 surviving siblings and our placement in the chronological order obviously affected our experience. My mother used to talk about having two families. She had five children after the death of the first, each roughly two years after the other, probably spaced as a result of lactational amenorrhoea. However, before I was born, as the eldest of the second five, there was a gap of four years after my brother Peter. I have never known why or even whether it was deliberate. She once said that she had planned the first five, but just let the second five happen.

I suspect that four year gap meant that I had greater access to my mother after Peter had started school and before the others were old enough to engage in conversation. A friendship and companionship developed with my mother, which has endured, though the more recent years when she has suffered from dementia have changed the character of our interactions. We tend to focus very much on the past because she cannot retain information about the present, despite giving very gracious and appropriate responses to contemporary news. I am grateful to the family members in Perth for the care they give her.

I was fortunate also in that I developed a good relationship with my father. He loved nothing more than to challenge my adolescent priggishness by playing devil's advocate. I recall many discussions with him and the peculiarly lateral nature of his thinking. Something that he taught me, and which we shared, was the ability to play chess with neither board nor players. It began in the car with a tiny plastic travelling chess set in which the pieces had spikes that held them in their positions. When others in the car became bored with playing chess with me, he would offer to continue, calling out his moves from the driving seat. Eventually I did away with pieces and then did away with the board and pieces altogether, retaining a memory of the moves made and the resultant position of the pieces. In the house there were books on chess, that taught me the different phases of the game, and I would work very hard to remember openings to use against him.

Those experiences came in handy later when I joined the Monash University chess club. My love of competitive chess was nearly my undoing, however. Soon after Mary and I met, I noted that her family home had a chess set and suggested a game. Mary's first move was to move her king's bishop's pawn, a move that opens the possibility for a sequence ending in the shortest possible game. Unable to resist such an extraordinary opportunity, I obliged. Somehow the relationship survived that savage check mate, but not by playing chess. We were more evenly matched for Scrabble.

My father had a short temper, and in those days it was accepted that parents would strike their children. I was to some extent frightened of his temper, though, as children, it was restricted to striking us with an open hand on the bottom, and, if the mood took him, he might do so indiscriminately without bothering to sort out who was in the wrong. I have heard other members of the family describe our shared childhood much more critically of my father. I guess the emotional impact of his style of parenting affected each of us differently. By the time I became a teenager and clearly challenging his authority, he had mellowed a great deal. I did not ever have the kind of stand-up conflict that I observed some of older my siblings having with him.

As a teenager I was very harsh on him, being very critical of his decisions and siding with my mother's complaints. By then he had become very tolerant, though I am sure that at times I hurt him with a teenager's almost complete disregard of the feelings of a parent. My regrets of that time in my life are about my conduct not his.

Despite his failings he was a very good father to me, and I miss him deeply, especially his quirky lateral mindedness that would always challenge my orthodoxies. I think I owe my interest in philosophy and theology largely to him, but also to my mother. Though they loved the Church they were both anti-clerical, and Sunday dinner after the morning mass was the time to deconstruct the sermon, including checking relevant texts, to explore the priest's errors and to suggest what he might have said instead, given the readings of the day. The game of what the sermon might have been became a lifetime habit. We always had copies of magisterial documents in the house, and the latest book by the Australian theologian Frank Sheed. My father had known Frank Sheed from when they both used to mount soap boxes for the Catholic Evidence Guild, on what is now Birrarung Marr Park on the edge of the central business district in Melbourne on the bank of the

Yarra River. People would promenade along the river on Sunday afternoons, when the shops were always closed, and the speakers would attempt to draw an interested crowd by their eloquence. It was a far cry from Tweeting, YouTube and Facebook, but serving similar ends.

Later, my father would spend much of his Sundays buried in the Bible, which was quite an unusual occupation for a Catholic of that era. In retrospect I realised that he took the two Vatican documents, *Gaudium et Spes* and *Lumen Gentium* very seriously and saw himself as part of the theological renewal based on Christ and the Scriptures, despite having had a very Thomistic Jesuit education of the kind that was offered in the 1930s. He was more interested in the Gospel than in traditional understanding of natural law, though he would readily express natural law reasoning when it suited him, and he was fascinated by the Old Testament.

Relevant to the topic of this work, I recall his explanation of the immorality of masturbation. I presume it was an explanation that he had been given as a teenager at Xavier College, or possibly earlier when he attended St Patrick's College, Ballarat, as a boarder. He said that when a postman was given his satchel of mail to deliver, it would be quite wrong of him to throw any of the letters into a creek. It was the postman's obligation to ensure that the mail was appropriately delivered to where it should go. I have to laugh now about some of the implications of what is a very poor analogy, and also what it implies about natural law reasoning. In retrospect though, I do love the fact that as a parent of a teenager he tried to deal with what is a most difficult topic. Faced with my own maturing sons, I know how difficult it was to initiate any such conversation, and can only wonder at the relationship that he and I shared that permitted him to discuss something so sensitive.

Not only did I have the opportunity to discuss matters of that kind with my father, even though I suspect at times my own contribution may have been silent hostility or disbelief, but my relationship with my mother also permitted discussion of sensitive matters, though never anything that would have intruded on my own private world as a developing adolescent. We would discuss matters of faith and doctrine at a much less personal level. However I was 12 when the very divisive document *Humanae Vitae*, on marriage and contraception, was published, and aware of the discussions, especially having older siblings with their own understanding of it, and being aware of the extent of theological dissent. My mother gave me a new pamphlet by Dr John Billings, with whom I was later privileged to work. The pamphlet was called, "Every Man a Lover" and published by the Australian Catholic Truth Society. It might seem strange that it was a great help to me at the time as I fumbled with my own sexuality. The crucial aspect that helped me was John's eloquent belief in the essential God-given goodness of sexuality.

Recently on reading the pamphlet again, published in 1969, I was amazed by how Christocentric it is and how John had grasped and given expression to what we now call Trinitarian anthropology. What is now regarded as a significant contribution that Pope John Paul II had made in his Catechesis on the Theology of the Body in the 1980s, Billings had already expressed when he wrote,

> In Christian marriage, the husband and wife become co-creative. They obtain the privilege of the closest act of human co-operation with God in His creative power. It is their love which is generative of a new person with an immortal soul to spend eternity with God. This is the purpose of the sexual union, the love of' the husband and wife becoming an echo of the Blessed Trinity itself where the Holy Spirit is generated by the mutual love of the Father and the Son.

and,

> In making men and women complementary to each other and creating the physical union of marriage, God intended that it should express a similar idea. They are one flesh, and this act symbolizes a perpetual surrender and sharing of their whole lives thereafter. It is when the physical act gives expression to a continuing attitude of mental unity and love that sex finds its fulfilment, and emotional and physical contentment become most exquisite. Here are joy and pleasure that the promiscuous individual has never experienced and scarcely understands.

and,

Love depends upon reverence, and the purest love flows from reverence for God, with reverence then for the work of His hands and the object of His love. Love is not blind, but looks deeply into the other to find a creature made in the image of God. When the husband says "With my body I thee worship", he is acknowledging the revelation of God's nature in the woman he is marrying."

Intellectually heady stuff for a thirteen-year-old, struggling as all young men must do, to come to terms with his own sexual imagination and desires, and my fascination with women and their bodies, as well as the usual fears that an adolescent has about his own sexuality and unexplored capacity. I travelled to Rome many times, and learned that the way to meet the Pope was to stand with John and Evelyn, because Pope John Paul II would immediately go to meet them upon entering the room. They were held in such high esteem.

At the earlier time I lived a dualism as teenagers are inclined to do. At one level there was a fascination with understanding sexuality and marriage intellectually and the intense discussions there were at that time among adults, given the political battles being fought within the Church over the encyclical. It should be borne in mind that the theologian Frank Sheed was a family friend and a visitor who stayed with us on occasion when he was in Australia. We were also regular visitors to Bishop Bernard Stewart, who had known my mother since when she worked in an office with him, where he was a young priest/lawyer, before the war. His housekeeper, Dorrie Smith, always made us as children welcome, and she had a television which we did not have at home. We could watch television while my parents met with the Bishop and his advisers, often then sharing afternoon tea or the mealtime with them. I remember being annoyed by Bishop Stewart voicing the view, no doubt intended to be humorous, that whenever an adult saw a boy he should thrash him, because if he had not just done something wrong, he was planning to do so. Clearly he saw boys and girls differently. I also recall him bemoaning what was then the mini-skirt era of Twiggy and what he said was a loss of womanly mystery.

When I reflect back on snippets of adult conversation that I recall, it is evident that the differences between the genders was a source of interest in an era of burgeoning feminism. My mother was not short of examples of sexism, such as being told that she would not be funded to attend university by her father, "Because the money was for the boys." She had two younger brothers. She did go to university, so I presume her father conceded.

Witnessing adult discussions at such a time was a great privilege. Other issues of moment were capital punishment and political assassination. I was 10 when Ronald Ryan became the last man executed by the Victorian government and 12 when Robert Kennedy followed his brother, President John F. Kennedy to a violent death at the hands of an assassin. That was the same year in which Martin Luther King was also assassinated, the latter death also having so much meaning for the equal rights movement. Our household literally buzzed with discussion.

I was especially privileged to be able to witness discussion of the intellectual issues, at least, between both my parents, but also between my older siblings, my older sister especially, who were emotionally involved with Ryan's execution and the assassinations and related issues.

The second part of the lived dualism was a fascination with the physical aspects of all things sexual, not least of which was my own body. Needless to say that the sacrament of penance was very helpful in reconciling that part of my dualism with the intellectual life, and assisting me to maintain a prayer life, even though at times it was full of hypocrisy.

All through that time, I never once doubted my sexual orientation. Many kinds of things can cause sexual arousal in a teenage boy, including thinking that might have been considered homosexual in nature, especially the kinds of things that are discussed in an all-male school environment, the jokes told and the name-calling, but I never doubted that the principal sexual fascination for me involved imagining making love to an woman. I remember that fear was an element, what I think is a particularly adolescent masculine fear, that I might be sexually abnormal in some way, of not being able to measure up, so to speak, to what a woman wanted in terms of performance. Sexual performance is a singular aspect of adolescent male fantasies and their conversation. They have little idea of the much gentler reality that awaits them and that the much greater demand of them as lovers will be for patience and self-mastery and giving themselves in so many other ways.

Some boys were teased for appearing effeminate and labelled with names that implied homosexuality. For some reason, though I did not articulate it, I understood that this was something to do with the discomfort of those doing the bullying, with their own feeling of attraction for boys who were more effeminate in appearance. I was sufficiently aware of the distinctions to not equate a boy's effeminate appearance with his sexual orientation.

As a teenager, my first encounter with definite homosexuality was when the older brother of one of my classmates, who had been a school prefect in the previous year, publicly announced his homosexuality soon after leaving school. The attitude amongst my peer group was very negative and I am sure as a group we gave the younger brother a very difficult time. I recall his defensiveness, which must have reflected negative attitudes. It was only years later that I became aware of homosexual orientation amongst my former classmates. At the time that we were still at school, the peer attitude was very negative about homosexuality. I wonder now what that meant for boys who had identified their own homosexual orientation and how they managed. I do not recall anything ever being said about sexual orientation by the teachers. It is cause for sadness now to think about how they must have suffered.

Many of the boys were from farming communities and well-informed about the biology. I recall a time, when I was about thirteen, when a young priest made an attempt at sex education in class. When he attempted to describe an erection it was too much for the boys and they literally laughed him out of the room. He left the room never to teach us again. I do not know what happened to him.

There was also a very negative attitude to masturbation. I do not recall any boy ever admitting to what was referred to very negatively by terms which all had a pejorative significance. I find it ironic now that the same pejorative words were used for lying and masturbating. The instinct seemed to be that masturbation reflected something false. I have noted a similar attitude amongst adult men to prostitution. In my experience in sporting clubs and other all male environments, I have never heard a man admit to engaging the services of a prostitute. It is clearly a shameful thing to do even in a liberal, secular society such as ours.

Pornography was something that was discussed. Some of the fellows possessed mildly pornographic images in the form of relatively discrete female nudity, and male places such as garages would often contain a "girly calendar". There was an acknowledged connection between the images and sexual arousal, though I never heard a connection expressed between pornography and masturbation, though it may have been implicit. My own explorations in that respect were limited to prose. That was safe enough territory in terms of discovery, as my parents did not have the time to be checking what we were reading, especially as I did read widely and frequently. Although I do recall my mother once deciding to read something that she had seen me reading. I was mortified that she might read an account of an explicit sex scene it contained, tame by contemporary standards. Whether she did or not, it was never mentioned. I feared that she would become aware of my prurient interest in such things.

On Saturday nights at the Vincentian secondary school I attended, the whole school would watch a film played on a 16mm projector. Being the projectionist was a privileged role for a senior boy. However, the priest who was appointed to the role of Dean would choose the films, and supervised the showing. It must have been difficult to choose films, from what was popularly available, to suit boys aged 12 to 18. I remember seeing many John Wayne westerns and some James Bond films. On one occasion we were watching one of the latter and there was a bedroom scene with one of the Bond consorts in a state of undress. The older boys reacted vocally, something along the lines of "Phwow!" The Dean at the time was Fr Murray Wilson CM, and I recall him stopping the film and standing in front of us and saying something along the lines, "If there is any more of that, the showing will be cancelled." The rest of the film was watched in silence.

I thought I knew Fr Wilson well. We had many conversations over my time at the school as I progressed through adolescence. However, the year after I left school an allegation was made that he had sexually molested one of the younger boys. I did not believe it at the time because he had had opportunity as far as I was concerned, and nothing like that was ever even suggested, but I guess that does not mean anything. I have since learned from work that I have done for the Church that it was not uncommon for paedophiles to pick vulnerable targets, boys who did not have fathers were especially vulnerable. I do not know whether that is due to cowardice in not having to confront a father, or because the perpetrator could offer to stand in for the absent male to meet a need.

I recall seeing Fr Wilson soon after the allegation was made and saying "hello" to him in the company of others. He had been suspended from teaching. Soon after that he was found dead in a room in one of the Order's houses. A gas heater was blamed for his death by the coroner, and poor ventilation, because the room had been used as a sewing-room and the vents were blocked with lint, and "death by misadventure" was the verdict. I always wondered whether he had suicided and wondered whether I might have made more of an effort to contact him after the allegation. I liked him and still pray for him. He was good to me at a time when I needed adult friendship and support, and he was a significant adult for me.

That experience gives me some insight into the terrible situation that occurs when an adult betrays a child's trust. I have no idea of the truth about the allegation made against him. But if it was true then I probably had a fortunate escape. As a result though, I can imagine something of what it must been like for a child to feel appreciated by an adult, and to like that person, and then have that relationship so distorted and made so confusing by sexual molestation. It must be devastating, and is now known to be a factor in the diagnosis of borderline personality disorder and other mental illnesses, such as depression, potentially having a devastating effect on self-esteem and on ability to relate normally.

There was one other time when I may have had a fortunate escape. At the age of eighteen I was asked to be cantor at a Mass that was being celebrated to mark the closure of a Mass centre that had been a parish church at the small town of Redesdale. The invitation came from Fr John Stockdale, the curate in our parish of St Therese's, Kennington, a suburb of Bendigo. The two priests in our parish also had coverage of Redesdale until they closed the Mass centre there.

Fr Stockdale was never convicted, but molestation allegations were later made after he died ignominiously, reportedly in a gay men's club.

Stockdale offered to take me to the Mass with him. My mother intervened and she and I travelled together in her car to Redesdale for the event, so I could sing. I guess she had her suspicions about him, though nothing was said to me. He used to be a frequent visitor to our home and I remember him as the only man I knew who would be wearing a top hat and white gloves as his usual clothing when he arrived on a visit, to be removed with his black overcoat with its red silk lining. He had a very pleasant tenor voice which also made him welcome at our home, where singing was an important aspect of what we did. Several family members performed publicly in a singing group we had formed, led by my mother, and we often would be rehearsing. I remember him singing a version of Helen Taylor's "Bless this House" and it must have made an impression on me because to this day if I go to sing that song a find myself parodying his rounded vowels and "plummy" intonation. The only point of criticism of him that I heard my mother make at the time was to say, "That one knows more than his prayers." At the time I did not understand her words as criticism. She may have intended to be complimentary. It may also have been intended as a warning about his homosexuality.

As a young man I was fortunate always to have a friend who was a priest. Towards the end of my time at school, I had befriended an elderly priest, Fr Fred Horne CM, when he led the debating. He had allocated to me the task of writing into a ledger a report of each debate: a popular task as it gave me a journalistic opportunity and I soon learned how much the fellows appreciated a flattering account of their arguments and performance. Soon after, he retired from teaching and then became quite ill. I used to take bottles of Guinness to him in hospital and later to his aged care facility. He had warned me against studying philosophy at university, which is possibly part of the reason why I did. His warning seemed somehow to endow philosophy with mystique and a challenge.

At university, the Master of Mannix College, an Islamist scholar and Thomist, Dr. Laurence Fitzgerald OP, was a friend, as was the Dean, a psychologist, Fr John Baron OP. Two more contrasting personalities could hardly be found. Fr Baron liked muesli and Mahler and was something of a loner within his religious community. He was also an Helenophile, especially Greek music and dance.

Some years later, I stayed with Fr. Baron at a flat he had taken near Sydney's notorious King's Cross. He was working as a psychologist with the NSW parole board by then. I recall a funny moment as we were both walking down the street looking for a place to eat. A prostitute propositioned us in bored fashion with the words, "Want a girl, love?" John responded for both of us with, "No thanks, love." To which she responded, "Good night, Father John."

Back at Mannix College, I recall a group of us as fellow members of the Senior Common Room, inviting the two priests, the Master and the Dean, to join us at a Greek restaurant. There was some tension between them, after the younger, Fr Baron, a very good Greek dancer, danced what was obviously a *pas de deux* celebration of betrothal, with the leading female dancer employed by the restaurant. I recall one segment in which she, in her long flowing skirts danced over the top of them as he literally bent over backwards to allow her to do so. It was a very beautiful and powerful dance, and well executed by them both. His superior, Father Fitzgerald, later made his displeasure known, drawing a distinction between the harmless activity of dancing generally, and what he saw as the unfortunate display of being so partnered in what was obviously intimate and sexually suggestive, even though in Greek style, there was no actual physical contact.

I enjoyed my friendships with both priests and, because I was studying philosophy, I returned to reading the *Summa* and being part of a discussion group that Dr Fitzgerald led. I had first begun reading the *Summa* to improve my Latin, while at school. I travelled interstate with John Baron and shared many occasions with him, many discussions of current issues. He was ten years older or so older, and in him I had a confidante about personal matters.

I guess these friendships were formative for me in learning proper boundaries for activity involving young adult men and women, at a time when I was fumbling my way as a young man from a sheltered all male school and a strong religious Catholic family. There is much for which I have little reason to be proud of in my early relationships with women, though I learned a great deal and experienced my share of broken-heartedness inflicted by young women of obvious sense and judgement. It was rare for me to wish the end of a relationship. The experience was most commonly in the other direction. The only thing I can really say in my own favour is that I did not treat relationships with young women exploitatively. I dated with an idea of possible permanence and not casually. Between being dumped and taking up with another, I often contemplated the possibility of priesthood and the religious life, but only fleetingly. I wanted to be married. I did also enjoy some good friendships with young women that were acknowledged as friendships but without romantic interest. I am grateful to them for that and remain friends with some of them to this day, now being able to include their husbands as friends also. We had much fun and I had a variety of interests, including music and sport, I played cricket for the university and coordinated a football competition between the college and the other halls of residence, Amnesty International, the Philosophy Society and the Psychological Society, and various student organizations, including the Chess Society, that meant that I had several different friendship groups. Living on campus for several years helped. Belonging to groups of friends is much safer than the later trend to require young people to pair off. The evidence suggests that the peer context is a most important element in relation to whether a young person becomes an early sexual initiate and thus at risk. Also important is whether a young person has opportunities to be of service to others and thus finds appreciation that reduces the need to give sex in order to gain love.

At school in the senior years, those who were seen as possible candidates for the priesthood, were treated to trips away to visit the Vincentian seminary at Eastwood in New South Wales, and the Order's holiday house at the beach. I knew from that experience that I was not at all attracted to living in an all-male community. I recall a sense of recoiling when at Eastwood, on one occasion, there had been a problem with the hot water supply and one of the resident members of the community paraded around in a bath towel, complaining that he was "all soaped up" when the water cut out. It was all a bit "camp" and I knew very definitely by then that my inclinations were not in that direction.

It might seem strange to say this now in our so very sexualised culture, but in the 1970s and early 1980s, sexual orientation was not normally a public matter at that time, and heterosexuality was presumed unless a person declared otherwise, either explicitly or by wearing what were considered to be symbols of homosexual orientation, which was rarely done. Sexual orientation was not part of ordinary conversation. Sexual orientation was never discussed with my friends and I simply enjoyed our friendships and that did not change, even if a person's homosexuality was made known. For two years I shared a house with a man who came out during that time. We remained friends. It was a time of sexual liberalisation, but explicit sexual sensuality and intimacy had not become as culturally dominant as it is now. My naïveté was such that I never really thought about what sexual intimacy between people of the same sex might involve until much later. In the mid-1980s, during the HIV/AIDS scare, government policy sought to normalize homosexual intimacy so as to facilitate the distribution of health messages related to the exchange of bodily fluids and the fact that sex between men was the major cause of spread of the retro-virus. We began then to tolerate much more explicit discussion of sexual practices and little was left unsaid. Years later, a member of a group of friends and tutors at Mannix College contacted me to say that he was gay, but that he had never had relationships within the College. Both admissions were interesting for the fact that he wanted to make them and he did so because he had seen from a website that I was the Australian representative for a group called Courage that served homosexuals who wished to be chaste. I had the role only because I had invited the founder of Courage, Fr John Harvey, to speak at a bioethics conference. Courage is modelled on Alcoholics Anonymous.

At university, I enjoyed my two very different friendships with Frs. Fitzgerald and Baron, and with other Dominican priests who served at Mannix College during that time. If I had ever contemplated religious life, I would have sought to be a Dominican, if they were willing to accept me. Fr. Fitzgerald wrote a glowing reference for me when he retired as Master of the College, telling someone else that his reference for me was the best reference he had ever written. My dualist hypocrisy still existed at that time and I am sure the reference was undeserved.

In 1982, my life was forever changed by being invited to assist the formation of the new bioethics centre at St Vincent's Hospital and meeting that wonderful group of people whose influence on my life I have discussed in earlier volumes. Again there were priest friends who continued to influence me, notably the late Rev Dr Frank Harman and the Rev Dr Tom Daly SJ. Later, there were young Dominican seminarians, such as now Bishop Anthony Fisher OP and the late Colin Stokes OP, both of whom the Order allowed to work with me at the St Vincent's Bioethics Centre. Fr.

Harman had a particular influence on me. A saner, more balanced man I have never known. As chief judge of the appeals Tribunal of the Catholic Church in Australia, he well knew the range of sexual perversions and the difficulties that people create for themselves. He was always capable of the most down-to-earth discussion but would always see in human weakness the way in which each person is called to goodness and is capable of it.

A constant throughout all my formative years were my parents. I often discussed with them my work in bioethics and they continued to be a sounding board, even long after I had surpassed them in scholarship in philosophy and theology, though I was never a match for my father's knowledge of Scripture and his constant effort to read and understand the Word of God. Apart from life itself, their greatest gift to me was their commitment to a very natural prayer life, both formal and spontaneous, but always with a strong Marian component inherited from their parents.

In this afterword and the preface, I have mentioned home life in terms of my parents and my relationship to them. I have mentioned my siblings only in passing, indicating that their recollections may be very different from mine, as may their experience of our shared childhood. I do not want to say any more than that, as I owe them their privacy. I am very grateful to my older siblings for the way in which they often took the place of parents when the latter were preoccupied, as they would necessarily be in dealing with the needs of 10 children. I am very grateful for the lifetime friendships formed in the way in which they have all contributed, both younger and older, to whom I am. I once heard a psychologist describe our family as enmeshed. I suspect that there have been times when that has been so been between some members. However in later life, communication between us has been much less common, as we developed our own families and independent lives. I have contact with some more than others.

So much of what we learn about our sexuality is observation of the relationship between our parents. In a large family, the relationships between siblings and their partners also contribute. There are tensions and hostilities within a large family and much is learned about conflict resolution. Siblings are likely to know more about our faults and failures as adolescents than anyone, and not necessarily with the underlying charity and tolerance that can usually be expected of parents. Siblings suffer perhaps the most from our mistakes, experiencing the rough edges as we develop and mature. I am sorry for what I inflicted on my siblings on the way through. I also know that there has been both joy and suffering in their lives, and much to be admired in their responses to what life has offered. I am proud of the family of my birth and the many and rich contributions that they have made. If I have made a worthwhile contribution to the wider community, much is due to those nine others who grew up with me in the family home and have continued to be part of my life since. We mean a great deal to each other and cannot avoid the fact that we share so much common identity. I do like to stay in contact, and Mary and I pray for each of our siblings and their families during our nightly prayer. Some have taken to emailing regular reflections and I enjoy reading those, especially the effort to apply the readings of the day to life around them.

I have made these comments about my own upbringing because it bears upon the topics of this book. My experience of motherhood in my own mother, in Mary's motherhood of our children, and my grandmothers has been very blessed. They are the women I most admire and they gave me an intimacy that was a window into a world of which I have no direct experience.

I have talked about my family of origin in this afterword because those experiences are relevant to my perceptions of gender, of sexuality and of motherhood. Gender differences are a significant aspect of this book. I do not mean to treat gender prescriptively. There are obviously men who are more effeminate than some women and women who are more masculine than some men. There are also people who have biological or psychological conditions that affect gender development and who consequently may not be clearly identifiable as male or female. There are so many variations in relation to gender.

On the other hand, there are some usual differences between men and women that provide some truth to male and female stereotypes. Further, how we identify ourselves with respect to gender is of great personal significance and, theologically, marriage is a concept that depends on acknowledging complementarity between a man and a woman. How that is expressed in any given relationship depends on the personality of that particular man and that particular woman. There are such different ways of being a man and of being a woman. However, there are obvious differences between motherhood and fatherhood biologically, and because there are those biological differences there are obvious impacts on the gender roles of the spouses. There are also obvious biological and psychological differences that are determinative of the relating between a man and a woman. Central to a theological analysis of marriage are the different ways in which men and women experience affectivity. We give and receive love differently, and in our love making we have different experiences and different priorities. Yet as a matter of faith, Christians recognize that men and women are equally *imago dei*.

Bibliography

Amba J.C. et al, "Fertility, Family Planning and Women's Health: New Data from the 1995 National Survey on Family Growth, National Centre for Health Statistics," *Vital Health Statistics* 23 (1997): 1–114.

American Academy of Pediatrics, Committee on Adolescence, "Contraception and Adolescents," *Pediatrics* 104.5 (November 1999): 1161–1166.

American Psychiatric Association, *Diagnostic and Statistics Manual of Mental Disorders* 4th Edition (2000). Accessed from ttp://www.psychiatryonline.com/resourceTOC.aspx?resourceID=1

American Psychiatric Association, *Diagnostic Services Manual IV*. http://www.psychiatryonline.com/referral.aspx?gclid=CNGV7LKczKECFRM3bwodF27ncQ

Aquinas, St Thomas, *Summa Theologiae*.

Aref I. et al, "Effect of Minipills on Physiologic Responses of Human Cervical Mucus, Endometrium, and Ovary," *Journal of Fertility and Sterility* 24.8 (August 1973): 578-583.

Aristotle, *Generation of Animals* 11.4 739b21-27

Aristotle, *On the Soul* 350 B.C.E Translated by J.A. Smith. http://classics.mit.edu/Aristotle/soul.1.i.html]

Ashley, Benedict and O'Rourke, Kevin, fifth edition *Health Care Ethics: A Catholic Theologiael Analysis*, Washington: Georgetown University Press, 2007, p. 111.

Ashley, Benedict and O'Rourke, Kevin, *Health Care Ethics: A Theologiael Analysis*, 4th ed. (Georgetown: Georgetown University Press, 1997), 253-54.

As-Sanie, S., Gantt, A. and Rosental, M., "Pregnancy Prevention in Adolescents," *American Family Physician* 70.8 (2004): 1517-1523.

Attorney-General for the Commonwealth & "Kevin and Jennifer" & Human Rights and Equal Opportunity Commission [2003] FamCA 94 (2 February 2003).

Australian Catholic Bishops Conference, "Bishops' Commission for Doctrine and Morals Preliminary Advice on Pregnancy Support and Counselling", 10/9/2006. Published on the Australian Catholic Bishops Conference website http://www.catholic.org.au/index.php?option=com_docman&Itemid=315

Australian Curriculum and Assessment Authority, *Draft Shape of the Australian Curriculum* Accessed 10/12/2012 from http://www.acara.edu.au/verve/_resources/Australian Government Department of Health and Ageing *Sixth National HIV Strategy 2010–2013* Australian Government, Canberra 2010.

Australian Institute of Health and Welfare (AIHW), "Australian Young People: Their Health and Wellbeing 2003," *Canberra: Australian Institute of Health and Welfare* (cat. n.

PHE50); M. Chen and B. Donovan, "Chlamydia Trachomatis Infection in Australia: Epidemiology and Clinical Implication," *Sexual Health*, 1.

Ayer, A.J., *Logical Positivism*, Dover Publications, 1952.

Bamhart K.T., Gosman G., Ashby R., Sammel M., "The medical management of ectopic pregnancy: a meta-analysis comparing 'single dose' and 'multidose' regimens", *Obstet Gynecol*, 2003, 101:778-784.

Barbieri, R.L., "Population Density and Teen Pregnancy," *Obstetrics & Gynecology*, 104.4 (2004): 741-744.

Barnet, B., *et al*, "Association Between Postpartum Substance Use and Depressive Symptoms, Stress and Social Support in Adolescent Mothers," *Pediatrics*, 96.4 (1995): 659-666.

BBC Relationships: Addicted to sex http://www.bbc.co.uk/health/physical_health/sexual_health/probs_sexaddiction.shtml

Bearman Peter S. and Bruckner, Hanna, "Promising the Future: Virginity Pledges and First Intercourse," *American Journal of Sociology*, 106.4 (January 2001): 861, 862.

Berti, E., "Multiplicity and Unity of Being in Aristotle", *Proceedings of the Aristotelian Society* Volume 101, 2001, pp.185-207.

Biddlecom, A.E., "Trends in Sexual Behaviours and Infections Among Young People in the United States," *Sexually Transmitted Infections*, 80 suppl. 2 (2004): 74-79.

Billings E.L. and Westmore, Ann, *The Billings Ovulation Method* (Melbourne: Anne O'Donovan P/L, 1998).

Billings Family Life Centre Melbourne in private correspondence, May 2010.

Billings, E.L., "The Simplicity of the Ovulation Method and Its Application in Various Circumstances," *Acta Europaea Fertilitatis* 22. (January-February 1991): 33-36.

Billings, Evelyn L. and Billings, John J., *Teaching the Billings Ovulation Method*, part 2, *Variations of the Cycle and Reproductive Health* (Melbourne: Ovulation Method Research and Reference Centre, 1997), 45.

Billings, J.J., "The Validation of the Billings Ovulation Method by Laboratory Research and Field Trials," *Acta Europaea Fertilitatis* 22. (January-February 1991): 9-15.

Blackwell, C.W., "Registered Nurses' Attitudes Toward the Protection of Gays and Lesbians in the Workplace", *Journal of Transcultural Nursing*, Volume 19, No. 4, 1 October 2008, pp. 347-353.

Blackwell, L.F., Brown, J.B., and Cooke, D.G., "Definition of the Potentially Fertile Period from Urinary Steroid Excretion Rates: Part II: A Threshold Value for Pregnanediol Glucuronide as a Marker for the End of the Potentially Fertile Period in the Human Menstrual Cycle", *Steroids* 63. (January 1998): 5-13.

Blake, D., *et al*, "Fertility Awareness in Women Attending a Fertility Clinic," *Australian and New Zealand Journal of Obstetrics and Gynaecology*, 37.3 (1997): 350.

Bonell, C.P., *et al*, "Effect of Social Exclusion on the Risk of Teenage Pregnancy: Development of Hypotheses Using Baseline Data from a Randomised Trial of Sex Education," *Journal of Epidemoilogy & Community Health*, 57.11 (2003): 871-876.

Borawski, Elaine *et al*, "Evaluation of the Teen Pregnancy Prevention Programs Funded Through the Wellness Block Grant (1999–2000)," Center for Health Promotion Research, Department of Epidemiology and Biostatistics, Case Western Reserve University, School of Medicine (23 March 2001).

Borgia P. *et al*, "Is Peer Education the Best Approach for HIV Prevention in Schools? Finding From a Randomised Controlled Trial," *Journal of Adolescent Health*, 36.6 (2005): 508-516.

Breeze, A.C.G., Lees, C.C., Kumar, A., Missfelder-Lobos, H.H., Murdoch E.M., "Palliative care for prenatally diagnosed lethal fetal abnormality", *Arch Dis Child Fetal Neonatal Ed*, 2007; 92:F56-F58.

Brener N.D. *et al*, "Reliability of the Youth Risk Behaviour Survey Questionnaire," *American Journal of Epidemiology* 141 (1995): 575–580.

Briken, P., Habermann, N., Berner, W., Hill, A., "Diagnosis and Treatment of Sexual Addiction: A Survey among German Sex Therapists", *Sexual Addiction & Compulsivity* Volume 14, 2007, pp. 131–145.

Brod, Harry and Kaufman, Michael, *Theorizing Masculinity*, Sage Publications, 1994.

Brown, J.B., "Timing of Ovulation," *Medical Journal of Australia* 2 (1977): 780-783; J.B. Brown *et al*, "New Assays for Identifying the Fertile Period," *International Journal of Gynaecology & Obstetrics* 1.suppl. (1989): 111-122.

Brown, J.B., Holmes, J., and Barker, G., "Use of the Home Ovarian Monitor in Pregnancy Avoidance," *American Journal of Obstetrics and Gynecology*, 165.6 (December 1991): 2008-2011.

Brown, Professor James B., conversation with author, June 2002.

Brown, Professor James B., conversation with author, 5 March 2004.

Buster J.E., Pisarska M.D., "Medical management of ectopic pregnancy", *Clin Obstet Gynecol*, 1999; 42:23-30.

Canadian *Crimes Act (Hate Propaganda) Amendment Act* was signed into law on 29 April 2004.

Canberra: AIHW.

Carr R.J., Evans R., "Ectopic pregnancy", *Prim Care* 2000; 27:169-183.

Catechism of the Catholic Church, St Paul Publications, 2000.

Cates, Willard Jr., "Contraception, Unintended Pregnancies and Disease: Why Isn't a Simple Solution Possible?", *American Journal of Epidemiology*, 143.4 (1996); John Murtagh, *General Practice*, 2nd ed. (Melbourne: McGraw-Hill, 1998).

Catholic Archdiocese of Melbourne, *Directives for Education in Sexuality*, East Melbourne: Catholic Education Office, 2002.

Catlin, Anita, and Carter, Brian, "Creation of a Neonatal End-of-Life Palliative care Protocol," *Journal of Perinatology*, 2002, 22:184-195.

Cheesbrough S., Ingham, R. and Massey, D., *Reducing the rate of teenage conceptions: A review of the international evidence on preventing and reducing teenage conceptions: The United States, Canada, Australia and New Zealand*. Health Education Authority, 1999; "Sexual Behavior [Journal Summary, ReCAPP]", in *Keeping the Faith: The Role of Religion and Faith Communities in Preventing Teen Pregnancy*, National Campaign to Prevent Teen Pregnancy, Editor, 2001: Washington, DC, Chapter 2, p. 245.

Childrens Medical Office of North Andover, P.C., "Masturbation in Early Childhood" http://www.chmed.com/mod.php?mod=userpage&menu=1907&page_id=142&PHPSESSID=a76dc0f6fb1882506f5666b63fb98062

Christ, Michael, Raszka, William V. Jr., and Dillon, Christopher, "Prioritizing Education about Condom Use among Sexually Active Adolescent Females," *Adolescence*, 33.132 (Winter 1998): 735-744.

Cohen, Marc, *Philosophy 320: History of Ancient Philosophy*, University of Washington Philosophy Department, 2006, http://faculty.washington.edu/smcohen/320/thforms.htm.

Concise Oxford Dictionary, English Edition, 1991.

Congregation for the Doctrine of the Faith, *Dignitas Personae: Instruction on Certain Bioethical Questions*, 2008, n. 19, 22.

Congregation for the Doctrine of the Faith, *Gaudium et Spes*, 5AAS 58 (1966), p. 1072.

Congregation for the Doctrine of the Faith, *Donum Vitae*, Vatican, 1987, http://www.vatican.va/roman_curia/congregations/

Congregation for the Doctrine of the Faith, *Letter To The Bishops Of The Catholic Church On The Pastoral Care Of Homosexual Persons*, 1986.

Cooper, L.C., Leland, N.L. and Alexander, G., "Effect of Maternal Age on Birth Outcomes Among Young Adolescents," *Social Biology*, 42 (1995): 22-35.

Couch, Murray, Dowsett, Gary W., Dutertre, Sophie, Keys, Deborah, Pitts, Marian K., "Looking for more: A review of social and contextual factors affecting young people's sexual health" http://www.latrobe.edu.au/arcshs/assets/downloads/reports/looking_for_more.pdf

Couple to Couple League International estimates based on its own studies and those completed by Nona Aguilar for her book, *No-Pill No-Risk Birth Control* (Rawson Wade).

Coyle K.K. *et al*, "Draw the Line/Respect the Line: A Randomised Trial of a Middle School Intervention to Reduce Sexual Risk Behaviours," *Research and Practice* 94.5 (2004): 843-851.

Curriculum Corporation, Carlton, Victoria, 1994.

Daly, T.V., SJ, "The Status of Embryonic Human Life: A Crucial Issue in Genetic Counselling," in Tonti-Filippini, Nicholas *Health Care Priorities in Australia*, St. Vincent's Bioethics Centre, 1985.

De' Liguori, Saint Alphonsus, *Theologia Moralis*, l. III, tr. 4, c. 1, dub.3.

Department of Education and Early Childhood Development 2008, *The state of Victoria's young people*, Department of Education and Early Childhood Development and Department of Planning and Community Development, Melbourne.

Department of Health and Ageing, Commonwealth of Australia, *National Sexually Transmissible Infections Strategy 2005–2008*, http://www.vicaids.asn.au/contentfilesuploaded/STI_strategy.pdf.

Descartes, René, *The Philosophical Writings of Descartes*, trans. John Cottingham, Robert Stoothoff, Dugald Murdoch and Anthony Kenny, Cambridge: Cambridge University Press, 3 vols, 1984-1991.

Detraux, J.-J., Gillot-de F.R., Vries, S. Eynde, Vanden, Courtois, A., Desm A., "Psychological Impact of the Announcement of a Fetal Abnormality on Pregnant Women and on Professionals", *Annals of the New York Academy of Sciences*, 5 February 2006.

Detsky A.S. *et al*, "Incorporating Variations in the Quality of Individual Randomised Trial into Meta-Analysis," *Journal of Clinical Epidemiology* 45 (1992): 255-265.

Diamond, J.J., "Abortion, animation and biological hominisation", *Theologiael Studies*, Volume 36, 1975, pp. 305-324.

DiCenso A. *et al*, "Interventions to Reduce Unintended Pregnancies Among Adolescents: Systematic Review of Randomised Controlled Trials," *British Medical Journal* 324 (2002): 1426-1433.

Doniger, Andrew S., "Impact Evaluation of the 'Not Me, Not Now' Abstinence-Oriented, Adolescent Pregnancy Prevention Communications Program, Monroe County, New York," *Journal of Health Communications* 6 (2001): 45-60.

Donnai P., Charles N., Harris R., "Attitudes of patients after 'genetic' termination of pregnancy", *British Medical Journal*, 1981, 282:621-622, p. 622.

Douglas, Carolyn J., Kalman, Concetta M., and Kalman, Thomas P., "Homophobia Among Physicians and Nurses: An Empirical Study", *Hospital and Community Psychiatry* Volume 36, December 1985, pp. 1309-1311.

Dunson, D.B., Colombo, B., and Baird, D.D., "Changes with Age in the Level and Duration of the Menstrual Cycle," *Human Reproduction* 17.5 (May 2002): 1399-1403.

Dunstan, Gordan "The moral status of the human embryo: a tradition recalled", *Journal of Medical Ethics* Volume 1, 1984, pp. 38ff.

Dyson S. and Mitchell, A., "Sex Education and Unintended Pregnancy: Are We Seeing the Results?", *Australian Health Review* 29.2 (2005): 135-139.

Editorial: "For Debate: Do fetuses feel pain?", *British Medical Journal* 313:7060 (28 September 1996) 795-798.

Elito J., Jr., Reichmann A.P., Uchiyama M.N., Camano L., "Predictive score for the systemic treatment of unruptured ectopic pregnancy with a single dose of methotrexate", *Int J Gynecol Obstet* 1999, 67:75-79.

Ellen, J., Aral, S., Madger, L., 1998, "Do Differences in Sexual Behaviours Account for the Ratial/Ethnic Differences in Adolescents' Self-Reported History of a Sexually Transmitted Disease?", *Sexually Transmitted Diseases*, vol. 25, pp. 125-129; Cf. H.R. Harrison, M. Costin, J.B. Meder, "Cervical Chlamydia Trachomatis Infection in University Women: Relationship to History, Contraception, Ectopy and Cervicitis," *American Journal of Obstetric Gynecology*, 153 (1985): 244-251; Aral (1998).

Escobar-Chaves S.L. *et al*, "Impact of the Media on Adolescent Sexual Attitudes and Behaviours," *Pediatrics*, 116.1 suppl. S (2005): 303-326.

Farquhar C.M., "Ectopic pregnancy", *Lancet*, 2005; 366:583-591.

Fawver, Patricia (01/10/2006). The Sexual Health Network. http://www.sexualhealth.com/question/read/love-relationships/sexual-addiction-compulsion/11608/

Federation Press/Sydney 2009. Accessed 9/710 from http://books.google.com.au/

Fehring R., Lawrence D., Sauvage C., "Self-esteem, spiritual well-being, and intimacy: a comparison among couples using NFP and oral contraceptives", *Int Rev*, 1989; 13: 227-36.

Fernandez H., Lelaldier C., Thouvenez V. *et al*, "The use of a pretherapeutic, predictive score to determine inclusion criteria for the non-surgical management of ectopic pregnancy", *Hum Reprod*, 1991; 6:995-998.

Fetro, J.V., 2010, "Health literate youth: evolving challenges for health educators", *American Journal of Health Education*, vol. 41, no. 5, pp. 258-264.

Fitzgerald, Denis, "The features of counselling in a Catholic agency", *Kairos*, Vol 2, No 3, 2007.

Flood M. and Hamilton, C., *Mapping Homophobia in Australia,* The Australia Institute, 2005. Accessed 9/2/10 from https://www.tai.org.au/documents/downloads/WP79.pdf

Flood, M. and Hamilton C., 2005, *Mapping Homophobia in Australia*. The Australia Institute, p. 5.

Ford C.A., *et al*, "Predicting Adolescents' Longitudinal Risk for Sexually Transmitted Infection," *Archive of Pediatric and Adolescent Medicine* 159 (2005): 657-664.

Ford, Norman M., *When did I begin?*, Cambridge University Press, 1988.

Fortenberry, J.D., "The Limits of Abstinence-Only in Preventing Sexually Transmitted Infections," *Journal of Adolescent Health* 36 (2005): 269-270.

Fox Keller, Evelyn, "Beyond the Gene but Beneath the Skin," in Susan Oyama, Paul

E. Griffiths, and Gray Russell D. (ed), *Cycles of Contingency: Developmental Systems and Evolution*. Cambridge, MA: MIT Press 2001, pp. 299-312.

Furukawa T.A. and Guyatt, G.H., "Sources of Bias in Diagnostic Accuracy Studies and the Diagnostic Process," *Canadian Medical Association Journal* 174.4 (2006): 481-482.

Geach, Mary, "Are there any circumstances in which it would be morally admirable for a woman to seek to have an orphan embryo implanted in her womb?", in *Issues for a Catholic Bioethic: Proceedings of the International Conference to celebrate the Twentieth Anniversary of the foundation of the Linacre Centre*, Gormally L. (ed.), The Linacre Centre, London, 1999, pp. 341-346.

Gerson, Lloyd P., *Aristotle and Other Platonists*, Cornell University Press, 2005.

Goldman, J.D.G., "Sexuality Education for Children and Pre-Schoolers in the Information Age," *Children Australia* 28.1 (2003): 17-23.

Goldman, J.D.G., "An exploration in health education of an integrated theoretical basis for sexuality education pedagogies for young people", *Health Education Research*, vol. 26, no. 3, (2011):526-541.

Goldman, J.D.G. and Bradley, G., "Sexuality information for older people in the technological age", *Australian Journal of Primary Health*, 10 (2004): 96-103.

Goodson P. *et al*, "Defining Abstinence: View of Directors, Instructors and Participants in Abstinence-Only-Until-Marriage Programs in Texas," *The Journal of School Health* 73.3 (2003): 91-95.

Gormally L. (ed.), *Issues for a Catholic Bioethic: Proceedings of the International Conference to celebrate the Twentieth Anniversary of the foundation of the Linacre Centre*, The Linacre Centre, London, 1999.

Grayson, N., Hargreaves, J., and Sullivan, E.A., "Use of Routinely Collected National Data Sets for Reporting on Induced Abortion in Australia," *AIHW National Perinatal Statistics* 17 (2005): 34.

Green J.M., "Obstetricians' views on prenatal diagnosis and termination of pregnancy: 1980 compared with 1993", *British Journal of Obstetrics and Gynaecology*, March 1995, 102(3):228-232, p. 231; and Mander R., *Loss and Bereavement in Childbearing*, Oxford: Blackwell Scientific Publications, 1994, p. 44.

Green, E.C., *The Impact of Religious Organizations in Promoting HIV/AIDS Prevention*. in *Challenges for the Church: AIDS, Malaria & TB*, 2001, Christian Connections for International Health, Arlington, VA.

Grimes, D.A., Raymond, E.G., "Emergency Contraception," *Annals of Internal Medicine* 137.3 (6 August 2002): 180-189.

Grisez, Germain, *The Way of the Lord Jesus Volume 3, Difficult Moral Questions*, Franciscan Press: llinois, 1997, pp. 239-244.

Grisez, Germain, *The Way of the Lord Jesus Volume One: Christian Moral Principles*, Franciscan Herald Press, 1983, pp. 3ff.

Grunseit A. *et al*, "Sexuality Education and Young People's Sexual Behaviour: A Review of Studies," *Journal of Adolescent Research* 12 (1997): 421-453.

Guttmacher Institute, "Choice of Contraceptives", *The Medical Letter on Drugs and Therapeutics*, Volume 34, No 885, 1992, pp. 111-114.

Guyatt G.H. *et al*, "Randomised Trial Versus Observational Studies in Adolescent Pregnancy Prevention," *Journal of Clinical Epidemiology* 53.2 (2000): 167-174.

Hagan J.F. *et al*, "Sexuality Educational for Children and Adolescent," *Pediatrics* 108.2 (2001): 498-502.

Hare, R.M., *Moral Thinking: Its Level, Method and Point*, Clarendon Press, Oxford, 1981.

Hatcher, R.A., Trussel, J., Nelson A.L., *et al*, *Contraceptive Technology* (19th ed.), New York: Ardent Media, 2007, http://www.contraceptivetechnology.com/table.html

Health and Physical Education, March 2012 Accessed 10/12/2012 from http://www.acara.edu.au/verve/_resources/

Hewitt, G. and Cromer, B., "Update on Adolescent Contraception," *Obstetrics and Gynecology Clinics of North America* 27 (March 2000): 143-162.

Horwood, Alice, Saya, Sibel, in discussion at a meeting on Perinatal Palliative Care, John Paul II Institute for Marriage and Family, East Melbourne, 7 December 2010.

http://apps.who.int/globalatlas/predefinedReports/EFS2008/full/EFS2008_UG.pdf

http://www.aeaweb.org/articles.php?doi=10.1257/pol.1.2.190

http://www.vatican.va/roman_curia/congregations/cfaith/documents/rc_con_cfaith_doc_20081208_dignitas-personae_en.html

Iles, Susan, and Gath, Denis, "Psychiatric Outcome of Termination of Pregnancy for Foetal Abnormality", *Psychological Medicine*, 1993, 23, 407-413.

Indian Council of Medical Research Task Force on NFP (1995). States of Uttar Pradesh, Bihar, Rajasthan, Karnataka and Pondicherry. "Field Trial of Billings Ovulation Method of Natural Family Planning," *Contraception* 53.2 (February 1996): 69-74.

Insurance Statistics Australia Limited, *Medical Indemnity Report Executive Summary*, Medical Indemnity Insurers Association of Australia, 29 March 2004, p. 6.

Internet Encyclopedia of Philosophy http://www.iep.utm.edu/descarte/#SH7b

Jadar *et al* (1999) cf. Streiner, D.L. and Norman, G.R., *Health Measurement Scales: a practical guide to their development and use*, Oxford University Press, 2008.

Jolly, M.C. *et al*, "Obstetric Risks of Pregnancy in Women Less Than 18 Years Old," *Obstetric Gynecology* 96 (2000): 962-966.

Jones O.W., Penn N.E., Shuchter S., Stafford C.A., Richards T., Kernahan C., Gutierrez J., Cherkin P., "Parental response to mid-trimester therapeutic abortion following amniocentesis", *Prenatal Diagnosis*, 1984, 4:249-256, p. 250.

Jones, R.K., Darroch, J.E., Singh, S., "Religious Differentials in the Sexual and

Reproductive Behaviour of Young Women in the United States," *Journal of Adolescent Health* 36.4 (2005): 279-288.

Jorgensen, Stephen R., Potts, Vicki, Camp, Brian, "Project Taking Charge: Six-Month Follow-Up of a Pregnancy Prevention Program for Early Adolescents," *Family Relations* 42.4 (October 1993): 401-406.

Kaczor, Christopher "Moral Absolutism and Ectopic Pregnancy," *Journal of Medicine and Philosophy* 26, no. (2001): 61-74.

Kaestle C.E. et al, "Young Age at First Intercourse and Sexually Transmitted Infections in Adolescent and Young Adults," *American Journal of Epidemiology* 161.8 (2005): 774-780.

Kahlenborn, C., Stanford, J.B., and Larimore, W.L., "Postfertilization Effect of Hormonal Emergency Contraception," *Annals of Pharmacotherapy* 36.3 (March 2002): 465-470.

Kingston, D.A., and Firestone, P., "Problematic hypersexuality: A review of conceptualization and diagnosis" *Sexual Addiction and Compulsivity*, Volume 15, 2008, pp. 284-310.

Kirby, Douglas, "Reflections on Two Decades of Research on Teen Sexual Behaviour and Pregnancy," *Journal of School Health* 69.3 (1999): 89-94.

Kirungi, W.L., Musinguzi, J.B., Opio, A., Madraa, E., *International Conference on AIDS*, 2002, 7-12 July; 14: abstract no. WeOrC1269. STD/AIDS Control Programme, Ministry of Health, Kampala, Uganda.

Kuhse, Helga, and Singer, Peter, "Individuals, Humans and Persons" in Peter Singer *et al Embryo Experimentation*, Cambridge University Press, 1990, pp. 65-75.

La Trobe University Australian Research Centre in Health and Society, "Secondary Students and Sexual Health", 2008. http://www.latrobe.edu.au/arcshs/download_reports.html#young_people

LaBarber, L.P., "Psychosocial aspects of NFP instruction: a national survey", *Int Rev* 1990; 14:34-53.

Lammers, Christina, Ireland, Marjorie, Resnick, Michael, Blum, Robert, "Influence on Adolescents' Decision to Postpone Onset of Sexual Intercourse: A Survival Analysis of Virginity Among Youths Aged 13 to 18 Years", *Journal of Adolescent Health*, Volume 26, 2000, pp. 42-48.

Laumann, Edward O., Gagnon, John H., Michael, Robert T., and Michaels, Stuart, *The Social Organization of Sexuality: Sexual Practices in the United States*, Chicago, 1994.

Lederman, R.P., Chan, W., Roberts-Gray, C., "Sexual Risk Attitudes and Intentions of Youth Age 12–14 Years: Survey Comparisons of Parent-Teen Prevention and Control Groups," *Behavioural Medicine* 29.4 (2004): 155-163.

Leonard, William, Mitchell, Anne, Patel, Sunil, Fox, Christopher, *Coming Forward: The underreporting of heterosexist violence and same sex partner abuse in Victoria*, Australian Research Centre in Sex, Health & Society, La Trobe University, December 2008. Accessed 16/2/10 from http://www.glhv.org.au/files/ComingForwardReport.pdf

Lipscomb G.H., Meyer N.L., Flynn D.E., Peterson M., Ling E., "Oral methotrexate for treatment of ectopic pregnancy", *Am J Obstet Gynecol* 2002; 186:1192-1195.

Long, Steven A., *The Teleological Grammar of the Moral Act, Introductions to Catholic Doctrine* (Naples, Florida: Sapientia Press of Ave Maria University, 2007), 95-102; 127-129.

Looking for more: A review of social and contextual factors affecting young people's sexual health http://www.latrobe.edu.au/arcshs/assets/downloads/reports/looking_for_more.pdf

Margaret C.A., Whit-van Mourik, J.M. Connor, M.A. Ferguson-Smith, "The Psychosocial Sequellae of a Second Trimester Termination of Pregnancy for Fetal Abnormality over a Two Year Period", *Psychosocial Aspects of Genetic Counselling*, John Wiley and Sons: New York, 1992, pp. 60-74.

Martin A. *et al*, "Early to Bed: A Study of Adaptation Among Sexually Active Urban Adolescent Girls Younger Than Age Sixteen," *Journal of American Academy of Child & Adolescent Psychiatry* 44.4 (2005): 358-367.

Mason, Gail, *The Spectacle of Violence: Homophobia, gender and knowledge*, London: Routledge, 2002, pp. 58-77.

Medical Board of Queensland, *Terminations of Pregnancies in Excess of 20 weeks of Gestation: Project Information Paper*, July 1997, p. 4.

Medline Encyclopedia accessed at http://www.nlm.nih.gov/medlineplus/ency/article/001669.htm

Miller, W.C., Ford, C.A., Morris, M., "Prevalence of Chlamydial and Gonococcal Infection Among Young Adults in the United States," *Journal of American Medical Association* 291 (2004): 2229-2236.

Milton J. and Berne, L., "Condom and Contraceptive Availability for Young People: Do Australian Teachers, Parents and School Counsellors Support Access in School Settings?", *ACHPER Healthy Lifestyle Journal* 51.1 (2004): 7-11; S. Yoo *et al*, "A Qualitative Evaluation of the Students of Service (SOS) Program for Sexual Abstinence in Louisiana," *Journal of School Health* 74.8 (2004): 329-334.

Milton, J., "Sexuality Education and Primary School: Experiences and Practices of Mothers and Teachers in Four Sydney Schools," *ACHPER Healthy Lifestyle Journal* 51.4 (2004): 18-25.

Mindel A. and Kippax, S., "A National Sexually Transmitted Infections Strategy: The Need for an All-Embracing Approach," *The Medical Journal of Australia* 183.10 (2005): 502-503.

Mittal S., "Non-surgical management of ectopic pregnancy", *Obs Gyn Com* 1999; 1:23-28; Cohen, M.A., Sauer, M.V., "Expectant management of ectopic pregnancy", *Clinical Obstetrics and Gynecology*, 1999.

Moraczewski, Albert S., "Managing Tubal Pregnancies: Part 2," *Ethics and Medics* 21, no. 8 (1996): 3-4.

Munson, David, Hudson, Martha, Kasperski, Stefanie, "Perinatal Palliative Care Initiative", Philadelphia Children's Hospital, Accessed 20/12/2010 from http://www.chop.edu/service/fetal-diagnosis-and-treatment/about-our-services/perinatal-palliative-care.html

Murray H., Baakdah H., Bardell T., Tulandi T., "Diagnosis and treatment of ectopic pregnancy" *CMAJ*, 2005; 173:905-912; Pansky M., "Methotrexate (MXT) treatment for ectopic pregnancy-systemic vs local injection", Scientific presentation at The First World Congress on Controversies in *Obstetrics, Gynecology & Infertility* Prague, Czech Republic, 1999. Available at: www.obgyn.net/firstcontroversies/prague1999pansky.doc

National Health and Medical Research Council, *National Youth Suicide Prevention Strategy. Setting the Evidence-Based Research Agenda for Australia: A Literature Review* (1999), http://www.nhmrc.gov.au/publications/synopses/mh12syn.htm.

National Health Service (UK), *Causes of gender dysphoria*. Accessed 21/12/09 http://www.nhs.uk/Conditions/Gender-dysphoria/Pages/Causes.aspx

National Perinatal Statistics Unit, "Australia's mothers and babies 2008" http://www.preru.unsw.edu.au/PRERUWeb.nsf/page/ps24

New South Wales Council for Civil Liberties, *Transexual Marriage in Australia*. Accessed from http://www.nswccl.org.au/unswccl/issues/transexual.php#StateOfLaw

New Zealand *Bill of Rights Act*; South African Promotion of Equality and Prevention of Unfair Discrimination Act.

NHMRC, *Ethical Guidelines for the Care of Persons in Post Coma Unresponsiveness (Vegetative State) or a Minimally Responsive State* http://www.nhmrc.gov.au/_files_nhmrc/file/publications/synopses/e81.pdf+NHMRC+unresponsive+state

NHMRC, *Ethical Guidelines on the Use of Assisted Reproductive Technology in Clinical Practice and Research*, Australian Government, June 2007, p. 9.

NHMRC, *National Statement on Ethical Conduct in Human Research*, Australian Government, 2007.

NHMRC, *Organ and Tissue Donation after death: Guidelines for Ethical Practice for Health Professionals*, Australian Government, 2007, p. 20.

Obermeyer, C.M., "Sexuality in Morocco: Changing context and contested domain", *Culture, Health & Sexuality*, Volume 2, No 3, 2000, pp. 239-254.

Odeblad, E., et al, "The Dynamic Mosaic Model of the Human Ovulatory Cervical Mucus," *Proceedings of the Nordic Fertility Society* (Umea, Sweden, January 1978).

Palliative care for prenatally diagnosed lethal fetal abnormality *Arch Dis Child Fetal Neonatal Ed*, 2007; 92:F56–F58.

Pallone, Stephen R., MD, and Bergus, George R., MD, "Fertility Awareness-Based Methods: Another Option for Family Planning", *Journal of the American Board of*

Family Medicine, 2009, Volume 22 (2), pp. 147-157. http://www.jabfm.org/cgi/content/full/22/2/147

Panzer, Claudia, *et al*, "Impact of Oral Contraceptives on Sex Hormone-Binding Globulin and Androgen Levels: A Retrospective Study in Women with Sexual Dysfunction", *Journal of Sexual Medicine*, 2006, Vol. 3, Issue 1, pp 104-113.

Pastrana, G., "Personhood and the beginning of life", *Thomist*, Volume 4, 1977, pp 247-94.

Pisarska M.D., Carson S.A., Buster J.E., "Ectopic pregnancy", *Lancet* 1998; 351:1115-1120.

Pope Benedict XVI, During the Flight to Africa Tuesday, 17 March 2009. http://www.vatican.va/holy_father/benedict_xvi/speeches/2009/

Pope Benedict XVI, Address to the Members of the Roman Curia for the Traditional Exchange of Christmas Greetings, Clementine Hall, Monday, 22 December 2008, Accessed from http://www.vatican.va/holy_father/benedict_xvi/speeches/2008/december/documents/hf_ben-xvi_spe_20081222_curia-romana_en.html

Pope Benedict XVI, Interview on plane to Africa, AFP, 3 October 2008.

Pope John Paul II, *Evangelium Vitae*, 1995.

Pope John Paul II, *Mulieris Dignitatem* (the Dignity of Women).

Pope John Paul II, Address to the participants in the Symposium on "*Evangelium vitae* and Law" and the Eleventh International Colloquium on Roman and Canon Law (24 May 1996), 6: *AAS* 88 (1996), 943-944.

Pope John Paul II, Apostolic Letter *Mulieris Dignitatem* (15 August 1988), 18: *AAS* 80 (1988), 1696.

Pope John Paul II, *Familiaris Consortio*.

Pope John Paul II, *L'Osservatore Romano*, 10 October 1983.

Pope Paul VI, *Humanae Vitae*, 1968, n. 9.

Pope Pius XI, *Casti Connubii*, 1930, n. 23-24.

Pope, Melissa, Haase, Asley Tm, "Transmission, acute HIV-infection and the quest for strategies to prevent infection", *Nature Medicine Review*, Volume 9, No. 7, July 2003, pp. 847-852.

President Museveni of Uganda, Interview with Jackie Judd, Kaiser Family Foundation, 14 June 2004.

Quinlivan J.A., Condon, J., "Anxiety and Depression in Fathers in Teenage Pregnancy," *Australian and New Zealand Journal of Psychiatry* 30.10 (2005): 915-920.

Reichert, Timothy, "Bitter Pill", *First Things*, May 2010.

Resnick, Michael, *et al*, "Protecting Adolescents from Harm: Findings From the National

Longitudinal Study on Adolescent Health," *Journal of the American Medical Association* 278 (10 September 1997): 823-832.

Resta R., Biesecker B.B., Bennett R.L., Blum S., Hahn S.E., Strecker M.N., Williams J.L., "A new definition of genetic counelling: NSGC task force report", *J Gen Couns.*, 2006, April;15(2):77-83.

Ring-Cassidy, Elizabeth, Gentles, Ian, "The Impact of Abortion After Prenatal Testing". Accessed 20 12 2010 from http://www.afterabortion.org/prenataltesting.html#6#6

Rose, Joanna, *A critical analysis of sperm donation practices : the personal and social effects of disrupting the unity of biological and social relatedness for the offspring*. PhD thesis, 2009. Queensland University of Technology. Accessed 9/1/2013 from http://eprints.qut.edu.au/32012/

Rostosky, S.C., Wilcox, B.L., Randall, B.A., "The Impact of Religiosity on Adolescent Sexual Behaviour: A Review of Evidence," *Journal of Adolescent Research*, 19.6 (2004): 677-696.

Royal Australia and New Zealand College of Obstetricians and Gynaecologists, *Amniocentesis and Chorionic Villus Sampling (CVS*, January 2007, www.mitec.com.au).

Sacred Congregation for the Doctrine of the Faith, *Persona Humana, Declaration On Certain Questions Concerning Sexual Ethics*, Vatican City, 1975.

Sauer, M.V., "Expectant management of ectopic pregnancy", *Clin Obstet Gynecol*, 1999, 42:48-54.

Seamark C.J., Pereira-Gray, D.J., "Like Mother, Like Daughter: A General Practice Study of Maternal Influences on Teenage Pregnancy," *British Journal of General Practice* 47 (1997): 175-176.

Second Vaticam Council, *Gaudium et Spes*.

Shao Zhen Qian and De-Wei Zhang, "Evaluation of the Effectiveness of a Natural Fertility Regulation Program in China," *Bulletin of the Ovulation Method Research and Reference Centre*, 24.4 (2000): 17-22.

Sheeran, P., *et al*, "Religiosity and Adolescents' Premarital Sexual Attitudes and Behaviour: An Empirical Study of Conceptual Issues", *European Journal of Social Psychology*, Volume 23, No. 1, 1993, pp. 39-52; 246.

Sheffer-Mimouni G., *et al*, "Ectopic Pregnancies following Emergency Levonorgestrel Contraception," *Contraception* 67.4 (April 2003): 267-269.

Sherman, Nancy. (2007) "Virtue and a Warrior's Anger", in R.L. Walker & P.J. Ivanhoe eds., OUP, 2007, pp. 251-278.

SIECUS, 1999, http://www.siecus.org

Silva, M., "The Effectiveness of School-Based Sex Education Programs in the Promotion of Abstinent Behaviour: A Meta-Analysis," *Health Education Research, Theory & Practice* 17.4 (2002): 471-481.

Singer, Peter, *Rethinking Life and Death*, Text Publishing, 1994.
Singer, Peter, *et al*, *Embryo Experimentation*, Cambridge University Press, 1990.
Skinner, S.R. and Hickey, M., "Current Priorities for Adolescent Sexual and Reproductive Health in Australia," *The Medical Journal of Australia* 179 (2003): 158-161.
Smith A., Agius P., Mitchell A., Barrett C., Pitts M., 2009, *Secondary Students and Sexual Health 2008*, Monograph Series No. 70, Melbourne: Australian Research Centre in Sex, Health & Society, La Trobe University
Somers, C.L. and Eaves, M.W., "Is Earlier Sex Education Harmful? An Analysis of the Timing of School-Based Sex Education and Adolescent Behaviours," *Research in Education* 67 (2002): 23-32.
Somers C.L. and Surman, A.T., "Sources and Timing of Sex Education: Relation with American Adolescent Sexual Attitudes and Behaviour," *Educational Review* 57.1 (2005): 37-54.
Sri Ramana Maharshi, Teachings of: The nature of Individual self and of liberation http://www.hinduism.co.za/mind1.htm
Stevenson, Betsey, and Wolfers, Justin, "The Paradox of Declining Female Happiness", *American Economic Journal: Economic Policy*, Volume 1, No. 2, 2009, pp. 190-225.
Stewart, D.C., "Contraception," in *Adolescent Medicine*, eds. A.D. Hofmann and D.E. Greydanus, 3rd ed. (Stamford, CT: Appleton & Lange, 1997), 566-588.
Stoneburner, R.L., Low-Beer, D., "Population-level HIV declines and behavioral risk avoidance in Uganda", *Science*, April 30; 304(5671):714-8, 2004.
Tabor, A., Philip, J., Madsen, M., Bang, J., Obel, E.B., Norgaard-Pedersen, B., "Randomised controlled trial of genetic amniocentesis in 4606 low-risk women", *The Lancet* (1986) 352: 1287-93.
The Concise Oxford Dictionary, 9th Edition, 1995.
Thiele, Pauline, "He was my son, not a dying baby", *J Med Ethics*, 2010, 36: 646-647.
Thompson, Judith Jarvis, "A Defense of Abortion", *Philosophy and Public Affairs*, Volume 1, No. Fall 1987, and reprinted in Peter Singer (Ed), *Applied Ethics*, Oxford University Press: Oxford, 1987, pp. 37-56.
Thornton, S.J., Pepperell, R.J., Brown, J.B., "Home Monitoring of Gonadotropin Ovulation Induction Using the Ovarian Monitor," *Fertility and Sterility* 54.6 (December 1990): 1076–82
Tonti-Filippini, Nicholas, *About Bioethics, Volume One, Philosophical and Theologiael Approaches*, Connor Court, 2011.
Tonti-Filippini, Nicholas, *About Bioethics, Volume Three, Transplantation, Biobanks and the Human Body*, Connor Court, 2012.
Tonti-Filippini, Nicholas, *About Bioethics, Volume Two, Caring for People Who are Sick or Dying*, Connor Court, 2012.

Bibliography 439

Tonti-Filippini, Nicholas, "Bioethics, Culture and Collaboration," *Solidarity: The Journal of Catholic Social Thought and Secular Ethics*. 2012, Vol. 2, Issue 1.

Tonti-Filippini, Nicholas, "Perinatal Palliative Care and Support", *Ethics Education*, Vol 18, Issues 1 and 2, 2012.

Tonti-Filippini, Nicholas, "Post-coital Intervention: From Fear of Pregnancy to Rape Crisis", *The National Catholic Bioethics Quarterly*, 4.2 (2004): 275-288.

Tonti-Filippini, Nicholas, "Gender Reassignment and Catholic Schools", *National Catholic Bioethics Quarterly*, Volume 12, No. 1, Spring 2012, pp. 85-98, and is here reproduced with permission as published.

Tonti-Filippini, Nicholas, "Professional Conscience", *Obstetrics and Gynaecology Magazine*, Vol 10, No 2, Winter 2008, pp. 27-8.

Tonti-Filippini, Nicholas, "The embryo rescue debate: impregnating women, ectogenesis, and restoration from suspended animation", *The National Catholic Bioethics Quarterly*, Volume 3, Spring 2003, pp. 11-137.

Tonti-Filippini, Nicholas, "The Pill: Abortifacient or Contraceptive? A Literature Review," *Linacre Quarterly*, 62, February 1995: 5-28.

Tonti-Filippini, Nicholas, *Health Care Priorities in Australia*. St. Vincent's Bioethics Centre, 1985

Trounson, Alan, and Wood, Karl, *Medical Journal of Australia*, Volume 146, 1987, pp. 338-40.

Twomey, D. Vincent, *Moral Theology after Humanae Vitae: Fundamental Issues in Moral Theory and Sexual Ethics*, Four Courts Press, Dublin 2010, p. 195.

Ugocsai, G., Rózsa, M., and Ugocsai, P., "Scanning Electron Microscopic (SEM) Changes of the Endometrium in Women Taking High Doses of Levonorgestrel as Emergency Post-coital Contraception," *Contraception*, 66.6 (December 2002): 433-437.

UK Section 4A of the *Public Order Act*, 1986, which was inserted by section 154 of the *Criminal Justice and Public Order Act*, 1994; *Prohibition of Incitement to Hatred Act*

United Nations *Convention on the Rights of the Child*.

University of Arkansas, *Daily Headlines*, "Disgust not fear drives homophobia, say UA psychologists", 7 June 2002.

VandeVusse L., Hanson L., Fehring R., Newman A., Fox J., "Couple's views of the effects of natural family planning on marital dynamics", *J Nurs Scholarsh* 2003; 35: 171-6.

Victorian Infertility Treatment Authority *2009 Annual Report* accessed from http://www.varta.org.au/www/257/1003057/displayarticle/1003573.html

Victorian Infertility Treatment Authority, *Annual Reports* Accessed July, 2010 from http://www.varta.org.au/www/257/1003057/displayarticle/1003573.html

Victorian Infertility Treatment Authority, *Annual Reports* Accessed July, 2010 from http://www.varta.org.au/www/257/1003057/displayarticle/1003573.html

Visser, A. and Van Bilsen, P., "Effectiveness of Sex Education Provided to Adolescent," *Patient Education and Counseling* 23 (1994): 147-160; C. Jacobs and E. Wolf, "School Sexuality and Adolescent Risk-Taking Behaviour," *Journal of School Health*, 65 (1995): 91-95.

Vitale, Anne, *Notes on Gender Identity Disorder*. Accesssed from http://webhome.idirect.com/~beech1/GENDERID.HTM

Wagner, K.D. *et al*, "Attributional Style and Depression in Pregnant Teenagers," *American Journal of Psychiatry*, 155.9 (1998): 1227-1233.

Weller, S., and Davis, K., "Condom Effectiveness in Reducing Heterosexual HIV Transmission (Cochrane Review)," *The Cochrane Library*, Issue 4, 2002.

WHO Epidemiological Fact Sheet on HIV and AIDS Core data on Epidemiology and response

"Why Defend Partial-Birth Abortion?", *New York Times*, 6 September 1996.

Wilmut, Ian, Schnicke, A.E., McWhir, J., Kind, A.J., and Campbell, K.H.S.L., "Viable offspring derived from fetal and adult mammalian cells", *Nature*,1997, 385, pp. 810-3.

Wilson, K.L. *et al*, "A Review of 21 Curricula for Abstinence-Only-Until-Marriage Programs," *Journal of School Health*, 75.3 (2005): 90-98.

Wilson, M.A., "The practice of natural family planning versus the use of artificial birth control: family, sexual, and moral issues", *Catholic Social Science Review*, 2002; 7.

Wood, Carl, and Westmore, Ann, *Test Tube Conception*, Hill of Content, Melbourne, 1983.

Woody, J.D. Randall, A.D. and D'Souza, H.J. "Mothers' Efforts Toward Their Children's Sex Education: An Exploratory Study," *Journal of Family Studies* 11.1 (2005): 83–87

World Health Organization (WHO), 1977-1981, Task Force on Methods for the Determination of the Fertile Period, Special Programme of Research, Development and Research Training in Human Reproduction. Multicenter–Auckland, Dublin, San Miguel, Bangalore and Manila. "A Prospective Multicentre Trial of the Ovulation Method of Natural Family Planning: I. The Teaching Phase," *Fertility and Sterility* 36 (1981): 152ff; "A Prospective Multicentre Trial of the Ovulation Method of Natural Family Planning: II. The Effectiveness Phase," 36 (1981): 591ff.

World Health Organization Task Force on Methods for the Determination of the Fertile Period, Special Programme of Research, Development and Research Training in Human Reproduction, "A Prospective Multicentre Trial of the Ovulation Method of Natural Family Planning: III. Characteristics of the Menstrual Cycle and of the Fertile Phase," *Fertility and Sterility* 40 (1983): 773-778.

Yeung, W.S.B., *et al*, "The Effects of Levonorgestrel on Various Sperm Functions," *Contraception* 66.6 (December 2002): 453-45.

Index[1]

abortifacience 162, 167, 169, 175, 178
Abortion Law Reform Act 2008 153, 155-6, 159, 161
abortion, foetal pain 130
abortion, incidence of 258
abortion, late term 6, 70, 128-37
abortion, morality 126
abortion, partial birth
abstinence 14, 229, 235, 237, 240, 245, 251, 353, 366, 370, 372
abstinence-only 371-2, 378
abstinence plus 251, 370
adolescent development 12
Adolescent Medicine 195
adolescent mother 362
adolescent pregnancy 360-1, 368
adolescent sexual behaviour 164-5, 247, 358-9, 363-4, 367
Agius, P. 356
Aguilar, Nona 344
AIHW National Perinatal Statistics 81, 84, 356, 360
Alexander, G. 359
Amba, J.C. 358
American Academy of Pediatrics 365
American Economic Journal: Economic Policy 252
Amnesty International 420
amniocentesis 40-1, 62, 67, 71

anthropocentric 202, 214-5, 221
anthropocentrism 201
anxiety 67, 110, 177, 292, 362
Applied Ethics 128
Aquinas, St Thomas 31, 38, 91-3, 101-2, 140, 187, 189, 197, 205, 229
Aristotle 86-7, 91, 100-1
Ashley, Benedict 144, 260, 263
assisted reproductive technology 44, 80-1, 84, 87, 91, 93, 95, 99, 101, 105, 107, 111, 149, 152, 303
Australian Catholic Bishops Conference 76-7, 141, 155, 332
Australian Constitution 153
Australian Curriculum 13
Australian Curriculum and Assessment Authority 342, 346
Australian Institute of Health and Welfare 356
Australian Medical Association 153
Australian Research Centre in Sex, Health and Society, La Trobe University 289

Baron, John 410, 419, 421
Bearman, Peter S. 373
beginning of life 86, 89, 92, 96
Bel Canto 400-1
Benedict XVI 1, 15, 220, 240, 272, 318, 326
Biddlecom, A.E. 359

---

1 Bibliography and endnotes are not included in this index, nor are words such as abortion, marriage and motherhood which occur frequently throughout the text.

Billings, Evelyn and John 82, 172-3, 236, 238, 388, 412

Billings Family Life Centre 135

Billings Ovulation Method 109, 256

biological marriage 299, 301, 304

birth control 258, 358

bisexual 264, 283-4

Borawski, Elaine 372

Borgia, P. 362

Bristol coupe 408

Brown, Louise 54

Brown monitor 170

Brown, Professor James B. 171-3, 176, 178

Bruckner, Hanna 373

Cahill, Des 313

Carvalho, David 406

Casti Connubii 31, 216

catechesis 17, 31, 38, 231, 339, 341

Catechism of the Catholic Church 193, 260

Catholic Education Office 335

cervical mucus 110, 168, 171, 256

Cheesbrough, S. 384

childbearing 254

China 52, 256

chlamydia 249, 355-6, 368-9

Chorionic Villus Sampling 40, 67, 69

Christocentric 1, 16, 335, 412

cloning 54-5, 60, 90, 99-100, 147

Clune, Frank 392, 396

cohabitation 35

condoms 7-8, 120, 164-5, 240, 242, 245-9, 251, 358, 366, 370, 385

Condon, J. 362

Congregation for the Doctrine of the Faith 41, 97, 113, 216, 240

conscientious objection 149, 151-161, 304

contragestion 8, 162, 360

Convention on the Rights of the Child 106, 326

corpus luteum 237

Creighton Method 229, 237

criminal law 11, 227, 266

Daly, Tom 421

Davis, Henry, SJ 31, 211, 216.

decision-making counselling 75-7, 122-3, 137, 408

Declaration on Procured Abortion, 97

Department of Education and Early Childhood Development 356

Department of Health and Ageing 353

depression 110, 255, 361-2, 417

Descartes, René 87

Diagnostic and Statistics Manual of Mental Disorders 264, 320

DiCenso, A. 366

direct abortion 98, 140, 144, 184-5, 225, 227

discovering gender 295

disorders of sex development 261-2

divorce 18, 35, 254, 257-8, 338, 376

Doniger, Andrew S. 372

donor gametes 51, 104, 108

Dunson, D.B. 174-5

Dunstan, Gordon 101

early abortion 6, 129, 134
early childhood 326
early induction 128-9, 131, 133, 135, 137, 156
early sexual initiate 346, 383, 420
ectopic pregnancy 6-7, 138-9. 141, 143-4, 156, 167-8, 356
education in sexuality, *see also* sex education 13-14, 342-3, 350-1, 373, 375-6, 378, 380, 382
electron-microscopic 166
embryo experimentation 54, 60
embryo loss 103, 164
embryo rescue 4, 112-3, 115, 117
emergency contraception 8, 162, 360
end of life 89
endometrium 126, 165-7, 178
equal respect for persons 16, 19, 35, 105, 386
Escobar-Chaves, S.L. 364
Ethical Guidelines on the Use of Assisted Reproductive Technology in Clinical Practice and Research 46
Eucharist 39, 391
Evangelium Vitae 140, 212
expectant management 139

false reassurance 65
Familiaris Consortio 30
family life 275
family of origin 423
family planning 124, 236, 239
fatherhood 1, 23, 120, 299-300, 424
fear of pregnancy 162

female happiness 252
fertile period 8, 170-2, 174
fertile window 163, 256
fertility 50, 229, 236
Filippini, Contessa 392
Filippini, Count Ercole 391-2, 397-8
Flood, M. 285
foetal abnormality 74, 131-2
foetus 7, 54, 58, 63, 65, 69, 71, 74, 79, 93, 97, 124, 130, 133-4, 142, 149, 156, 186, 207
Ford, Norman M. 99-100
Fortenberry, J.D. 366
foundations of education in sexuality 380-1
freedom of speech 288-9
freedom of conscience 8, 151
Furukawa, T.A. 368

Gaudium et Spes 97, 193, 221, 391, 411
gay, gays 283-4, 286, 289-290, 299, 417, 421
Geach, Mary 114
gender dysphoria 10. 263-5, 269-70, 278-9
gender identity disorder 23, 261, 264, 268, 270
gender reassignment 10, 260-281
genetic counselling 50, 74
genital herpes 120, 248, 250, 358, 370-1
genital warts 248, 250, 358, 370
Gay, Lesbian, Bisexual, Transexual or Intersex (GLBTI) 283, 285, 287-90, 293
gonococcal infection 356, 359

gonorrhoea 249, 356, 358-9
Gonzales Opera Company 391, 397
Goodson, P. 366
Gospel of Life, The (see *Evangelium vitae*)
Grail, the 391
Grisez, Germain 114, 181, 183, 186, 189-90, 195-6, 199-201, 206-8, 210, 213, 215, 220, 223, 225, 227
Grunseit, A. 371
Guttmacher Institute 244
Guyatt, G.H. 368
gynaecology 6-7, 125, 146, 148

Hamilton, C. 285-6
Harman, Frank 388
Harris, Lee 266
Hart, Archbishop Denis 332
Health and Physical Education 342-4, 346, 349
health care 151, 177, 359
Health Care Ethics 260
health education 164, 350
health practitioners 151-2, 154, 160
health sciences 344
hepatitis 8, 136, 353
Hinduism 88
HIV (Human immunodeficiency virus) 240-1, 243-9, 358, 360, 362, 395
homophobia 11, 283-93
hormonal treatment 10, 260, 264, 272, 279
human chorionic gonadotrophia 139, 178
human embryo experimentation 54
human life 3, 8, 42, 88, 90-1, 97-8, 101-2, 113, 125, 127, 134, 143, 178, 193, 220, 231, 274

human papilloma virus (HPV) 250, 371
Human Reproduction 100
Humanae Vitae 31, 38, 220, 229-30, 411

indirect abortion 184, 227
indirect marriage 35
induced abortion 5, 62, 72-3, 258, 360
infertility 4, 37, 43, 80-3, 108-12, 163, 171, 177, 249
integration of sexuality 289, 295, 308, 377
intersex 9-10, 22, 24, 261-3, 277-9, 283-4
intra-uterine devices (IUD) 229, 257
Ireland, Marjorie

John Paul II 1, 5, 15, 17, 24-5, 28-31, 64, 113, 118, 124, 140, 199, 206, 213, 217, 221, 242, 413
Jorgensen, Stephen R. 373
Journal of Medical Ethics 69

Kaczor, Christopher 142
Kanawa, Dame Kiri te 400
Kelly, Paul 400
Kennedy, President John F. 414
Kennedy, Robert 414
key learning areas 349, 380
Kuhse, Helga 54-8, 98

late abortion 79
late term abortion (late term termination of pregnancy) 128-37
Lederman, R.P. 362
lesbians 283-4, 289-90, 292, 299

levonorgestrel 165-9, 178
Lumen Gentium 411
Lysaught 180-227

MacKillop, Mary 394
mammalian eggs 92
Mary (the Mother of Jesus) 88, 96, 388
Mary Magdalene 387
masculinity 20, 28
masturbation 11-12, 110, 306-9, 411, 415
maternal danger 181-227
McParland, Nancy 391
medical indemnity 7
menstrual cycle, menstruation (129, 170, 174-5, 268
methods of education in sexuality 381
Methotrexate (MXT) 7, 138-9, 144-5
Migliore, Lucia 110
Milton, J. 363
Moraczewski, Albert 144
moral status of the embryo 86-102
morality and prenatal diagnosis 41-42
morning after pill, the 8, 159, 162, 358, 360
Mulieris Dignitatem 30
Mumford, Roy 401
Murdoch Children's Research Institute 64, 74
Museveni, Yoweri 244-5

mutual love 25, 296, 305, 308

Naprotechnology 237
National Campaign to Prevent Teen Pregnancy 354, 385

National Curriculum 13-14, 280, 342-389
National Health and Medical Research Council 44, 64, 152, 376, 382
National Longitudinal Study on Adolescent Health 359
National Perinatal Statistics Unit 82
natural family planning 170, 172, 174, 236, 239, 258-9
natural law 16-17, 31, 38, 195-6, 222, 335, 411
neonatal death 73
New York Times 130

Obermeyer, C.M. 385
obstetrics 67, 125, 146-150, 187
Odeblad, E. 171-2
oestrogen 163-4, 167-8, 171 229, 256
oral contraceptives 9, 60, 120, 163, 252-9
oral sex 357-8, 367
orphan embryo 114
ovary 142, 256
ovulation 163, 165, 171-175, 236-7, 256
Ovulation Method Research 109

paedophilia 12-13, 148, 311-340
parenthood 1-2, 14, 32, 37, 55, 80, 105, 115, 117, 126, 244, 295, 301, 304, 326
partial-birth abortion 6
partners in sex education 378-9
perinatal palliative care 3, 61-79
personhood 29, 101, 378
physical education 342-4, 346, 349
Pinkerton, Steven D. 366

Plato 86
pledge programs 371
Pope Anastasius 92
Pope Benedict XVI 1, 15, 240, 318, 326
Pope Gregory XV 398
Pope John Paul II (see John Paul II)
Pope Paul V 398
Pope Paul VI 230-1
Pope Pius XI 31, 216, 232-3
population density 361
pornography 12, 110, 306-310
post-coital intervention 7-8. 162-78
post-partum women 131
post-abortion syndrome 5
pregnancy avoidance 170-5
pregnancy counselling 76, 123, 161
pregnancy scares 176-7
pregnancy support 76, 121-3
pregnanediol glucuronide 170, 179
primary schools 108, 277
progesterone 125, 163-4, 167, 170-1, 173, 179, 229, 237-8, 256
prophylaxis 119, 250, 351, 354, 370, 387
prostaglandin 126
psychosocial 45, 131, 146, 258, 384

qualitative evaluation 367
Quinlivan, J.A. 362

rape crisis 8, 125, 162-3, 171, 173, 175, 177-8, 397
Redesdale 417
Reichert, Timothy 253-4
religious education 349

reproductive behaviour 365
reproductive discrimination 3, 44, 46-8, 133
Resnick, Michael 372
Rhonheimer, Martin 181
risk behaviours 14
Royal Australia and New Zealand College of Obstetricians and Gynaecologists 7
RU486 360
Ryan, Ronald 414

safe sex 120, 240, 251, 370, 381
same sex attraction 11, 294-8
school counsellors 367
Second Vatican Council 1, 15, 26-7, 31, 97, 319, 339, 341, 393
secondary students and sexual health 383
self-esteem 361, 375
sex education 5, 13-14, 120-1, 125, 241, 342-389
sexual addiction 307
sexual attitudes and behaviour 362
sexual health 343, 348. 357, 384
sexual intercourse 138, 168, 172, 174, 179, 254, 308, 356, 359-60, 367
sexual intimacy 1, 11, 34, 38, 107, 127, 228, 232, 235, 238, 241, 270, 272, 279, 285, 297, 370, 374-5, 387
sexually transmitted diseases, infections 80, 246, 352, 359
Sheed, Frank 410
SIECUS (Sexuality Information and Education Council of the United States) 354

Index

Singer, Peter 54-8, 60, 98, 101-2, 128
sociology 406
Somers, C.L 363
step-children 302-3
Stevenson, Betsey 252
Stewart, Bishop Bernard 407, 413
Summa Theologiae 197
Surman, A.T. 364
surrogacy 43, 106-8, 114, 303
Sutherland, Dame Joan 400
Sympto-Thermal Method (STM) 229, 236

teen pregnancy 354
teenage mother 362
Theology of the Body 17-19, 22, 30-1, 36-40
Thomists 221, 223, 418
Thompson, Judith Jarvis 128
transgender 266-7, 284
transsexual 267, 269, 283
treatment of ectopic pregnancy 156
Triardo, Ray 406-7
Trounson, Alan 99
Twomey, D. Vincent 229-30

Uganda 243-4, 246
unintended pregnancies 254
unruptured ectopic pregnancy 139
urban adolescent girls 367

Veritatis Splendor 191, 193, 196, 201, 206, 208, 215-6, 224-5
Victorian Assisted Reproductive Treatment Authority 4, 81, 86
Vienna Boys' Choir 399
Vincentian seminary 420
virginity 372

Walsh, Mary 83, 162
Wilmut, Ian 55
Wilson, K.L
Wilson, M.A. 258
Wilson, Murray 416-7
Wolfers, Justin 252
womb 94-5, 106, 114, 265, 303
Wood, Carl 99, 116
World Health Organization (WHO) 371

Yeung, W.S.B. 168

Acknowledgements

I have acknowledged those who have assisted my writing of these volumes and my career that made it possible. However, I would like to make a special place for those who actually carry out the project. First, I express my gratitude to Connor Court and Dr. Anthony Cappello particularly for publishing the series. Anthony was responsible for the idea of publishing not one book but a series of volumes. I am grateful too to Michael Gilchrist for his tireless efforts to edit the manuscript, including dealing with my several rounds of finding new corrections. In that respect I must acknowledge Mary who is a comma friend. I also express my gratitude to Madge Fahey and Jewel Starr of the Catholic Women's League, Anna Krohn from Anima and Marcia Riordan from the Melbourne Catholic Archdiocesan Life, Marriage and Family Office who contributed ideas and encouragement, and reviewed material along the way.

www.ingramcontent.com/pod-product-compliance
Lightning Source LLC
Chambersburg PA
CBHW061341300426
44116CB00011B/1935